THE QUILTER'S BIBLE

The indispensable guide to patchwork, quilting and appliqué

LINDA CLEMENTS

D&C
David and Charles
www.rucraft.co.uk

For my darling son Rory, who puts up with piles of fabric all over the house and always seems to find pins with his bare feet before I even know I've lost them. And for my dear sister Jan, who waits patiently (not) in the car while I pop into yet another fabric shop for 'just a minute' (hour).

A DAVID & CHARLES BOOK
Copyright © David & Charles Limited 2011

David & Charles is an F+W Media Inc. company
4700 East Galbraith Road, Cincinnati, OH 45236

First published in the UK and US in 2011

Text and 'Make It Now' projects copyright © Linda Clements 2011
Layout and photography copyright © David & Charles 2011

Linda Clements has asserted her right to be identified as author of this work in accordance with the Copyright, Designs and Patents Act, 1988.

A catalogue record for this book is available from the British Library.

ISBN-13: 978-0-7153-3626-7 paperback
ISBN-10: 0-7153-3626-6 paperback

Printed in China by RR Donnelley
for David & Charles
Brunel House   Newton Abbot   Devon

Commissioning Editors Jane Trollope and Cheryl Brown
Assistant Editor Jeni Hennah
Project Editor Heather Haynes
Design Manager Sarah Clark
Designer Sarah Underhill
Photographers Karl Adamson and Kim Sayer
Illustrator Ethan Danielson
Production Controller Kelly Smith
Pre-Press Natasha Jorden

David & Charles publish high quality books on a wide range of subjects. For more great book ideas visit: **www.rucraft.co.uk**

CONTENTS

Foreword

For many years Linda Clements has edited a wide range of patchwork and quilting books, including my own, and I couldn't work without her. Her knowledge and experience of so many techniques has resulted in this thorough and comprehensive reference book – anything you need to know about, it's here.

This is my specialist craft area, but just leafing through the book I found whole sections that I knew very little about and strategies for dealing with them that I will immediately adopt.

Within the three broad definitions of patchwork, appliqué and quilting, traditional techniques and designs lie alongside contemporary textile treatments plus fabric manipulation, decorative stitchery and embellishment – so much inspiration!

A bonus is the series of small projects dotted throughout the book, each one based on the technique that is being described and placed with it in the text.

The step-by-step diagrams are clear and helpful, while the ravishing photography (always one of David and Charles' strengths) makes this book both lovely to look at and an essential resource for every quilter's library.

Lynne Edwards MBE
Quiltmaker, teacher, author
and quilting journalist

Combining patchwork, appliqué and quilting can create striking designs, and panels printed with attractive scenes are a quick way to create a quilt. This koi and waterfall panel has been edged by a braided border (see page 135) and two plain borders. Fusible web appliqué was used to add flowers over the borders and the wall hanging is finished with simple machine quilting and a narrow binding.

Introduction

Patchwork, appliqué and quilting are crafts that have endured over centuries and continue to be re-invented as more and more people find pleasure and satisfaction from creating something for themselves, their family and friends. This book is a comprehensive guide to creating beautiful work with fabric, with an encyclopedia of techniques to inform and inspire everyone, from the complete beginner to the more experienced stitcher.

The book covers a vast subject area and is divided into five sections, although there is much overlap between patchwork, appliqué and quilting.

Getting Started – This first section describes the tools and materials you may need and basic techniques such as choosing fabrics, working with colour, marking methods, using templates and drawing and cutting shapes.

Patchwork – Here we look at quilt design using blocks, and then at specific shapes, building from simple squares and rectangles to triangles, diamonds, polygons and curves. Many styles of patchwork are described and illustrated.

Appliqué – This section explores some of the many forms of appliqué, including traditional needle-turn, fusible web, shadow appliqué and bias-strip appliqué.

Quilting – All you need to know about hand and machine methods of quilting is covered in this section, including free-motion quilting, sashiko, corded quilting and other decorative forms of quilting.

Finishing Off – This final section shows you how to add the finishing touches to quilts and other projects, describing various edging treatments and how to display and care for quilts.

You can use this book in many ways. You can dip into it randomly to explore some of the many techniques covered or use it as a workbook, working through it and building up your skills. Throughout the book there are small projects, called Make It Now, which are intended to provide practice for some of the techniques described.

The book has hundreds of detailed diagrams, explaining the techniques and giving ideas for designs. The abbreviations 'rs' and 'ws' have been used to indicate the right side and wrong side of fabric. Where possible, both imperial and metric measurements have been provided. These are not interchangeable so use one or the other. Imperial inches have been used as first choice – see page 250 for converting imperial to metric. There is also a section on useful stitches (see page 245) which contains descriptions of the specific stitches mentioned in the book. To increase your knowledge further, some books are suggested on page 252, and of course there are many more wonderful books and magazines available to help you.

It is hoped that this book will become a treasured resource, answering questions you may have about patchwork, appliqué and quilting and, above all, encouraging you to make lovely quilts and other projects you will be thrilled with. Although there is detailed guidance throughout, there is no ultimate right or wrong way to sew and new ways of doing things are being devised all the time. The most important thing is to have a go, explore what takes your fancy and enjoy what you create.

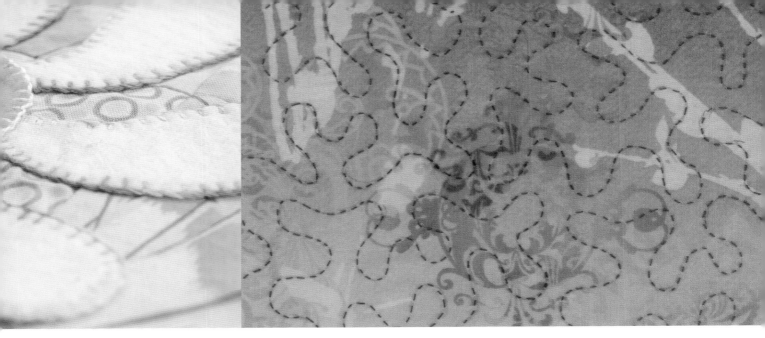

There are so many wonderful effects that can be achieved with patchwork, appliqué and quilting and this book provides plenty of inspiration – so dip in and enjoy!

FEATURES OF A QUILT

The techniques in this book can be used to create whatever lovely projects you choose. For those new to quiltmaking the diagram below identifies the main features of a quilt, explaining the basic terms you will encounter in the book.

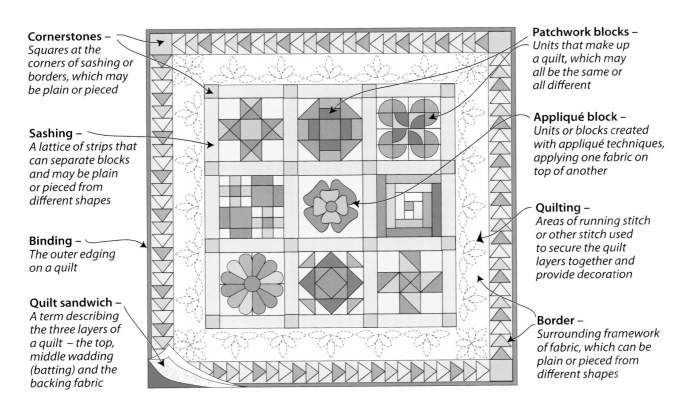

Cornerstones –
Squares at the corners of sashing or borders, which may be plain or pieced

Sashing –
A lattice of strips that can separate blocks and may be plain or pieced from different shapes

Binding –
The outer edging on a quilt

Quilt sandwich –
A term describing the three layers of a quilt – the top, middle wadding (batting) and the backing fabric

Patchwork blocks –
Units that make up a quilt, which may all be the same or all different

Appliqué block –
Units or blocks created with appliqué techniques, applying one fabric on top of another

Quilting –
Areas of running stitch or other stitch used to secure the quilt layers together and provide decoration

Border –
Surrounding framework of fabric, which can be plain or pieced from different shapes

Getting Started

This section contains useful information on the tools, materials and basic skills needed for successful patchwork, appliqué and quilting. We begin with descriptions of some of the equipment that is available to make our quilting lives easier and more fun – those wonderful gizmos and gadgets that help us design, mark, measure, cut, sew and press.

Moving on, we look at some of the fabulous fabrics we can use in our work and how to choose them, make colour selections and prepare them for sewing.

Finally, there are helpful techniques describing the skills fundamental to patchwork, appliqué and quilting, such as preparing and using templates, drawing and cutting basic shapes and using technology to make designing and sewing easier.

TOOLS

This section looks at some of the tools and materials you might need for patchwork, appliqué and quilting, describing their uses and showing illustrations where relevant. The tools are grouped according to their function, and include design tools, marking tools, measuring and cutting tools, sewing tools, pressing tools and miscellaneous gizmos and gadgets.

If you are a complete beginner, the sheer volume of tools and gadgets available can be overwhelming but you really only need the basics in the Tool Kit listed here to get going. After you discover which areas of patchwork, appliqué and quilting interest you most you can add to your supplies.

> **BASIC TOOL KIT**
> - Rotary cutter and mat
> - Quilter's ruler
> - Tape measure
> - Fabric, embroidery and paper scissors
> - Selection of hand sewing needles
> - Fine dressmaker's pins and safety pins
> - Thimble
> - Sewing machine
> - Selection of machine sewing needles
> - Selection of hand and machine threads
> - Erasable markers
> - Fusible web
> - Freezer paper
> - Graph paper and isometric paper
> - Standard ruler
> - Pens, pencils and eraser
> - Steam iron and ironing board
> - Thin card
> - Template plastic

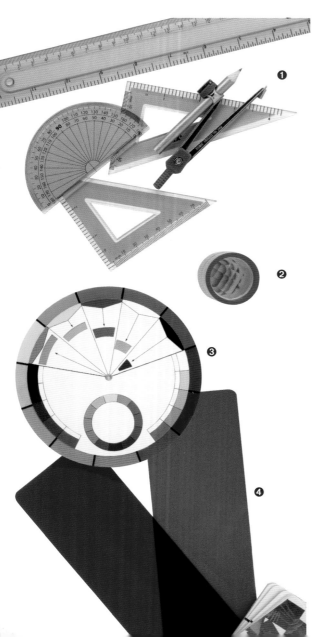

DESIGN TOOLS

There are various items that are useful for drafting and designing in many areas of patchwork, appliqué and quilting. See page 29 for more on drawing shapes.

- **Geometry tools** – A compass is needed for drawing circles and semi-circles, a protractor for measuring angles and drafting triangles and a standard ruler with ⅛in (3mm) and 1/16in (1.5mm) markings for drawing shapes. ❶
- **Multi-image lens** – This allows you to see multiplied images and thus imagine how grouped blocks might look. ❷
- **Colour wheel** – This will help with making colour choices when designing blocks and quilt settings, showing which colours are complementary and which are analogous – see page 19 for more advice on colour. ❸
- **Value finder** – Red and green lenses can be used to show relative dark and light tones in fabrics. ❹
- **Pens and pencils** – These will be needed for various tasks, including sketching design ideas, drafting shapes and blocks and creating templates. Coloured pens and pencils are useful for planning colour schemes.
- **Papers** – Various types of paper are useful, including plain paper for drawing ideas and sketches, graph paper for planning blocks and quilt layouts, isometric paper for drafting triangles, hexagons and diamonds, and tracing paper for copying designs and templates.
- **Card** – Sheets of card can be used for making templates and thin card is handy for English paper piecing.
- **Calculator** – When designing and working out fabric requirements, a calculator makes the maths much easier.
- **Design board** – Having somewhere to display work in progress is vital so you can judge how a design is working. This might be a piece of fabric fixed to a wall where work can be pinned, or a board that folds away when not in use. A closed curtain can be a temporary display area.
- **Lighting equipment** – It is important to have good lighting as you design or sew, to see the work properly and avoid straining your eyes. An overhead lamp with a head that can be angled is most useful and many are available with a magnifying attachment. Using a 'daylight' type bulb will help to produce real light conditions and make choosing thread colours easier.

MARKING TOOLS

There is a wealth of tools available for marking, and new ones being devised all the time. The basics are described here. See page 25 for further information.

- **Chalk** – Chalk is available in various forms and colours, including chalk pencils, blocks and in powder form distributed through a wheel. ❶
- **Hera** – This is a useful tool for creasing lines on fabric. ❷
- **Flexicurve** – This flexible rubber tool can be bent into curved shapes and is useful for marking semi-circles or S-shapes. ❸
- **Templates and stencils** – These are really useful for marking. They can be made in any shape and many basic shapes are available commercially. See page 26 for examples of template materials. ❹
- **Template plastic** – Available in sheets of plastic for making templates, in clear or marked patterns, such as grids or triangles. ❺
- **Pencils** – Use a hard pencil for marking a fine clean line around templates and a soft pencil for marking quilting patterns.
- **Pens** – There are many types of removable markers, including water-soluble, air-fading and iron-off. The sort you choose depends on your project and personal preference. A fine permanent fabric pen is useful for writing labels for quilts. See page 25 for more on using marking pens.
- **Dressmaker's carbon paper** – This can be used for tracing with templates and stencils. The marks are usually removed by washing. Various colours are available for different coloured fabrics, including white, yellow, red and blue.
- **Masking tape** – Low-tack tape is useful for marking straight lines.

MEASURING AND CUTTING TOOLS

Today's measuring and cutting tools are easy to use, fast and efficient. See page 29 for advice on rotary cutting.

- **Snips** – These are short scissors that work with a squeezing action and are useful for snipping threads and cutting off 'dog ears' (small areas of fabric that show when seams are joined on pieced units). ❶
- **Rotary cutter** – Although scissors can be used for cutting fabric, a rotary cutter will make the task easier and quicker. These have very sharp blades that can slice through many layers of fabric simultaneously. They are available in several metric sizes, with the small 28mm and larger 45mm diameter sizes being the most useful. Handle shapes vary so choose one that is easy to operate and comfortable to use. Circle cutters are also available. ❷
- **Acrylic rulers** – There are dozens of rulers, often called quilter's rulers, including square, rectangular, triangular, hexagonal and diamond rulers. There are specialist rulers for all sorts of tasks, for example, making half-square triangles and piecing designs such as Double Wedding Ring (see page 44). To begin with you really only need a 24½in x 6½in (62cm x 16.5cm) or 18in x 3in (46cm x 7.5cm) rectangular ruler and a 12½in (32cm) square ruler. Normal rulers are fine for designing but should not be used for rotary cutting as they are not robust enough. ❸
- **Cutting mat** – Mats with a self-healing surface are used with rotary cutters and are available in many sizes. Choose the biggest and best you can afford with clearly marked measurements and grids – an 18in x 24in (46cm x 61cm) size is useful. Store mats flat and away from direct heat and sunlight. ❹
- **Scissors** – A large pair of sharp fabric shears will be needed, plus smaller sharp-pointed embroidery scissors. Keep a pair of scissors just for paper and card.
- **Tape measure** – A standard tape measure with imperial and metric measures will be needed. Use a good quality one that will not stretch.

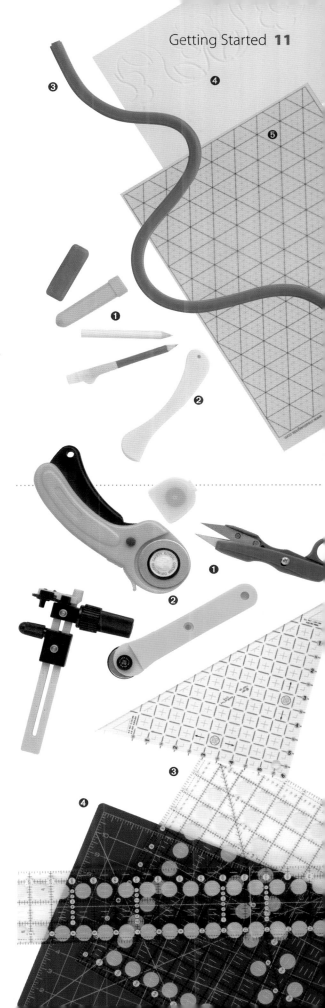

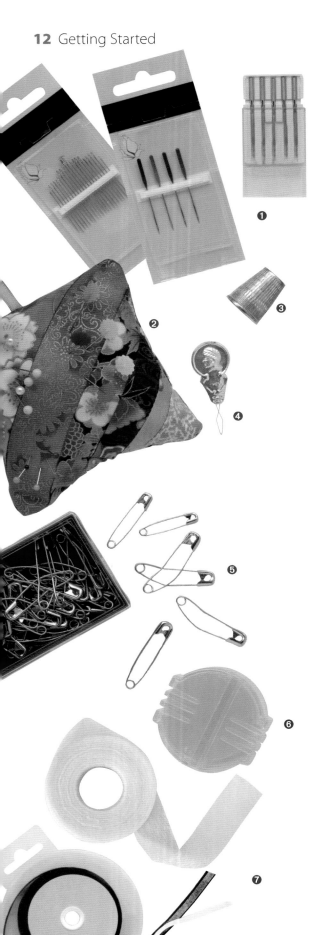

SEWING TOOLS

These are the tools you will probably use the most. Use the best you can afford and experiment to find the types that suit you.

- **Needles** – There are many types of needle for machine and hand sewing, each designed for specific types of thread or fabric. Choose the needle to suit the task – see page 23 for more advice. ❶
- **Pins** – Beginners will be amazed at the different types of pins available – there are glass-headed pins, plastic-headed pins, flower-headed pins, silk pins, appliqué pins and even sequin pins! For general patchwork and quilting, all you really need are pins that are sharp and fine, can be easily sewn over by a sewing machine and where the heads can be seen easily. Glass-headed pins don't melt with the heat of a hot iron, while flower-headed pins are easy to pick up. Longer pins are useful for securing the layers of a quilt. Having several pincushions around your work area will help keep pins under control, as will magnets – see opposite. ❷
- **Thimble** – You will need a thimble (or several) to protect your fingers as you sew and quilt. Various types are available, including those made from metal, leather and plastic. Choose one with deep indentations so the end of the needle doesn't slip off the thimble. Thimbles may be closed-ended or open-ended, for long nails. Finger guards help protect the underneath finger as you quilt. ❸
- **Needle threader** – A needle threader may not always be needed but fatigue or age can make threading a needle awkward at times. ❹
- **Safety pins** – Safety pins are primarily used to fix the layers of a quilt together, ready for quilting. Safety pins come in various guises. There are straight ones, curved ones and those with different finishes, including anodized and brass. Choose safety pins that are sharp, rust proof and about 1in (2.5cm) long. Curved pins can make pin-tacking (basting) a quilt easier. ❺
- **Wax block** – Beeswax or silicone wax is available in a block form and is used to coat threads to help prevent tangling and knotting. Threads are available that are already silicone coated. ❻
- **Fusible bias tape** – Bias tape is used in stained-glass appliqué and Celtic appliqué. Commercially made bias tape with a fusible web backing allows easy fusing to fabric. Fusible web for gluing one fabric to another is also available in reels. ❼
- **Fabric glue** – Glues suitable for fabric come in liquid, solid (glue stick) and spray form and can be used for permanent hold for attaching braids and embellishments, as a temporary adhesive for tacking (basting) fabrics together, or for holding the layers of a quilt together prior to quilting.
- **Piping cord** – This will be needed for piped edges and for corded Italian quilting. It is available in different widths and also in a fusible format. Quilting wool is also useful for corded quilting.
- **Polyester stuffing** – This may also be called toy stuffing and fiberfill and is used for puffed patchwork, three-dimensional appliqué and stuffed quilting.
- **Hoops and frames** – These are available in different types and sizes, hand-held and floor-standing, and are used to keep fabric taut. They are useful for embellishing work with hand embroidery and for quilting.
- **Freezer paper** – This has a shiny, plastic-coated side that will stick to fabric when ironed, and can be removed and reapplied several times. It is excellent for appliqué and for marking quilting designs.
- **Sewing machine** – Any sewing machine that has a zigzag function and a variable stitch length can be used for patchwork, appliqué and quilting. See page 24 for more advice.

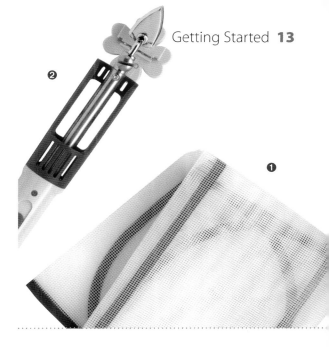

PRESSING TOOLS

- **Press cloth** – This is a sheet, usually made from non-stick Teflon, which can be used to protect delicate fabrics and also to protect the iron from sticky fusible web residue. A sheet of greaseproof paper could also be used. ❶
- **Mini iron** – This is a heated tool with a small, pointed plate that makes precision pressing easier, especially for bias-strip appliqué. A small travel iron could be used instead, although its plate is bigger than that of a mini iron. ❷
- **Starch** – Spray starch helps to firm up fabrics and makes cutting and sewing easier. Avoid over-spraying as this can distort the fabric as you press it.
- **Steam iron** – An iron is essential for all forms of patchwork, quilting and appliqué. In most cases it will be used dry but a steam function may be needed at times. See pressing fabrics on page 23.
- **Ironing board** – Use a standard ironing board with a tapered end for ironing creased fabrics and pressing work at all stages. A small or portable ironing board is useful for placing near the sewing machine for pressing patches as they are sewn. Boards are also available with a rotating surface.

GIZMOS AND GADGETS

There are some wonderful specialist products available for patchwork, appliqué and quilting. Many of these items are not essential but can make tasks easier and quicker. Whether you buy them or not depends on your budget and how much you think you will use them. A few are listed here.

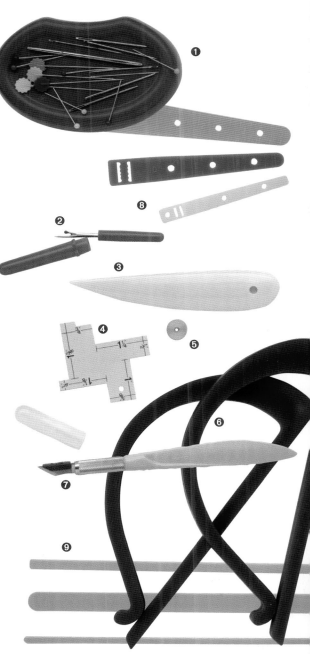

- **Magnets** – Magnets are useful for keeping errant needles and pins under control and having several means that you can keep pins on one, needles on another and safety pins on a third. Be sure to keep magnets away from computerized sewing machines. ❶
- **Seam ripper** – No one plans to unpick their work but mistakes happen and a seam ripper is useful for removing stitches without damaging fabric. Most sewing machines have one in the tool kit. They can also be used for holding down patchwork pieces as you sew them. ❷
- **Point turner** – This is a gadget with a sharp point that is used to make sure corners are pushed out properly when 'bagging-out' a quilt or project. A knitting needle could also be used. ❸
- **Measuring gauge** – A useful gadget marked with the commonly used seam allowances. ❹
- **Seam guide** – This little brass circle with a hole in the centre can be used to draw a ¼in (6mm) seam around a shape, especially for templates. ❺
- **Quilting clips** – These are plastic rings that clip together and hold a rolled-up quilt together while you are quilting. ❻
- **Double-bladed stencil knife** – This is a useful gadget if you want to make your own quilting stencils. The double blade cuts a narrow channel. ❼
- **Elastic threader** – Available in different sizes, these can be used to thread elastic or for webbing when making bag handles. ❽
- **Bias bars** – These are also called bias press bars and are useful for bias-strip appliqué – see page 178 for use. ❾
- **Bias maker** – This is handy for making bias strips as the edges emerge from the gadget already turned under – see page 178 for its use.
- **Tweezers** – Useful for fine positioning of embellishments, particularly beads.
- **Tack gun** – A handy gadget for those who hate tacking (basting) a quilt sandwich. It shoots little plastic tags through the quilt layers, securing them ready for quilting.

MATERIALS

This section looks at the materials you may need for patchwork, appliqué and quilting, including fabrics, threads, wadding (batting), interfacings, stabilizers, fusible web and embellishments. Obviously, a whole book could be devoted just to this subject so further reading is advised.

FABRICS

Fabrics are what draw people to patchwork, quilting and appliqué – glorious, versatile fabrics in all their many types and hues. Who is not drawn to crisp, clean cottons and linens, softly shimmering silks and satins or plush, strokeable velvets and cords? The fabrics used for patchwork and appliqué can come from many sources. Originally, they were recycled from old clothing and household linen but today are more likely to be bought new from patchwork and quilting stores and increasingly via websites. Pure 100 per cent cottons are top of the list for patchwork and quilting but there are other fabrics that can be used, particularly for appliqué and crazy patchwork. Some of the common fabric types are described below but quilt artists are increasingly stretching the boundaries on fabrics and materials that can be used.

Just as fabrics chosen for quilt tops vary, so too can backing fabrics. A quilt backing is usually chosen to coordinate or link with the front of the quilt and may be calico or a plain or printed cotton in a similar weight to the quilt top. Increasingly, though, quilt backs are being pieced to make them nearly as interesting as the front of the quilt. See pages 22 and 187 for more on backings.

FABRIC TYPES

Cottons – Cotton fabric is the first choice for quilt making because it is easy to work with, does not fray too badly and drapes well. Cottons dye and print readily, resulting in plain colours, mottled, marbled and colour-on-colour effects. Cottons can be solid-dyed, tie-dyed and random-dyed, not to mention wax-dyed, the process that creates wonderful batiks. The range of printed cotton available today is overwhelming, and prints can be tiny or large, subtle or bold, monochrome or multicoloured. You can also dye and print your own fabric.

Silks and satins – These are a little more temperamental than cotton but well worth using for the wonderful sheen and glamour they create. Silk dupion is a good material to try as it irons well and comes in a good range of colours, including shot effects with two colours. Silks and satins are more prone to fraying but careful handling reduces this, as does using a wider seam allowance of ½in (1.3cm).

FABRIC THEMES

When buying fabric, especially when visiting websites, you will often see that it is themed. Themes reflect popular tastes and can help you select fabrics that work well together. Themes come and go but popular categories might include reproduction, patriotic, Asian, floral, animals, children, batiks, seasonal and contemporary. Some theme examples are shown right.

Batiks

Nursery

Reproduction

Sheers – There are many sheer and transparent fabrics that can be used, particularly for shadow appliqué work, including voile, organza, net, nylon, organdie, tulle, chiffon and georgette. They are usually soft and delicate but not the easiest fabrics to work with. Fraying can be a problem and they are not durable enough for normal patchwork but they can create some lovely special effects. When pressing, always use a cool iron and a press cloth on top of the sheer fabric.

Metallics – Many metallic fabrics are available today, as well as cottons shot through with metallic threads. They bring a touch of opulence to quiltmaking and a visual quality not often appreciated by a photograph. They are also fabulous for techniques such as stained-glass appliqué and crazy patchwork. The behaviour of metallics varies, depending on the synthetic content. Some are quite biddable, particularly those blended with cotton; others are very wayward, fraying badly and melting at the mere suggestion of an iron, so experiment with small pieces first.

Synthetics – Fabrics made from synthetic or man-made fibres also have a place in patchwork and appliqué, especially for creating special effects. These include Lurex fabrics, those with plastic surfaces and those mimicking silks and satins. Sequin- and diamanté-studded fabrics can also be great fun to use. As with sheers and metallics, these types of fabric need careful handling and testing.

Craft felt and wool felt – These fabrics are not useful for traditionally pieced quilts but are very popular for small projects and appliqué work. Felt does not fray because it is a bonded rather than a woven fabric. Wool felt is made from a mixture of wool and rayon. It is softer and more flexible than craft felt and is available in a wider range of colours.

Specialist fabrics – Some fabrics have been developed to create special effects, for example water-soluble fabrics, fabrics that can be printed on and shrinkable fabric for ruching. Shrinkable fabric is activated by steam and is available with different shrinkage rates, including 15 per cent and 30 per cent. Specialist fabrics can be used creatively, especially for quilt art.

THREADS

There are many amazing threads today, from all-purpose cotton and polyester to shiny rayons and metallics and glorious variegated and hand-dyed creations. Thread labels give details of the fibre and weight or gauge. The higher the gauge the finer the thread.

Threads for sewing – An ordinary cotton or all-purpose sewing thread in a medium gauge (50 weight) can be used for piecing, by hand or machine.

Threads for quilting – Stronger threads are needed for quilting, so use 100 per cent cotton quilting thread for hand quilting. For more decorative effects try embroidery threads and crochet cottons. Thicker threads, such as perle cottons, can be used for big stitch quilting (see page 200). For machine quilting, 100 per cent cotton thread is popular. Monofilament nylon thread is often used for quilting in the ditch, as it is nearly invisible.

Threads for embellishment – The sky's the limit here as threads for embellishment can be surface couched as well as sewn. Try bouclés, viscose knits and metallic rayons, particularly for crazy patchwork and decorative quilting (see pages 100 and 228).

WADDINGS (BATTINGS)

Wadding or batting is the material layered between two fabrics to form a quilt's padding. There are many types, made from different materials. Wadding is made by bonding or needle punching, both intended to secure the fibres together. When bonded, a resin is used and the wadding may be completely bonded or only surface bonded. A needle-punched wadding has the fibres pieced by needles, which causes them to tangle together.

The wadding you choose depends on the type of quilting planned and how the item will be used. Some are fine for machine quilting but are more difficult to hand quilt through, while others are very puffy and work best for tied quilts. Some need to be quilted at tightly spaced intervals of 2in (5cm) while others may only need to be quilted every 10in (25.4cm) or so. Waddings are also available with a heat-resistant layer, useful for table and kitchen linen. Some waddings are fusible, which helps when securing the layers of a quilt together. Generally, try to match the wadding with the quilt material, for example, cotton wadding for cotton fabrics, silk for silk and so on. Waddings often shrink when washed, producing the attractive crinkled quality of old quilts. If you don't want this effect then wash the wadding before use. Wadding is available in pre-cut pieces to fit standard mattress sizes – see page 250.

'Loft' refers to the weight and thickness of a wadding. Low-loft waddings are thinner than high-loft ones, which are puffier. 'Bearding' is a term used to describe how a wadding can break down, allowing fibres to work their way to the right side of the fabric. This may occur with cheap waddings so always buy the best you can afford. 'Request' weight waddings are lightweight with low loft and are good for hand quilting.

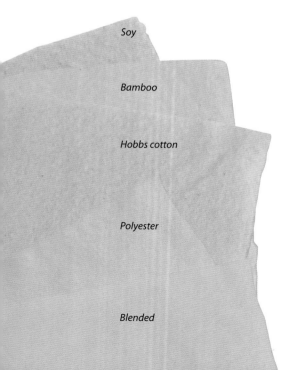

Soy

Bamboo

Hobbs cotton

Polyester

Blended

TYPES OF WADDING (BATTING)

Cotton – This is finer, heavier and warmer than polyester wadding and is very suitable for machine quilting. It can be hand quilted, though this needs to be quite close, about 2in (5cm), between lines. Cotton waddings do not work well as tied quilts as the wadding can break up unless secured at closely spaced intervals.

Wool – Natural fibre waddings breathe well and are usually comfortable all year long. Wool waddings are suitable for hand quilting, being easy to stitch through.

Silk – This natural fibre wadding is expensive so isn't the first choice for a large quilt, however its fineness makes it perfect for quilted garments.

Bamboo – This natural fibre product has a low loft and quilts well. It is very soft and has antibacterial properties so could be useful for baby quilts.

Polyester – This is made from synthetic fibres and is available in different weights, including a thin 2oz (60g) and a thicker 10oz (300g). It is usually the least expensive, washes well and creates a lightweight quilt. Bearding may be a problem. Lower loft polyester waddings can be hand or machine quilted but thicker weights will be difficult to machine quilt. High loft types are great for tied quilts. Do *not* use a hot iron on polyester wadding.

Blended – Wadding may also be made from blended fibres, for example, 80 per cent cotton and 20 per cent polyester or 50 per cent cotton and 50 per cent soy protein. Blended waddings tend to be more stable and less apt to shift.

INTERFACINGS, STABILIZERS AND FUSIBLE WEBS

Interfacings and stabilizers are used to line, stiffen and stabilize fabrics, while fusible web is used to glue one fabric to another and is particularly useful for appliqué work. These materials are available in different weights, usually light, medium and heavy. As a general rule, match the weight with the fabric weight.

Interfacings – This may be sew-in or fusible, the fusible sort having a heat-activated coating on one side, which allows it to be glued to a fabric. It is usually single sided but double-sided types are available. In patchwork, appliqué and quilting an interfacing such as Vilene is used to stiffen or give shape to fabrics, particularly delicate ones or those that fray badly. It can be used as a base when foundation piecing or for crazy patchwork. Different weights are available and stiffer (heavy) weights are useful in bag making and for three-dimensional patchwork.

Stabilizers – These materials are used to stabilize fabrics, making them firmer to stitch on, and are available in different weights. Stabilizers can be temporary, being torn away or dissolved when stitching is finished, or be permanent and left in place. They can be sew-in or fusible. Interfacing may sometimes be referred to as a stabilizer. Muslin and calico can also be used as stabilizers.

Fusible webs – These are made of an ultra-thin sheet of adhesive backed with a special paper. The heat of an iron causes the adhesive to melt and so fuse two fabrics together. Once fused, it forms a secure bond and prevents edges fraying. It comes in different weights, usually light, medium and heavy. Many brands are available and may vary slightly, so always read the manufacturer's instructions before use. See page 152 for more on using fusible web.

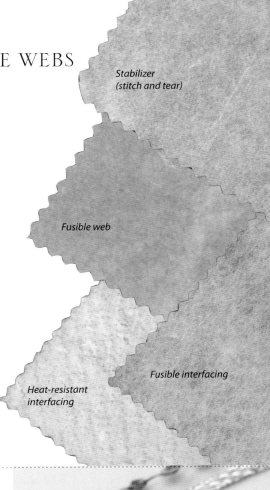

Stabilizer (stitch and tear)

Fusible web

Heat-resistant interfacing

Fusible interfacing

EMBELLISHMENTS

Embellishment is decoration, adornment and ornamentation and can be anything you choose to beautify your work – from using unusual threads for decorative embroidery stitches to adding trims and three-dimensional objects. Collecting embellishments is highly addictive as there are so many gorgeous braids, trims, ribbons, beads, buttons and charms available. See Crazy Patchwork and Decorative Quilting (pages 100 and 228) for more on embellishing. Embellishments generally fall into the following types but mixing and matching is fun.

- Ribbons, tapes, braids, cords, ricrac and thousands of other decorative trims.
- Bows, lace and broderie anglaise.
- Sequins and beads.
- Buttons, charms and shells.

WORKING WITH FABRICS

There are many aspects to consider when working with fabric, the most important being choosing them in the first place! This section takes a look at selecting fabrics and using colour, as well as practical aspects such as estimating how much fabric will be needed and preparing fabric for use. For information on hand and machine piecing, see pages 50 and 54.

CHOOSING FABRICS

Choosing fabric is arguably the hardest part of making a quilt or other project. With almost limitless choice, where do you start? It is also one of the most exciting parts, with so many gorgeous colours and prints to choose from and combine in fresh and interesting ways. This is the time when guilt over a large stash of fabric can turn into relief that there is so much to choose from – a collection of fabric seen together can yield interesting combinations that you might not have thought of otherwise. When choosing fabrics it might help to take the following points into consideration – colour, value, contrast and variety.

COLOUR, VALUE, CONTRAST AND VARIETY

Colour is a driving force for quilters. Many people select fabrics after a colour scheme and quilt design have been decided but not always; falling in love with a particular fabric can be the starting point for a whole design and its colour scheme. Think about what works for you colourwise. What colours are you drawn to or repelled by? Do you like bold or subtle prints, bright or muted colours? If you are a beginner, it is usually best to work with colours you like and feel comfortable with.

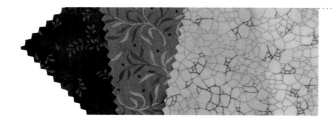

Value – This is the lightness or darkness of a colour and many quilters find that a mixture of light, medium and dark colours produces the most visually satisfying result. A quilt that has fabrics all with the same colour value can look dull and boring. Fabric viewed through coloured lenses can reveal differences in value. Use a red lens for warm colours and a green lens for cool colours (see colour wheel opposite and picture on page 10).

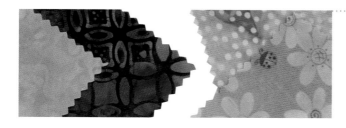

Contrast – This is often what gives a quilt additional interest, and contrast can be the juxtaposition of many things, warm against cool, light against dark, print against plain, large motif against small. Once you have chosen a preliminary collection of fabrics, look at them again to see if there is sufficient contrast.

Variety – This refers to the mix of fabrics used, as these can make a quilt more visually stimulating. Consider the style and scale of fabrics, mixing small prints with larger ones, and combining styles, such as florals with stripes, or geometrics with curves. Plain (solid) colours can work with busy prints to tie a design together.

BRIGHT IDEA

TO GET IDEAS ABOUT COLOURS AND FABRIC VARIETY, LOOK AT FABRIC COLLECTIONS BY FABRIC MANUFACTURERS. A COLLECTION WILL BE THE RESULT OF MUCH HARD WORK BY A DESIGNER BLENDING COLOURS, VALUE, CONTRAST AND VARIETY.

USING COLOUR

A successful quilt design depends on many elements and colour choice is near the top of the list of things to get right. Probably the best advice is to choose the colours you like, especially if the project is to be used in your own home. It also helps to observe colour combinations you see around you and make a note of those that appeal to you. Taking a closer look at a colour wheel can also help you make colour decisions.

The colour wheel is a tool used to help make colour choices, showing the relationships between colours.

WARM

yellow-green   yellow

green   yellow-orange

blue-green   orange

blue   red-orange

blue-violet   red

violet   red-violet

COOL

primary   *secondary*   *tertiary*

analogous   *complementary*   *split complementary*

hue   *tint*   *tone*   *shade*

THE COLOUR WHEEL

This is a tool that artists have used for centuries and is useful for quilters too. A colour wheel is a way of arranging colours so their relationships can be seen. At its simplest the colour wheel is based on twelve colours. Three of these – blue, red and yellow – are described as primary colours (see circles above). These are pure colours seen when light is split and they cannot be created from other colours.

When primary colours are combined in equal amounts they create three secondary colours of violet, green and orange (blue + red = violet; blue + yellow = green; red + yellow = orange).

When primary colours are combined with secondary colours in equal amounts they create six tertiary or intermediate colours of yellow-orange, red-orange, red-violet, blue-violet, blue-green and yellow-green.

These twelve colours are the ones seen in the colour wheel above. Colours are also described as 'warm' or 'cool' and having a 'value', that is, a lightness or darkness. Colour becomes even more interesting once you start creating tints, tones and shades. A tint is a colour with white added. Tints are often called pastels and are normally soft, light and airy. A tone is a colour with grey added. Tones have a similar muted quality and can be a bit dull but act as a foil to brighter colours. A shade is a colour with black added. Shades can be rich, dark and imposing. The intensity of a colour also plays a part and highly saturated colours, such as a really brilliant red or yellow, can be too forceful and overwhelming and are best used in moderation.

Colours can be further described by their position on the colour wheel. Colours next to each other are the most similar and are described as analogous (see above). Those colours that are opposite each other are the most different and are called complementary. Sometimes a finished quilt can seem flat and dull and this may be because it has been made with fabrics all having the same value or with too many colours with the same tone. A mixture of light, medium and dark will create more visual interest, as will a splash of a complementary colour. A view finder is a useful tool for judging the value and tone of a fabric's colour.

COMMON COLOUR TERMS

It is helpful to learn some basic terms describing colour.

Hue – another name for colour.
Primary colours – blue, red and yellow.
Secondary colours – violet, green and orange.
Tertiary colours – yellow-orange, red-orange, red-violet, blue-violet, blue-green and yellow-green.
Analogous colours – colours next to each other in the colour wheel.
Complementary colours – colours opposite each other in the wheel.
Value – a colour's lightness or darkness.
Tint – a colour with white added.
Tone – a colour with grey added.
Shade – a colour with black added.

BRIGHT IDEA

TO HELP MAKE DECISIONS ABOUT COLOUR AND BLOCK DESIGN MAKE A SAMPLE BLOCK USING COLOURS AND FABRICS YOU THINK MIGHT WORK WELL.

COLOUR COMBINATIONS

There are many colour combinations that work, and many books devoted to the subject. Try the following suggestions for choosing a scheme.

One colour – Choose just one colour and find fabrics in that colour in darks, mediums and lights, some with small prints, some with large. For a different look this single colour could have a white or black added to it for a fresh feel.

Side by side colours – Look at the colour wheel and choose three colours that are next to each other in the colour wheel. These colours will harmonize well together. You could widen the range to five colours side by side or even seven.

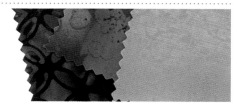

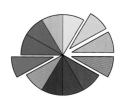

Side by side colours with a complementary – Choose three colours next to each other in the wheel and then choose a fourth colour that is complementary to one of the three, often called an accent colour. You could extend this to five colours and an accent.

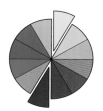

Complementary colours – Choose a colour and find its opposite colour in the colour wheel. Rather than having equal amounts of both colours, try having a 'major' colour, which occurs the most, and a 'minor' complementary colour that occurs less.

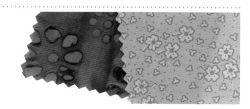

Triangle colours – Choose three colours equal distances apart in the colour wheel, often called a triad, to create a harmonious mix with a modern twist.

Multiple colours – Choose a colour from each segment of the wheel, varying the tints, tones and shades to create a multi-hued scheme. Scrap quilts often use this scheme successfully.

Neutral colours – These are colours that work well with many other colours. Black, white, grey, ivory, cream, beige and brown are all neutrals.

BRIGHT IDEA

THE SELVEDGE MIGHT BE A BIT OF A NUISANCE AT TIMES BUT IT INCLUDES USEFUL PRINTED INFORMATION ABOUT THE FABRIC AND THE COLOURS USED. IF YOU KEEP THESE INFORMATION STRIPS YOU CAN USE THEM LATER NOT JUST TO IDENTIFY THE FABRIC YOU HAVE USED BUT ALSO AS A WAY OF CREATING ATTRACTIVE COLOUR COMBINATIONS.

BUYING AND STORING FABRIC

Fabric isn't just available by the yard or metre but in a sometimes bewildering array of pre-cut sizes. You can buy fat quarters, thin quarters, fat eighths, thin eighths, 5in (12.7cm) squares, 10in (25.4cm) squares, strips in different widths, triangles, rectangles and more, not to mention large-scene panels. These pre-cuts can save you time in measuring and cutting and many quilt patterns have been devised using them. Indeed, whole books have been written about the many uses of these handy pre-cuts (see Further Reading, page 252).

FAT QUARTERS

A quilt design usually requires small quantities of several fabrics and for most quilters fat quarters are a convenient and affordable way to buy fabric for a design. A fat quarter is half a yard or metre of fabric cut in half across the width, yielding a piece that is normally 18in x 22in (46 x 56cm), which is much more useful and versatile than a thin quarter, which is approximately 9in x 42in (23cm x 106cm). Fat eighths are also more useful than thin eighths. For the number of squares yielded from a fat quarter see Useful Information on page 250.

COMMONLY AVAILABLE PRE-CUTS

Squares – Squares are readily available in a 5in (12.7cm) size, often called charm squares, and in a larger 10in (25.4cm) size (called Layer Cakes™ by Moda). These squares are usually a selection of twenty or forty different fabrics from one collection. They can be used as squares or to create other units, such as half-square and quarter-square triangles.

Strips – Pre-cut strips are popular and are commonly available 2½in (6.3cm) wide x 44in (112cm) long. Strips this size may be called 'roll-ups'. Moda call these strips Jelly Rolls™. Narrower strips 1½in (3.8cm) wide x 44in (112cm) long are also available (Moda call theirs Honey Buns™). Pre-cut strips are usually twenty to forty-two fabrics from a single collection. They can be used to piece many units and blocks and one roll of forty-two 2½in (6.3cm) wide strips is usually sufficient for a single bed-sized quilt, depending on how the strips are pieced.

Triangles – Pre-cut triangles may be offered by some fabric manufacturers, usually eighty 6in (15.2cm) half-square triangles, with two triangles each of forty different fabrics from the same collection. Moda call their pre-cut triangles Turnovers™.

Panels – Panels, sometimes called cheater cloths, are available in various sizes printed with a scene or other pictorial element. They can be a quick way to create a quilt or wall hanging (see page 4).

Kits – There are many quilt patterns available as kits complete with instructions, patterns and fabrics.

STORING FABRICS

Those of us addicted to fabric often find it hard to organize our stash, especially after a marathon auditioning session where failed candidates are strewn all over the bed or sofa. Storage really depends on the size of your stash and space available. Fabrics need to be stored out of direct sunlight and kept safe from insects so plastic or canvas boxes with lids are a good idea, especially if they can be kept under a bed. Keeping fabric pieces folded neatly will take up the least space and allow you to quickly see the colour and pattern. Storage can be by colour, by fabric type or pattern (for example, batiks, florals, polka dots) or by tone.

ESTIMATING FABRIC REQUIREMENTS

If you are creating designs of your own or making a sampler quilt from different blocks you will need to be able to estimate fabric amounts – there's nothing worse than running out of a crucial fabric before a project is completed. If you are making a project from a book or magazine, the fabric requirements are usually provided, although some lists may be very general. Making a sketch of the overall quilt design and the block designs (see diagrams A and B below) is a good starting point as you can then list the separate elements that will need fabric, including those needed for blocks, sashing, borders, backing and edging. Estimates need to be generous to allow for seams, fabric grain and mistakes.

Overall quilt size – The finished size of a quilt depends on the bed it needs to fit and whether you wish it to just drape over the top or reach the floor on all sides. There are tables of standard bed sizes (see page 250) and wadding (batting) is also sold in these standard sizes. For a customized fit, measure the bed the quilt is needed for.

Blocks – Make a sketch of the block you want to make, labelling each part that will use a different fabric (B). Make a list of the total number of pieces needed in each colour for the block and multiply this by the total number of those blocks in the quilt. Make another sketch to estimate how many pieces can be cut from a yard, half yard or fat quarter. Do this for each different block.

Sashing and borders – These are normally cut on the straight grain and are usually rectangles, so draw a sketch of the pieces needed in each colour (C). Decide what size each piece will be and sketch the pieces side by side to see how many will fit across the fabric. Remember the selvedge, subtracting about 2in (5cm) from the width.

Backing – Backing fabric normally needs to be about 6in (15.2cm) wider than the quilt top. Whether it is seamed or not depends on the overall size of your quilt and the width of backing you are using. Seams can be horizontal or vertical. Fabric is normally 42in (106.7cm) but extra wide backing fabric is available, which means fewer seams. See page 187 for more on backing.

Binding – Fabric needed for binding depends on the width of the binding and whether it is to be single or double, cut on the straight grain or on the bias – see page 236 for more on binding. There are tables of binding fabric requirements and an example is given here. Double-fold binding cut on the straight grain 2½in (6.3cm) wide sufficient for a double (full) bed = 270in (686cm) approximately and would require ½yd (0.5m) of fabric or ⅔yd (0.75m) if cut on the bias.

Appliqué motifs – The easiest way to calculate how much fabric you need for appliqué work is to draw the motif within an easy geometric shape, such as a square and then measure the geometric shape – see page 139 for more details.

A *Quilt sketch*

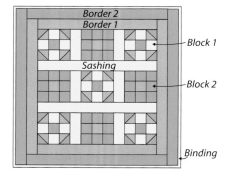

B *Block sketch*

Block 1
Fabric A = 1 piece per block
Fabric B = 4 pieces per block
Fabric C = 4 pieces per block
Fabric D = 4 pieces per block

Pieces in whole quilt for Block 1
Number of blocks in quilt = 5
Fabric A = 5 pieces
Fabric B = 20 pieces
Fabric C = 20 pieces
Fabric D = 20 pieces

C *Sashing and borders sketch*
Sashing

Border 1

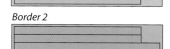

Border 2

← *Width of fabric* →

PREPARING FABRICS

It pays to take a little time preparing fabrics before use in order to reduce unpredictable results later on in the quilt-making process.

WASHING FABRICS

Some people always wash their fabrics before use to check for shrinkage and colourfastness, but others do not, preferring to do this after a quilt is finished to achieve that attractive, slightly crinkled antique look. Some pre-cut fabrics, such as charm squares or triangles, should not be washed before use as being small they might distort.

- If you think a fabric may shrink or bleed colour then wash separately before use in warm water and a mild detergent. If no dye runs occur rinse the fabric in cold water, dry and then iron.
- If the dye does run, put the fabric in a bowl with one part white vinegar to three parts cold water and leave for an hour or so. If the fabric continues to bleed then either discard it or use it for a project that won't require washing.
- Once washed, straighten fabric by hand whilst still damp to re-establish the fabric grain, pulling it gently into shape from opposite corners.

PRESSING FABRICS

In patchwork pressing means *pressing*, not sweeping over the fabric as in ironing. It is a restrained action, moving the iron in a lifting and pressing motion so seams lie in the right direction.

- Iron fabrics at the appropriate temperature to remove creases before use, so measuring and cutting will be more accurate.
- Steam from the iron can be used on stubborn creases though take care that you don't stretch and distort bias edges.
- Spray starch is useful to stabilize fabrics and give more body, especially if stacking fabrics ready for multiple layer cutting.
- Don't forget that many stages of piecing can be finger pressed, particularly for small units. Finger press on a hard surface using the flat area of the thumbnail so the seam lies flat. A hera or other firm tool can also be used.
- Press work first as it comes off the sewing machine to 'set' the stitches and help them settle into the fabric and reduce small puckers. Then press towards the seam allowance. Press seams so they lie in opposite directions as the work will then lie flatter and be easier to quilt – see diagrams below.

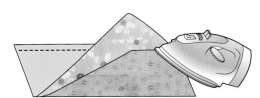

Press towards the seam allowance

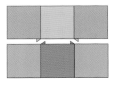

Press seams in opposite directions wherever possible so they 'nest' together neatly.

Press towards darker fabrics where possible so darker colours don't show through lighter colours on the right side.

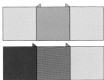

Press away from heavily pieced blocks with many seams where possible.

Press towards narrow strips to avoid the narrow area sinking.

PREPARING EDGES

Check all fabric pieces for straight edges. It may have been cut accurately but this isn't always the case.

- If fabric isn't straight, use your rotary cutter and ruler to trim it.
- Some loosely woven fabrics can be straightened by pulling a crosswise thread from the weave and then cutting along the gap. Tearing fabrics is rarely accurate enough for patchwork.

- Fabrics such as stripes and plaid patterns may have skewed grain lines. These can be straightened out by pulling on the two short sides of the fabric to return the warp and weft threads to right angles (see diagram below).
- Trim off the selvedge, that is, the tightly woven edge on a fabric. It is often more than ¼in (6mm) wide so may well appear in your patchwork without you intending it to.

USING FABRIC GRAIN

Fabrics are made with lengthwise threads called warp threads and crosswise threads called weft threads. Warp threads are on the straight grain and are the strongest with the least stretch. Weft threads are also firm but with a little more give. At a 45 degree angle to these threads is the bias grain, which has the least strength and the most stretch (see diagram below).

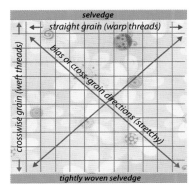

Cutting and sewing fabric on the straight grain causes the least stretching and distortion, which means that patches and units will align more accurately. When edges are on the bias they are likely to distort and stretch with handling and pressing, so when in doubt have the straight grain on the edges.

A fabric's tendency to stretch can be a positive benefit in some cases, for example, when cutting strips for bias-strip appliqué and bias binding, when you want the fabric to ease around curves easily. Bias-cut edges can also be of benefit for needle-turn appliqué, where edges need to be turned under smoothly. Bias-cut edges are also useful for slashing and chenilling to encourage fabric to fray and 'bloom'.

USING THE RIGHT NEEDLE

Before sewing you need to check you are using the right needle for your fabric. If you use too fine a needle in thicker fabrics it will break: use too thick a needle in a fine fabric and it will punch holes that will weaken the fabric. Generally, use larger needles for thicker threads and finer needles for thinner threads.

Needles are made of high carbon steel wire and, to resist corrosion, are plated with nickel, gold, platinum or titanium alloys. Needle sizes are in metric (European) and universal (American). For example, for a needle size 80/12, 80 is the metric size and 12 is the universal size (see the needles table on page 250). The higher the number, the thicker and longer the needle.

Needles are given various names that reflect their function or characteristics. Embroidery, or Crewel needles, are sharp, pointed needles with a longer eye than Sharps, making threading thicker threads easier. Betweens, or Quilting needles, are shorter than Sharps or Embroidery, with a small round eye and are good for detailed work on slightly heavier fabrics. Tapestry needles have a blunted tip and a large eye, making them suitable for wool thread and canvas stitching. Chenille are sharp-pointed with a large eye and are good for hand sewing with thicker threads or for ribbon embroidery. For machine sewing, Universals are available in a wide range of sizes and are suited to woven or knitted fabrics. Topstitch or Microtex needles are useful for general sewing. Metallic are designed for use with metallic threads and have a large eye, sharp point and fine shaft. Twin/Triple are double- or triple-pointed needles used in a sewing machine to create double or triple rows of stitching for decorative effect. Wing needles have a flared shaft that creates a decorative hole in fabric and so are useful for decorative machine stitching.

CHOOSING NEEDLES

When choosing needles the following guides may help.
Hand sewing and piecing – Sharps 60/8–65/9.
Hand quilting – Betweens 65/9, 70/10 and 80/12.
Hand appliqué – Sharps or Betweens 60/8–65/9.
Decorative hand stitches – various, depending on thread.
Machine piecing – Universal 80/12 or 70/12 for straight stitching.
Machine quilting – Universal 75/11–90/14.
Machine appliqué – Universal 70/10 or Embroidery 75/11 for satin stitch.
Decorative machine sewing – Embroidery 75/11 for 40 weight threads and 80/12 for 30 weight threads.
Italian quilting – Large-eyed Tapestry needle for threading the wool cord through channels.

SEWING MACHINE BASICS

Advice on using a sewing machine for patchwork, quilting and appliqué is given throughout the book, especially in Machine Piecing on page 54 and Machine Quilting on page 212.

Stitch length – This is the length in millimetres of each stitch that makes up the pattern. For machine quilting most people use a stitch length of about 10–12 stitches per inch (2.5cm) but this may be varied depending on fabric and threads being used. The thicker the fabric, the longer the stitch required.

Machine tension – This is the tightness the stitches are formed under and can affect how the work looks from the front and back. The upper and lower tensions should balance, so thread used in the bobbin should not show on the top of the work, and vice versa. The bottom bobbin thread tension is controlled by a screw on the bobbin case, which can be loosened or tightened. The top tension is controlled on most machines by a dial, the position of which will vary. If the bobbin thread is showing through on the top of the work, the tension is too tight, so loosen it by selecting a lower number. If the top thread is showing through on the back of the work and even creating loops, the tension is too loose, so tighten it by selecting a higher number.

Machine tools – There are some accessories that make sewing easier, including a walking foot or even-feed foot for machine-guided quilting, a ¼in (6mm) foot for ¼in (6mm) line spacing, a darning foot for free-motion quilting, a dual-feed foot to help ensure even stitching and a quilting guide to stitch parallel rows of stitching. See page 212 for more information.

CHOOSING A SEWING MACHINE

Buying a sewing machine or upgrading to a new one can be a little daunting as there are so many makes and models, all at different prices. Decide first what you intend to use the machine for and what you might need it for in the future.

• Will it be used mainly for patchwork and quilting or also for dressmaking and decorative sewing?
• Will you be doing a lot of quilting? If so, useful features include a large throat area to manoeuvre a bulky quilt through, a walking foot or fabric-feed mechanism and feed dogs that can be lowered for free-motion quilting.
• If you are interested in creative machine sewing try out decorative stitches including wing needle stitches.
• Take the time to 'test drive' several makes and models before you buy. Watch demonstrations at quilt shows and visit dealers with some fabrics to try.
• Once you have your machine, take the time to study the manual and practise using the machine.

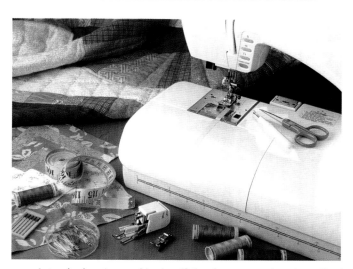

A standard sewing machine is sufficient for most patchwork, appliqué and quilting tasks and there are many makes and models available.

MARKING FABRICS

Designs can be transferred or marked on fabric ready for cutting out or quilting in various ways but there are things to consider. Should the marks be permanent or temporary? Can the marks be ironed, or does this set them? How do markers react with different fabrics? To be safe, always test a marking method on scrap fabric.

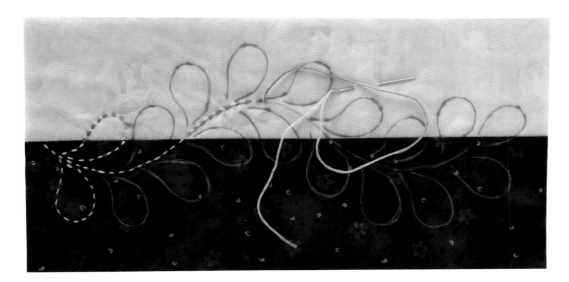

Select a marker to suit the fabric and its colour. Here a water-soluble pen has been used on the pale fabric, with a white watercolour pencil on the darker fabric. Both markers are easily washed out. A chalk marker would also have been suitable for the darker fabric.

Pencils – Normal graphite pencils and water-soluble coloured pencils can be used for marking. Marks should wash out with laundering. Quilter's or dressmaker's pencils are available in various colours. They have a wax content so may not be as easy to remove but should wash out.

Removable marking pens – These include water-soluble, iron-off and air-fading. The sort you choose depends on your project and preference. Some water-soluble markers can be set by the heat of an iron, so care needs to be taken to avoid this. Water-soluble markers can require more than a dab of moisture to remove them. Air-erasable markers may not stay in place long enough to complete a larger project but would work well with quicker projects. As the long-term effects of markers on fabric are not yet known it might be wise to rinse finished projects.

Chalk – This is easy to remove with a soft toothbrush, though take care with pink and blue coloured chalk on very light fabrics. Chalk is available in various colours and forms, including chalk pencils, blocks and as powder distributed through a wheel (Chaco liner). Chalk lines may need to be re-marked on large projects or those that have been handled a lot.

Hera – This plastic or bone tool is great for scoring temporary lines on fabric.

Masking tape – Low-tack masking tape is ideal for marking straight lines for quilting. Stick the tape in position and quilt along the edge of the tape. Remove the tape promptly to avoid stickiness on the fabric.

Compass – This is useful to mark circles. Circles can also be marked using templates cut from card or plastic or by drawing around plates, cups and even the plastic bases from pizzas. Curves can also be marked using a flexicurve.

Tracing – If tracing a design for quilting you will need to do this *before* layering the quilt into a sandwich in order to be able to see through the fabric. A light box is useful. See page 195 for tracing technique.

Dressmaker's carbon paper – This can be used for tracing or with templates and stencils. Most marks can be removed with washing. Various colours are available to suit different-coloured fabrics. Place the coloured side face down on top of the right side of the fabric and use a hard pencil to draw the design, checking to see it is transferring. You could use a spoked marking wheel instead, which will leave dots rather than a continuous line.

Embroidery transfer marker – This method is suitable for designs that will be cut out or where stitching will obscure the marked line. Draw the design on paper with a pencil. Turn the paper over and draw the design again, following the pencil line with an embroidery transfer marker. Position the design on the right side of the fabric with the marker line down. Use a warm iron to transfer the marked line on to the fabric.

Needle marking – Also called needle tracking, this method temporarily scores the fabric. Place the quilt top on a padded surface so the needle point can be pressed into it. Use the tip of a blunt tapestry needle to score the design on the fabric.

Perforated paper – Perforated paper and chalk powder are used in a technique called pierce and pounce, where chalk is pushed through holes in the paper. It can be used to mark dark fabrics. Draw the quilting design on paper and follow the lines with an unthreaded sewing machine to pierce holes. Place the paper on the fabric, sprinkle chalk over it and use a pad of cottonwool to push the powder through the holes. Use a chalk marker to go over the dotted lines.

Stencils and templates – These are very popular ways to mark designs and quilting patterns – see Using Templates overleaf and Marking Designs on page 194.

USING TEMPLATES

Templates are invaluable for patchwork, appliqué and quilting and can be made from various materials. Uses for templates are suggested throughout the book but in the main they are used to mark fabric pieces that make up patchwork blocks, to mark shapes for appliqué ready for cutting out, and to mark quilting patterns on a quilt top.

There are many commercial templates available to help make all sorts of blocks, including curved blocks, so it is worth checking quilting shops and online stores for templates that will help make work faster and easier. Check that any templates you plan to use are the correct size and shape and fit together as they should before you cut dozens of fabric pieces. Store templates flat and uncreased. They can be stored according to shape and labelled so you can quickly see what size they are. Marking the centre point and the centre lines of a template shape can also help when positioning it on fabric.

TEMPLATE MATERIALS
The following materials can be used for making templates.
- **Thin card or thick paper** – Trace the design on to the card or paper and cut it out on the line. Templates made from card are fairly robust so can be used many times.
- **Plastic** – Sheets of thin, clear plastic are available. The transparency makes it useful for 'fussy cutting' fabrics and its durability means that templates can be used over and over. Some stationery stores have large A1 sheets of plastic, which are slightly thicker than the plastic used for patchwork and quilting but are much cheaper.
- **Metal and plastic** – Pre-cut metal and plastic templates are available for English paper piecing. The materials are hard wearing and can be used as master templates, allowing many paper templates to be made from them.
- **Freezer paper** – This has a waxy side that can be temporarily stuck to fabric. It is useful for appliqué, allowing you to cut out designs, fold the seam allowance on to the waxy side, and stick in place – see page 151 for more details. It can also be cut to a shape and used as a quilting outline.

USING ISOMETRIC PAPER

Isometric paper is composed of triangles of equal dimensions and is useful for drafting designs and creating templates, especially for English paper piecing. It is available in metric sizes.

To use isometric paper to create a hexagon, use a ruler to draw the shape on the paper following the printed lines (see diagram below). Cut the hexagon from the paper, following the marked lines. Use a glue stick to glue the shape to stiff card and cut it out, again making sure you cut on the line. Label the template ready for use. See also page 84.

A range of templates made from different materials. Clear plastic templates are useful to place over a specific area of a fabric piece or patchwork block.

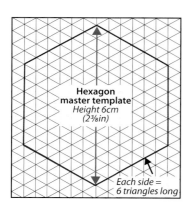

Hexagon master template
Height 6cm (2⅜in)

Each side = 6 triangles long

ENLARGING AND REDUCING

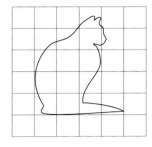

By far the easiest method of changing the scale of a template or image is to use a photocopier or a computer scanner. When reducing or enlarging a pattern or template shape a percentage is used to describe the amount by which the shape has been changed – a number under 100 means it has been reduced in size; a number over 100 means it has been enlarged. Three easy percentages are 75 per cent, 50 per cent and 25 per cent: a pattern reduced by 75 per cent will be three-quarters of its original size; a shape reduced by 50 per cent will be half the original size and one reduced by 25 per cent will be a quarter of its size. When enlarging an image, enlarging by 200 per cent will double the size of the original. Enlarging by 150 per cent will make the shape half as large as the original.

If you don't have a photocopier or scanner you can use graph paper or a drawn grid to enlarge or reduce a design. Draw the design on a grid of, say, ¼in (6mm) squares. Now use a grid with squares twice the size (½in/1.3cm), and copy the lines of the drawing in the same places on the grid. This doubles the size of the design. To reduce a design reverse the grid sizes. Many types of graph paper can be downloaded free from websites – search for 'download graph paper' for sites.

MAKING A SIMPLE TEMPLATE

Making your own templates is a useful skill. These instructions use a cat motif but the principles are the same for any shape.

1 Start by creating the shape or motif you require at the size needed. There are several methods you can use to do this, as follows.
- If the shape is already the size you want, simply trace it with a pencil on to tracing paper.
- If the shape is a geometric one, draw it following the instructions on pages 31–33.
- Some polygon shapes can be drawn using isometric paper (see opposite).
- If the shape is too large or too small, reduce or enlarge it using a photocopier or computer scanner, and print it on to thick paper or thin card. If you don't have access to a photocopier or scanner, follow the instructions above for enlarging and reducing designs.

2 Once you have your shape or motif, create a master template from it by copying it on to sturdy material such as thick paper, thin card or template plastic. Use a pen with a fine point so the shape stays true to the original. Cut it out with sharp paper-cutting or household scissors. Take care that you don't inadvertently enlarge the shape as you cut it out – cut exactly on the line or just inside to avoid this. Label the shape 'master' and add its finished size, if relevant. ▼

3 Place the template on the right side of the fabric and trace around the shape lightly with a pencil or erasable marker. ▼

4 If the shape is being used for appliqué, remove the template and cut out the fabric piece ⅛in–¼in (3mm–6mm) beyond the marked line if a seam is required or on the line if no seam is required. ▼

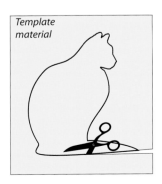

Template material

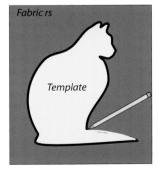

Fabric rs

Template

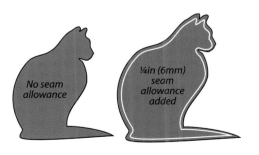

No seam allowance

¼in (6mm) seam allowance added

MAKING A MULTI-PART TEMPLATE

In appliqué, many motifs consist of more than one shape and some of the shapes overlap, so templates are needed for each part. A sunflower motif is used as an example here but designs can be much more complex.

1 This motif has eight petals, each overlapped by a central circle. Two templates will be needed – one circle and one petal shape – so prepare these as in step 1 on page 27. ▼

2 Choose your fabrics – one for the background, one for the centre circle and one for the petals (or the petals could all be different fabrics). Use the circle template to cut one circle from fabric and use the petal template to cut eight petals. If using an appliqué method that requires a seam allowance (such as needle-turn), cut the fabric pieces ⅛in–¼in (3mm–6mm) beyond the marked line. ▼

3 Position the pieces on the background fabric. Add the central circle last as it covers the ends of the petals. Place the circle template on the background fabric and lightly draw around it to mark its position. Sew or fuse the petals in place, making sure their lower edges overlap the circle. If petals are being sewn in place with a seam allowance only turn under the edges marked in green on the diagram, as the lower end will be covered by the centre circle. Sew the circle in place to finish. ▼

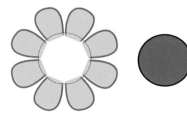

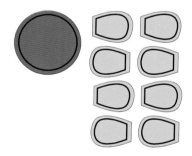

SEAM ALLOWANCE OR NO SEAM ALLOWANCE?
Templates can be drawn with or without a seam allowance depending on their purpose. The basic guidelines are as follows.
Do use a seam allowance if the shape needs to be turned under all round, as in needle-turn appliqué and freezer paper appliqué. Simply draw another outline, normally ¼in (6mm) further out from the original all round.
Do use a seam allowance if the shape is being used to cut fabric pieces for patchwork.
Don't use a seam allowance if the shape is being used for fusible web appliqué; the edges are protected by the web and may also be stitched over in some way.
Don't use a seam allowance if the shape is being used as a quilting pattern.

This delightful scene, part of a gorgeous quilt by Mandy Shaw, uses multi-part templates to create the appliqué characters.

DRAWING AND CUTTING SHAPES

Being able to draw shapes and cut them out accurately is a fundamental skill in patchwork, appliqué and quilting and this section gives advice on drawing common shapes and how they can be cut using rotary cutting equipment. See the Patchwork section for additional guidance and tips.

Fabric can, of course, be cut with scissors but by far the easiest, quickest and most accurate method is with rotary cutting equipment. A self-healing cutting mat and acrylic quilter's ruler, the larger the better, and a rotary cutter with a large blade are really all you need for basic cutting. If you love drafting and designing, there are many excellent books on the subject – see Further Reading on page 252.

Fabric doesn't have to be cut in rigid lines and patterns. Free-form cutting without a ruler, with a rotary cutter or scissors, in softly waving lines can create attractive and unusual designs. Freedom from the ruler can be very liberating!

Combining shapes in attractive blocks and patterns is one of the most exciting aspects of patchwork and quilting. Accurate drawing and cutting will lead to the best results. This beautiful quilt by Christine Porter was inspired by a Victorian tiled floor and uses squares, rectangles and triangles in a striking arrangement.

ROTARY CUTTING

The following points should lead to successful rotary cutting. See also Cutting Safety, overleaf.

- Press fabrics before cutting them to remove creases.
- Cut on a firm surface on a self-healing mat. Avoid straining your back with a surface that is too low.
- A 45mm diameter blade is useful for most cutting tasks, while a smaller 28mm blade is more manoeuvrable for cutting around curves and templates.
- Hold the cutter firmly in the same hand you write with at a 45 degree angle, with the blade vertical. Hold the ruler in place with your other hand, keeping fingers away from the edge. Do not use a normal ruler for rotary cutting, only a thick acrylic type. Standing up to cut usually gives more control.
- Cut with the blade firmly against the side of the ruler – on the right if you are right-handed and on the left if you are left-handed. The patchwork piece you are cutting should be under the ruler.
- When making a long cut, 'walk' your hand down the ruler when it needs to be steadied in a different place, rather than taking your hand off, as this will help stop the ruler moving.
- Do not cut over pins as they will damage the blade and may cause it to jump.

- Clean your mat regularly to stop the build-up of lint. Using the marked lines on the ruler rather than the mat will also reduce cutting in the same place each time and prolong the mat's life. Store the mat flat or hang it vertically, out of direct sunlight.
- Use the same ruler throughout a project as small measurement differences can occur between rulers.
- When rotary cutting around templates, position the cutter along the template and cut out the shape, taking care that you do not shave thin slivers off the template.
- Gentle curves can be cut with a normal rotary cutter although circle rotary cutters are available.
- When cutting strips of fabric from a folded piece of fabric, check that the first cut strip is not kinked in the middle. If it is, re-fold the fabric.
- When cutting multiple layers of fabric (sometimes called 'stack and whack'), take care how many layers you stack as too many can cause shifting and inaccuracy. Press each fabric with a little spray starch, pressing one fabric on top of the other to form a firm sandwich. Place the layers carefully on the cutting mat and trim the edge off first.

CUTTING SAFETY

A rotary cutter has an *extremely* sharp blade and it is easy to accidentally cut yourself or others so you must treat this equipment with great respect at all times and follow these safety tips.

- Place the mat on a firm surface such as a kitchen counter or sturdy table and stand up to cut. Wear something on your feet when you cut, in case you drop the cutter.
- Always cut away from yourself and keep your fingers well away from the edge of the ruler as you cut.
- Always replace the safety guard on the cutter after every cut. Some cutters have an auto-retract mechanism.
- Use a sharp blade that is free from nicks. Using a dull blade requires more pressure when you cut and risks the blade slipping. When a blade starts skipping threads it is time to replace it.
- Keep cutting equipment well away from children and pets, and never let children use them.
- Dispose of old blades carefully, either in the plastic container they came in or taped within thick card.

CUTTING STRIPS

Cutting fabric strips is the first step towards cutting other shapes and is required for many forms of patchwork, including Seminole and string patchwork. Fabric strips can be cut crosswise, at right angles to the selvedge, or lengthwise, which is parallel to the selvedge (A). Many quilters are used to cutting crosswise but there are advantages to cutting lengthwise. ▼

Cutting a crosswise strip – To cut a crosswise strip fold the fabric in two smoothly, right sides out, with selvedges aligned. Place it on the cutting mat with the fold aligned with a horizontal mark on the mat and cut a narrow vertical strip to straighten the edge (B). Now move the ruler to the right and cut a second strip to the desired width. If left-handed, cut from the right side instead of the left. Fabric can be folded more than once for multiple-layer cuts. ▼

A

B

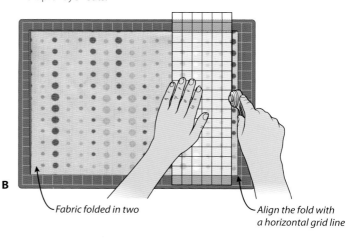

Fabric folded in two

Align the fold with a horizontal grid line

Cutting a lengthwise strip – Cutting fabric this way produces more stable strips because the straight grain is less stretchy than the crosswise grain. In addition, the print on a fabric follows the lengthwise grain, so when cut the pattern is less likely to be skewed. Fabrics can be stacked, usually four layers, and then be cut without folding, as shown here. Trim off the selvedge first (C) and then cut strips to the desired width (D). ▶

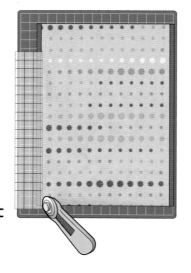

C

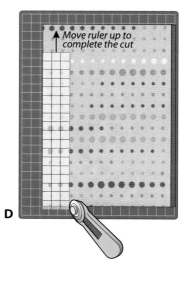

Move ruler up to complete the cut

D

SQUARES AND RECTANGLES

A square is a four-sided shape with four equal sides and four angles each 90 degrees. To draw a square with seam allowances = finished size + ½in (1.3cm) (A). ▶

A rectangle is a four-sided shape with two matching pairs of sides and four angles each 90 degrees. To draw a rectangle with seam allowances = finished width + ⅝in (1.6cm) and finished length + 1¼in (3.2cm) (B). ▶

Cutting – Cut the fabric into strips first and then re-position the ruler to cut the strips into squares or rectangles of the desired size (C). ▼

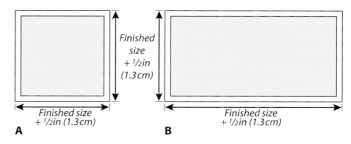

A — *Finished size + ½in (1.3cm)*, *Finished size + ½in (1.3cm)*

B — *Finished size + ½in (1.3cm)*

Cutting an individual square – If only one or two squares are needed, these can be cut individually rather than cutting many from a strip. Position a square ruler on one corner of the fabric and make two cuts along the two edges of the ruler, making the size slightly bigger than required (D). Take the cut square and turn it, re-positioning the ruler so the cut edges line up with the desired measurement on the ruler. Cut the other two sides of the square so the square is now true (E). ▼

C

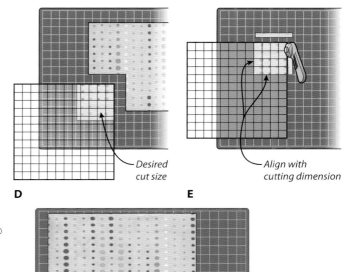

D — *Desired cut size*

E — *Align with cutting dimension*

Cutting multiple patches – It is far quicker and more efficient to cut patches from stacked strips. When a strip has been cut from several layers of fabric (as described previously) leave the strip in place on the mat and carefully move the rest of the fabric to one side. Rotate the mat 90 degrees and use the rotary cutter to trim a scant amount from the short end to tidy the strip. Re-position the ruler to cut the desired size of patch, and sub-cut in this way all along the length of the strip (F). ▶

F

HALF-RECTANGLE TRIANGLES

A half-rectangle triangle is a rectangle divided on the diagonal to produce a tall triangle. It has three unequal sides and one 90 degree angle.

To draw the shape with seam allowances = finished height + ⅝in (1.6cm) and finished width + 1¼in (3.2cm). Cut this rectangle once on diagonal to yield two units. ▶

Alternatively, draw a rectangle on paper without seam allowances and mark it into two triangles. Add a ¼in (6mm) seam allowance around all three sides of one of the triangles. Cut the fabric to this size.

Cutting – Cut fabric into strips first and then into rectangles of the desired size (as calculated in diagram). Re-position the ruler so the 45 degree line aligns with the edge of the rectangle and cut across the diagonal. Check the diagonal cut is sloping in the direction you require.

Finished size + ⅝in (1.6cm)

Finished size + 1¼in (3.2cm)

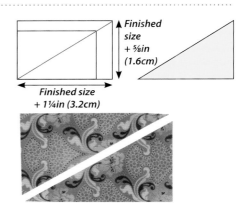

HALF-SQUARE TRIANGLES

A half-square triangle is created by dividing a square on the diagonal. The triangle has two equal sides and one 90 degree angle (A). To draw the shape with seam allowances = draw a square with a finished height + 7⁄8in (2.2cm) and divide the square once diagonally to yield two units. ▶

Cutting – Cut fabric into strips first and then into squares of the desired size. Re-position the ruler so the 45 degree line aligns with the edge of the square and cut across the diagonal (B). In quilt instructions a symbol may be used to indicate when a square is to be cut into half-square triangles. ◻ ▶

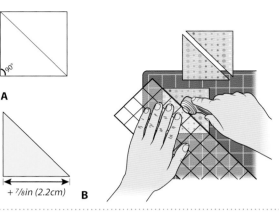

A

+ 7⁄8in (2.2cm) B

QUARTER-SQUARE TRIANGLES

A quarter-square triangle is created by dividing a square on both diagonals. It has two equal sides and one 90 degree angle (A). To draw the shape with seam allowances = draw a square with a finished base + 1¼in (3.2cm) and divide the square twice diagonally to yield four units. ▶

Cutting – Cut this shape in the same way as half-square triangles but make a second cut across the other diagonal (B). In quilt instructions a symbol may be used to indicate when a square is cut into quarter-square triangles. ⊠ ▶

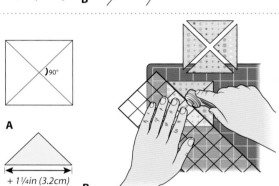

A

+ 1¼in (3.2cm) B

EQUILATERAL TRIANGLES

An equilateral triangle has three sides each the same length, with three angles each 60 degrees. To draw the shape with seam allowances = finished height + ¾in (1.9cm) (A). ▶

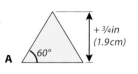

A 60° + ¾in (1.9cm)

Cutting – Cut a fabric strip to the desired width. Use a rotary ruler, positioning the 60 degree line along the top edge of the fabric strip (B). Make the cut and discard the end piece. Re-position the ruler so the other 60 degree line is along the bottom edge of the fabric strip (C). Make the cut – this is the first triangle. Re-position the ruler again as in B, with the 60 degree line along the top edge of the strip, and make the cut (D). Continue alternating the ruler position along the strip. ▼

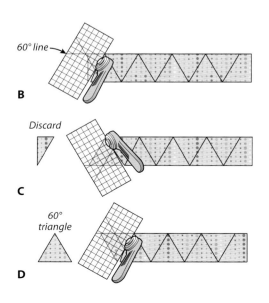

60° line

B

Discard

C

60° triangle

D

DIAMONDS

Diamonds commonly used in patchwork are those with 60 degree and 45 degree angles, making a short diamond and a long diamond (A). See also Patchwork with Diamonds and Polygons on page 84.

To draw the shapes with seam allowances = finished height + ½in (1.3cm) and finished width + ½in (1.3cm). ▼

Cutting – Diamonds can be cut in a similar way to triangles. First cut the fabric into strips that are ½in (1.3cm) wider than the finished height of the diamond. Use the 60 or 45 degree line on the ruler to cut diamonds of the desired angle and width (B). ▼

A 60° + ½in (1.3cm) + ½in (1.3cm) 45° + ½in (1.3cm) + ½in (1.3cm)

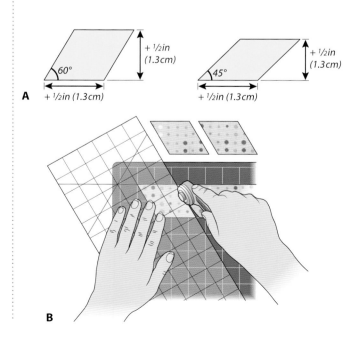

B

HEXAGONS

A hexagon has six equal sides and six equal angles. The shape can be created by cutting away two equilateral triangles from a 45 degree diamond (A). See also Patchwork with Diamonds and Polygons, page 84. ▶

Cutting – Start by cutting a strip ½in (1.3cm) wider than the desired finished height of the hexagon. Cut the strip into 45 degree diamonds. Lay a diamond horizontally as shown (B). Cut two equilateral triangles off each side of the diamond – these will be half of the diamond's height (C). ▶

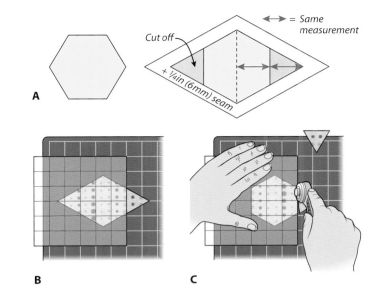

↔ = Same measurement

Cut off

+ ¼in (6mm) seam

A

B   **C**

OCTAGONS

An octagon has eight equal sides and eight equal angles. The shape can be created by cutting the corners off a square (A) so all sides are equal. See also Patchwork with Diamonds and Polygons on page 84. ▼

Cutting – Start by cutting a square ½in (1.3cm) larger than the desired finished height of the octagon. On the wrong side of the square mark the diagonal lines (B). Rotate the square so it is on point. Cut the four corners off the square by finding the line on the ruler that is equal to half the cutting height of the square, aligning this with the vertical line drawn on the square (C). ▶

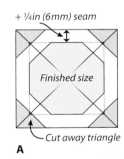

+ ¼in (6mm) seam

Finished size

Cut away triangle

A

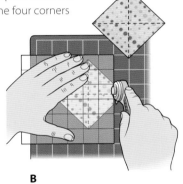

B

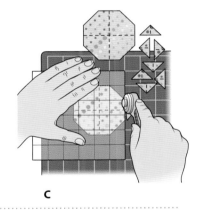

C

TRAPEZIUMS

A trapezium or trapezoid is a quadrilateral (a shape with four sides) which is actually based on a triangle. See also Patchwork with Diamonds and Polygons on page 84. The shape can be created by cutting the top off a triangle (A). ▶

Cutting – The size of the triangle to be cut off can be determined by drawing diagram A on graph paper, adding the seam allowance as shown and then cutting off the grey-shaded triangle (B). ▶

Cut off

Finished size

+ ¼in (6mm) seam allowance

A

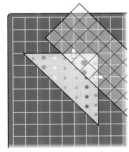

B

KITES

A kite is a quadrilateral based on a triangle. See also Patchwork with Diamonds and Polygons on page 84. A kite can be created by cutting away one side of a triangle (A). ▶

Cutting – Cut a kite shape by first cutting a half-square triangle (as described opposite). Draw diagram A on graph paper with the seam allowances, cutting off the shaded triangle (B). ▶

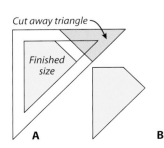

Cut away triangle

Finished size

A

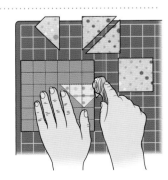

B

USING TECHNOLOGY

There are many pieces of equipment that most of us use routinely that can also be of help for patchwork, appliqué and quilting, including computers, scanners, printers, photocopiers, digital cameras and mobile phones. There are also software programs that are brilliant for planning and designing quilts.

USING COMPUTERS, SCANNERS AND PRINTERS

If you have a computer, scanner and printer you can use them in many ways when designing and stitching a quilt or other project. Here are a few suggestions.

- Having a computer, scanner and printer takes a lot of the drudgery out of copying designs and makes enlarging and reducing them quick and easy. Designs can also be flipped or reversed (as the teddies have been here), rotated and repeated (as the flower motif) without having to be taken to a photocopy shop.

- If you can't decide whether a selection of fabrics would work well together in a block and don't want to waste precious fabric making a block then fake it. Scan each fabric and make a colour printout. Cut up the paper fabric and assemble the pieces into the block, sticking them on to paper.
- If you have many templates to cut from paper or freezer paper for English paper piecing, copy the template into a word processing or drawing file. Repeat the shape as many times as you can on a page and then print. If printing on to freezer paper, print directly on to the non-shiny side. The printer must be a desk-jet type that works without heat, not a laser.

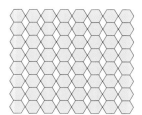

- A word processing program can be used to print quilt labels. Type in the details you want to include (see page 243) and arrange the text in a pleasing way – a 'centred' format looks good. Print the label on to fabric prepared to accept printer ink.

Print details here

- If you have skills in using drawing programs such as Adobe Illustrator or Corel Draw you can draw quilting patterns and print them out on to fabric. This would work for fabric pieces A4 size or smaller. Draw the pattern actual size in the drawing program using a grey line in a dashed form that mimics your desired quilting size. Press the fabric and use temporary spray glue to fix it right side up on to stiff card. Place the card in the printer and print out the pattern. Remove the fabric. Consult your printer manual to check for any problems associated with printing on materials other than paper.

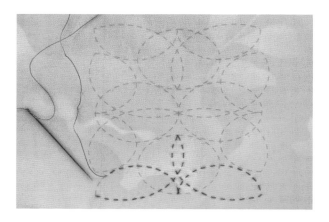

- Specially prepared fabrics are available for direct printing and can be used to print messages, photographs and other images on fabric.

USING QUILT DESIGN SOFTWARE

Designing quilts and projects can be achieved with drawing programs such as Adobe Illustrator and Photoshop and Corel Draw but there are dedicated software programs, such as Electric Quilt, which are more comprehensive and adaptive to patchwork, quilting and appliqué and would be worth exploring.

USING DIGITAL CAMERAS AND MOBILE PHONES

Apart from taking pictures of gorgeous quilts at shows to inspire you later, digital cameras and mobile phones can be used at home to help in designing and sewing.

- If trying to decide on a quilt layout, arrange all the blocks on the bed or floor and take a photo. Rearrange the blocks in another layout and take another photo. Reviewing the photos together makes it easier to decide which layout works best.
- Pictures of projects taken with digital cameras can easily be shared with other quilters, either as hard copy print-outs or posting as files on the web. Digital files can also be sent to patchwork magazines, competitions and organizations. If doing this, take the photo with the camera set on the highest resolution to produce a good quality print-out. The file size will be large, probably over 1MB.

USING THE INTERNET

Probably the most dramatic change in the way we use technology has taken place through the internet, not just increasing the information we have access to but vastly increasing the products we can review and purchase.

Interacting via the web

Interacting with other quilters via websites and blogs can be very enjoyable and a great way to swap useful information. The web is increasingly being used for social interactions and to share ideas, inspirations and photos. Most sites will allow you access as a guest and registration is normally free. There are many well-known social networking sites and thousands can be found via sites such as International Friendship Quilters (http://www.friendshipquilters.com). A list of quilting forums can also be found at (http://www.quiltinggallery.com) In fact, there are groups for every conceivable aspect of patchwork, appliqué and quilting.

Sites are an invaluable source of advice, ideas, free patterns, videos and much more. Most quilting authors have their own websites and blogs and these are useful not just for interacting with the author but for receiving information about work in progress, upcoming events and books being published.

E-SAFETY

While the web is exciting and informative it also contains hazards. Computer viruses are easily transmitted and can cause much damage, so before browsing make sure your anti-virus protection is the most comprehensive you can find and always keep it up to date. Be vigilant about the amount of personal information you give and *never* give your financial details unless you are sure the site is secure.

E-shopping

Shopping through websites has been with us for a long time. While nothing can quite take the place of seeing and touching fabrics on the bolt, websites selling fabrics and sewing equipment are exciting to visit. The majority of sites are safe and reputable but caution is always advisable, and the following points may help.

- ✓ *Always choose reputable sellers, checking they have a physical address and can be contacted by phone. Check their privacy policy and returns policy to ensure that the information you give them about yourself is respected and that faulty or unsatisfactory goods can be returned and refunded easily.*
- ✓ *Ensure that your payment is protected. Using debit, credit or charge cards through a secure website is normally the safest, with information verified by a third party, such as WorldPay or Verified by Visa. PayPal is another widely used service. When you come to enter card details a padlock sign in the web browser's window frame is an indication of trustworthiness but always be vigilant. Never give your personal or financial details to unsolicited emails. This is called 'phishing'.*
- ✓ *If dealing with a seller for the first time, especially an overseas one, limit your order so if anything goes wrong you don't lose large sums. A small initial order will also allow you to assess delivery times and the quality of the goods.*
- ✓ *When ordering from overseas be sure to assess the postage costs before you commit to buy, as you may find that these are shockingly high. Orders from home may be free over a certain order size.*
- ✓ *Keep a written note of what you are ordering and the cost. Although 'checkouts' and 'view basket' facilities are common it's always safer to do your own maths, especially if you decide not to buy an item and need to delete it from your basket. Once orders are processed the web retailer will normally send you an email confirmation of the order too, so print a copy of this.*
- ✓ *When the goods arrive, check them against your original order that they are all there and the correct price has been charged. If any items are delayed due to being out of stock then note whether they have already been charged for and when they are due to arrive.*
- ✓ *Some websites are easier to use than others, so if it's confusing or doesn't show clear pictures of the fabrics or items you want to buy then leave and find a better site.*

Patchwork

Patchwork is magical: take a few fabrics, cut them into pieces, sew them together and *voila*, something unique and wonderful is produced. Patchwork is one of the most exciting, inventive and utilitarian craft forms. It's also highly addictive and there seems to be no end to the fun and fascination of designing, combining and arranging fabrics in gloriously unique combinations.

This section begins by looking at some of the many settings or arrangements for patchwork and how working with blocks can produce an almost never-ending array of designs. We move on to seeing how certain shapes can be pieced together to create beautiful designs, including squares, strips, triangles, diamonds, polygons and curved shapes.

Other distinctive patchwork techniques explored include Seminole patchwork, crazy patchwork, puffed patchwork and folded patchwork. The section also includes special fabric techniques, such as slashing, gathering and weaving, which can be used with patchwork and appliqué to create highly tactile work. We also look at how sashing and borders can be used to develop a design.

Whether you are making a simple scrap quilt or an heirloom sampler quilt, there are some fabulous techniques to explore here.

PATCHWORK SETTINGS

A setting is the layout that the units, blocks or sections of a quilt or project are arranged in – and the choice is excitingly wide. By far the most common and easiest arrangement is using blocks, which are based on a grid, and over the centuries a vast number of block patterns have been developed. Block patterns, which are repeated to form more complex arrangements, have been with us for a long time and can be seen in art and architecture the world over – from Islamic mosques to Victorian tiled floors.

Blocks not only allow you to break a quilt design down into simpler units but the combination of different blocks and alterations in colour and pattern allow fascinating secondary patterns to become apparent. The majority of blocks are square, the easiest shape to combine, but the principles of arranging the layout of a quilt are the same whatever the block shape. Some of the most common quilt settings are described in this section. We also look at types of quilt with descriptions of the most popular ones, some of which you may be familiar with, such as sampler quilts and scrap quilts.

The way that patchwork units and blocks can be arranged is almost limitless, giving opportunities for wonderful combinations of colour and tone. The more varied the shapes, the greater the scope for unique designs.

Patchwork settings can be very simple yet still have impact, as this elegant quilt by Julia Davis and Anne Muxworthy shows. Each square has a border and the whole design is then set on point with triangles added to return the shape to an overall square.

COMMON QUILT SETTINGS

There are so many books, magazines and online articles on quilt settings that many books could be devoted to the subject (see Further Reading on page 252 for suggestions). Examples of the most usual layouts are given in this section to give you a taste of what you might try. Of course, diagrams with plain colours can only hint at the effects that can be achieved and this subject comes to life once gorgeous fabrics are used.

STRAIGHT SETTING

Straight quilt settings, that is arranging the blocks vertically or horizontally, are the most popular way to arrange a quilt. Straight settings, sometimes called edge to edge, may repeat the same block throughout the design of the quilt or feature different blocks. The blocks can be presented in the same way or rotated one way or the other, and often combined to create secondary patterns. The blocks can be joined to one another or be separated by 'frames' or sashing.

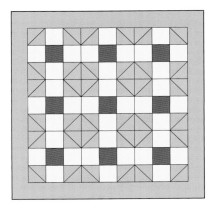 

ON POINT SETTING

Rather than arranging quilt units or blocks straight, they can be turned 45 degrees, which is called 'on point'. This type of layout can either be extended to the edge or border of the quilt with half blocks at the edges, as shown in the first diagram right, or corner triangles and setting triangles can be added to make the overall shape into a square or rectangle, as shown in the second diagram.

ALTERNATING SETTING

These quilt settings alternate a main block with another block, often a plain or simpler block, as shown in the first diagram. This means less piecing work and allows the main block to be shown off. If plain blocks are used this allows greater scope for quilting. Four-patch and nine-patch blocks are often alternated with plain blocks in this way. Quilt layouts can be in four quadrants, each rotated 90 degrees, as shown in the second diagram.

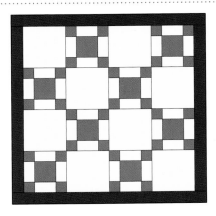 

TESSELLATING SETTING

Quilt settings with tessellating patterns are those that repeat a particular unit or pattern all over the quilt to make designs that interlock and create areas of positive and negative space. Tessellating patterns are visually stimulating and appear never-ending. They often use a single shape, such as a diamond, or a block, such as the Friendship Star block and the T block shown here. Tumbling Blocks and Inner City are two other blocks often used (see page 193).

 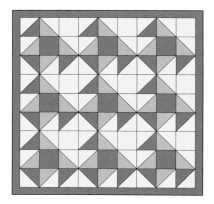

MEDALLION SETTING

A medallion setting is one where a central square, rectangle or circle forms the focal point of the quilt, with patchwork 'frames' or borders building out from this centre point. Printed panels, such as the Kona Bay one shown in the second diagram, can make very attractive focal points of a medallion-style quilt. See also the picture opposite.

TILTED SETTING

Many blocks can be tilted quite easily by adding pieced sections to each side, with the block then re-cut so the central pattern is at an angle. Square-within-a-Square and Log Cabin are blocks that look good in this type of arrangement. Tilted settings create great movement within a quilt. See page 134 for creating a tilted block.

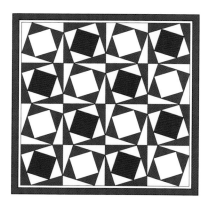 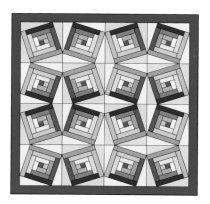

SASHED SETTING

The way that the blocks within a quilt are arranged can be enhanced by the use of sashing. Sashing, sometimes called lattice, is used to frame and separate blocks and can make a big difference to the look of a finished quilt. Sashing can be plain or pieced and can also have the addition of keystones and cornerstones (see second diagram). See pages 126–129 for more details on sashing and keystones.

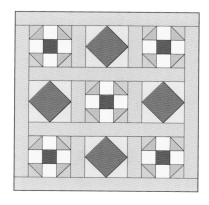 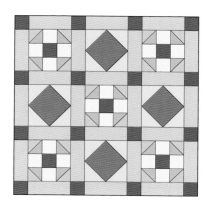

TYPES OF QUILT

Quilts are often given different names to describe their structure or purpose and you may come across some of the following terms in quilting books, magazines and on the internet.

ALBUM QUILTS

These quilts are personal creations, made up of blocks with all sorts of images meaningful to the maker, rather like a scrapbook of memories. The blocks may be patchwork, appliqué or a combination and the settings vary with the maker.

MEDALLION QUILTS

These quilts are characterized by a central square or rectangle that forms the focal point of the quilt, with patchwork 'frames' added to it and building out from the centre. The quilts are usually highly balanced and symmetrical.

SAMPLER QUILTS

These quilts feature a number of recognizable blocks in a unified design that shows the skill of the maker in coping with different techniques. See page 48 for more on sampler quilts.

SCRAP QUILTS

These quilts are literally made up of scraps of fabric, pieced together in any design. Because they use fabrics already to hand they usually have a colourful quality. See page 46 for more on scrap quilts.

This medallion quilt by Petra Prins features a central star panel surrounded by six borders, some plain and some pieced.

CHARM QUILTS

These are quilts where each piece of fabric used is different – in the past the aim was to use 1,000! Charm quilts often use the same shape throughout, commonly a square, rectangle or triangle. Many fabric manufacturers today supply ranges of fabric cut as 'charm squares', usually 5in (12.7cm) square. People often use the internet to find like-minded quilters to swap fabrics with.

FRIENDSHIP QUILTS

Friendship quilts developed in America from around 1840 onwards as people moved and settled westwards. Quilts were given to family or friends to show love and affection. They often use fabrics given by loved ones and are usually signed by the maker.

ROUND ROBIN QUILTS

These are fun quilts made by whole groups of quilters and are often medallion types. Everyone in the group makes a quilt centre and this is passed along to another person in the group who adds a border. It is passed on again to another quilter who adds the second border and so on. Eventually the quilt is returned to the originator, who can see how it has developed.

WORKING WITH BLOCKS

Most blocks are designed on geometric principles so a great many can be categorized as types (although even these categories have subdivisions!). There are thousands of block names, and many have more than one name, but the good news is that you don't have to know the names of any of them to create wonderful patchwork. There are more than 100 blocks illustrated in this book – plenty to experiment with!

Blocks made from small units, such as the equilateral triangles used here, allow plenty of scope for playing with fabrics.

Some block names describe a shape the block may represent, such as Eight-Point Star, Spider Web and Streak o' Lightning. Some are named after the pattern they represent, such as Pine Tree, Bow Tie and Pinwheel. Others are named after historical and religious subjects, such as Lincoln's Platform, Clay's Choice and Walls of Jericho. Some names are just fanciful, their origins lost in the past, such as Toad in a Puddle, Corn and Beans and Dove in the Window. When American magazines started publishing patchwork patterns from the 1830s onwards there was an explosion in new block designs and names. To make things easier, blocks are usually categorized into various types – see opposite and overleaf.

This book shows how to make many blocks, beginning with simple shapes, such as squares, rectangles and triangles, and moving on to more complex shapes, including diamonds, trapeziums and polygons. By working through the book you can increase your knowledge and skills and tackle all sorts of block.

BRIGHT IDEA

IF YOU ARE CREATING A QUILT OR OTHER PROJECT COMPOSED OF VARIOUS BLOCKS AND CAN'T DECIDE WHICH ARRANGEMENT WOULD WORK BEST, ARRANGE THE BLOCKS ON THE FLOOR OR BED AND USE A DIGITAL CAMERA OR MOBILE PHONE TO TAKE A PICTURE. CHANGE THE LAYOUT AROUND AND TAKE ANOTHER PICTURE. DO THIS AS OFTEN AS NECESSARY. YOU CAN THEN SCROLL THROUGH THE PICTURES TO DECIDE WHICH ONE YOU LIKE BEST.

Just two blocks were used in this quilt by Pam and Nicky Lintott made from a Jelly Roll™. The alternating setting and colour combinations create a vibrant and interesting quilt.

BLOCK TYPES

The way that blocks are classified depends on the books you read and how deep you want to delve into the subject. Blocks range from simple one-patch designs to complex multi-patch arrangements using a mixture of shapes. The idea of a quilt made up of the same one-patch units or blocks may seem limited but the exciting thing about patchwork is that a single shape repeated over and over but in different colours and fabric patterns can create a vibrant design. As experience grows so too does the thrill of combining different types of block, creating patterns within patterns. Of course, blocks don't have to be regular and they may also be made up of appliqué motifs rather than be pieced. The following general categories are often used to describe block types, with diagram examples below and overleaf. Subsequent sections in the book show how to create such blocks.

ONE-PATCH BLOCKS

These can be made up of various shapes, including squares, rectangles, triangles, diamonds and hexagons, and when combined in certain patterns are given names. These blocks lend themselves well to interlocking, mosaic patterns called tessellations, where combinations of positive and negative space or light and dark tones create fascinating visual illusions.

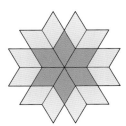
Six-Point Star

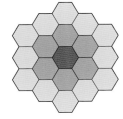
Grandmother's Flower Garden

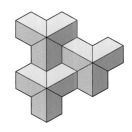
Inner City

FOUR-PATCH BLOCKS

These are easy to sew and so versatile. A four-patch block is made up of four units, but these can be subdivided to create many more patterns. A combination block of four different blocks might also be described as a four-patch block if it is used repetitively in a quilt layout.

Four patch

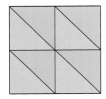
Pinwheel

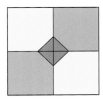
Bow Tie

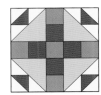
Dutchman's Puzzle

FIVE-PATCH BLOCKS

These are constructed on a five x five grid, so each block would contain a total of twenty-five units. Subdivisions of the elements of the grid can create many more variations. These units do not have to be the same size and the central one can be narrower or wider than the flanking ones.

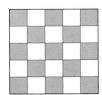
Five patch

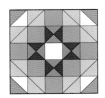
Handy Andy

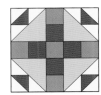
Duck and Ducklings

SEVEN-PATCH BLOCKS

These blocks are constructed on a seven x seven grid, so each block would contain forty-nine units and so can build into very complex patterns. As with five-patch blocks, the units in seven-patch blocks do not have to be of equal size.

Seven patch

Lincoln's Platform

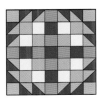
Dove in the Window

NINE-PATCH BLOCKS

Along with four-patch blocks, nine-patch blocks form the backbone of so many quilt designs. These blocks are made up of nine units, three x three, and are usually made up of squares and rectangles, with subdivisions creating triangles.

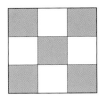
Nine patch

Shoo Fly

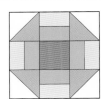
Churn Dash

Card Trick

SQUARE-IN-A-SQUARE BLOCKS

There are many blocks made up of squares within squares, frequently with inner squares turned on point. Amish quilts make a bold feature of this type of design. Other designs, such as Log Cabin and Snail's Trail (see pages 63 and 89) are often classified as square-in-a-square designs.

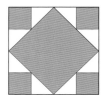
Art Square

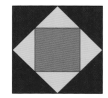
Economy Patch

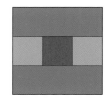
Boxed Square

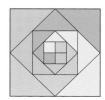
Snail's Trail

STAR BLOCKS

There are dozens of star blocks and a wealth of variations and many are based on a nine-patch format. Friendship Star blocks were traditionally drawn around a square so that names could be stitched in the centre. Some block designs are more irregular and eccentric and would make good subjects for English paper piecing.

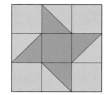
Friendship Star

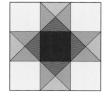
Aunty Eliza's Star

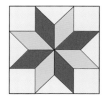
Le Moyne Star

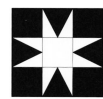
Eight-Point Star

CURVED AND FAN BLOCKS

Curved blocks are very popular and create some interesting interlocking patterns. Some classic blocks use curves and fan shapes, including Dresden Plate and Double Wedding Ring. See page 93 for more examples of curved blocks.

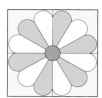
Dresden Plate

Dresden Fan

Fool's Puzzle

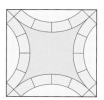
Double Wedding Ring

POLYGON BLOCKS

Any type of polygon can be used as the basis of a patchwork block but the most common multi-sided shapes used are hexagons, which have six sides, and octagons, which have eight sides. Patterns created with these shapes tend to be composed of triangles, diamonds and trapezoids, as the examples here show.

Six-sided Star

Octagon

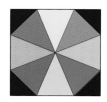
Kaleidoscope

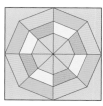
Spider's Web

PICTORIAL BLOCKS

These blocks are also called realistic or representational and favourite motifs include buildings, trees, flowers and animals. They can use various shapes but geometric ones are the most common. Many objects can be reduced to a simple grid representation. Cross stitch embroidery patterns can be good sources of inspiration.

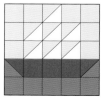
Sailing Ship

House

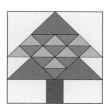
Tree

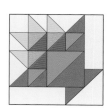
Grape Basket

BLOCK SETTINGS

The way that blocks are combined in an arrangement or setting is fascinating and varied, and part of the fun of patchwork is deciding on how blocks will be combined. Some magical effects can be created when blocks begin to be sewn together. Some basic arrangements are shown here.

REPEATING BLOCK SETTINGS

Perhaps the simplest design of blocks is a repeating grid pattern. Even this repetition can create interesting secondary patterns. Alternatively, blocks can be repeated horizontally or vertically with plain areas left in between.

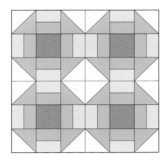 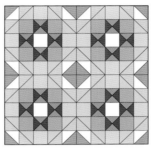 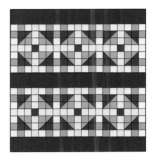

MIRRORED SETTINGS

Mirroring and rotating blocks can create quite a different look. Rotations of 45 degrees produce pleasing effects, especially when combined with plain blocks or very simple ones.

 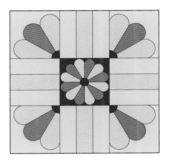

ON POINT SETTINGS

It is amazing how different a block can look when set on point, that is diagonally, and it is well worth trying this effect. Blocks set this way will need triangles added at the sides and corners. By offsetting a row half a block down, zigzag background patterns can be created.

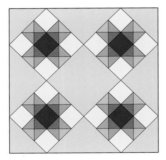 

COMBINATION BLOCK SETTINGS

The sky's the limit when it comes to combining different block designs. Sometimes the combination of just two blocks can create the cleanest look; alternatively, just adding plain squares or simple four-patch blocks is equally successful.

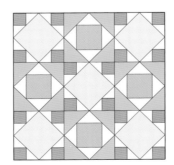 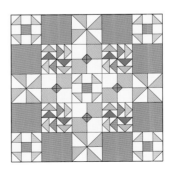

SCRAP QUILTS

Scrap quilts are traditionally made up of small pieces and offcuts of fabric, pieced together in a chosen arrangement. These quilts often have a colourful quality but scrap selection can also be within a specific colour range. Some people define a scrap quilt as one where little or no new fabric is bought for the project. String patchwork (see page 76) is often described as scrap work. Making a scrap quilt is a really easy way to begin quiltmaking, but even if you are experienced just feeling free to delve into your fabric stash or use up small remnants is a relaxing way to work. In addition to providing a great way to use up your excess fabric, scrap quilts can also produce some wonderful results.

DECIDING ON COLOURS

For many people a true scrap quilt is one that uses random scraps in random colours – just put two piles together, one of darks and one of lights, and select from each pile in turn as you stitch them together. This casual approach often leads to some interesting effects, with colour combinations that might not otherwise have been discovered.

SELECTING THE SCRAPS

The scraps used in this type of quilt can come from many different sources, including those from newly purchased fabrics, offcuts from fabrics used for other projects or pieces cut from old clothing and household textiles. Take care when using old fabrics that you use unworn areas, such as shirt tails. You could also base a scrap quilt around units and blocks previously made and not used, using sashing to unify them all.

CUTTING PATCHES

You can use rotary cutting to obtain a good selection of patches. Try using just fat quarters, stacking four together and cutting one or two strips lengthwise from the stack. Choose another four fat quarters and stack and cut again, and so on. These strips can then be sub-cut into different shapes and should yield a wide variety of colours and prints for you to play with.

Bright, multicoloured scraps are beautifully combined in this scrap quilt by Katharine Guerrier. Only two star blocks were used – Friendship Star and Eight-Point Star – but the scrap arrangement of fabrics creates the illusion of many more blocks.

CHOOSING A PATTERN

The setting for a scrap quilt can be anything you like and perhaps one of the easiest methods is to choose a single block shape, repeated over the whole quilt. One-patch blocks that could be used include squares, rectangles, triangles, diamonds and hexagons. One-patch blocks can form tessellating patterns, where light and dark tones create visually interesting designs – see the diagrams and picture below for some ideas and also Block Types on page 43. Of course, scrap quilts can also use more formal arrangements, especially those that emphasize light and dark tones – see Common Quilt Settings on page 39 for ideas.

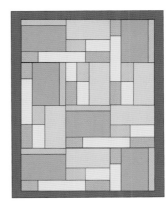

A scrap quilt can easily be created from a single rectangular pieced block, in whole and half units. These can be recombined to produce an irregular look.

Half-square triangles paired in a combination of lights, mediums and darks create a pleasing scrap quilt design.

A repeated block, such as Friendship Star, can create an all-over, tessellating pattern that would be ideal for a scrap quilt.

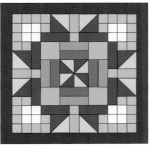

Small units or blocks left over from other projects can be combined in a scrap quilt. If the different scales are a problem, use sashing to bring the units or blocks up to sizes that can then be pieced together.

This scrap quilt made by Jenny Lankester uses light and dark values to telling effect, with squares and a few half-square triangles combined to produce a striking pattern.

SAMPLER QUILTS

Sampler quilts are very popular, not just because they are fun and rewarding to do but because they offer the opportunity to learn new techniques and build skills. A sampler quilt is made up of different blocks, set together in a pleasing design, usually with the addition of sashing and borders. The blocks can be a mixture of anything you like, pieced and appliqué. Many teachers use sampler quilts as a way of teaching quiltmaking skills because so many fundamental techniques can be included (see Further Reading on page 252).

Sampler quilts allow the development of many skills, such as quilt design, fabric selection and colour choices. They can be true scrap quilts, where fabrics are selected from your stash, or planned carefully around a particular colour scheme. They can be an eclectic mixture of blocks or focus on a specific theme, such as curved or appliqué blocks.

This sampler quilt by Mary Harrowell, made during a Lynne Edwards' sampler quilt course, displays a wealth of techniques in a beautifully coloured and balanced design. It features twenty different blocks, including pieced and appliqué. The blocks are framed with sashing and setting stones and then with two borders.

CHOOSING BLOCK SIZES

Some thought needs to be given to the finished block sizes in a sampler quilt, so all the blocks balance visually with each other – see examples opposite. The use of sashing often solves size problems, allowing blocks to be framed with sashing and so brought up to the same sizes. If sashing is to be used, consider this early in the design, so the chosen fabric links well with the fabrics in the blocks.

The size of the blocks will not only dictate the finished size of the quilt but also how many blocks can be used. For example, if you want to make a single bed-sized quilt, say, 50in x 80in (127cm x 203cm), and you choose to make 12in (30.5cm) square blocks, there will be space to allow approximately three blocks wide x five blocks long, once sashing, borders and binding are added. You might then want to reduce the block size to allow the inclusion of more blocks in the quilt. See page 250 for more information on standard quilt sizes.

DECIDING ON FABRICS AND COLOURS

Audition lots of fabrics for a sampler quilt as some of the best results are obtained by mixing prints in different scales and themes with tone-on-tone and plain fabrics. You need to end up with a final choice that gives you sufficient scope to create some interesting and varied effects but not so many that the design is a mishmash. See also pages 14 and 18 for further advice on choosing fabrics and colours.

SELECTING A SAMPLER QUILT DESIGN

A sampler quilt can be anything you choose and making one is a great opportunity to be creative in your design. The patchwork blocks selected can be favourites you've made before or new ones you'd like to try. You could choose just rectilinear blocks, curved blocks or appliqué blocks – or a combination of all types.

Layouts for sampler quilts are as varied as the blocks. A first attempt at this type of quilt could have the blocks arranged in a simple grid pattern, allowing you to concentrate on the blocks, with perhaps some simple sashing and a final border. Setting the blocks on point can create a dynamic-looking quilt, while a medallion-style setting can also work well. Some design suggestions are illustrated here and see also Patchwork Settings on pages 38–40 for ideas.

A simple grid design is often the easiest sampler quilt setting and displays all the different blocks well. A Flying Geese border makes a striking addition.

The blocks used in a sampler quilt can be whatever you choose – perhaps a mixture of rectilinear, curved and appliqué, or all based on curves and circles as shown here. Wide horizontal sashing gives opportunities for quilting.

An 'on point' setting looks so attractive and works well with appliqué blocks balanced with areas of quilting.

Sampler quilts based on a medallion arrangement can look very striking and allow for the addition of decorative sashing and borders.

HAND PIECING

We have become so accustomed to using sewing machines for piecing patchwork together that it's sometimes easy to forget just how easy and portable hand piecing is, particularly for some techniques, such as English paper piecing. Certain blocks, such as Grandmother's Fan and Dresden Plate were traditionally sewn by hand as the curved seams were easier to stitch that way. Hand sewing is also useful for appliqué work. Most of the techniques described in this and other sections of the book can be stitched by hand, and advice is given where relevant.

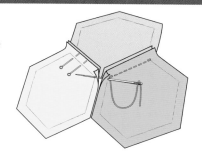

For many people, Grandmother's Flower Garden is their first experience of patchwork. It looks very pretty worked in bright, contemporary fabrics.

When sewing patches together a simple running stitch will suffice or use a backstitch. The smaller and closer the stitches the firmer and more secure the seam will be. For extra security, start and finish with a knot and also a backstitch. If sewing pieces together that have been placed over card or paper templates, as in English paper piecing, a whip stitch is easier to use.

>>> related topics... *Pressing Fabrics 23 • Sewing Points 52*   >>

THE TECHNIQUES

HAND SEWING PATCHES

1 Cut your fabric pieces to the size required, ensuring they are square. Place two patches right sides together, aligning edges and corners. Use a pencil to mark the seam line, usually ¼in (6mm) and pin the patches together. ▼

Fabric ws

Marked seam line ➔

2 Start with a knot and sew along the seam line using short running stitches and the occasional backstitch for stability. Finish with a backstitch or two. ▼

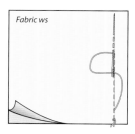

Fabric ws

HAND SEWING ROWS

1 Place the pieced patches right sides together, aligning edges and corners. Use a pencil to mark the ¼in (6mm) seam line (or use pins). Pin the sections together. ▶

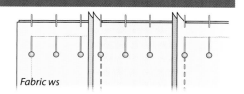

Fabric ws

2 Start with a knot ¼in (6mm) from the edge and sew along the seam line using short running stitches. When you reach a seam, make a backstitch or knot and then put the needle through the seam to the other side and continue sewing – this leaves the seam free to be pressed. Finish with a knot or backstitch ¼in (6mm) from the edge. ▶

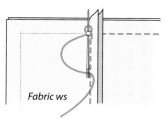

Fabric ws   *Fabric ws*

HAND SEWING MULTIPLE SEAMS

When sewing multiple seams or set-in seams, sew two patches together, as before and then pin the third in place as shown. Take the needle through from the edge of one seam across the corner into the third patch, and then continue on to sew that final seam. ▶

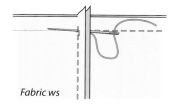

ENGLISH PAPER PIECING

This type of patchwork, also called English patchwork, is often one of the first techniques that beginners learn. The patchwork uses templates, usually made of thick paper, thin card or freezer paper, which fabric pieces are wrapped around and tacked (basted) to (or pressed in the case of freezer paper). The fabric patches are then hand sewn together, usually with whip stitch and the papers removed.

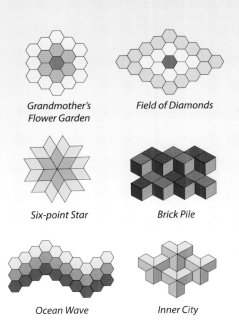

These master templates are used for cutting papers for English patchwork. These are also useful for 'fussy cutting', where you want to feature a specific motif.

This technique may be slow but one of its big advantages is that it is portable. It also allows complex designs to be built up and some lovely effects achieved. You can buy templates for English paper piecing or make your own (see page 27). Templates are available in various shapes and sizes and in different materials. 'Master' shapes made from acrylic or metal are very durable. Accurate shapes can also be created using isometric paper, which is composed of 60 degree triangles (see page 26).

CREATING PATTERNS

The most common and useful shapes are triangles, diamonds and hexagons, which allow you to create many patterns. These shapes can be combined with squares and rectangles to produce many innovative patchwork designs.

Grandmother's Flower Garden

Field of Diamonds

Six-point Star

Brick Pile

Ocean Wave

Inner City

Designs created with English paper piecing can be used as appliqué and attached to a plain or pieced background. This wall hanging was created this way, using elongated octagons. The shapes were edged with narrow ricrac braid but a machine satin stitch or hand blanket stitch could be used instead. The octagon shape was used again for the hand quilting.

> > > related topics... *Making a Simple Template 27 • Using Technology 34 • Hand Piecing 50 • Freezer Paper Appliqué 151* > > >

THE TECHNIQUES

PAPER PIECING CUTTING AND ASSEMBLY

If you are new to English paper piecing it is best to use 100 per cent cotton fabrics as they crease well. Sew using a thread that matches the main fabric colour or use beige or mid-grey as these blend with most shades.

1 Calculate how many paper templates you will need for the design and create them from your master template. Pin a template on the wrong side of the fabric and by eye cut ¼in (6mm) further out all round for the seam allowance. Freezer paper could also be used as a template, ironed in place. Repeat the process as often as necessary. ▼

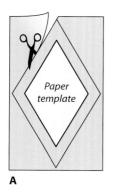

1/4in (6mm) seam allowance

Paper template

Cut

Fabric ws

2 Pin a template to the wrong side of a fabric piece and fold the seam allowance over the template edges, tacking (basting) in place through all layers. Repeat with all pieces. ▼

3 Assemble the design. Place two pieces right sides together, aligning edges. Using small whip stitches sew together along one edge through the folded fabric, but not through the paper. Don't pull the stitches too tight or the finished work may not lie flat. Flip the patch over to the right side when it is sewn. ▼

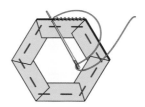

4 Continue adding patches in this way, flipping the sewn patches over to their right side. Once a patch is sewn around all its edges remove the tacking (basting) and the template. Alternatively, leave the template in place until all work is complete. ▼

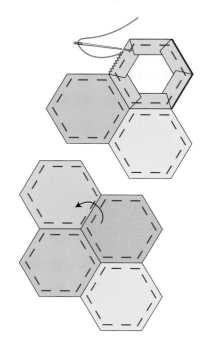

SEWING POINTS

Some shapes, such as triangles, diamonds and trapeziums have acute points and when tacking (basting) these shapes over paper templates you will need to make sure that the seam allowance extends beyond the template at the point, in order to allow it to be sewn to other shapes.

DEALING WITH DIAMONDS

A diamond shape cut out (A) and a tacked (basted) diamond (B).

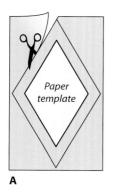

Paper template

A

B

Several diamonds sewn together to create a unit (C).

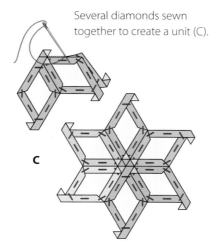

C

DEALING WITH TRIANGLES

A triangle shape cut out (A) and a tacked (basted) triangle (B).

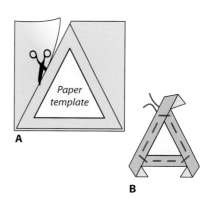

Paper template

A

B

make it now
Summer Cushions

These bright cushions in contemporary fabrics use easy shapes and English paper piecing. The making of the two round cushions is described here. The templates can be enlarged or reduced to any size you like.

profile

Skills practised: English paper piecing; hand sewing; adding trims
Project layout: Hexagon cushion uses six hexagons; triangles cushion uses eight triangles
Finished size: Hexagon cushion 12in (30.5cm) diameter; triangles cushion 15in (38cm) diameter
Fabrics: Selection of brightly coloured fabrics; two fat quarters of white fabric; polyester stuffing
Threads: Hand sewing threads
Embellishments: Bobble or lace trim edging

METHOD

- Use the templates on page 251, enlarged to the desired size. Cut sufficient templates from paper for your cushion.
- Tack (baste) your fabric shapes to the paper templates. Hand sew the sections together, remove the papers and press.
- For the hexagonal patchwork turn under a ¼in (6mm) seam all round and appliqué it to a circle of fabric larger than the patchwork.
- For the triangles cushion add a white appliqué circle (see Gathered Edge Appliqué on page 147), padded with wadding (batting) if desired.

- Use the patchwork as a template to cut backing fabric for each of the cushions, adding ¼in (6mm) all round for seams. Pin the front and back right sides together and sew around the edge, leaving a gap for turning through.
- Turn through to the right side, press and stuff each pillow with polyester stuffing or use a pad. Sew up the gap.
- For the triangles cushion the bobble edging is a knitting wool (yarn). The hexagon cushion uses a gathered voile trim hand sewn around the edge.

MACHINE PIECING

Machine sewing is a fast, accurate and secure method of piecing patchwork. We all live busy lives yet the need to create something with our own hands is as strong as ever and machine piecing allows us to complete projects in a reasonable time frame. This section describes the basic techniques required for successful machine piecing, and shows how to sew a wide range of seams, which will allow you to piece all sorts of shapes.

SETTING UP THE MACHINE

When beginning a patchwork project, spending a little time preparing the machine for piecing will save time in the long run. The following points should help.

- Insert a new needle for each project and use a Sharps size 80/12 for straight stitching.
- Select a straight stitch with a length of 10–15 stitches per 1in (2.5cm). This forms stitches that are close enough to make a secure stitched line but not so densely packed that the stitches can't be unpicked if the need arises. For piecing smaller fabric pieces reduce the length to 10–12.
- Use top thread and bobbin thread in colours to match your fabrics or choose neutral shades of grey or beige which will blend with most colours.
- Do some test stitching to check that the machine tension is correct.
- Fill several bobbins to reduce interruptions while piecing.

When machine piecing bear in mind that seams don't always have to be hidden. Make a feature of them by sewing patches right sides together so the seams show on the outside. Snip into the seam at intervals and fluff up for a cozy chenille effect.

Machine piecing creates a very professional look and a durable finish. This beautiful little bag by Susan Briscoe uses a Log Cabin block in delicate coffee and cream colours.

STARTING AND FINISHING MACHINE SEWING

There are various ways to start and finish sewing securely and the following are the most popular.

- Start and finish each line of stitching by stitching forwards for a few stitches and then in reverse for a few. Trim the thread ends and feed them into the wadding.
- Start and finish each line of stitching by reducing the stitch length to zero, which means the machine will stitch on the spot. Trim the thread ends and feed them into the wadding.
- Modern machines have a built-in 'fix' or 'secure' function, which when selected will secure the thread ends. Trim thread ends as before.
- When cutting through seams to make smaller pieces no finishing off is possible. Stitching with a shorter stitch length will help keep stitching secure.

>> related topics... *Using Fabric Grain 23 • Sewing Machine Basics 24 • Working out Piecing Order 87* >>>

THE TECHNIQUES

SEWING STRAIGHT SEAMS

Seams for pieced work are normally ¼in (6mm) and sewing a consistent and accurate seam is important if units and blocks are to fit together neatly. Many teachers of patchwork suggest that a *scant* ¼in (6mm) seam is used, to allow for the thickness of the thread and the tiny amount of space taken up when the seam is pressed to one side. There are several ways to ensure your seam allowance is accurate.

- Use a presser foot called a quilter's foot. This comes with most machines and is ¼in (6mm) wide, which means it can be aligned with the fabric edge to sew an accurate seam.
- With a normal machine foot, try moving the needle position from the centre to the right to reduce the seam width.
- Use a stitching guide. The simplest method is to stick a strip of masking tape on to the machine plate exactly ¼in (6mm) away from the needle and line the fabric edge up against this.
- Check your seam allowance is accurate with this test. Take a 2½in (6.3cm) strip and cut off three segments 1½in (3.8cm) wide (A). Sew two segments together down the longer side (B) and press the seam to one side. Sew the third segment across the top (C). It should fit exactly. If it is too long, your first seam allowance is too wide so move the machine needle to the right. If it is too small, your seam allowance is too narrow so move the needle to the left. ▶

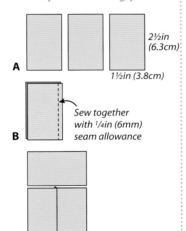

2½in (6.3cm)

1½in (3.8cm)

A

B Sew together with ¹⁄₄in (6mm) seam allowance

C

SEWING INTERSECTING SEAMS

The perfect alignment of seam junctions is the goal of most patchworkers, and there is something very satisfying about opening out a newly sewn seam to find it perfectly aligned. Begin by cutting all your patches and units accurately – even an ⅛in (3mm) difference will affect how well seams align. If pieces are meant to be right-angled, make sure they are. Pin pieces together well, especially at seam junctions, to stop one layer of fabric moving in relation to the other. 'Nesting' seams together whenever possible will help to create neatly aligned seams. Follow the diagram sequence here.

1 When joining two pairs of fabric, pressing seams in opposite directions will help when joining the units together as the seams will 'nest' together more neatly. ▶

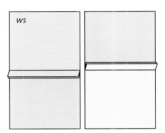

2 Place units right sides together, nesting the seams and ensuring seam lines match. Place pins at intersection. Sew the seam. ▼

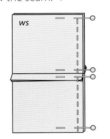

3 Open out the completed block and press the seam to one side. ▼

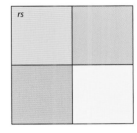

SEWING INTERSECTING SEAMS WITH POINTS

When sewing seams together with angled seams that have points it's important not to lose the points.

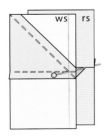

1 Place the units right sides together, with seams going in opposite directions so they nest. Insert a pin in the seam line of the top layer, at the point at which the existing seams cross, and through into the bottom layer at the same point. ◀

2 Pin the two units together, making sure edges are aligned, and sew the seam. The sewing line needs to go through the points marked by the first pin. Remove the pin as the machine reaches it. ◀

3 Open out the block and press the seam to one side. ▼

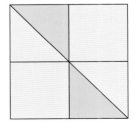

SEWING PARTIAL SEAMS

These sorts of seam are also called right-angled seams or part-sewn seams and are used when piecing right-angled pieces of fabric. Such seams are also used to create woven effects in patchwork, where it is hard to see where sewing begins or ends. Follow the diagram sequence here.

A Position the first rectangle right sides together with the square and aligning only one side edge. Sew the seam only to the centre and press outwards, away from the square.

B Pin the second rectangle right sides together with the centre square, as shown, and stitch the complete seam. Press outwards as before. Repeat this with the third rectangle, again sewing the complete seam.

C Position the final rectangle along the remaining edge of the square and sew the complete seam.

D Only the partially unsewn seam now remains to be sewn. Working from the back, pin the hanging portion in place against the rest of the block and sew the remainder of the seam.

E Press the completed block.

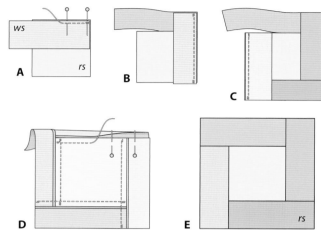

SEWING OFFSET SEAMS

When pieces of fabric need to be joined with oblique angles, such as rhomboids, diamonds and triangles, the seam needs to be offset or the result will be a mismatched seam.

For a rhomboid shape, offset the shapes at both ends of the seam as shown (A) and then press open (B).

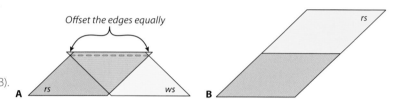

Offset the edges equally

JOINING 60 DEGREE TRIANGLES

Joining equilateral triangles into rows requires that each triangle added is offset alternately in order that the finished row is straight. This principle also applies to other acute-angled shapes, such as trapeziums.

1 Sew triangles 1 and 2 together with a ¼in (6mm) seam, aligning edges (A). Press the seam to one side. Position triangle 3 so it is aligned with triangle 2 at the top but projecting slightly at the base (B). Sew in place and press. Position triangle 4 but this time align it with the base of the previous triangle and projecting slightly at the top (C). Sew in place and press. Continue in this way, alternating how the triangles are offset.

2 To join rows of triangles together, place the rows right sides together, aligning edges, and sew with a ¼in (6mm) seam (D). Press the seam to one side.

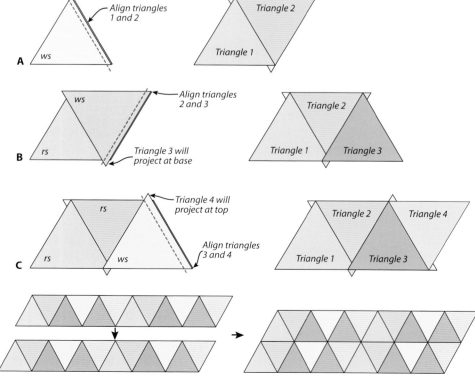

SEWING SET-IN SEAMS

Attic Windows – This block is composed of two pieces joined at a 45 degree angle, with a square set into the angle. Follow the diagram sequence here.

1 Using ¼in (6mm) seam allowances, mark the corners of the seams on all pieces on the wrong side with a pencil dot (shown in red on diagram A).

2 Pin one long piece right sides together with the square, aligning edges and dots. Sew a straight seam from the edge to the inner dot (B). Stop at the dot and secure with a backstitch or stitching on the spot. Press the seam to one side.

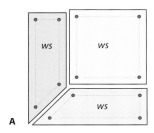

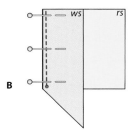

3 Pin the second long piece on the other side of the square, right sides together and aligning edges and dots. Sew a straight seam from the edge to the inner dot (C). Secure with a backstitch or stitching on the spot. Press the seam.

4 Fold the unit across the diagonal, right sides together and tucking the seam allowance and window fabric out of the way. Align the two angled edges and pin together. Sew the final seam from the edge to the dot (D). Press the finished unit (E).

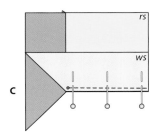

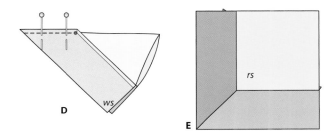

Tumbling Blocks – This block is composed of three diamonds. Follow the diagram sequence here.
A Using ¼in (6mm) seam allowances, mark the corners of the seams on all pieces on the wrong side with a pencil dot (shown in red on the diagrams).
B Pin two diamonds right sides together, aligning the dots.
C Sew a straight seam from dot to dot. Secure the thread ends with a backstitch or stitching on the spot.
D Press the seam open on these two pieces.
E Position the third diamond right sides together with the sewn pieces, aligning the dots and pinning as shown. Stitch from one corner dot to the other, pivoting slightly at the centre point.
F Press the unit open to finish.

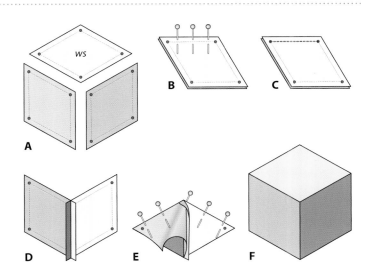

Eight-Point Star – This block is composed of eight diamonds. Follow the diagram sequence. For an alternative piecing method, where squares and triangles are added to make the star into a square block, see page 79.

A Using ¼in (6mm) seam allowances, mark the corners of the seams on all pieces on the wrong side with a pencil dot (shown in red on diagrams).

B Pin two diamonds right sides together, aligning the dots, and sew a straight seam from dot to dot. Secure thread ends with backstitch. Do the same with three pairs of diamonds. Press seams open.

C Place two units right sides together, aligning the dots, and sew the seam from dot to dot. Press the seam open. Repeat with the other two units. You now have two halves of the star.

D Trim off the dog ears and place the two halves of the star right sides together. Place a pin vertically through the centre seam on both pieces, aligning the dots. Pin the pieces together, leaving the first pin in place. Sew the seam towards this pin, removing it as you reach it. Continue on to sew the rest of the seam. Press open.

E The completed star should now have all points of the diamonds aligned at the centre.

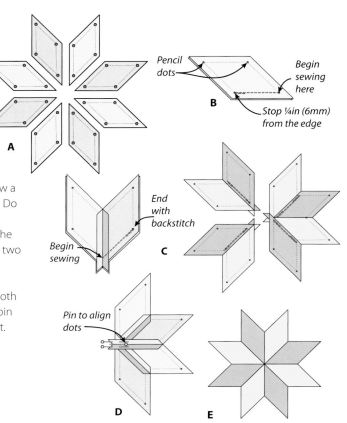

SEWING CURVED SEAMS

Sewing curved seams is needed for many blocks, including Drunkard's Path, Orange Peel and Tobacco Leaf. You will need to use a curved template – see page 27 for making templates and page 90 for more details on sewing curves. Follow the diagrams below.

A Using your curved template mark and cut the fabric pieces. If possible, try to have the straight grain of the fabric on the edges. Mark the centre of both curves – find this by folding each piece in half. You could make additional marks along the curves.

B Place the fabric pieces right sides together, with the concave shape (inward curving one) on top of the convex one. Pin together at the centre, matching the marked points. Align the straight edges and pin together at these points. Continue pinning the pieces together, stretching the top fabric so it fits the curved shape beneath.

C Stitch the pieces together with a ¼in (6mm) seam, removing the pins as you go. The seam can be stitched by machine or by hand.

D When the seam is sewn, press it towards the concave shape. If the curve is quite tight or is a complete circle, clip the seam at regular intervals to help it lie flat.

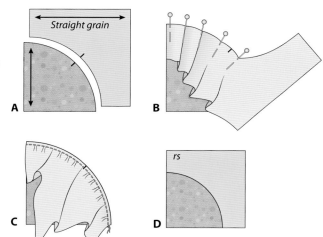

CHAIN PIECING

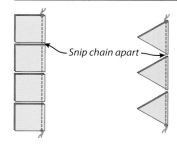

Chain piecing is a form of speed piecing on the sewing machine that saves time and thread. Patchwork pieces are fed through the machine one after the other and sewn together in a chain. Sew one set of pieces together and stop at the end of the fabric. Don't cut the thread or lift the presser foot but position the next set and continue sewing. Do this as many times as needed. When sewing is finished cut the chain apart. When chain piecing some shapes, such as triangles, it may be easier to lift the presser foot slightly and re-position on the next set.

SPEED PIECING

Patchwork blocks tend to be made up of repeated units, so finding quicker ways of producing these units usually leads to faster patchwork. Techniques that achieve this are often referred to as speed piecing. Time and effort can be reduced if larger pieces of fabric are sewn together first and then cut into smaller units. Some examples are shown here. A number of nine-patch blocks can be speed pieced by preparing pieced strips first. ▼

Sandwich piecing speeds up the production of half-square triangles. Working in this way results in two pieced units. Place two squares right sides together and mark the diagonal line. Pin the squares together and sew ¼in (6mm) either side of the marked line. Cut the two triangles apart with a rotary cutter or scissors on the marked line and press open. ▼

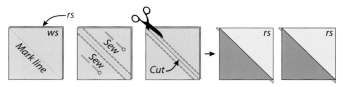

Quarter-square triangles can be speed pieced in a similar way resulting in two pieced units. Place two half-square triangle units right sides together with their diagonal lines going in the same direction and mark a diagonal line in the opposite direction across the top square. Sew ¼in (6mm) either side of the marked line. Cut the two triangles apart on the marked line and press open. ◀

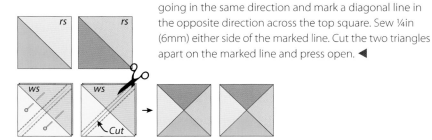

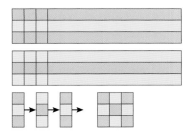

PIECING BLOCKS

Blocks are generally sewn together in a specific and logical order and most books and magazines will illustrate the piecing order, often using arrows to indicate how the units are built up. The way that a block is pieced depends on the shapes it is composed of. Wherever possible sew together smaller units and then sew these units together. These smaller units may be sewn together in a square format, in rows or quadrants depending on the block. Two examples are shown here: the Windmill Star block has four identical units so is simpler to piece than the Road to Paradise block which has three different units. Before sewing, lay out all the pieces in the shape of the block. See also page 87 for more on piecing order.

Windmill Star block

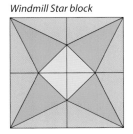

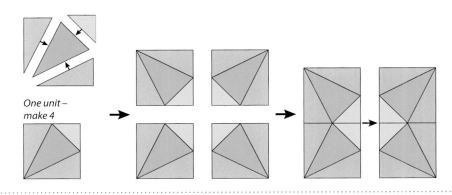

One unit – make 4

Road to Paradise block

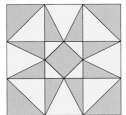

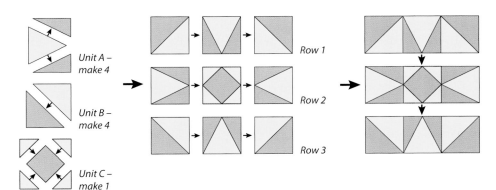

Unit A – make 4

Unit B – make 4

Unit C – make 1

Row 1

Row 2

Row 3

PATCHWORK WITH SQUARES AND RECTANGLES

It is obvious why most beginners start patchwork by piecing together squares and rectangles – they are very easy shapes to draw, cut and sew, they showcase some of the gorgeous fabrics available and they are very versatile, allowing you to create a wide range of patchwork blocks. They also work well as spacer blocks within more complex designs. Many fabric ranges are available as pre-cut 5in (12.7cm) and 10in (25.4cm) squares, which makes pieced work and designing even easier (see page 21).

Squares and rectangles are easily combined to make highly versatile four-patch and nine-patch blocks.

This section takes a look at patchwork designs achieved with just squares and rectangles, showing how these shapes can be pieced together and used to create interesting designs. Some blocks that can be created this way are shown opposite. This section also takes a closer look at the ever-popular Log Cabin block, which is a favourite with so many quilters.

Narrow rectangles are really strips and can also be pieced using a technique called strip piecing. This highly inventive and versatile method of patchwork is dealt with in detail in Patchwork with Strips on page 66 and Seminole Patchwork on page 70.

Probably the easiest way to start patchwork with squares is with simple but oh-so-effective four-patch and nine-patch blocks. These blocks also provide a foundation for appliqué and quilting. Piecing strips together is really easy, resulting in adaptable blocks such as Rail Fence. You can then really start to have fun by combining squares and rectangles in blocks such as Log Cabin and Basket Weave.

This elegant quilt, made by Pauline Bugg, uses a square within a square block, showing how squares and rectangles can create some striking effects, especially when combined with great colour choices. This block is useful if you wish to work with a limited colour palette.

SQUARE AND RECTANGULAR BLOCKS

This page gives some examples of blocks that can be created using just squares and rectangles. The design possibilities come alive depending on the fabrics you use and how colour and value are arranged. See overleaf for the techniques for making these blocks.

Squares

The humble square is such a versatile shape, whether used as similar-sized units alone or combined with variable-sized squares. Squares work perfectly with many other blocks – see Common Quilt Settings on page 39 and Block Types on page 43.

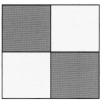

Four-patch

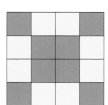

Puss in the Corner block

Autumn Time block

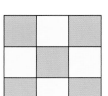

Nine-patch

Patience Corner block

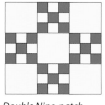

Double Nine-patch

H Square block

Red Cross block

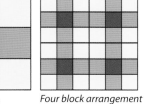

Four block arrangement of Red Cross

Sixteen-patch

Chequerboard block

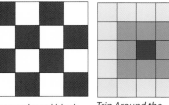

Trip Around the World block

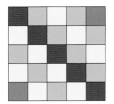

Brick Wall block

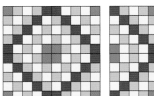

Four-block arrangements of Brick Wall

Rectangles

Blocks made from rectangles or oblongs can be combined to create designs that not only have a repetitive pattern but also a sense of movement and direction.

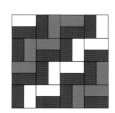

Streak o' Lightning (Endless Stair) block

Four-block arrangement of Streak o' Lightning

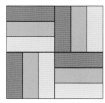

Roman Square block

Four-block arrangements of Roman Square

Rail Fence block

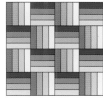

Four-block arrangements of Rail Fence

Squares and Rectangles Combined

When squares and rectangles are combined the design possibilities expand even further. Try some of these.

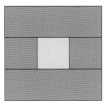

Boxed Square block

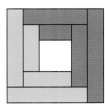

Log Cabin block

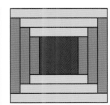

Courthouse Steps block

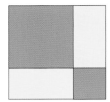

Basket Weave block

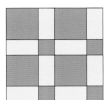

Four-block arrangements of Basket Weave

> > > related topics... *Squares and Rectangles 31 • Straight Strip Piecing 67 • Using Sashing 126 • Using Borders 130* > >

THE TECHNIQUES

JOINING SQUARES AND RECTANGLES

Joining these shapes together is the most basic technique in patchwork and can help you perfect crucial skills, such as cutting patches accurately and at right angles and matching seams perfectly. The technique is also used when joining blocks together. A four-patch block is used here as an example but other multi-patch blocks can be made in the same way.

1 Cut four right-angled squares to the size required. Place two squares right sides together, exactly on top of each other, and sew together with a ¼in (6mm) seam. Open out the joined squares and press the seam to one side, usually towards the darker fabric. ▼

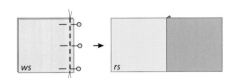

2 Repeat this process with the other two squares but this time press the seam in the opposite direction. Now place the two sets of squares right sides together and match up the seams accurately. Pin in place and sew together. Open out and press. ▼

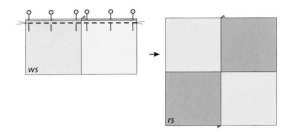

MAKING A STREAK O' LIGHTNING BLOCK

An arrangement that represents a streak of lightning can be created with rectangles or with triangles (see page 80). A simple block like this comes into its own when combined in a repeating pattern, creating a really bold design. Alternatively, use a graded colour palette for a more subtle result.

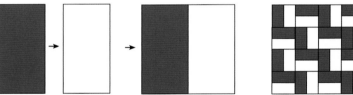
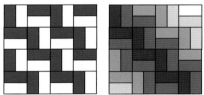

MAKING A BASKET WEAVE BLOCK

Some interesting woven patterns can be created with the Basket Weave block when it is combined in four-block units. Turning the blocks on point changes the look completely.

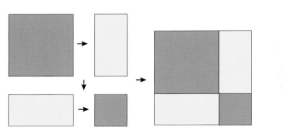
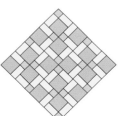

MAKING A BOXED SQUARE BLOCK

This easy block combines three squares and two rectangles. Sew the three squares together first and then add a rectangle on each side. To accentuate the square-in-a-square look use the same colour for the fabrics surrounding the inner square. Colourways can be subtle or bold and a multicoloured version is a great way to use up scraps of fabric.

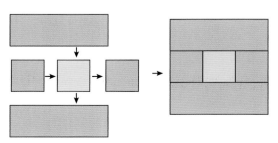

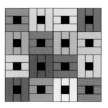

LOG CABIN

Log Cabin is one of the simplest but most rewarding blocks to make. The number of variations that can be achieved is amazing and a few are shown overleaf. The design is worked around a centre square, with strips added around this, usually with light on one side and dark on the other. The design is hundreds of years old and was probably taken to America in the early days of British and European settlement. The centre square is traditionally red to represent the fire in the hearth, or yellow for the light in the windows; the surrounding 'logs' represent the house or cabin.

Some stunning quilts can be created using just this block (see the table topper on page 65). The centre piece doesn't have to be square – it could be a rectangle, triangle or diamond, or be pieced. It can also be any size and be fussy cut.

The block is sewn from the centre outwards, in rounds, and can be machine pieced, foundation pieced or hand pieced. The technique for machine piecing Log Cabin is described here. Many other designs derive from Log Cabin, including Courthouse Steps (overleaf) and Pineapple (page 97). Specialist rulers are available for cutting Log Cabin strips.

The strip width for Log Cabin can be any size, and the wider the strips the bigger the finished block will be. Strips can be cut using templates or a rotary cutting mat and ruler. You can sew the strips in place and trim to length as the block is built up, or calculate beforehand how long each strip should be – in which case a full size master template needs to be drawn before you begin sewing.

FABRICS FOR LOG CABIN

Log Cabin designs achieve their impact by the combination of dark and light fabrics. You could use the same fabric for the 'light' half of the block and a different fabric for the 'dark' half, or grade the fabrics. Contrast can also be achieved using complementary colours, such as blue and gold or red and green. The juxtapositions can be vibrant or more subtle, so experiment. For advice on colour combinations see page 20.

THE TECHNIQUES

MAKING A LOG CABIN BLOCK

These instructions show a block with twelve strips of 'logs' but you could stop at eight if preferred. Overleaf are suggestions for arranging Log Cabin blocks, plus some variations.

1 Select your fabrics for the centres and for two sets of contrasting strips. Arrange your strips into two sets – one dark set and one light set. Measure and cut out the square for the centre and then cut the strips to the desired width.

2 For the first 'round' (strip 1 on the diagram below), select a fabric strip from your 'dark' pile. Cut the strip equal to the length of the centre square (or slightly longer and trim it to size after it has been sewn and pressed). Pin and sew the strip right sides together with the centre square using a ¼in (6mm) seam. Press the seam open, or towards the darker fabric. ◄

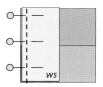

3 For the second round, take the second fabric strip from the 'dark' pile (number 2 on diagram), cut it to size and pin it right sides together with the pieced unit. Sew together and press. ▼

4 For the third round you will be starting to add the alternate colour, so take the third fabric strip from your 'light' pile, cut it to size and pin it right sides together with the pieced unit. Sew together as before and press. ▼

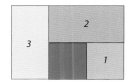

5 Continue adding rounds, changing the strip colour according to your master diagram. As you proceed, check the block size to make sure it is staying square and right angled. The outer strips on the finished block will be slightly wider than the inner ones due to the seam allowance. ▶

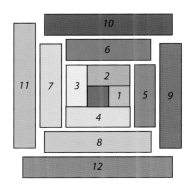

JOINING LOG CABIN BLOCKS

Log Cabin blocks are often joined in groups of four and these blocks can then be combined in various ways to create different sets or arrangements. Join two blocks by placing them right sides together, matching seams, and sew together with a ¼in (6mm) seam. Press seams open or towards the darker fabric. Repeat with a second pair of blocks. Place the pairs of blocks right sides together, matching seams and particularly the centre point carefully. Sew together with a ¼in (6mm) seam and press towards the darker fabric as before.

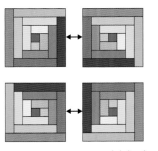
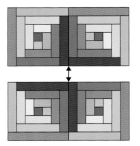

Joining Log Cabin blocks

LOG CABIN SETTINGS

The Log Cabin block can be arranged in many ways, depending on how the blocks are turned and the juxtaposition of light and dark. Some common settings are shown here.

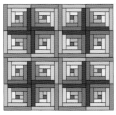
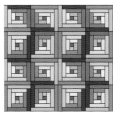

Barn Raising   *Streak o' Lightning*

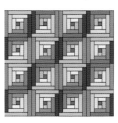
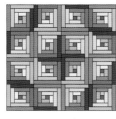

Straight Furrow   *Starry Night*

LOG CABIN VARIATIONS

There are many variations of Log Cabin and other block designs that are derived from it. A few are shown here but there are many more to discover. For example, a Pineapple block is a more intricate interpretation of Log Cabin – see page 97.

HALF LOG CABIN

In this variation the centre square is placed in a corner and the strips added outwards from there (first diagram). Different effects can be achieved by varying the colour combinations. The pattern creates interesting interlocking effects when blocks are set together. The other diagrams show groups of four.

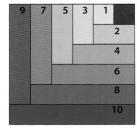
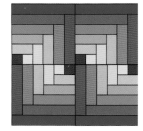
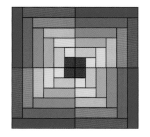

OFF-CENTRE LOG CABIN

Here the strips sewn around the centre square are of two different widths (right), which can create the illusion of curves when blocks are set together (centre and far right). The centre piece can be a triangle or diamond (see page 97).

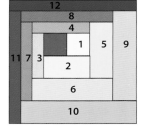
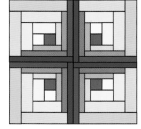
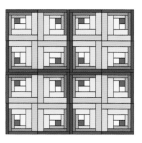

COURTHOUSE STEPS

This is very similar to Log Cabin, but with the strips, the 'steps', added on alternate sides. The centre piece was traditionally black, to represent a judge's robes and this can vary in shape and size. Block arrangements can look more dynamic when set on point (far right).

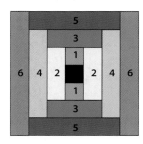
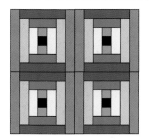
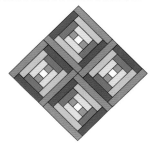

make it now
Log Cabin Table Topper

This striking but easily made table topper will allow you to practise making Log Cabin blocks. It would be a good project to use up fabrics from your stash. You could also make it up as a large floor cushion. It has a mitred border and easy machine quilting.

profile

Skills practised: Log Cabin blocks; simple machine quilting; mitred border; binding
Project layout: Four Log Cabin blocks each 11½in (29.2cm) finished size, with one border 2in (5cm) wide
Finished size: 27in (68.6cm) square
Fabrics: Log Cabin blocks – gold fabric for the centre squares and two sets of strips in contrasting colours; border – four strips of black 30in (76.2cm) long x 2½in (6.3cm) wide; wadding (batting) and backing each 30in (76.2cm) square; binding fabric 2½in (6.3cm) x 116in (295cm)
Threads: Machine quilting thread, invisible and pale gold

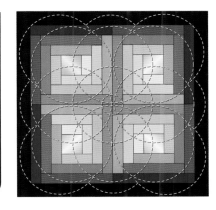

METHOD

- For each Log Cabin block cut a 3in (7.6cm) centre square, six dark strips 2in (5cm) wide and six light strips 2in (5cm) wide. Follow the technique on page 63 to make four blocks. Sew them together.
- Cut four strips of fabric, each 30in (76.2cm) long, and sew to the centre panel as a mitred border (see page 135) or straight border (see page 134).

- Make a quilt sandwich of the top, wadding (batting) and backing (see page 188). Use invisible or matching thread to machine quilt in the ditch between the blocks and around the border. Use pale gold thread to quilt a pattern of circles over the top – see diagram above.
- Bind the patchwork to finish (see page 238).

PATCHWORK WITH STRIPS

Strip piecing is a very simple technique of sewing strips of fabric together but is amazingly versatile, depending on whether the strips are sewn and cut on the straight grain of the fabric or on the bias, and whether the segments cut off are cut straight or at an angle. A great many blocks and patchwork designs can be created with strip piecing, as the next few sections of the book will show. Strip piecing is fast and accurate, especially if rotary cutting equipment is used. It needs to be machine sewn as hand stitches would unravel where seams are cut across. For an even quicker result a quilt can be pieced in no time using just strips across the fabric width. Simply find a range of gorgeous fabrics, cut a selection of different width strips and sew them together.

A super-quick quilt can be created using just strips cut across the fabric width. Pre-cut fabric strips, such as those found in Jelly Rolls™, are perfect for strip work – see page 21 for more on pre-cuts.

This elegant quilt made by Lynne Edwards puts fabric strips to good use with Magic Lantern blocks arranged as a lap quilt. The hand-dyed suede-effect fabrics used create a lovely autumnal colour scheme.

Strip piecing not only allows the creation of blocks such as Rail Fence and Chevron but also speed piecing of Nine-Patch blocks, which can be combined with other units to form more complex arrangements. Strip piecing forms the basis of many patchwork styles, including Seminole designs, bargello patchwork and string patchwork, and all of these are described in more depth on pages 70–77. The strip piecing technique can also be used to create a pieced fabric which can be cut up into different shapes and used as backgrounds, patchwork units, appliqués and for borders. Once pieced together, strips can be cut into curved shapes for a more irregular look.

When sewn and cut on a 45 degree angle, strip piecing creates sets of diamonds, which can be used to piece together a number of blocks and designs, including Chevron and Lone Star.

Bias-strip piecing is a method of joining fabric strips cut on the fabric bias. Once seams are sewn on the bias edge in this way, squares cut from the strip have the straight grain on the outer edges. This means they do not stretch and so assist with very accurate piecing. This is ideal for creating beautiful Feathered Star designs – see page 81 for details.

>> related topics... *Cutting Strips 30 • Bias Strip-pieced Triangles 81* > > >

THE TECHNIQUES

STRAIGHT STRIP PIECING

1 Press fabrics if necessary before cutting. Using a rotary cutter, cut your strips to the width required across the straight grain of the fabric, from selvedge to selvedge, to avoid too many stretchy bias edges. Stacking fabrics together will make cutting faster but for accuracy be careful how many you stack. ▶

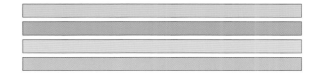

2 Pin two strips right sides together and sew together using a ¼in (6mm) seam. Press each pair as you sew them. When sewing fabric strips together bowing or rippling can occur, especially if there are bias edges, but sewing the strips together in pairs and pressing after each seam can prevent this. Sewing seams in opposite directions also helps. Pressing seams open can give greater accuracy. Do this with all the pairs and then sew the pairs together. ▼

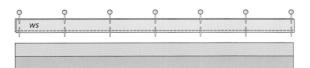

3 Once all the strips are sewn together, the pieced unit is ready to be cut into segments and used to create blocks or form part of other, more complex, arrangements. ▼

BRIGHT IDEA

USE A SHORTER STITCH LENGTH THAN NORMAL FOR STRIP PIECING TO HELP PREVENT SEAMS COMING APART WHEN THE PIECED STRIP IS CUT.

MAKING A RAIL FENCE BLOCK

A Rail Fence block can easily be created by strip-pieced segments as shown here. Making more than one set of strips will provide more design choices. ▼

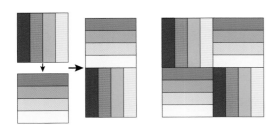

Different patterns can be created depending on how the Rail Fence blocks are arranged. ▼

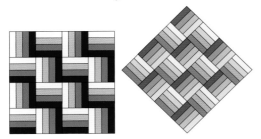

MAKING A NINE-PATCH BLOCK

Creating strip-pieced units with alternating colourways is an easy way to build up a Nine-Patch block, and quicker than joining nine separate squares. ▼

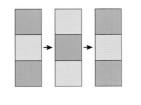

Nine-Patch blocks are so versatile – even simple alterations in colour placement can create a very different look. ▼

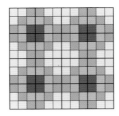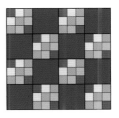

USING STRIP PIECING AS A FABRIC

Once a strip-pieced unit has been sewn you can use it like any other fabric, to cut units for other blocks or motif shapes for use in appliqué. Templates can be used to trace the shapes on to the strip-pieced fabric. You could also use freezer paper: prepare the freezer paper shape, iron it on to the strip-pieced fabric and cut out around the edge. If a seam is needed, cut ¼in (6mm) further out all round. ▶

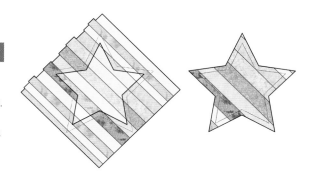

ANGLED-CUT STRIP PIECING

Once fabric strips have been pieced they can be crosscut, that is cut at an angle, to create diamonds. Cutting at 45 degrees is very common in Seminole patchwork (see overleaf) but you could also experiment with 30 and 60 degree cuts. These angles are included on most rotary rulers.

1 Prepare your striped pieced unit in the colours and widths of your choice, as described on the previous page. Once the unit is finished and pressed use the 45 degree angle on your rotary ruler to cut the unit at that angle all along the length. ▼

2 Take the angled strips and rotate and rearrange them into a pleasing design. Sew them together using a ¼in (6mm) seam, pressing seams carefully. ▼

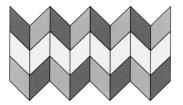

CHEVRON BLOCK

Creating a Chevron block is easy with strip piecing cut at a 45 degree angle. A pleasing three-dimensional quality is achieved by careful colour and value placement, especially if two different colourways are combined. ▶

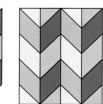

Introducing a third colour common to both sets emphasizes the chevron pattern even further and would make a striking arrangement for a quilt. ▶

Strip piecing is a speedy way of piecing blocks. This picture shows a detail from a quilt by Shelagh Roberts, which uses alternating strip-pieced units to create a strong geometric design.

MAKING A LONE STAR BLOCK

The Lone Star block (also called Star of Le Moyne) can be made with angled-cut strip-pieced units, plus four additional squares and triangles, which need to be sewn with set-in seams – see page 57. The block can also be pieced by bias-strip piecing – see page 81. ▶

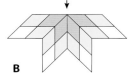

A

B

C

D

The Lone Star block can form the centre of a medallion quilt or be repeated in a 3 x 3 or 3 x 4 arrangement. ▲

This quilt, designed and made by Chris Porter and quilted by Rosemary Archer, shows just how effective angled-cut strip piecing can look. The chevron pattern and beautifully graded colour palette create a striking piece of work.

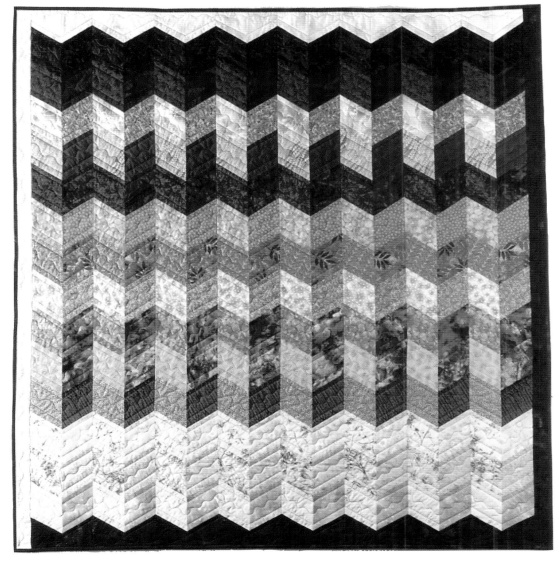

SEMINOLE PATCHWORK

Seminole patchwork is a highly inventive form of machine strip piecing and is named after the Seminole Indians of Florida, USA, who by the late 1800s had developed a form of patchwork that used strips to produce distinctive designs. Seminole patchwork appears complicated but is actually straightforward and is produced quickly, especially with rotary cutting equipment. See also pages 66–69 for strip-piecing techniques.

Seminole patchwork creates fresh, bright designs and there are many bands to try.

Seminole patchwork uses strips of fabric, joined together to create a 'strip set'. This is then cut into various segments or larger sections and re-combined in bands. An amazing number of variations can be created depending on the width of the strips, the angles they are cut in and how the pieces are rearranged and sewn back together. Seminole bands can be roughly classified into four main types: stairstep bands, alternate bands, angled bands and floating bands. Examples of each are shown in the techniques opposite and overleaf.

   Colour contrast in Seminole work can be high, resulting in striking designs, or can be low contrast, resulting in more subtle patterns. Scale and repetition of patterns also play a big part. Both plain and patterned fabrics can be used, but solids create the maximum impact. Cotton fabrics often give the best results.

This Seminole block was made by Heather Jackson during a sampler quilt course taught by Lynne Edwards. It features two different bands, with one repeated. Added sashing and borders create an elegant, mirrored arrangement.

>> related topics... *Using Colour 19 • Rotary Cutting 29 • Straight Strip Piecing 67* >>>

THE TECHNIQUES

SEWING SEMINOLE PATCHWORK

The Seminole technique described here is for a straight-cut stairstep band – see overleaf for other Seminole bands. Numbers on the diagrams indicate suggested ratios for strip width and segment width.

1 Cut your strips of fabric across the fabric width in the width you require. Sew them together with ¼in (6mm) seams. Use a rotary cutter and ruler to cut the pieced strip into straight segments. The width of these segments needs to allow for the centre colour shape to end up as a square. ▼

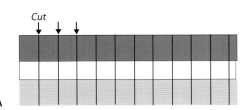

A

2 Take the segments and rearrange them to create a pattern – in this case the segments have been stepped down by one colour. Sew the segments together using ¼in (6mm) seam allowance. Press the band. ▶

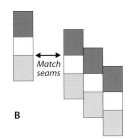

B

3 Place the band on a cutting mat, aligning the top points with a horizonal mat line. Position a rotary ruler vertically on the band through the centre of a diamond and cut through the band (C). Take one section and move it to the other end of the band (D) and sew back together (E). The band ends are now straight. ▼

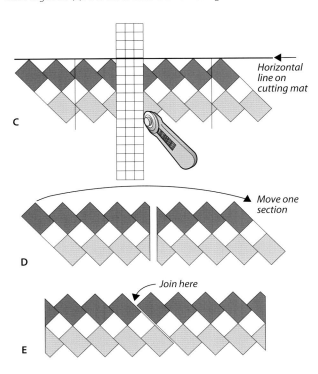

Horizontal line on cutting mat

C

Move one section

D

Join here

E

4 Rotate the band and use a rotary cutter and ruler to trim off the triangles at the top and bottom of the band, leaving ¼in (6mm) seams. ▼

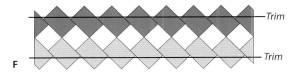

Trim

Trim

F

5 Measure the length of the band and cut plain strips to the same length and sew them to the top and bottom of the band using a ¼in (6mm) seam. ▼

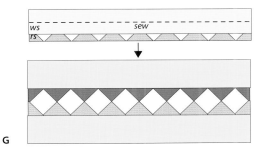

ws

sew

rs

G

Even the basic types of band described in this section can be combined to create striking Seminole quilts and the variations are endless. Bold designs are shown here as examples but you can create your own unique look with colours of your choice.

SEMINOLE BANDS

Instructions on making three alternate bands, one angled band and one floating band are given here. Some strip width and segment width ratios are suggested.

Alternate Band – Piece strips into one set and cut into straight segments. Rotate every other segment 180 degrees and then sew the segments together. The strip width ratios here are 4:1:1:4 with a segment width of 3. ▼

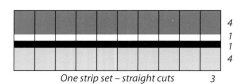

One strip set – straight cuts

Alternate Band – Piece two strips sets and cut into straight segments. Arrange one segment from the second strip set between two segments from the first strip set and then sew the segments together. As an alternative, add spacer strips to either side. ▼

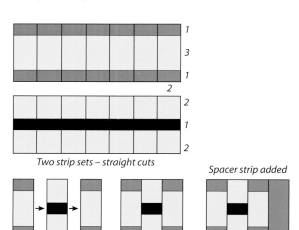

Two strip sets – straight cuts

Spacer strip added

Alternate Band – Piece two strip sets to create nine-patch blocks. Sew the blocks together, adding a spacer strip between blocks. ▼

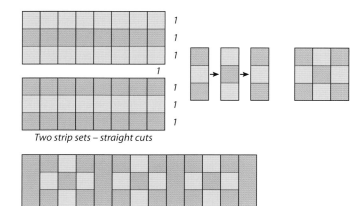

Two strip sets – straight cuts

Angled Band – Piece one strip set and cut into 45 degree segments. Arrange the segments into a chevron pattern and sew together. Trim off the points top and bottom or sew a spacer band to the top and bottom. ▼

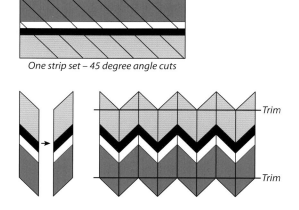

One strip set – 45 degree angle cuts

Floating Band – Piece two strip sets to create nine-patch blocks (see page 67). Cut spacer blocks the same height as the nine-patch blocks but twice as long, and sew together in a band. Cut the band into sections with 45 degree cuts. Move the end section to the beginning and sew in place. Turn the segments and sew together. The band ends can be straightened as described in step 3 on page 71. ▼

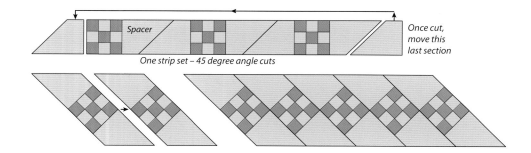

Spacer

Once cut, move this last section

One strip set – 45 degree angle cuts

make it now
Seminole Scarf

This scarf has four different Seminole bands, repeated at each end, with prairie points as decoration. The scarf was not padded as it is for summer use but you could add wadding (batting) for a winter scarf.

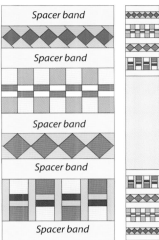

profile

Skills practised: Seminole patchwork; prairie points
Project layout: Four Seminole bands separated by spacer bands, repeated at each end
Finished size: 67in x 8in (170.2cm x 20.3cm)
Fabrics: Assorted strips of coordinating prints and plains; toning fabric for spacer bands; backing fabric
Threads: Machine sewing thread

METHOD

- The bands were created in an 18in (45.7cm) width and cut into two narrower widths once stitched. Make the bands of your choice (see techniques on pages 71–72). Use ¼in (6mm) seams.
- Cut spacer bands and join these together with the Seminole bands. Cut the completed band into two 9in (22.9cm) widths. Making the scarf wider than required allows you to trim the bands so they look balanced.
- Decide on the scarf length and cut sufficient spacer fabric to join the two ends. The joined bands for this scarf were each 19in (48.3cm) and 29in (73.6cm) was added between them, making a total length of 67in (170.2cm).
- Make prairie points for the scarf ends (see page 112) – seven for each end. Make up the scarf as described on page 248.

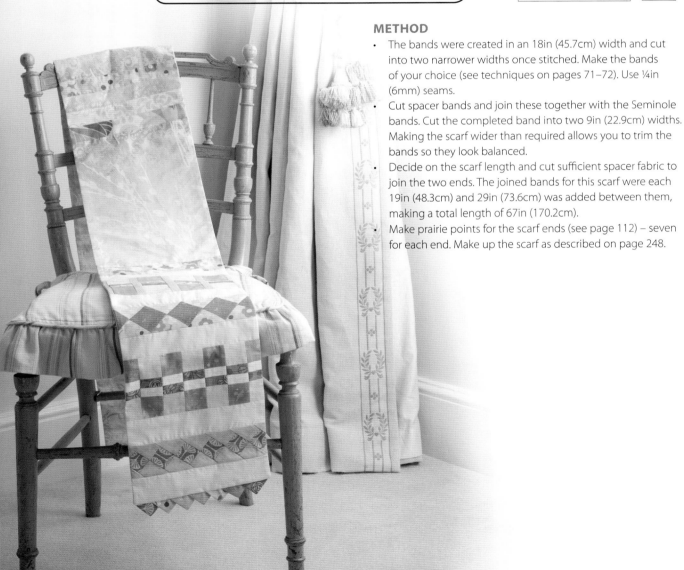

BARGELLO PATCHWORK

Bargello is a word normally associated with Florentine embroidery, where flame-like, wavy patterns are created with stitches on canvas. Inventive patchworkers soon realized that they could adapt the idea for pieced work and a whole new world of fabulous designs was born, and continues to be developed and re-invented.

Bargello designs use squares and rectangles in rising and falling patterns of graded colours and some extremely complicated and visually stunning designs can be created. The piecing of so many squares and rectangles does require accurate seam alignments for the best results but strip piecing helps greatly in achieving this – see page 67 for strip-piecing techniques.

FABRICS AND COLOURS FOR BARGELLO

Fabrics used can be prints or plains, and prints can be small or large. Batiks are often a good choice as they have an overlying colour but with variations in each fabric. Fabric selection will take time. Decide on your overall colour scheme to begin with. It might help to look at your stash to see what colour you have most of and then select a dozen or more fabrics in this range, from pale to dark. For the basic technique described opposite just six colours are used but once you have learnt the technique you can become more adventurous with your choices.

This vibrant quilt, designed by Marion Brown, uses contemporary fabrics to spectacular effect. The undulating patterns have great movement across the quilt.

>> **related topics...** *Using Colour 19 • Rotary Cutting 29 • Cutting Strips 30 • Straight Strip Piecing 67*

THE TECHNIQUE

PIECING BARGELLO PATCHWORK

The example illustrated here is a simple one, using strips of the same width and just squares to make up the design. Bargello designs can be much more varied but the same principles apply. The width of the cut strips depends on the finished size required. In this example, the result is a finished square of 34in (86.4cm) square. Each strip started out as 2½in (6.3cm) wide x 20in (51cm) long.

1 Choose your fabrics, grading the colours from light to dark. You will need to cut two strips of each colour. Cut the strips 2½in (6.3cm) wide x 20in (51cm) long or to the width of your choice. Number the colours as shown. Strip piece fabric strips 1 to 6 together using ¼in (6mm) seams. Repeat with the other set of strips and then join the two sets of strips together into one long band. ▶

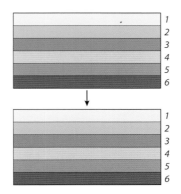

2 The band can now be cut into the widths required using a rotary cutter and ruler. In this example the vertical strips were cut 2½in (6.3cm) wide but other bargello designs may use a combination of squares and rectangles of varying widths so read instructions carefully. ▶

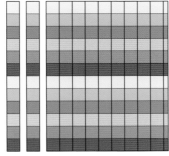

3 Referring to the diagram and the large layout diagram and beginning with Row 1, prepare each row. Place the narrow strips of colours in the right order, joining strips where indicated in the diagram using ¼in (6mm) seams. The strips will also need to be split at certain points, so undo the seam where indicated. Reserve the separated segment – in this design it can be moved to form the top part of the next row. Assemble all the rows in this way. ▶

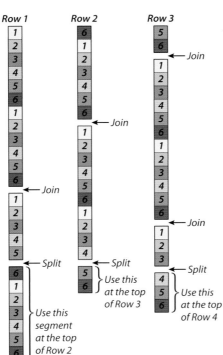

Bargello layout diagram

Rows

	R1	R2	R3	R4	R5	R6	R7	R8	R9	R10	R11	R12	R13	R14	R15	R16	R17
1	6	5	4	3	2	1	2	3	4	5	6	5	4	3	2	1
2	1	6	5	4	3	2	3	4	5	6	1	6	5	4	3	2
3	2	1	6	5	4	3	4	5	6	1	2	1	6	5	4	3
4	3	2	1	6	5	4	5	6	1	2	3	2	1	6	5	4
5	4	3	2	1	6	5	6	1	2	3	4	3	2	1	6	5
6	5	4	3	2	1	6	1	2	3	4	5	4	3	2	1	6
1	6	5	4	3	2	1	2	3	4	5	6	5	4	3	2	1
2	1	6	5	4	3	2	3	4	5	6	1	6	5	4	3	2
3	2	1	6	5	4	3	4	5	6	1	2	1	6	5	4	3
4	3	2	1	6	5	4	5	6	1	2	3	2	1	6	5	4
5	4	3	2	1	6	5	6	1	2	3	4	3	2	1	6	5
6	5	4	3	2	1	6	1	2	3	4	5	4	3	2	1	6
1	6	5	4	3	2	1	2	3	4	5	6	5	4	3	2	1
2	1	6	5	4	3	2	3	4	5	6	1	6	5	4	3	2
3	2	1	6	5	4	3	4	5	6	1	2	1	6	5	4	3
4	3	2	1	6	5	4	5	6	1	2	3	2	1	6	5	4
5	4	3	2	1	6	5	6	1	2	3	4	3	2	1	6	5

4 When all the rows are prepared in the right colour order, begin to sew them together. Sew together in pairs, pinning right sides together and matching seam junctions carefully. Use ¼in (6mm) seams and press after each seam. Sew the pairs together and so on until all the rows are joined. The bargello piece can be treated as any other block and be trimmed, bordered, backed and quilted. ▼

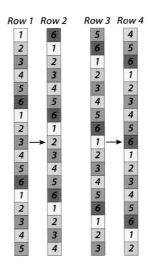

STRING PATCHWORK

String patchwork uses a technique of piecing narrow 'strings' or strips of fabric together, usually in a repeated shape, on a base fabric or foundation material. The foundation can be permanent or temporary. Originally, this form of piecing was a way of using up every scrap of fabric, particularly the narrow strips left over from dressmaking. Recycled fabrics were also used and the quilts created in this way were true scrap quilts. Strings can be trimmed to be symmetrical or be left asymmetrical, as seen in crazy patchwork. Using a foundation material means that very fine or flimsy fabrics can be used if desired.

This type of patchwork is very suitable for beginners as it uses a relaxed method, with very little measuring and piecing angst. Strings are cut long enough to cover the foundation length, while strip widths can be various, upwards of 1in (2.5cm). A scrap approach is a good place to start as most quilters have strings left over from other projects, which can be collected together. You could also cut a strip or two off new fabrics as you buy them and start a collection to make a string quilt. String patchwork is similar to strip piecing, except that strip piecing is used to create a fabric, rather than sewing strips to a foundation – see page 67 for strip piecing.

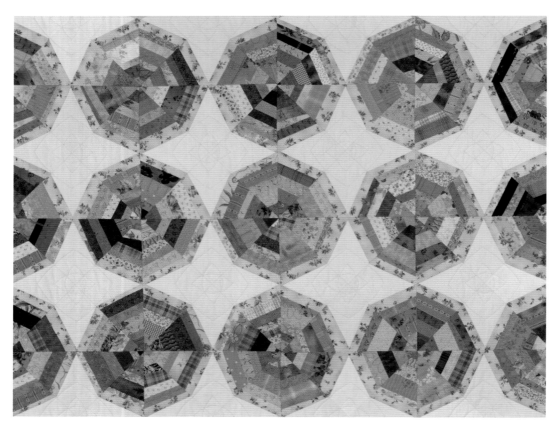

This quilt was made by Carolyn Forster using a string patchwork technique to create Spider's Web blocks which, when combined, create a secondary star-like pattern. The cream fabric was used as a permanent foundation, on to which the other strips were sewn.

USING A TEMPORARY FOUNDATION

Temporary foundations are those only needed while the patchwork block or unit is being constructed. Materials that could be used include newspaper, freezer paper, tear-away stabilizers and water-soluble foundation paper. Temporary foundations do not require a seam allowance as they are not sewn into the block. The foundation is cut to the actual size and shape required and the edges act as sewing lines for joining the unit or block to other blocks later.

USING A PERMANENT FOUNDATION

These foundations are left in place within the quilt so light materials are generally used, such as calico, thin cotton, lightweight sew-in interfacing and foundation sheets, which are made from a blend of rayon and polyester. Permanent foundations can also be chosen to be seen in the final quilt as part of the piecing – see Spider's Web String Patchwork opposite. In this case you could use calico or a thin cotton fabric as the foundation.

>> related topics … *Cutting Strips 30 • Foundation Piecing 96 • Crazy Patchwork 100* >>>

THE TECHNIQUES

PIECING STRING PATCHWORK

This technique is the same one used in a technique called stitch and flip. There are numerous variations of the technique and a few are shown in the Varying String Patchwork technique below.

1 Each strip needs to be cut long enough to cover the foundation, overlapping slightly at each end. Pin the first strip right side *up* on the foundation, ensuring the ends overlap the foundation edges. ▼

2 Pin the second strip in place, right side *down*, with its edge aligned with the first strip, as shown. Sew along the edge using a ¼in (6mm) seam. ▼

3 Flip the second strip over so the right side is showing and finger press the seam. Pin and stitch a third strip in place against the second strip. Sew and finger press open, as before. You can add strips on either side of the first strip. ▶

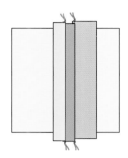

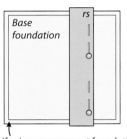

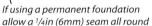

If using a permanent foundation allow a 1/4in (6mm) seam all round

4 Once the whole foundation is covered, trim the block to the size and shape required, trimming from the wrong side, following the foundation shape: if using a permanent foundation trim to the edge; if using a temporary one trim ¼in (6mm) further out to allow for a seam. Once all blocks are made, remove the temporary foundation. When the quilt top is finished, it can be padded, backed and quilted as normal. ▶

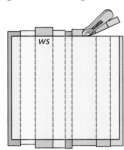

VARYING STRING PATCHWORK

There are numerous variations to piecing string patchwork. Here are a few suggestions.

A The foundation shape can be anything you choose.
B You can vary the angles of the strips.
C You can add strings in more than one direction.

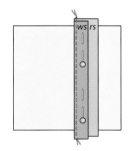

SPIDER'S WEB STRING PATCHWORK

A spider's web pattern is a really popular design to use for string patchwork. The colour scheme can be whatever you like. In the example shown below, the pale blue fabric forms part of the finished unit so needs to be either added as a wide strip or be the permanent foundation to which the other strings are sewn.

A Use the basic technique described above to create a right-angled triangle unit.
B Make three more units and sew together into a block.
C Create as many blocks as you need for a quilt and sew them together to create the spider's web design.

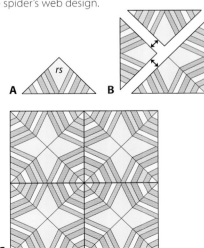

PATCHWORK WITH TRIANGLES

After squares, rectangles and strips, triangles are the next easiest shape to piece and create some wonderful quilts, both on their own and in combination with other shapes. Triangles form the basis of many patchwork units, including half-square triangles, quarter-square triangles and flying geese. They can also be used extensively in sashing and borders to create additional interest.

The techniques described in this section will allow you to make all sorts of blocks based on triangles, and include making half-square triangles, bias strip-pieced triangles, quarter-square triangles, joining 60 degree triangles, sewing flying geese units, joining triangles to squares, creating triangles from folded corners and using setting triangles. A selection of blocks is given overleaf for you to try.

Triangles can be cut with a rotary cutter and ruler, usually layering several fabrics together or can be sandwich or grid pieced – see pages 31–32 for details on cutting triangles. There are many specialist rotary rulers that can be bought for cutting triangles. Commercial templates and pre-printed foundation piecing kits are also available for triangle piecing and making blocks, such as Pineapple.

KNOW YOUR TRIANGLES

Thankfully, a knowledge of geometry is not essential to create lovely patchwork but being able to recognize different shapes is useful. A few you will come across in patchwork and quilting are shown here. See also Drawing and Cutting Shapes on page 29.

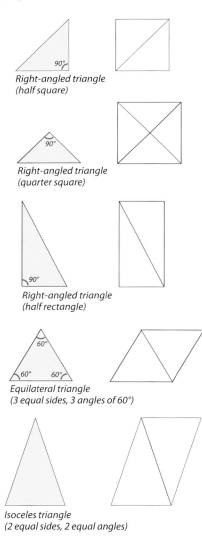

Right-angled triangle (half square)

Right-angled triangle (quarter square)

Right-angled triangle (half rectangle)

Equilateral triangle (3 equal sides, 3 angles of 60°)

Isoceles triangle (2 equal sides, 2 equal angles)

Irregular triangles

A wonderful combination of blocks and fabulous colour choices can be seen in this quilt by Katharine Guerrier. Triangles take centre stage, with different-sized blocks of Friendship Star, Eight-point Star and Ohio Star.

HALF-SQUARE TRIANGLE UNIT

These patchwork units are magic and are *so* versatile as they can be combined with squares, rectangles and other polygons to create an almost infinite number of patchwork blocks. Half-square triangles are known by various names, including pieced triangle squares, two-triangle squares, split squares and bias squares. They can be made in many different ways, including sandwich piecing and bias-strip piecing (see overleaf for techniques). When used alone the variations are endless: the simple Pinwheel block, once rearranged, becomes Broken Dishes, Barn Raising, Streak o' Lightning and many more.

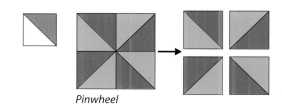

Pinwheel

QUARTER-SQUARE TRIANGLE UNIT

Quarter-square triangle units look great on their own in a quilt, showcasing attractive colour combinations. They also make great partners with half-square triangles, squares and rectangles, creating many wonderful blocks, including Ohio Star, Milky Way and Handy Andy. Quarter-square triangles are made up of four triangles and clever colour choices can create interesting secondary patterns in a quilt.

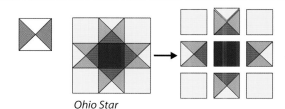

Ohio Star

FLYING GEESE UNIT

This is another simple patchwork unit that is easy to make and has so many uses. It can appear alone in blocks such as Dutchman's Puzzle; it can be combined with other shapes and make blocks such as Indian Star, Art Square, Woodland Path and Stacked Stars. Flying Geese are also popular for sashing and borders and can give powerful visual direction within a quilt.

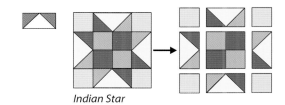

Indian Star

TRIANGLE-IN-A-SQUARE UNIT

This unit is the basis of many star blocks, including the well-loved Eight-point Star shown here. The basic unit can be drawn in a stretched and distorted format to create different-shaped triangles. This unit also works well with square-in-a-square units.

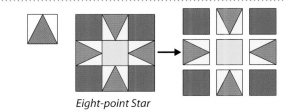

Eight-point Star

ECCENTRIC UNIT

Triangles come in all shapes and sizes and can be combined in more unusual or eccentric patterns to create a number of interesting blocks. The piecing of such blocks as Interlaced Star can look puzzling but once again triangles come to the rescue and instead of being pieced in rows the block is created by joining four pieced triangles. Eccentric units have the ability to fool the eye and interesting kaleidoscopic patterns arise when Interlaced Star blocks are combined.

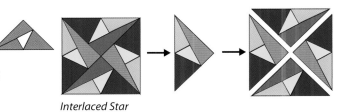

Interlaced Star

BLOCKS USING TRIANGLES

The repertoire of blocks becomes infinitely greater once the skill of piecing triangles is mastered and a few are shown here, some combined with squares and rectangles. Some of the easiest are four-patch and nine-patch arrangements and most can be pieced in units and then rows using the techniques described in this section.

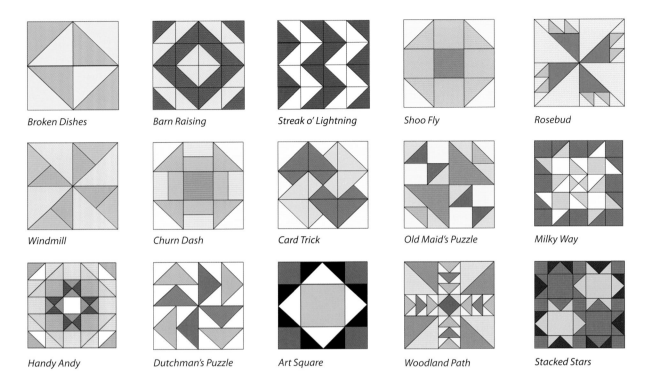

Broken Dishes   Barn Raising   Streak o' Lightning   Shoo Fly   Rosebud

Windmill   Churn Dash   Card Trick   Old Maid's Puzzle   Milky Way

Handy Andy   Dutchman's Puzzle   Art Square   Woodland Path   Stacked Stars

> > > **related topics...** *Drawing and Cutting Shapes 29 • Machine Piecing 54*   > >

THE TECHNIQUES

SEWING HALF-SQUARE TRIANGLES

A square composed of two right-angled triangles can, of course, be made by sewing two triangles together but a much quicker way is to start with two squares and use a technique called sandwich piecing, which results in two pieced units. To make two half-square triangle units, start with two squares, each ⅞in (2.2cm) larger all round than the finished size you want.

1 Place two squares right sides together and mark the diagonal line. Pin the squares together and sew ¼in (6mm) either side of the marked line. These lines can be marked too if desired. ▼

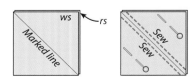

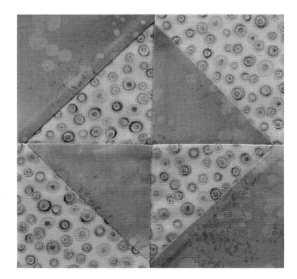

2 Cut the two triangles apart on the marked line. Press to set the seams and then press open, usually towards the darker fabric. ▼

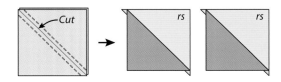

BIAS STRIP-PIECED TRIANGLES

This is another method of creating half-square triangles developed by Marsha McCloskey, an expert in feathered star designs, which use many half-square triangle units that need to be accurately pieced. Here, strips are cut on the bias from a large square. The strips are sewn together and squares are cut from the strips which then have the straight grain on the outer edges, meaning they are less likely to stretch and distort. The number of units obtained depends on the size of the starting square and the width of the bias strips.

1 Decide on the size of your starting squares and the width of strips to cut. Take the two different squares and layer them right sides together, with the fabric grain as shown (A). Using a rotary cutter and ruler cut strips on the bias, starting diagonally from corner to corner and working outwards (B). ▼

3 Using a square ruler with a 45 degree marked line, begin to cut squares from the strips beginning at the lower edge, placing the 45 degree line on the ruler on the first seam line. At this point, cut a few threads larger than the finished size required. Two cuts will be needed for each square (D). When the first set has been cut, go back and cut a second set, and so on (E). ▼

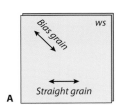

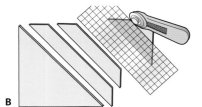

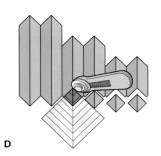

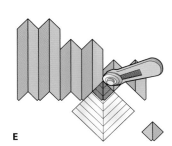

2 Without disturbing the paired strips, take each pair in turn and sew them together down the long bias edge using a ¼in (6mm) seam. Press seams open. Arrange the paired strips (C) and sew them together. Place the joined strips back on the cutting mat, with the bottom V shapes aligned. ▼

4 Trim all the units to the exact size, aligning the diagonal line of the ruler with the seam line of the square (F). The bias-pieced triangle squares are now ready for further piecing. ▼

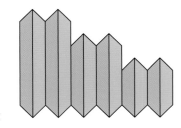

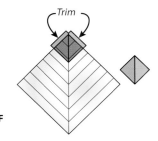

SEWING QUARTER-SQUARE TRIANGLES

As with half-square triangle units, quarter-square triangles can be created more quickly by sandwich piecing. To make two quarter-square triangle units, start with two squares each 1¼in (3.2cm) larger all round than the finished size you want. This method begins with half-square triangle units.

1 Start with two half-square triangle units. Place them right sides together with their diagonal lines going in the same direction and mark a diagonal line in the *opposite* direction across the top square. Sew ¼in (6mm) either side of the marked line. ▶

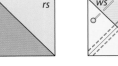

2 Cut the two units apart on the marked diagonal line. Press the units to set the seams and then press open, usually towards the darker fabric. ▶

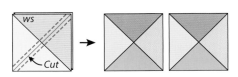

BRIGHT IDEA

JOIN A HALF-SQUARE TRIANGLE UNIT WITH A SQUARE TO MAKE A UNIT WITH ONE LARGE TRIANGLE AND TWO SMALL ONES. WHEN JOINED TOGETHER THESE CAN CREATE A BRAIDED LOOK.

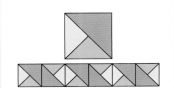

JOINING TRIANGLES TO SQUARES

The points on a triangle can make it difficult to sew at times, especially if these edges are on the bias. To join a triangle to a square, align the pieces along one edge, matching the centre points (A), and then trim off the triangle points at the edges (B). The seam can now be sewn and the triangle flipped back and pressed (C). A point trimmer is a useful gadget that can be used before sewing. Removing points reduces bulk and minimizes show-through.

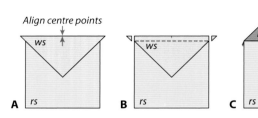

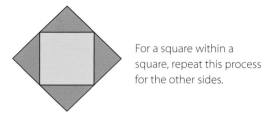

For a square within a square, repeat this process for the other sides.

SEWING TRIANGLE CORNERS

A quick way to add triangles to a square or rectangle is to sew a square to the corner and fold it over along the diagonal, so it becomes a triangle. Triangle corners can be added to pieced blocks in the same way.

1 Cut the large square to the size required then cut a smaller square. The size of this smaller square needs to be half the size of the bigger one plus ¼in (6mm). So if your large square is 5in (12.7cm), the smaller square needs to be 2½in (6.3cm) + ¼in (6mm) = 2¾in (7cm) square. Place the small square right side down on the large square, aligning edges. Pencil a diagonal line through the small square and pin the squares together. Sew along the line. Flip the smaller square over and press. Trim excess fabric at the back. ▼

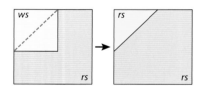

2 To create a second triangle corner, repeat in the opposite corner. This square will overlap the one already sewn in place. Sew along the centre line as before and press. ▼

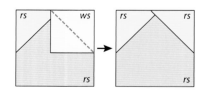

For a square on point within a square, repeat this stitch and flip process on all corners. ▼

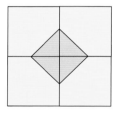

Sewing triangle corner blocks together can create secondary patterns, as in the quilt on page 217. ▼

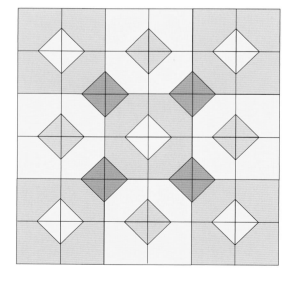

BRIGHT IDEA

CREATE OTHER TRIANGLE-IN-A-SQUARE UNITS, FOR EXAMPLE, THOSE NEEDED FOR A STORM AT SEA BLOCK AND OTHER KALEIDOSCOPIC DESIGNS, BY USING A FOUNDATION PIECING TECHNIQUE (SEE PAGE 96) OR SPECIALIST RULERS.

seam allowance

SEWING A SINGLE FLYING GEESE UNIT

Flying Geese units can be made in the same way as triangle corners (left) but starting with a rectangle not a square.

1 Cut a rectangle ½in (1.3cm) wider and longer than the required size of your unit. Cut two squares the same size as the short side of the rectangle. So if the finished unit is to be 4½in x 2½in (11.4cm x 6.3cm), cut the rectangle 5in x 3in (12.7cm x 7.6cm) and cut the two squares each 3in (7.6cm).

2 Place the square right side down on the rectangle, aligning the corners. Draw a diagonal line through the square and pin the squares together. Sew along this line. Flip the smaller triangular part over, along the stitched line and press. Trim excess fabric at the back. ▶

3 Sew the second square to the rectangle in the same way in the opposite corner, aligning the top and side edges. Once sewn and pressed, this square will overlap the one already sewn in place. ▶

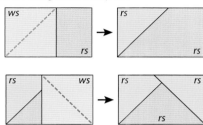

SEWING MULTIPLE FLYING GEESE UNITS

This method makes four Flying Geese units simultaneously and is useful for making blocks that require sets of four.

1 Decide what finished size you want your units to be and cut a square 1¼in (3.2cm) larger than the longest finished side. Cut four squares from a different fabric each ⅞in (2.2cm) larger than the shortest finished side. For example, if the finished unit is to be 5in x 3in (12.7cm x 7.6cm), cut the large square 6¼in (15.8cm) and the four smaller squares 3⅞in (9.8cm).

2 Draw a diagonal line through each small square. Place the large square right side up and pin two of the smaller squares right sides down on this, aligning corners and matching the drawn lines. Sew a line ¼in (6mm) away from the drawn line on either side. ▶

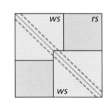

3 Cut the unit apart on the drawn diagonal line (shown in red on diagram). Open out and press the individual units. ▶

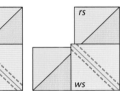

4 Position the remaining two small squares on the units with the marked line running diagonally. Sew either side of the line, cut the units apart and press. You now have four units. ▶

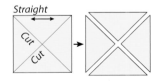

USING SETTING TRIANGLES

In a diagonal or on point quilt setting, triangles, called setting triangles, are needed to bring the quilt shape back to a straight square or rectangle. These setting or filler triangles are of two shapes – corner triangles and side triangles.

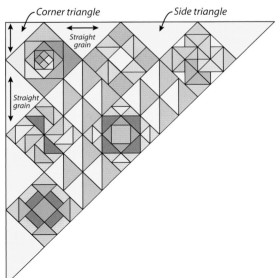

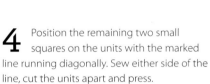

Corner triangles

Four of these will be needed. Cut a square diagonally in one direction to yield two triangles. To calculate the size of square needed, measure the finished block and divide this by 1.414, then add 0.875in (⅞in/2.2cm) for seam allowances. Round up the final number. Taking a 12in (30.5cm) block as an example: 12 ÷ 1.414 = 8.48 + 0.875 = 9.36 (rounded up to 9½). So the square needs to be 9½in (24cm).

Side triangles

The number of side triangles depends on the quilt size. Cut a square diagonally in both directions to yield four triangles. To calculate the size of square needed, multiply the finished block size by 1.414, then add 1.25in (1¼in/3.2cm) for seam allowances. Round up the final number. Taking a 12in (30.5cm) block as an example: 12 x 1.414 = 16.96 + 1.25 = 18.21 (rounded up to 18¼in). So the square needs to be 18¼in (46.3cm).

PATCHWORK WITH DIAMONDS AND POLYGONS

The beauty of patchwork and appliqué is that *any* shape, regular or irregular, straight or curved, can be used to create fabulous quilts, and the huge range of techniques in this book gives guidance on the many ways that these shapes can be used. This section looks at designs made with diamonds and more unusual shapes, such as kites, trapeziums, hexagons and octagons. Combining many different shapes can produce far more eccentric and irregular designs, with greater scope for creativity.

Some stunning quilts can be created with diamonds, as this quilt by Pam and Nicky Lintott shows. The large eight-point stars are composed of diamonds made by strip piecing. Each large star block is framed with narrow sashing, pieced together from fabrics used in the blocks.

ISOMETRIC PAPER FOR UNUSUAL SHAPES

Many shapes can be drawn easily using isometric paper, which is divided into 60 degree triangles. If scaled up, the paper shapes can be cut out, glued to thin card and used as templates (see page 26). Isometric paper is also useful for English paper piecing (see page 51).

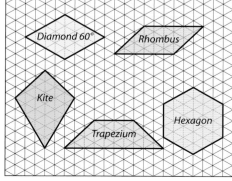

DIAMONDS AND RHOMBOIDS

After triangles, diamonds and rhomboids are the shapes most often used to make star designs in patchwork and some fabulous quilts can be created with them, either alone or combined with other quadrilateral shapes, such as kites and trapeziums, and with polygons, such as hexagons and octagons.

Diamond – A 45 degree diamond is symmetrical, with four equal sides and with opposite sides parallel. If these diamonds are to fit together accurately, careful cutting and piecing is required, especially if they are used as one-patch blocks. Bias edges can cause the fabric to stretch and affect accurate piecing. For this reason many designs with diamonds are created from templates. If using diamonds pieced en masse as a background fabric, they will be more stable if the fabric grain runs vertically and horizontally.

Diamonds are sometimes described as 'short' and 'long' diamonds. A short diamond is cut at a 90 degree angle, which means it is really a square turned on point. A long diamond is cut at a 45 or 60 degree angle. See page 29 for more on cutting shapes. There are specialist rotary rulers available for cutting diamonds and commercial templates in many sizes. A diamond can also be created by piecing two opposing triangles cut from the same fabric.

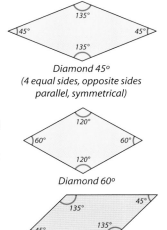

Diamond 45º
(4 equal sides, opposite sides parallel, symmetrical)

Diamond 60º

Rhombus
(2 long sides, 2 short sides, asymmetrical)

Rhombus – This shape is similar to a diamond but is not truly symmetrical, having two long sides and two short sides. This lack of symmetry means that when cutting numerous rhomboids for a pattern, some of the shapes need to be reversed. Instructions vary but will usually say 'cut four and cut four in reverse'. The term 'rhomboid' is used to mean a shape that is like a rhombus, but may not be geometrically accurate.

A diamond or rhombus can also be created by piecing two opposing triangles cut from the same fabric.

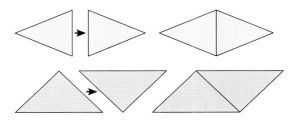

KITES AND TRAPEZIUMS

Kites and trapeziums are quadrilaterals, that is, shapes with four sides. These two shapes are both based on triangles, as seen in the diagrams below, and so work well combined with triangles in block designs. See page 33 for cutting kite and trapezium shapes.

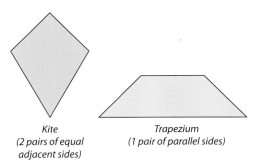

A trapezium can be created by cutting the corner off a right-angled triangle and a kite by cutting two corners off an equilateral triangle.

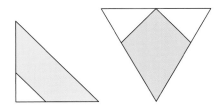

Kite
(2 pairs of equal adjacent sides)

Trapezium
(1 pair of parallel sides)

HEXAGONS AND OCTAGONS

Hexagons are polygons, that is, many-sided shapes. There are many polygons but six-sided hexagons and eight-sided octagons are very useful in patchwork and they often occur as one-patch designs and can create interesting tessellating effects. See English Paper Piecing on pages 51–52 for more on hexagons.

Hexagon
(6 equal sides and equal angles of 120º)

Octagon
(8 equal sides and equal angles of 135º)

A hexagon can be created from a 60º diamond and an octagon from a square.

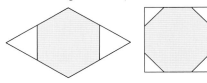

BLOCKS WITH UNUSUAL SHAPES

A selection of blocks is shown here featuring diamonds, rhomboids, kites, trapeziums, hexagons and octagons. Some are shown as repeat arrangements to show how secondary patterns appear when the blocks are combined. Try rotating grouped blocks 45 degrees for on point settings.

Diamonds

Le Moyne Star

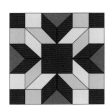

Six-point Star

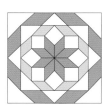

Merry Kite

Four Merry Kite blocks on point

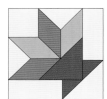

Texas Cactus

Chevron

Swallows in the Window

Star and Chains

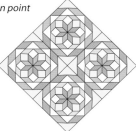

Four Star and Chains blocks in an on point setting

Kites and Trapeziums

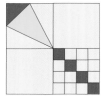

The Kite

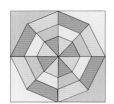

Spider's Web

Trials and Troubles

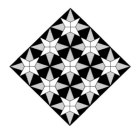

Trials and Troubles tessellating

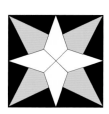

Double Star

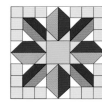

Double Star on point

Pillar to Post

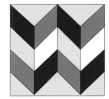

Pillar to Post in a group of four

Hexagons and Octagons

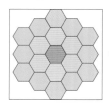

Grandmother's Flower Garden

North Star

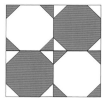

Snowball

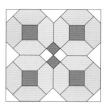

Memory Chain

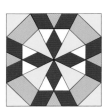

Hawaii

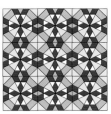

Hawaii in a group of nine

>> related topics... *Drawing and Cutting Shapes 29 • Tessellating Setting 40 • Machine Piecing 54* >>>

THE TECHNIQUES

SEWING UNUSUAL SHAPES

Many techniques covered in other sections described how to sew different shapes together. For the shapes in this section a combination of techniques is needed.

- Piece by hand (see page 50) – tricky shapes are sometimes easier to piece by hand.
- Piece over papers (see page 51) – useful for designs that repeat the same shape or tessellate. See page 52 for advice on dealing with points on shapes such as diamonds and triangles.
- Use templates (see page 26) – for greater accuracy, especially for shapes such as diamonds and kites.
- Use machine piecing (see page 54) – intersecting seams, set-in seams and partial seams are all used when piecing unusual shapes. The techniques used for piecing triangles (see pages 80–83) are also invaluable.
- Use strip piecing (see page 67) – this is useful for creating multiple shapes quickly, particularly diamonds, and would work well for blocks such as Chevron, Six-Point Star and Spider's Web.
- Use foundation piecing (see page 96) – some blocks have many units that would be complicated to piece so foundation piecing can make this easier and aid accuracy. Try this for blocks such as Trials and Troubles, North Star and Hawaii.

WORKING OUT PIECING ORDER

It is easy to work out the piecing order for many blocks based on a grid system. Normally they are pieced in squares or rectangles; these are then sewn into rows and these rows are then sewn together – see page 59 for examples. Some blocks are more complex and those that use unusual shapes can seem to defy understanding. Generally, such blocks are still pieced in smaller units; those units may not be square but might be triangular or trapezoid in shape. Two examples are shown here using two blocks from this section, and an eight-point star block is shown below.

North Star

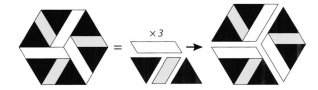

Trials and Troubles

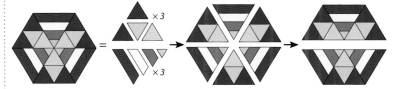

PIECING AN EIGHT-POINT STAR

An Eight-Point Star block, also called a Le Moyne Star, is a very popular design. It can be repeated in a quilt arrangement or form the central focus, as it does in many medallion quilt designs. The one shown here has half-square triangle corners but these could be plain squares or four-patch blocks if preferred. See page 57 for details on stitching set-in seams.

Begin by making four half-square triangle units (see page 80) as in diagram A. Stitch two diamonds together and add a triangle using a set-in seam (B). Remember that shapes with acute angles, such as diamonds and triangles, must be joined by offsetting the edges by ¼in (6mm), in order that edges align properly (see page 56). Join these two units together (C) and make another three units this way. Now join these units together to create four larger units (D). Join these together to create two halves of the block (E). Join the two halves to complete the block. ▼

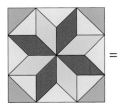
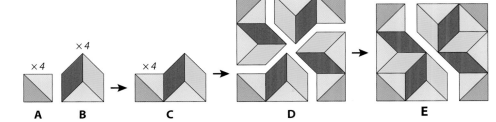

A **B** **C** **D** **E**

BRIGHT IDEA

WHEN CHOOSING FABRIC PRINTS FOR DIAMONDS, CONSIDER THE PATTERN DIRECTION. A STRIPE, FOR EXAMPLE, MAY LOOK ODD AT DIFFERENT ANGLES FOR EACH DIAMOND BUT WITH PLANNING THE PATTERN CAN WORK WELL.

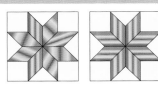

PATCHWORK WITH CURVES

Patchwork doesn't have to be all straight lines and geometric shapes. Some exciting designs can be created once you begin to use circles and curves. There are dozens of blocks with curvilinear elements. Sewing curved seams takes a little practice but once you understand the principle, the technique is straightforward. Fabrics cut in curved shapes look fine but the act of taking these curved shapes and putting them right sides together means that the curves then bend in opposite directions and no longer look so biddable. However, a careful approach, and much pinning and easing, will yield results and you will be pleased with the stunning effects you can achieve with curves. Designs can also be created using a combination of patchwork and appliqué techniques.

Curved seams can be sewn by hand or machine but if you are new to curved piecing you might find it easier to begin with hand sewing to get the feel of how the fabric behaves. Curves and circles can be marked with various tools, including templates, a compass and a flexicurve – see page 11 for more information on equipment. An easy way to use curved shapes in your work is to appliqué them in place on top of pieced work, using needle-turn appliqué or fusible web appliqué. Refer to pages 144 and 152 for details of these techniques.

Once mastered, the techniques in this section will allow you to make many different curved blocks, how to match curved seams, how to hand and machine sew a curved seam, how to cut and sew freehand curves, how to set a circle into fabric and how to sew shell patchwork. A selection of blocks is given on pages 93–94 for you to try.

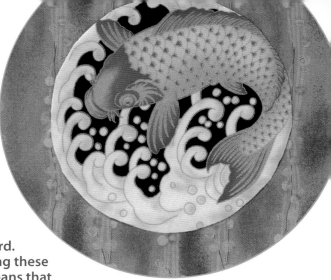

An interesting motif can become a feature if set into a background fabric as a circle.

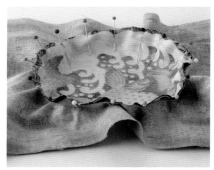

Setting a circle into a background fabric is a little fiddly and looks strange once pinned together, but you will soon get the hang of it – see technique on page 91.

This pretty bag by Susan Briscoe was made using foundation piecing with the circle appliquéd in place, but it could be pieced with the circle joined to the fan with a curved seam.

CUTTING CURVED SHAPES

Curves are best cut with sharp fabric scissors but they can also be cut with a circular rotary cutter. Templates are also available.

- When cutting curves with scissors, follow the smooth shape of the marked curve by moving the fabric rather than the scissors.
- Use a small diameter rotary cutter as this will sweep round tighter curves more easily and accurately.
- Use a separate cutting mat if possible, as a mat used for cutting straight shapes may have minute ruts in the surface which will hinder or interrupt the smooth cutting of curves.

CREATING THE ILLUSION OF CURVES

There are some patchwork blocks that are made up of straight lines but when repeated or combined with other blocks can create the illusion of curves. Four block examples are shown here – Road to Paradise, Windmill Star, Snail's Tail and Storm at Sea. Some blocks, such as Storm at Sea, are more easily pieced using a foundation piecing technique or with specialist rulers.

Road to Paradise

Windmill Star

Snail's Trail

Storm at Sea

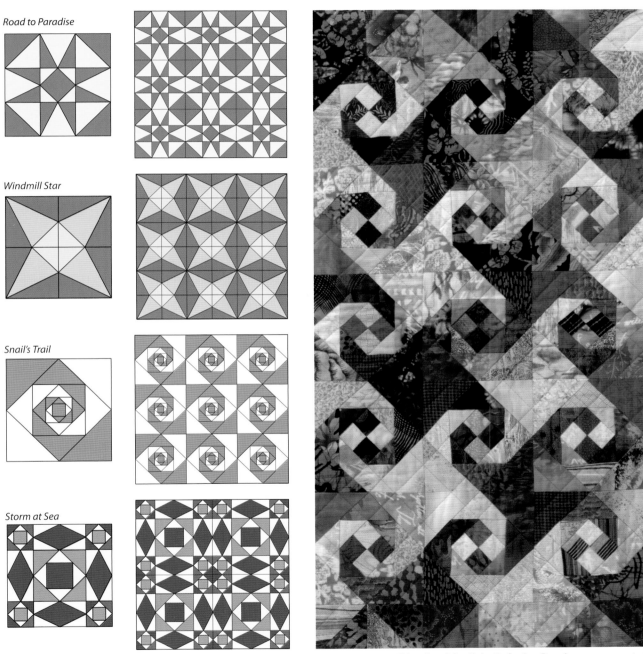

This colourful quilt by Katharine Guerrier uses a repeated Snail's Trail block, which creates the illusion of curves when pieced like this. The effect is highlighted by the contrast between the medium and dark values of the fabrics used.

related topics... *Using Fabric Grain 23*

THE TECHNIQUES

MATCHING CURVED SEAMS

Sewing curved seams is made easier by marking matching indicators across the planned seam. Do this after the curved shape has been marked on your fabric but before the fabric is cut. If these lines are marked at the centre point and then regularly along the seam line they will provide guidelines when the two sections are cut out, pinned and sewn together (A). You could also mark ¼in (6mm) seam lines if you wish. The more irregular the curve, the more seam matching indicators are needed, especially on tight curves (B). ▶

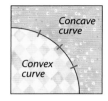

A

B

BRIGHT IDEA

WHEN SEWING CURVED SEAMS, MATCHING BIAS EDGES WILL ALLOW MORE 'GIVE' IN THE FABRIC PIECES AND MAKE IT EASIER TO PIECE THEM TOGETHER.

HAND SEWING A CURVED SEAM

This technique, and its machine-sewn equivalent below, works well for all curved seams and would be suitable when piecing blocks such as Drunkard's Path, Love Ring, Around the World, Fool's Puzzle and Grandmother's Fan – see block diagrams on page 93. See opposite for setting a complete circle into fabric.

1 Mark the fabric pieces and mark the seam indicators, as described above. Cut out the pieces. Place the fabric pieces right sides together, with the convex shape (the outward curving one) on top of the concave one (the inward curving one). Pin together at the centre, matching the marked points. Now align the fabric pieces at the edges and pin together at these points. ▼

2 Working across the curve, continue pinning the pieces together, easing the excess fabric so that it fits the curved shape. ▼

3 Stitch the fabric pieces together by hand with a ¼in (6mm) seam, using closely spaced stitches for a secure seam. Remove the pins as you stitch. Press the seam from the back towards the darker fabric or the concave shape (whichever is easier). If the curve is tight, clip the seam at intervals to help it to lie flat. Press from the front, checking there are no pleats. ▼

BRIGHT IDEA

YOU MAY FIND IT EASIER TO PIN THE FABRIC PIECES TOGETHER IN THE OPPOSITE WAY TO THAT DESCRIBED IN STEP 1, THAT IS, WITH THE CONCAVE SHAPE (INWARD CURVE) ON TOP OF THE CONVEX ONE.

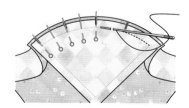

MACHINE SEWING A CURVED SEAM

If unfamiliar with curved piecing by machine, take your time with this technique, practising on scrap fabrics first.

1 Follow step 1 and 2 above for marking, cutting and pinning the fabric pieces. Machine stitch the pieces together with an accurate ¼in (6mm) seam. If you remove the pins as you stitch, it will be easier to manoeuvre the machine. ▶

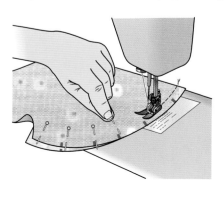

2 Press the seam from the back towards the concave shape. If the curve is quite tight, clip the seam at regular intervals to help it to lie flat. Then press from the front, checking there are no pleats.

CUTTING AND SEWING FREEHAND CURVES

Some interesting effects can be created with freehand curves, and irregular designs created this way are becoming popular. If long strips are joined in this way they can be cut up to create blocks, which can then be pieced into a design. Start with gentle curves as they are easier to piece. This method results in two sets – one the reverse of the other.

1 Cut two different fabrics in the width required and slightly longer than the required finished length. Place the two pieces on top of each other, wrong sides up, and cut a freehand curve along the length using a small-diameter rotary cutter. You will now have four pieces. Take one from each pair and place together so they match along the curve. Mark indicators along the curve. ▼

2 Pick up the fabric pieces and begin to match them right sides together, pinning together at the indicator marks and then in other places along the seam to match edges carefully. Sew together with a ¼in (6mm) seam, removing the pins as you go. ▼

3 Press from the back, pressing towards the darker fabric, and then press from the front, ensuring there are no pleats. ▼

SETTING A CIRCLE INTO FABRIC

Being able to set a circle into another fabric with hand or machine piecing rather than by appliqué is a useful skill.

1 Start by creating a circular template in thin card or plastic ½in (1.3cm) wider than the desired finished size. Mark the template at eight points – north, south, west and east, and then four more marks equidistant between these (A). Make a second circular template with a diameter 1in (2.5cm) wider than the first template. Mark it in the same way (B). ▶

2 Place the smaller template on the background fabric, draw round it and mark all indicators (C). Place the larger circle on the fabric chosen for the circle. Draw round and mark indicators (D). ▶

3 Cut out the smaller circle (E) and set it aside, leaving the outer section to be used. Ensure the markers are still visible on the fabric. ▼

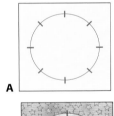 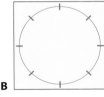

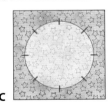 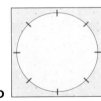

5 Using a ¼in (6mm) seam, machine or hand sew around the circle, removing the pins as you go. Take your time to check that the fabric pieces and marks stay aligned (G). When the stitching is finished, work from the back and use the point of the iron to nudge the seam allowance outwards, over to the background. Clip the seam if need be. Once the seam is flat, press the complete piece from the front, ensuring there are no pleats (H). ▼

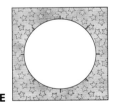 

4 Put the fabric pieces right sides down, with the background shape on top of the circle. Pick up the two shapes and place together so their raw edges are aligned at the north mark and pin together. Now pin the south point, then east and west and the remaining marks (F) (see also photo page 88). Add more pins between those already in place. ▶

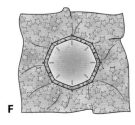 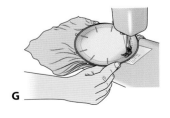 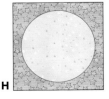

SEWING SHELL PATCHWORK

Shell and fish-scale designs make attractive patchwork and can be used as all-over patterns or constructed as single blocks. This method uses templates, creating shell shapes that have a seamed edge along the top, and could be used to create a Clamshell block.

1 Two shell templates are needed: template 1 is the finished size of the shell, while template 2 is ¼in (6mm) bigger all round for cutting out fabric shapes. You can use those supplied here, enlarged to the size you require. ▼

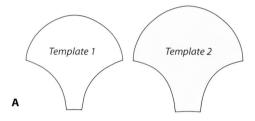

A

2 Using template 2, place it on the wrong side of the fabric and mark all around the edge with a pencil. Cut out the shape from the fabric following the drawn line. Now use template 1, placing and pinning it centrally within the fabric shape and mark around the edge. ▼

B

Some blocks, such as Clamshell, are easier to piece by hand. This shell shape could also be created using appliqué.

3 From the wrong side turn a hem over along the top, following the curve of the marked line and tack (baste) in place (C). Press the shape from the right side, ensuring it is smooth (D). Remove the template. Prepare as many shells as you need in this way. ▼

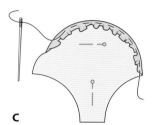

C

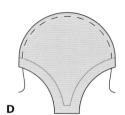

D

4 Pin the shells in position on the background fabric, in the colour sequence of your choice, beginning with the top row of the design. Tack (baste) in place if desired. Using small slipstitches, sew the first row of shells to the background fabric along the curved edge. Position the second row of shells so their curved tops cover the bases of the first row. Sew in place through the first row of shells and the background fabric. Continue until all rows are complete. ▼

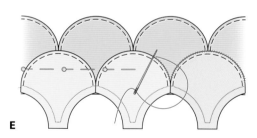

E

5 When all the shells are stitched in place use a rotary cutter and ruler (or scissors) to trim the edges straight, allowing for a seam as desired. ▼

F

BRIGHT IDEA

ADD EXTRA ROWS OF CLAMSHELLS SO THE OVERALL DESIGN IS WIDER AND TALLER AS THIS WILL ALLOW YOU TO TRIM THE FINISHED WORK NEATLY.

CURVED BLOCK EXAMPLES

Curved designs in patchwork and appliqué have a long history and there are hundreds of blocks and countless variations to play with. Popular design themes include fans, plates, shells and rings. Some examples are shown here and overleaf, with diagrams showing how the block is made up. These sorts of block can be constructed in a number of ways, including piecing, foundation piecing and appliqué methods. Templates are useful in their construction.

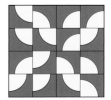

Drunkard's Path – This is a very versatile block, with many different patterns created from rotating and rearranging the curved pieced units. The curved seam can be sewn by hand or machine and it is a good block to practise the technique on. Numerous other blocks are created by rearranging the units and are given different names, including Tumbleweed, Love Ring, Around the World and Fool's Puzzle. When combined in groups of four or more, the curved seams create interesting secondary patterns.

Two shapes make up a unit

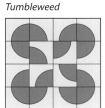
Tumbleweed

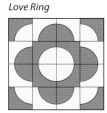
Love Ring

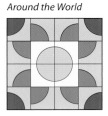
Around the World

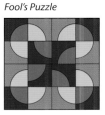
Fool's Puzzle

Grandmother's Fan – This block has long been a favourite. It is versatile with many variations. and is ideal for using up scraps. At its most basic, it is composed of just three shapes – a corner quadrant, a fan 'stick' and a background piece. To piece the block begin by sewing the eight 'sticks' together with straight seams. Next, using a curved seam, sew the corner quadrant to the pieced fan. Finally, sew the background shape in place with a curved seam.

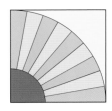

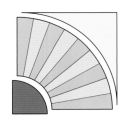

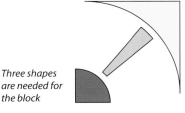
Three shapes are needed for the block

Dresden Fan – Many pages could be devoted to fan and sun designs. At their simplest they usually radiate out from a corner or centre point but some wonderful variations can be found. The simple one shown here is also called Fan of Friendship and Art Deco Fan. It is made up of three shapes – a corner quadrant, a petal shape and a background piece – and is best created with a combination of patchwork and appliqué. Sew the petals together and appliqué this unit to a background square using either needle-turn appliqué or fusible web appliqué (see pages 144 and 152). Finally, appliqué the corner quadrant in place or sew it with a curved seam.

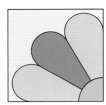

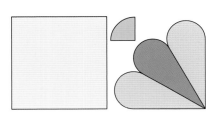

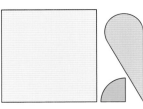
Three shapes are needed for the block

Dresden Plate – There are many, many variations of this block, and the number of segments vary between eight and sixteen. The shapes making up the 'plate' are also variable and may be petal-shaped or more geometric or twisted in a swirling pattern. The design shown here is made up of three shapes, in a similar way to the previous Dresden Fan design, repeating the quadrant to create a full circle.

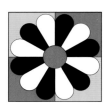 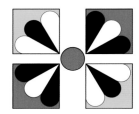

Three shapes are needed for the block

Clamshell – Shell and fish-scale designs are very popular and the Clamshell block can be used as an all-over design, either straight or in rotating patterns, or be built into a specific shape as shown here, adding circles to the centre line. See the technique on page 92 for sewing shell patchwork.

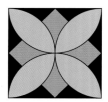 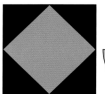

Two shapes are needed for the block, plus a background

Tobacco Leaf – Designs that feature petal shapes, such as Tobacco Leaf and Melon Patch are best pieced with a combination of patchwork and appliqué. For Tobacco Leaf, piece a square within a square first (see technique on page 82) and then add the petals with appliqué.

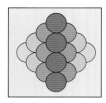

One petal shape and a square within a square is needed for the block

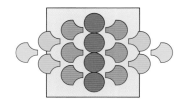

Melon Patch – For this block, piece a four-patch block to start and then add the petals with needle-turn or fusible web appliqué.

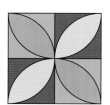

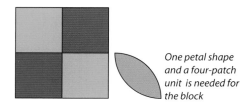

One petal shape and a four-patch unit is needed for the block

Combining and rotating blocks creates secondary patterns

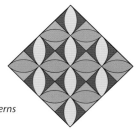

PICTORIAL PATCHWORK

Patchwork blocks that represent familiar objects have long been used to create fun quilts and are especially useful for quilts for children. Pictorial designs may also be referred to as representational and motifs that occur frequently include buildings, ships, trees, flowers and animals. Alphabet letters can also be created from pieced work. Piecing pictorial patchwork requires a number of techniques depending on the individual shapes or units that make up the motif, which may be geometric, curvilinear, irregular or a combination. Piecing and sewing these types of units has been covered in previous sections so this section gives examples of pictorial blocks you may like to try.

Of course, pictorial quilts and other projects using representational images don't have to be solely made up of pieced blocks but can be combined with appliqué to create some fantastic 'story' or 'event' quilts. A specific family celebration or a pictorial record of a happy home or favourite place can be the starting point for some wonderful work that will always be a talking point. Don't forget to add a label giving details of the quilt and its maker – see page 243.

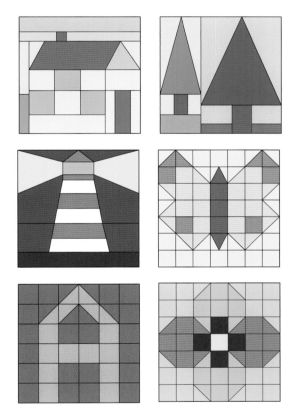

Some of the easiest pictorial blocks can be created by combining squares and half-square triangle units, as these examples show. The blocks can be scaled up or down, depending on the size of the units.

This sunny quilt by Jenny Hutchison features a colourful beach hut block. The block uses the distinctive elements of a beach hut but is easy to piece. The quilt was created using a Jelly Roll™ – see page 21 for more on using pre-cut fabrics.

BRIGHT IDEA

MANY MOTIFS CAN BE REDUCED TO A GRID REPRESENTATION. CROSS STITCH EMBROIDERY PATTERNS ARE GOOD SOURCES OF INSPIRATION FOR PICTORIAL PATCHWORK AS THESE TYPES OF CHART REPRESENT OBJECTS IN A SIMPLISTIC WAY. 'SQUARING UP' ELEMENTS OF A DESIGN.

FOUNDATION PIECING

Many forms of patchwork use foundation piecing to piece shapes together quickly and extremely accurately. Foundation piecing is particularly useful for intricate blocks, such as Pineapple, Storm at Sea and Mariner's Compass but it can be used for any piecing. The basic method uses a base fabric or foundation material, which can be temporary or permanent. Foundation piecing uses one of two main methods – under-pressed piecing and top-pressed piecing – and both have advantages, depending on what sort of patchwork is required. Under-pressed piecing is described in this section and is a technique well worth learning as it will allow you to piece complex blocks with super accuracy. Top-pressed piecing can be a more random approach and is popular for crazy patchwork and string patchwork where matching exact sewing lines isn't quite as important.

The sewing order is important with foundation piecing in order that the raw edge of one patch is concealed by the seam of another. Some patterns, such as Log Cabin and Pineapple, work from the centre outwards, while others can be stitched diagonally or from side to side. Curvilinear designs, such as Mariner's Compass, can be stitched in quadrants, which are then sewn together. Some blocks are made up of many pieced units, such as Storm at Sea, and these can be foundation pieced in segments or rows, which can then be sewn together.

FOUNDATION PIECING METHODS

Under-pressed piecing – This is a very accurate method of piecing where the fabric is positioned *under* the foundation material. The pattern is drawn on the back of the foundation and fabric patches are pinned to the front, unmarked side. Stitching is then done in a specified order from the printed side of the foundation, with the marked lines becoming seam lines. In this method the foundation pattern needs to start as a mirror image one, because sewing patches in place in this way means that the finished block will be a reverse of the foundation paper pattern. This upside down approach sounds confusing but it is actually very easy to do.

Top-pressed piecing – Top-pressed piecing is sometimes called 'stitch and flip' piecing and in this method the fabric is placed on *top* of the foundation material. This method normally uses a permanent foundation material such as muslin but a pattern isn't always marked on the material. Instead, strips or pieces of fabric are sewn to the foundation material using a ¼in (6mm) seam. This piece of fabric is then flipped over to the right side and pressed in place. Further patches or strips are added in the same way. See page 102 for this technique.

This fun tablemat by Mandy Shaw uses a foundation piecing technique for the chickens' bodies and blanket stitch appliqué for the wings, beaks and central flower.

FOUNDATION MATERIALS

Temporary foundations – These are removed after the block or unit has been constructed. Materials used include newspaper or other thin paper, freezer paper, tear-away stabilizers and water-soluble foundation paper. Temporary foundations do not require a seam allowance and are not sewn into the seam allowance, as this would make them impossible to remove. The foundation is cut to the actual size and shape required and the edges act as sewing lines for joining the unit or block to other blocks later. Remove temporary foundations after all sewing is complete. To ensure easy removal, sew with a shorter stitch length than normal and with a larger needle (for example, size 90/14).

Permanent foundations – These foundation materials are left in place within a project, so lightweight fabrics are generally used to reduce overall weight and allow quilting to be done. Materials used include calico, thin cotton, lightweight sew-in interfacing and commercially available foundation sheets, which are made from a blend of rayon and polyester.

MARKING PATTERNS

Patterns can be marked on the foundation material in a number of different ways.
- Tracing is one of the easiest methods, using a ruler and sharp pencil or marking pen to trace the lines of the design.
- Needle-punching using an unthreaded sewing machine can also be used for marking. The block pattern is placed on top of the foundation material and the lines of the design are sewn (without thread) to punch holes through into the foundation.
- Printing the pattern on to paper or freezer paper is another option, but not for permanent foundations, which are frequently made from fabric.

CUTTING PATCHES

In foundation piecing fabric patches need to be large enough to cover the shape on the pattern and allow for the seam, so cut them at least ½in (1.3cm) larger all round. Even though foundation piecing stabilizes cut bias edges it is still helpful to follow the straight grain where possible when cutting the pieces, trying to have the edges of a block on the lengthwise grain. Once the strips or patches are sewn in place excess fabric can be trimmed off with scissors or by folding the foundation out of the way and using a rotary cutter.

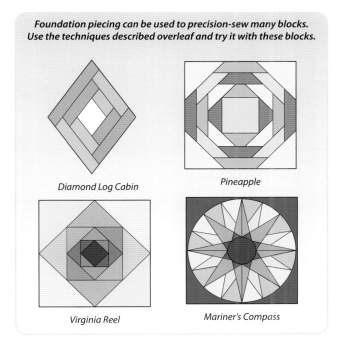

Foundation piecing can be used to precision-sew many blocks. Use the techniques described overleaf and try it with these blocks.

Diamond Log Cabin

Pineapple

Virginia Reel

Mariner's Compass

A single Log Cabin block made with foundation piecing forms the basis of a padded jewellery pocket by Gail Lawther. Simple long stitches and beads were used for embellishment.

> > > **related topics...** *Using Templates 26 • Drawing and Cutting Shapes 29 • String Patchwork 76 • Crazy Patchwork 100* > >

THE TECHNIQUES

MAKING A FOUNDATION PIECING PATTERN

You may prefer to use a pre-printed foundation piecing pattern but making your own is easy and will allow you to create many more patterns than are available commercially.

Select the block pattern you wish to make, in the size you require (A). Patterns can be reduced or enlarged on a photocopier. Choose what foundation material you wish to use. Mark the pattern in reverse on to the back of the foundation material (B). Use a light box if you have one to trace the design; if not, tape the pattern to a window, flipping it over first so it is in reverse. Tape the foundation centrally in place on top. Using a ruler and marking pen or pencil, draw the lines of the pattern *accurately* on to the foundation.

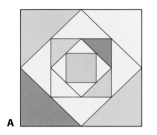
A

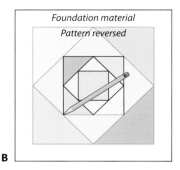
Foundation material
Pattern reversed
B

UNDER-PRESSED FOUNDATION PIECING

Once the block or pattern is marked on the foundation material you can begin sewing.

1 Decide on the sewing order and mark the foundation pattern with numbers on the *back* of the foundation. ▼

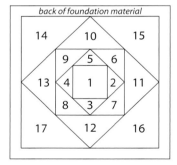

2 With the *front* of the foundation upwards, position patch 1, right side up, over its shape on the foundation, ensuring it overlaps the shape all round and pin it in place. Hold it up to the light if need be to check the position. ▼

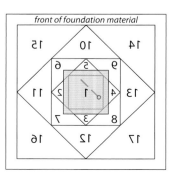
front of foundation material

3 Position and pin patch 2 right side down on patch 1, edges aligned. Turn the foundation over to the marked side and sew patch 2 in place *exactly* along the marked line on the foundation pattern. ▼

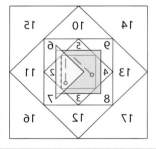

4 Hold the work up to the light to check it is sewn in the right place. Remove pins, flip patch 2 over with right sides up and press. Trim excess fabric to a ¼in (6mm) seam allowance. ▼

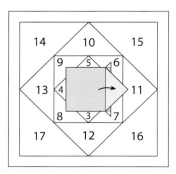

5 Using this same pin, sew and press method, continue on, adding patches 3, 4, 5 and so on until all sewing on the block is complete. After the final pressing trim the block square. ▼

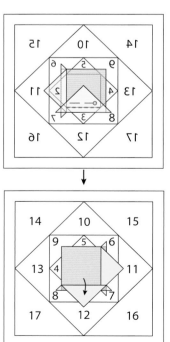

FOUNDATION PIECING MARINER'S COMPASS

Mariner's Compass is an old block design that has many variations. It is best pieced using templates or foundation piecing. The foundation piecing method is outlined here.

1 For a finished block of 10in (25.4cm) enlarge the template here to the size you want (305 per cent will make the circle 7in (17.8cm) in diameter). ▼

Foundation piecing template

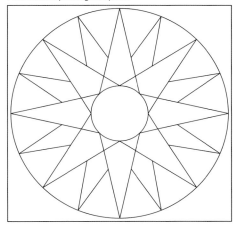

2 Using the under-pressed foundation piecing technique described left, piece the block in four segments. Follow the sewing order given in the diagram. The dark turquoise points (north, south, east and west) can be pieced with a straight edge for the moment as the edge will be covered by the central circle later. Ensure the finished segment has at least ¼in (6mm) seam allowance all round the edge. ▼

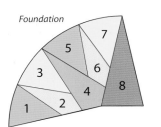
Foundation

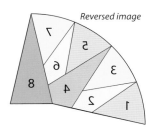
Reversed image

3 When all four segments have been pieced, sew two segments together with a ¼in (6mm) seam. Sew the other two segments together, and then sew the two halves together. ▼

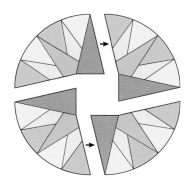

4 When the compass is complete, cut the centre circle from fabric, adding ¼in (6mm) all round for a seam allowance, and appliqué the centre circle in place (see Gathered Edge Appliqué on page 147). ▼

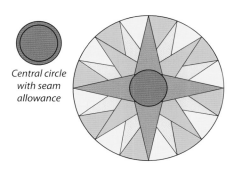
Central circle with seam allowance

5 Once the compass has been fully pieced it can be set into a background square. This can be done either using a needle-turn appliqué method or by using a circular seam as described on page 90. ▶

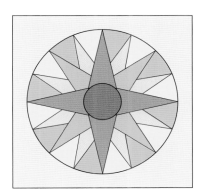

CRAZY PATCHWORK

Crazy patchwork is characterized by irregularly shaped patches sewn together in a random way. It is great fun and a wonderful collage-type technique, perfect for using up fabric scraps and embellishing work. The style was inspired by Japanese art and craft design, which to European and American eyes in the 19th century appeared unusual, almost haphazard. It was very popular during Victorian times and was used on quilts, household items and clothing. All types, colours and textures of fabric can be used, including velvet, silk, brocade and dressmaking and upholstery fabrics. A distinctive feature is the use of embroidery stitches and a huge variety of braids and trims to decorate the patches or along the seams.

Using just ginghams, checks and stripes creates a rustic look and this is emphasized by the use of ricrac braid, broderie anglaise and tape trimmings. The patches were cut and fused on a foundation. The trims were glued and stitched in place.

Some wonderfully vibrant and interesting quilts can be created using crazy patchwork. The easiest way is to make a collection of blocks. These can be sewn together or separated by other, plainer blocks or sashing. The shapes of the patches are often straight-edged but curved and irregular shapes can add a further 'crazy' dimension. Due to the amount of decorative stitching and embellishment that is often used on crazy quilts, they are best secured by tying (see page 223) rather than by traditional quilting.

Crazy patchwork is normally worked on a foundation fabric, usually calico or other thin cotton, and there are four main methods: stitch and flip, turned-edge, raw-edge and appliqué. All are described in the techniques opposite and overleaf. See also Foundation Piecing on page 96.

Crazy patchwork using black and white fabrics would suit any modern interiors. This was made using a strip-piecing technique, with the unit cut up and rearranged in a more random design. Decorative machine stitching is worked along the seams in red and gold.

Fabrics for Crazy Patchwork

The sky is the limit when selecting fabrics for crazy patchwork. Glitzy prints, brocades and Lurex, homely checks, spots, stripes and ginghams, traditional tweeds, tartans and paisleys or sumptuous silks, velvets and lace are all candidates. Try the following sources.

✓ *Your own home – most of us accumulate old clothing and worn-out home furnishings that could be used for crazy patchwork. Quilts made from old clothes can become heirloom pieces, filled with memories.*

✓ *Fabric offcuts – start saving offcuts from your normal patchwork fabrics. Anything larger than 3in (7.6cm) square will be useful. Store them in a bag and when you have enough tip them out and see what colour ideas jump out.*

✓ *Friends, family and quilting friends – once it becomes known you want spare fabric you will be inundated. Even a lace hanky or old silk scarf can provide just the right patch.*

✓ *Second-hand sales – jumble sales, garage sales and car boot sales are excellent places to look for unusual fabrics and trims, especially vintage pieces such as Eastern robes or Indian saris.*

✓ *Markets – markets are held regularly in most towns and whether it's a Christmas market or just a flea market there are bound to be stalls with all sorts of clothing and bric-a-brac.*

✓ *Charity shops (thrift stores) – when visiting these places try to see clothing in a new light. For example, a blouse may be too worn but the lace trim may be fine. An old cardigan may not be useful but the mother-of-pearl buttons will be.*

✓ *Fabric stores – shops selling dressmaking fabrics often have mixed bags of offcuts and samples, which are sometimes given away or sold cheaply, so ask at your local shops.*

CRAZY PATCHWORK DECORATION

After the precision of traditional pieced patchwork, crazy patchwork offers an exciting and liberating change. It can be decorated in various ways. Adding stitches or embellishments along seams is the most common but the patches themselves can also showcase appliqué motifs or embroidered designs. Decorating the seams in crazy patchwork is a really exciting part of the process and can lead to some gloriously creative effects. See Decorative Quilting on page 228 for ideas. Experiment with plain, solid-colour fabrics to really allow stitches and embellishments to take centre stage. For a different look create a faux crazy patchwork look by working embroidery stitches on a single piece of fabric in a crazy pattern.

Stitches – Crazy patchwork is the perfect technique for showcasing decorative machine stitches and hand embroidery stitches. The threads used can be different colours to contrast with the individual fabric patches or be a single colour to unify the design. Gold is a popular and traditional thread colour.

- Embroidery threads are perfect and include silky rayons, matte and variegated cottons and shiny metallics.
- Wool yarns, crochet cottons and narrow ribbons can also be used to create a bolder look.
- Popular hand stitches to use are herringbone, blanket, feather, chain, cross, fern, fly, cretan and sheaf stitches. See page 245 for working these stitches and page 229 for decorative machine stitching.

Anything goes when choosing fabrics for crazy patchwork. Go bright and glitzy or soft and romantic – and anything in between. Choose two you really love and plan another six or so around them. Select threads and embellishments to work well with your fabrics. Busy prints will camouflage threads so start planning early.

Embellishments – These generally fall into the following types but mixing and matching is one of the most exciting features of crazy patchwork.

- Ribbons, tapes, braids, ricrac and thousands of other decorative trims.
- Bows, lace and broderie anglaise.
- Sequins and beads.
- Buttons and shells.

BRIGHT IDEA

INCREASE YOUR FABRIC CHOICES BY HAVING A SWAPPING SESSION WITH FRIENDS, LETTING THEM PICK SOME FABRICS FROM YOUR STASH IN RETURN FOR SOME FROM THEIRS.

>>> related topics... *Straight Strip Piecing 67 • String Patchwork 76 • Fusible Web Appliqué 152 • Decorative Quilting 228* >>

THE TECHNIQUES

STITCH AND FLIP PATCHWORK

This is an easy technique that is also used in string patchwork and strip patchwork. The sewn strips can be in a lengthwise direction or rotate around a central patch. Patchwork blocks are easily created with this method and some well-known blocks, such as Log Cabin, can be given a crazy treatment. Stitch and flip can be done alone or on a foundation material such as calico or thin cotton. This method favours straight seams so using very irregular patches isn't as easy as with the other methods described opposite.

1 Begin with a multi-sided piece of fabric. Place a strip of another fabric on top, right sides together, with one outer edge aligned and sew together with a ¼in (6mm) seam (A). Flip the fabric strip over and press or finger press the seam (B). Add another strip of fabric, in the same way, aligning its outer edge with the central patch and stitch in place (C). Flip the newly added patch over and press again (D). ▶

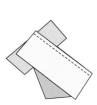
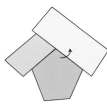

A   **B**   **C**   **D**

2 Continue in this way (E–J) until the crazy patchwork panel is the size you desire. Give the panel a final press and trim to a square, or the shape required, using a rotary cutter and ruler. ▶▼

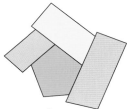

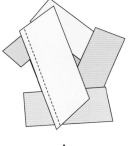
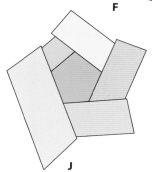

E   **F**

G   **H**   **I**   **J**

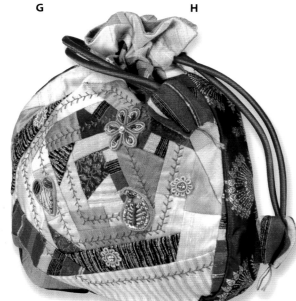

This little drawstring bag was made using a stitch and flip technique. Susan Briscoe created it from scraps of shot silk, prints and Indian fabrics, with small glittery motifs appliquéd in place. The decorative stitching, worked in the same bright pink throughout, unifies the design and in this piece is worked through the centre of the fabric pieces rather than along the seams.

TURNED-EDGE CRAZY PATCHWORK

In this method the patches are cut to allow for seams to be turned under and are sewn into place by hand or machine. This makes the seams very secure and the patchwork item most durable. Patches can be cut into even more irregular shapes than with the stitch and flip method.

1 Cut a piece of foundation fabric to the size required for the finished piece or block. Pin the first patch in position, right side up, near one corner of the foundation fabric. Pin a second patch in place, right side up, with one edge overlapping the first patch by at least ½in (1.3cm). ▼

2 Continue in this way, cutting and pinning further patches in place across the foundation, always overlapping other patches by at least ½in (1.3cm). ▼

3 Tack (baste) the patches in place, about ½in (1.3cm) from the edge, making sure the tacking (basting) for each patch only secures that patch and not others beneath it. Remove pins as you go. Alternatively, use small dots of temporary glue to secure the patches. ▼

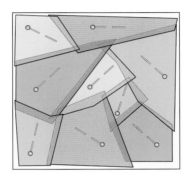

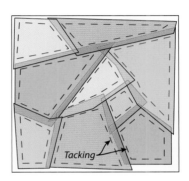

4 Begin to turn under the seams on the patches and press in place with an iron. Not all seams will need to be turned as some patches will overlap others, or will be at the edges of the block and sewn into later seam allowances. Work across the patches, making sure none of the foundation is showing and that all raw edges are covered. Using small slipstitches or a machine straight stitch in toning or invisible thread, stitch the seams down (shown in red on diagram). Remove tacking (basting) when patches are secure. Decorate seams with embroidery stitches and/or braids and trims as desired. When all work is finished trim the edges of the panel neatly. ▼

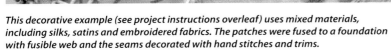

This decorative example (see project instructions overleaf) uses mixed materials, including silks, satins and embroidered fabrics. The patches were fused to a foundation with fusible web and the seams decorated with hand stitches and trims.

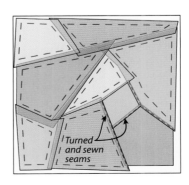

RAW-EDGE CRAZY PATCHWORK

This method works well with fabrics that do not fray too badly. The raw edges are also protected with decorative stitches or by decorative trims couched along the junctions. The method is similar to the turned-edge method but patches are not overlapped as much and no seams are turned under.

1 Use a foundation fabric as before and cut the first patch, pinning it in place, right side up. Cut and pin a second patch in place, right side up, with one edge barely overlapping the first patch. Tack (baste) or use a temporary glue to fix the patches in place. Alternatively, use freezer paper as a foundation, to temporarily stick the patches in place (see page 151). ▼

> ### BRIGHT IDEA
>
> IF USING BRAIDS AND TRIMS THAT FRAY AT THE ENDS, TURN THE ENDS UNDER BEFORE SEWING TO KEEP THEM NEAT. ALTERNATIVELY, USE A FAST-TACK CRAFT GLUE TO SEAL THE ENDS UNDER BEFORE SEWING.

2 Continue in the same way, cutting patches in the shapes you like and pinning (or gluing) them in place across the foundation fabric. ▼

3 Work hand embroidery stitches or decorative machine stitching along each edge, making sure the stitches pierce both fabric patches. If using decorative trims, couch these in place. When finished, press and trim edges neatly. ▼

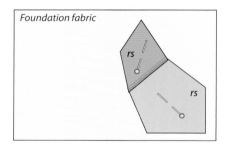

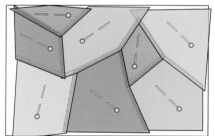

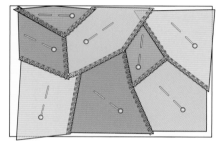

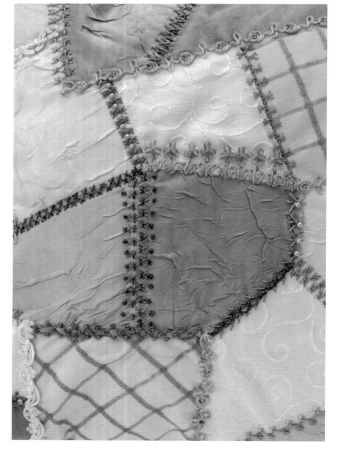

APPLIQUED CRAZY PATCHWORK

In this method patches are appliquéd into place on a base fabric using fusible web. It is worked in the same way as raw-edge, above, but using fusible web makes the patchwork more secure and protects cut edges. Try using fussy cutting motifs for a different look.

Back your fabrics with fusible web and then cut your patches, laying them on a foundation and piecing them together in a random jigsaw pattern. Once you are happy with the arrangement, fuse the patches in place, very slightly overlapping them as described above. Allow the work to cool and then begin the surface decoration. When all work is finished, press and then trim the edges of the panel neatly.

> ### BRIGHT IDEA
>
> TAKE CARE WHEN PRESSING THE FINAL WORK THAT YOU DON'T SCORCH OR MELT BRAIDS AND TRIMS. SOME HAVE A HIGH NYLON OR MAN-MADE FIBRE CONTENT AND NEED A COOL IRON. USE A PRESS SHEET IF IN DOUBT.

Appliquéing crazy patches to a foundation fabric results in a more secure and durable finish. It also makes the crazy patchwork more stable for the addition of trims and beads.

make it now
Memories Box

A hand-painted and decorated box is perfect for displaying crazy patchwork, and wooden and cardboard boxes are available in many shapes and sizes. The fabric scraps, including silks, satins and brocades, were fused on to a base fabric with fusible web but you could use another method of crazy patchwork, as described on pages 102–104.

profile

Skills practised: Fusible web appliqué; crazy patchwork; decorative stitches
Finished size: 9in x 8in (22.9cm x 20.3cm)
Fabrics: Scraps of different fabric types
Threads: Embroidery threads to suit fabrics
Embellishments: Trims and braids as desired

METHOD

- Measure your box lid and cut a piece of base fabric at least 2in (5cm) larger all round. Use a pencil to mark the lid shape on the fabric. Prepare your box, painting it if required.
- Create your crazy patchwork, overlapping the edge of the marked shape slightly. Embellish the seams with hand embroidery stitches, decorative machine stitches and trims, as desired.
- Cut out the patchwork along the marked line and use fabric glue to glue it in place on the box. Glue trim around the edge to protect the patchwork and hide any trim ends.

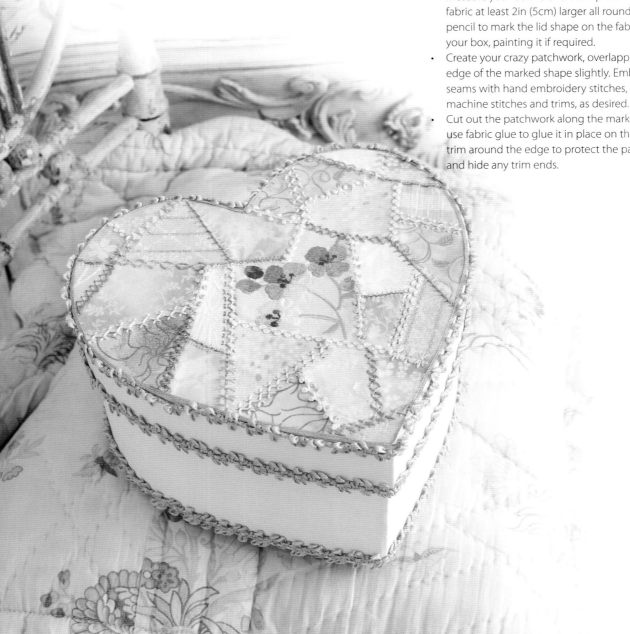

PUFFED PATCHWORK

Puffed patchwork is an interesting technique that looks really attractive, creating a wonderfully plump and tactile quality that is almost impossible not to squeeze. It looks great on its own but can also be combined with other more conventional forms of patchwork and appliqué. The technique is really easy to do and although normally stitched by machine it could be worked by hand too. Essentially, one square of fabric is sewn to a slightly smaller square, with little pleats made in the sides of the top square. The resulting shape is stuffed lightly with polyester filling. A number of puffs are then sewn together and the quilt is backed.

Puffed patchwork is great fun. All sorts of fabrics can be used, and fussy cutting to select a specific motif can add an extra dimension.

This form of patchwork is over 150 years old and is also called biscuit patchwork because the stuffed shapes were thought to resemble biscuits. The technique creates a quilt that is warm and snuggly – perfect for cold winter nights. The three-dimensional quality of this type of work means that it is not usually quilted but layers can be tied together.

PUFF SIZE

The size of the puff in this type of patchwork, and thus the filling needed for it, can be varied depending on the size of the top square compared to the base square. For average-sized puffs, cut a top square that is ½in (1.3cm) larger than the base square. For fuller, deeper puffs, cut a top square that is 1in (2.5cm) larger than the base square. The technique described opposite uses the slightly smaller measurement. Seams are usually ¼in (6mm). The back of the puffs won't be on show so you could use a plain, inexpensive fabric or scraps.

PUFFED PATCHWORK DESIGNS

Puffed patchwork can create interesting effects depending on the fabric colours and arrangements used – here are some suggestions.

- Themed effects can be created if fabrics are 'fussy cut', that is, selected for a specific motif. The puffs could also be created from pieced fabrics or appliquéd blocks – you may have such blocks left over from another project that could be used in this way.
- Make a puffed patchwork quilt or project using up scrap fabrics from your stash.
- Try using shapes other than squares, such as rectangles and triangles.

This detail from the Puffed Play Quilt overleaf shows puffed patchwork being used with plain blocks decorated with yo-yos to create a very pretty and tactile effect.

Try using plain, solid colours, graded in tones and combined in a striking pattern.

Using patterned fabrics you could copy a traditional block arrangement, such as Rail Fence.

Try combining puffed patchwork blocks with normal patchwork blocks, such as the star blocks shown here.

>> related topics... *Chain Piecing 58 • Tied Quilting 223* >> >> >

THE TECHNIQUES

SEWING PUFFED PATCHWORK

The technique described here uses a cut top square that is ½in (1.3cm) larger than the base square. As an example, if you want each finished puff to be 4in (10.2cm) square, then the top square needs to be cut 4½in (11.4cm) and the bottom square 4in (10.2cm). When the puffs are joined together this will result in finished squares of 3½in (8.9cm) if ¼in (6mm) seams are used.

1 Cut the number of top and base squares required for your project. Place a large square on top of a smaller one, align all the corners and pin at these points. Fold pleats on three sides and pin these, leaving one side open. Using a ¼in (6mm) seam, sew round the three pleated sides using a thread to match your fabric. ▶

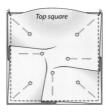

2 When making rows of puffs use a chain piecing technique (see page 58) to sew them together without breaking the thread each time. Once a row is sewn, stuff the squares with polyester filling (fiberfill), fold the final pleat on each square and pin it closed. ▶

3 Sew up the final sides on the puffed squares. Cut the puffs apart when the row is sewn. Begin to join the puffs together. Start by joining pairs, placing right sides together and using a slightly wider seam allowance than before so the previous stitching is covered. ▼

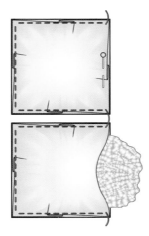

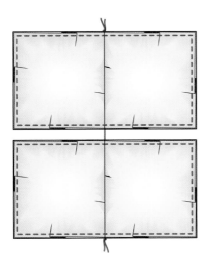

4 In the same way join rows of puffs together. Alternating the direction of seams in each row will help the rows lie flatter on the back. Once all the puffs are joined together the quilt can be backed and finished – see below. ▼

BRIGHT IDEA

DON'T STUFF THE PUFFS TOO FIRMLY OR THEY WILL BE DIFFICULT TO SEW TOGETHER. CONVERSELY, IF YOU DISCOVER AFTER JOINING THEM THAT THEY AREN'T FULL ENOUGH, CUT A SLIT IN THE BACK OF THE PUFF, INSERT MORE STUFFING AND SEW THE SLIT CLOSED.

FINISHING PUFFED PATCHWORK

Once the quilt top has been created you can add a wadding (batting) layer, if desired, and a backing. Puffed patchwork isn't normally quilted so the best way of securing the layers together is by tying. You could also experiment with different types of edging. For example, you could add a puffed border, thick piping or a frill all round the edge of the quilt top before sewing the quilt layers together. The edge could also be bound: if the puffs make this difficult, try flattening them at the edges with pins before sewing the binding in place. Creating the puffs with a wider seam allowance will also help.

To finish the quilt with a 'bagging out' technique follow the instructions on page 235. Once the quilt has been bagged out and the gap sewn up, use strong thread to tie the three layers together at regular intervals over the quilt, placing the ties within the 'valleys' of the puffs. Alternatively, you could stitch the layers together with simple backstitches or cross stitches or quilt in the ditch.

make it now
Puffed Play Quilt

This sweet little quilt is beautifully soft for a young baby to play on. It could be made with all puffed squares or be larger.

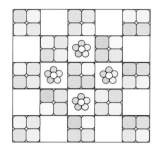

profile

Skills practised: Puffed patchwork; yo-yos; gathered edging
Project layout: Four-patch puffs alternating with plain padded squares
Finished size: 28in (71cm) square
Fabrics: Assorted prints (about ¾yd (0.75m) in total); ½yd (0.5m) white fabric; ¾yd (0.5m) pale fabric; twelve 6in (15.2cm) squares of wadding (batting); 30in (76cm) square of backing fabric; fabric for frill
Threads: Machine sewing thread and strong thread for gathering

METHOD

- Cut fifty-two 3¼in (8.2cm) squares from assorted prints and fifty-two 3¾in (9.5cm) backing squares. Make the puffs (see page 107). Sew together in groups of four to make thirteen four-patch units.
- Cut twelve 6in (15.2cm) squares of white fabric, twelve of backing fabric and twelve of wadding. Place a backing fabric square right side down, a wadding square on top and a white square right side up. Sew together using a ¼in (6mm) seam. Note: seams are on the outside. Repeat to make eleven more padded squares.
- Placing right sides together, sew the four-patch puffs and padded squares together in an alternating arrangement.
- Cut twenty-four 3½in (8.9cm) diameter circles from assorted prints and make twenty-four yo-yos (see page 121). Sew the yo-yos to four of the plain squares in groups of six.
- Make up the quilt with a frill – see page 248.

SAFETY NOTE

BABIES CAN EASILY OVERHEAT SO TAKE CARE WITH THICK QUILTS.
IF IN DOUBT USE STANDARD BEDDING AT NIGHT.

FOLDED PATCHWORK

Making patchwork by folding fabrics into different shapes and then layering them together creates a wonderfully textured look and visually striking designs. Squares folded into triangles form the basis of prairie points and folded star designs, while Japanese folded patchwork, Cathedral Windows and Secret Garden are reminiscent of stained glass windows. Once the units or blocks are created by folding and manipulating the fabric they can be stitched together and so many types of folded patchwork do not need to be quilted further. This section looks at four techniques but for more inspiration see Lynne Edwards' books (Further Reading on page 252) which contain further techniques and a wealth of gorgeous folded designs.

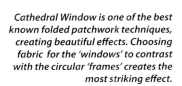

Cathedral Window is one of the best known folded patchwork techniques, creating beautiful effects. Choosing fabric for the 'windows' to contrast with the circular 'frames' creates the most striking effect.

PRAIRIE POINTS

Triangles can be used decoratively and prairie points are a popular way to bring texture and interest to work. Prairie points are also referred to as dogtooth borders, sawtooth edging or shark's teeth. They start out as a square of fabric and finish as a folded triangle. They can be made in a single colour or print, or be made of various colours to match the quilt, and if made this way are perfect for using up scraps. They can be a single-fold arrangement or double-folded to create a central pleat. Prairie points are normally created in a row and can be added to a seam or to decorate the edge of a quilt or project. The height of the points can also be varied, giving additional interest.

To calculate the size of the starting square, decide on the finished height of a prairie point, double it and then add sufficient for a seam allowance. The finished length will be twice the height of the triangle. For example, for a finished prairie point 2in (5.1cm) tall, it would be: 2in + 2in = 4in + ½in = a 4½in cut square. In metric it is: 5.1cm + 5.1cm = 10.2cm + 1.3cm = an 11.5cm cut square.

Gail Lawther made double-fold prairie points from brightly coloured silk dupion and sewed rows of them into the seams of this fun party bag. The prairie points not only add texture and interest but can be embellished with beads.

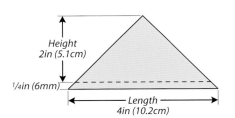

Height
2in (5.1cm)

¼in (6mm)

Length
4in (10.2cm)

FOLDED STAR

This patchwork may also be called mitred or Somerset patchwork. Folded stars look complicated but are actually very easy to make, being composed of prairie points that radiate out from a central point. The edges can be inset into a fabric circle, or bound with bias or fusible binding, or edged with a border. The colour scheme is important to achieve the right effect, and contrasting rounds of colour have the most impact.

This pillow by Gail Lawther uses folded star patchwork as the centrepiece, edged with silver binding. The star effect is emphasized by the contrasting blue and white colours used.

JAPANESE FOLDED PATCHWORK

Folded patchwork has much in common with origami, the ancient Japanese art of paper folding. In this technique wadding (batting) could be used to give further texture and dimension. The work starts off as a circle, which is then folded over to create a square. Each square created is a separate unit, which is then joined to others. The technique can also be adapted to a hexagon shape. Originally, the technique was a hand-stitched one, which involved gathering fabric circles around card and then stitching two circles together, but working by machine is quicker.

Bags are a great way to try out a technique. These bags by Lynne Edwards use Japanese folded patchwork in sophisticated colours, where the fabrics for the central design are chosen to contrast with the outer frames. Buttons added to the centres of the 'flowers' create extra detail.

CATHEDRAL WINDOW

Cathedral Window folded patchwork creates some stunning designs and many variations of it have been developed. Cathedral Window work involves folding and re-folding squares and using a different-coloured fabric as an insert. It looks complicated but is actually straightforward. The finished units are joined together without wadding (batting) or backing and no conventional quilting is needed. The technique can be worked by hand or machine, as described on pages 115–116.

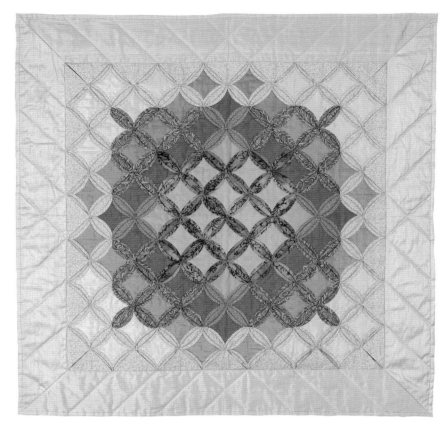

This wall hanging by Janet Covell uses silks and cotton prints to create a beautiful stained-glass effect in Cathedral Window. The graded colours contribute to the ethereal look.

SECRET GARDEN

This lovely block is a four-petal version of Cathedral Window. While Cathedral Window reveals a curved diamond at the centre of each unit, Secret Garden creates a four-petalled flower (shown in the four corners of this picture). The two types of folded patchwork combine well together.

This striking piece was made by Marjory Dench using colourful batik fabrics. It uses Cathedral Window blocks in the centre with four Secret Garden blocks in bolder colours at each corner.

>>> related topics... *Hand Piecing 50 • Fabric Special Effects 118 • Adding a Prairie Point Edging 240* >>

THE TECHNIQUES

MAKING SINGLE-FOLD PRAIRIE POINTS

Simple single-fold points can be made individually and assembled into a row, as described here, or be created in a continuous arrangement (see below).

1 Fold a square of fabric across a diagonal and finger press (A). Now fold this triangle in half diagonally and press with an iron (B). ▶

2 To create a row, make as many folded triangles as required and slip one inside the other, pinning them together (C). Tack (baste) together and then remove the pins. The row can be applied in a similar way to using piping – see page 240. ▼

MAKING DOUBLE-FOLD PRAIRIE POINTS

Double-fold prairie points are created with a central fold so they have a little more visual impact. This type works well with two different colours.

1 Fold a square of fabric across the width to create a rectangle and finger press (A). Fold each folded corner down to the centre of the rectangle to create a triangle shape and press with an iron (B). ▶

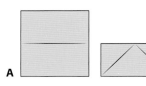
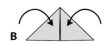

2 Create a row as shown, overlapping them so the pointed edges meet at the centre folds of each neighbour (C). Tack (baste) the triangles together and remove the pins. ▼

MAKING CONTINUOUS PRAIRIE POINTS

Prairie points can also be made in a continuous strip, which is useful for edging large quilts. The technique instructions below describe a finished width of 2in (5cm); for a wider strip of prairie points increase the starting width.

1 Cut a strip of fabric 4in (10.2cm) wide by the length required (joining lengths if required). Fold in half lengthwise, wrong sides together, and press the fold. Open out flat, wrong side up and use a pencil to mark the centre line along the strip. Mark lines at 2in (5cm) intervals along the strip, staggered as shown and then cut these lines up to the centre marked line. ▼

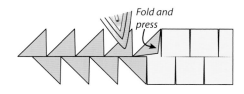

Discard

2 Begin folding each cut portion on the diagonal to create a triangle shape, pressing with an iron. Do this along the top and then along the bottom. ▼

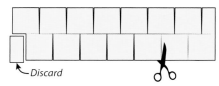

Fold and press

3 Now fold the triangles again in the opposite direction, creating smaller triangles and enclosing raw edges. Press firm creases again. ▼

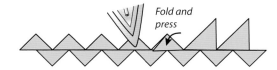

Fold and press

4 Finally, fold the whole strip in half lengthwise, so the triangles on the bottom row intersect with those on the top row. Press well and secure with pins and then tacking (basting). The strip of prairie points is now ready for use. ▼

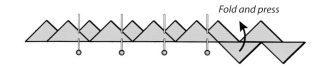

Fold and press

FOLDED STAR

The folded star described here has three 'rounds' of double-fold prairie points but could have more. Decide on your colour scheme, contrasting the rounds of colour for most impact. Mounting the base fabric in an embroidery hoop will keep the work stable.

1 Calculate how many 'rounds' you want for your project and how many prairie points you will need for each round. Round 1 starts with four prairie points, Round 2 has eight points and Round 3 has eight points. A fourth round would need sixteen points. Make double-fold prairie points as described opposite in the colours required. ▶

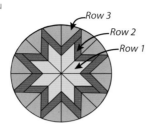

2 Cut a square of base fabric 2in (5cm) larger than the finished size of the project. Mark the vertical, horizontal and diagonal lines on the fabric. Place four prairie points together in the centre aligned with the diagonal lines as shown. Machine or hand sew in place around the edges and use matching thread to slipstitch the points in place at the centre. ▶

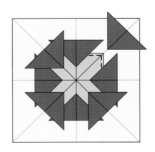

BRIGHT IDEA

MOUNTING THE BASE FABRIC IN AN EMBROIDERY HOOP WILL
KEEP IT FIRM AND STABLE AS YOU SEW THE ROUNDS OF
PRAIRIE POINTS IN PLACE.

3 Take eight prairie points in a contrasting colour and position these in a second round. Place those at the north, south, east and west positions first, with the points of the triangles about ½in–¾in (1.3cm–1.9cm) from the centre, and then place the other four. Stitch down as before. ▶

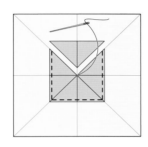

4 Take eight prairie points in a contrasting colour (or the same colour as Round 1). Position and stitch these in a third round in a similar way. Add more rounds if desired. Once complete, trim away all excess fabric. ▶

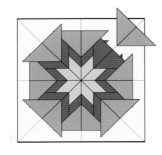

5 Set the star in a circle to finish. Draw a circle on tracing paper a little smaller than the width of the star. Trace this on to the fabric chosen for the surround and cut out the circle. Tack (baste) the fabric in place over the star and stitch in place with a machine zigzag or bias binding or use fusible bias tape. ▶

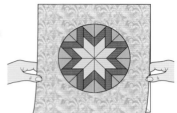

Folded star patchwork looks really striking if complementary colours are used and if the points are allowed to stand proud of the surface of the fabric – see page 20 for advice on colour combinations. For this pillow, Gail Lawther set the patchwork into a circle to create even more impact.

JAPANESE FOLDED PATCHWORK

This technique is shown to best advantage if two contrasting fabrics are used – those from opposite sides of the colour wheel would be most striking.

1 Decide on the size of the finished square and prepare a square template to this size using thin card. Measure the square from corner to corner and prepare a circular template with the same diameter as this measurement, plus ¼in (6mm) for a seam allowance. For example, a 3in (7.6cm) square has a diagonal measurement of 4¼in (10.8cm), so make the circle 4¼in (10.8cm) in diameter, *plus* ½in (1.3cm) for seams, which is 4¾in (12cm) in diameter in total (A). ▼

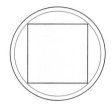

A

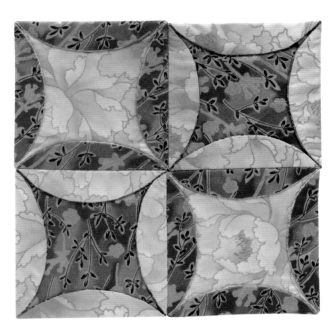

Japanese folded patchwork is very portable. You could create the units by hand in odd moments and then sew them together for a small project, such as a bag or cushion. The 'windows' can be all the same or some can be in reversed colours, as shown in this sample.

2 Calculate how many circles you need and cut this many in one type of fabric (Fabric 1). Cut the same number in a contrasting fabric (Fabric 2). Place a Fabric 1 circle right sides together with a Fabric 2 circle and stitch ¼in (6mm) in from the edge all the way round (B). Trim the seam with pinking shears if possible or to ⅛in (3mm). Cut a slit in the back of the circle through one layer only and turn through to the right side (C). Flatten the seam and press well. The slit won't show so it can be left as it is or closed by ladder stitch. Prepare half of the circles with Fabric 1 on top and half with Fabric 2. ▼

B   **C**

BRIGHT IDEA

WHEN FOLDING OVER THE CIRCLE EDGES, DO IT NEAR A ROTARY CUTTING MAT SO YOU CAN CHECK THE SQUARE IS REMAINING SQUARE.

4 Prepare the rest of the circles in the same way but, if desired, have half of them showing Fabric 1 in the centre and half with Fabric 2. When all squares are prepared sew them together from the wrong side with neat oversewing (F). Press the finished work (G). Back the finished work using wadding (batting) if required. Quilting can be worked through all layers as normal. ▼

3 Place the template on top of the prepared circle. Fold the circle over the template along one side and press in place (D). Repeat on the other three edges (E). Remove the template. Pin, and then slipstitch the curved edges in place through the top fabric only. ▼

D   **E**

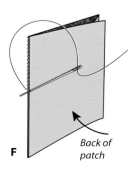

Back of patch

F

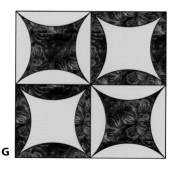

G

CATHEDRAL WINDOW BY HAND

The technique described here shows four square Cathedral Window units but make as many as you require for your project. The finished unit ends up just under half the size of the starting square, so for a finished unit of 4in (10.2cm) square begin with an 8½in (21.6cm) square. Cathedral Window blocks can also be rectangular, or a combination of square and rectangular.

1 Cut a square of fabric on the straight grain and tack (baste) a ¼in (6mm) hem on all sides. Press the square flat. ▶

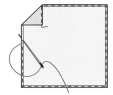

2 Lightly mark the centre of the square. With wrong side up, fold each corner of the square so the points meet the centre. Press into place and then tack (baste). ▶

3 Fold the corners into the centre again, press and this time secure the corners with a small cross stitch in matching thread through all layers. ▼

4 Repeat steps 1–3 to create three more squares. Sew the squares together in pairs by placing two squares right sides together and whip stitching. Sew the pairs together in sets of four and press. ▶

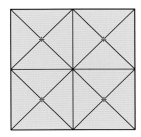

5 Measure one vertical seam (shown in red on diagram) and cut four squares with a diagonal measurement slightly smaller than this using a contrasting fabric. Pin one square on point over a seam. ▶

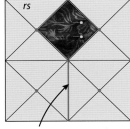

Measure vertical seam

6 Starting at the top corner of the square begin to roll the surrounding border on one side of the window over it, creating a curve. Pin the curve in place and then secure with tiny hem stitches or backstitches. Do the same on the other side. Add a small horizontal tack (called a bar tack) to secure the window fabric at the corners. Repeat this on the other two sides of the square. ▶

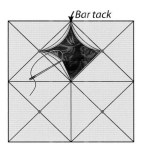

7 Continue in this way to sew all the windows. If desired, the sides can have windows added. Cut the same size square as in step 5 but fold it in half to create a triangle. The folded edge will match the edge of the piece. Trim the under layer back to ¼in (6mm) from the fold. Secure as shown. ▶

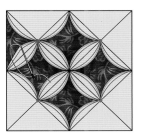

This wedding album cover by Elaine Hammond shows just how effective even a small Cathedral Window panel can be. Some of the windows have been used to display little gold charms.

CATHEDRAL WINDOW BY MACHINE

The early stages of Cathedral Window can be sewn by machine and are described here. Once the square blocks have been made the 'windows' are added in the same way as Cathedral Window by Hand (see steps 5–7 on the previous page).

1 Fold a fabric square in half, right sides together to form a rectangle, and machine stitch along the short sides with ¼in (6mm) seams. Clip corners. ▶

2 Pick up the rectangle, pull the open edge apart and bring the seams together at the centre. Pin and sew the raw edges, leaving a small gap. Clip corners, turn the square to the right side through the gap, push out the corners and then slipstitch the opening closed. ▼

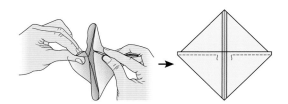

3 Press the square and then fold over the corners to the centre, pressing them to crease. Repeat steps 1–3 to create as many square blocks as required. ▶

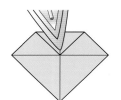

4 Start to sew the square blocks together as follows. Place two squares with smooth sides facing. Open up the top flap on each and, with creases matching, pin the blocks together. Use matching thread to sew the blocks together along the crease. Continue in this way to join the blocks into rows. Press the corners of the stitched seams towards the block centre and pin as shown. ▼

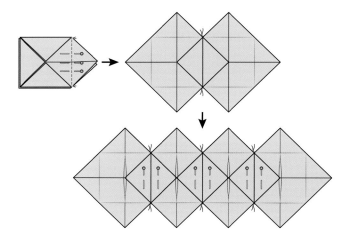

5 Now join the rows together as follows. Pin the two top rows together, matching the mid points. Using matching thread, stitch the rows together, making sure as you sew that the junctions remain matched. Press the corners of the blocks to the centre and stitch in place. Repeat for the rest of the rows. The windows can now be added – follow steps 5–7 on the previous page. ▼

Match mid points

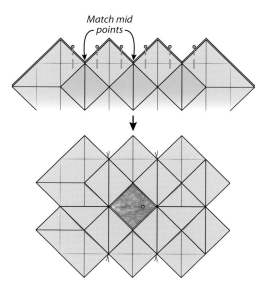

This piece by Lynne Edwards uses fabulously bright batiks in a combination of square and rectangular Cathedral Windows, which creates a more complex design.

SECRET GARDEN

Secret Garden is a pretty variation of Cathedral Window and many of the stages of construction are similar. The finished unit ends up just under half the size of the starting square, so for a finished unit of 4in (10.2cm) square begin with an 8½in (21.6cm) square.

1 Prepare the folded squares as described in steps 1–3 of Cathedral Windows by Hand (see page 115) but do not stitch the folded corners down. ▼

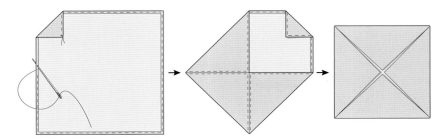

2 Using a contrasting fabric cut a square to fit inside the folded block and tack (baste) it in place centrally. ▼

3 Fold all four triangular flaps over the window square and secure at the centre with a cross stitch in matching thread. Secure each outer corner with a bar tack. ▼

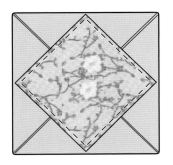

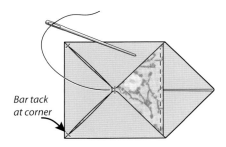

Bar tack at corner

Secret Garden is perfect for a small project as this elegant wall hanging by Birgitte Bennett shows. The main area is worked with Cathedral Windows with little Secret Garden units hanging from it.

4 Starting in one corner of the square begin to roll the edge, pulling on the bias edge so it curves and reveals the fabric beneath. Pin the curve in place and then secure with tiny stab stitches or backstitches. Do the same on the other parts. Add a small bar tack to secure the window fabric at the corner points. Repeat this on other blocks. ▼

5 Multiple blocks can be sewn into rows in the same way as step 5 of the Cathedral Windows technique opposite. ▼

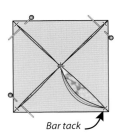

Bar tack

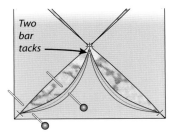

Two bar tacks

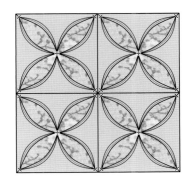

FABRIC SPECIAL EFFECTS

Fabric is so good natured and just invites experimentation. Apart from being sewn together as in conventional patchwork it can be gathered, ruched, ruffled, slashed, chenilled, pleated, tucked and woven – to mention just a few. There are so many exciting ways of manipulating fabric that result in interesting, textural and three-dimensional effects and these are increasingly being used in patchwork, appliqué and quilting. New products, such as self-ruching shrinkable fabric, are being developed all the time and these too are finding their way into mainstream sewing. This section looks at some of the most popular techniques and suggests ways you can use them.

Yo-yos can be used as a simple embellishment or be grouped together to become a feature in their own right. They can even be used to create an entire quilt.

GATHERING AND RUCHING

Gathering and ruching fabric can take many forms and produce many lovely effects and more patchworkers are experimenting with the interesting three-dimensional appearance that can be achieved. Gathering in any form uses more fabric than is used in flat work, so as a general rule allow at least double the normal amount.

Gathering – In general sewing, gathering is used to fit a longer length of fabric on to a shorter one, such as waistbands on skirts, or in preparation for smocking, but it has decorative uses in patchwork and appliqué too. For example, puffing is a gathered technique that can be used as in insert in patchwork. When fabric is gathered along one long edge it is called ruffling and may be used to edge a quilt – see page 242. Gathering small circles of fabric to create yo-yos is a great way to decorate patchwork and appliqué.

Ruching – This is a form of gathering that may also be called furrowing or waffles. The gathers are made across the width and length of a piece of fabric in a grid-like arrangement, forming a crinkled effect that is very attractive. Fabric treated this way can be used as decorative panels. Ruching can also be done in a circular fashion to produce a crinkly flower-like effect. If fabric is ruched with elastic it is called shirring, which is the basis of smocking. You can also create a ruched effect by using shrinkable fabric.

Yo-yos – Yo-yos are sometimes called Suffolk puffs or rosettes and are easy to make, being simply a circle of fabric gathered around the edge to form a puffy centre. The puffy quality can be emphasized by adding polyester stuffing. Yo-yos are usually circular but can be heart shaped or flower shaped and there are commercial yo-yo makers available in different sizes and shapes. The centres can be left as gathers or decorated with buttons, beads or decorative stitches. Different fabrics react differently to being gathered, so experiment with various types. Yo-yos are often used as embellishments to patchwork, appliqué and quilting but can form the basis of a whole quilt or wall hanging. If used in a grouped design, yo-yos are stitched to a background fabric and then sewn to each other at their edges.

Simple ruching set into patchwork blocks creates interesting textured effects. You might try creating a sampler quilt using folded and ruched effects. A quick ruching can be created with shrinkable fabric, which crinkles up when steamed.

SLASHING AND CHENILLING

These techniques can be used in combination with traditional patchwork and appliqué and are very popular for bag making and soft furnishings, such as cushions and table runners.

Slashing – Slashing fabric with short cuts to reveal other fabrics and colours beneath is a very old technique and dates back to Renaissance times. Tudor costumes in England used slashing, where parts of the lining would be pulled through the cuts in the fabric and puffed out, to create a contrast of colours and textures.

Chenilling – Chenille is a tufted, velvety cord or yarn and its shaggy look is mimicked in fabric by taking slashing a stage further and cutting channels in layers of fabric and fluffing up the fabric edges. Dagging is a term used to describe the cutting of patterns in the edges of fabric, sometimes long V shapes or more complex leaf-like patterns.

The techniques for slashing and chenilling are quite simple but the effects are striking, creating interesting variegated textures and colours. The basic technique involves layering fabrics together, usually between three and six, and stitching channels on the bias grain. Small cuts or long slashes are then made along these channels through one or more layers, but not the base layer. Cuts may be straight or curved. Cut fabric edges are encouraged to fray and 'bloom' usually by washing and tumble-drying the work. There are specialist tools available for slashing and chenilling, including rotary cutters and mats, which make the work easier and faster.

Further visual interest can be created, especially when chenilling, by including random little 'hits' of odd chunks of fabric. These will be more noticeable if they contrast with surrounding fabrics, either by colour, finish or texture. The position of such fabrics matters too – the higher up the layer a fabric is, the more obvious it will be.

The most successful fabrics to use are those that fray or fluff easily, including silks, rayons, denim and loosely woven cottons. Because fraying is encouraged by washing and drying it is advisable to test combinations of fabric beforehand for shrinkage, bleeding and so on. For the base or foundation fabric it is best to use a more stable, firm fabric.

This fun bag by Gail Lawther uses simple chenilling to great effect. Small areas of chenilling such as this are really easy to do and a good way to experiment with the technique. Layers of brightly coloured fabrics create the most contrast.

BRIGHT IDEA

WASH AND DRY THE SLASHED FABRIC UP TO THREE TIMES TO GET THE DESIRED EFFECT AND WASH WITH ITEMS THAT ARE ROUGH, SUCH AS JEANS. USE DRIER BALLS IN THE TUMBLE DRIER, IF YOU HAVE THEM, TO FURTHER BASH UP THE FABRIC. ONCE DRY, USE A STIFF BRUSH TO DEVELOP THE TEXTURE FURTHER.

PLEATS AND TUCKS

Pleats and tucks are systematic folding of fabric and are increasingly being used to add detailing and decoration to patchwork, appliqué and quilting projects. Modern sewing machines are making the process even easier. As with gathering, pleating uses more fabric than is used in flat work.

Pleats – These are measured folds in a piece of fabric and there are many types of pleat, including knife, box, inverted, pinched and piped. For patchwork and appliqué they are useful for creating texture, particularly twisted pleats, as interesting patterns can be created depending on how the fabric is folded and secured. Wave-like panels can be produced and used as inserts to patchwork blocks. These look most striking if contrasting light and dark fabrics are used.

Tucks – These are essentially slender pleats that are sewn in place along their length. As with pleats, there are many types but the most useful for patchwork are wide tucks, narrow tucks (also called pin tucks) and corded tucks, which have a fine cord encased within them. Tucks can also form 'waves' in fabric by being turned back in alternate directions.

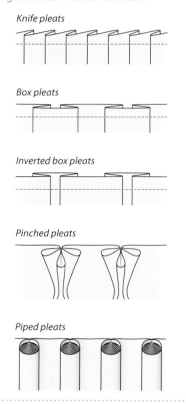

Knife pleats

Box pleats

Inverted box pleats

Pinched pleats

Piped pleats

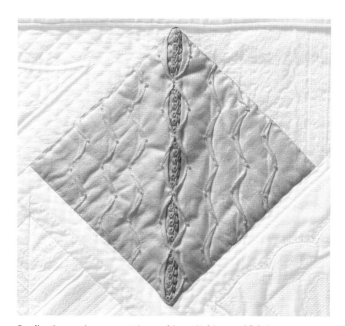

Pauline Ineson is an expert in machine stitching and fabric manipulation. Tucks are raised to the level of an art form in her 'Heirloom Quilt' (see Further Reading on page 252). This detail shows twisted corded tucks decorated with beads, with a central area of linear Cathedral Window.

WEAVING

Weaving is great fun and the end result is creating your very own fabric. It is amazing how three strips can look quite ordinary but when woven together create something really special. For good contrast choose a dark, medium and light fabric. The technique is very simple, quick and surprisingly addictive. When a woven piece is finished it can be used as a panel for a project or as a block within other patchwork blocks.

Marbled fabrics and batiks are useful for weaving as the variable colours and patterns create interesting effects. A machine zigzag was used here to secure the raw edges but you could use a transparent thread or hem the strips before using them.

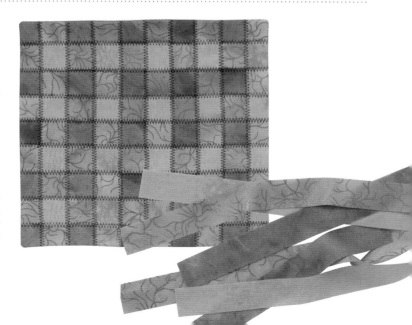

> > > **related topics...** *Folded Patchwork 109 • 3-D Appliqué 148* > > >

THE TECHNIQUES

MAKING A YO-YO

Plates, bowls and cups can be used as quick templates for circles, or if you plan to make lots of yo-yos create some circular templates from template plastic. The basic technique is simple – just stitch, gather and flatten. To work out the starting size of the circle of fabric needed, multiply the diameter of the desired finished size by two and then add ½in (1.3cm). So, for a finished puff of 2in (5cm) diameter, start with a circle of 4½in (11.4cm).

1 Take your circle of fabric and finger press a narrow hem about ⅛in–¼in (3mm–6mm) all around the fabric edge. If the fabric is thick, such as velvet, then use a ¼in (6mm) hem. Choose a strong thread or a double thread in a colour to match the fabric and, starting with a knot, use even running stitches to sew around the folded edge. The length of these stitches determines the size of the opening. Large running stitches will result in a small opening, while small stitches will produce a larger opening. ◄

2 Leave a long length of thread at the end and then pull up both ends of the thread to gather the fabric tightly. Tie the two ends in a secure knot. Trim the thread ends to about 2in (5cm), thread a needle with them and feed the ends inside the yo-yo, trimming the excess. ◄

3 Keeping the gathers around the centre of the yo-yo with your left thumb and forefinger, pinch and pull the edges with your right hand to straighten and even out the gathers (or vice versa if you are left-handed). Flatten the puff with your palm or an iron for a flatter look. Sew the yo-yo in position on your project. ◄

MAKING A YO-YO FLOWER

These are a lovely variation of the standard yo-yo and create a very pretty look. Four lines will create four petals but five will look more like a flower. Starting with a circle at least 5in (12.7cm) in diameter is easier to sew.

1 Follow steps 1–2 left for making a basic yo-yo. ◄

2 Start to create petals by sewing a line of running stitch from the centre to the edge of the yo-yo. Pull up the thread to gather the fabric and then tie off at the back of the work. Start again at the centre with another thread and repeat to create as many petals as you want. ◄

BRIGHT IDEA

IF CREATING A FLOWER YO-YO WITH FIVE OR SIX PETALS, USE PINS TO MARK WHERE THE PETAL LINES NEED TO BE SEWN, SPACING THEM OUT EVENLY. REMOVE THEM AS YOU GATHER EACH LINE.

YO-YO VARIATIONS

Once you know how easy it is to make yo-yos you can play around with all sorts of variations. Here are some suggestions.

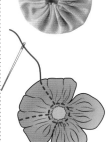

- Decorating the centres or gathers – yo-yos can be left plain but it's great fun to embellish them further, perhaps with French knots or cross stitches within the gathers or clusters of beads or buttons in the centre.

- Filling the centre with another fabric – thick fabrics cannot be gathered as tightly as thin ones, leaving a bigger 'hole' in the centre. Placing another fabric inside adds interest.

- Heart-shaped yo-yos – changing the shape of the fabric from a circle to a heart is easy and creates a cute variation.

- Yo-yos from trims – try using decorative trims and lace to create different yo-yos. Simply run a gathering stitch along the trim and pull up. Sew the two ends of the trim together neatly and decorate the centre if desired.

RUCHING FABRIC

The ruched area will end up much smaller than your starting piece so begin with a square of fabric at least twice the size you require the finished ruching to be.

1 Use a strong thread, such as 100 per cent polyester in a colour to match the fabric and cut a length longer than the width of the fabric. Knot the thread at the start and sew a line of running stitches across the fabric, making small stitches on the front of the fabric and longer ones on the back. Leave a long tail of thread at the end. Cut the thread and stitch another row of stitching about 1in (2.5cm) further up. Continue in this way over the whole fabric. ▶

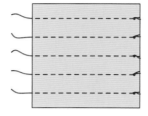

2 Turn the fabric 90 degrees and stitch rows in the opposite direction. ▼

3 Starting on one side begin to pull on the thread tails to gather up the fabric (A). When the gathers are to your liking, tie off the threads. Repeat this with the threads on the other side. The fabric is now ruched (B). The ruched fabric is easier to handle and use in a project if it is stabilized, so place it on a square of the same fabric and tack (baste) it to the flat fabric. ▶

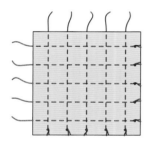

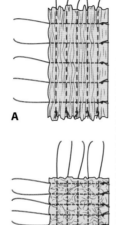

A

B

CHENILLING FABRIC

1 Layer up to five fabrics together, right sides up. Cut the base fabric at least 1in (2.5cm) larger all round than the other fabrics. Machine stitch the layers together diagonally on the bias grain, about ½in–1in (1.3cm–2.5cm) apart, using a straight stitch or short zigzag. For fine fabrics, stitch channels ½in (1.3cm) apart and wider for coarse fabrics. Stitch adjacent rows in opposite directions to minimize shifting of the layers. ▶

2 Use very sharp, pointed scissors to cut through the fabric layers between the channels of stitching but do *not* cut the base layer. Cut one channel at a time. ▶

3 Shake the work well to begin the fraying process. Use a nail brush or toothbrush to fray the cut fabric edges, or wash the piece in a washing machine and dry in a tumble drier. If you plan to use the chenilled piece as a block, it is best to border it with another fabric to protect the outer edges, or sew it to other blocks before washing it. ▶

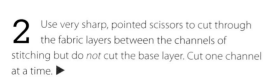

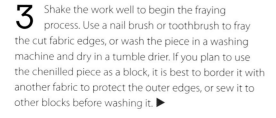

SLASHING FABRIC

When slashing fabric for a frayed effect, fit a sturdy needle to your sewing machine before sewing the layers together – one suitable for denim will be strong enough for multiple layers.

1 Layer up to five fabrics together, right sides up. Cut the base fabric at least 1in (2.5cm) larger all round than the other fabrics. Machine stitch the layers together in a grid pattern, 1in–1½in (2.5cm–3.8cm) apart. Using a walking foot will help the layers to feed together evenly. ▼

2 Use sharp, pointed scissors to cut through the fabric layers but *not* the base layer. Cuts can be diagonal or in a cross, all in one direction or in a pattern. If the base layer is accidentally cut, fuse a patch of fabric to the underside using fusible web. ▼

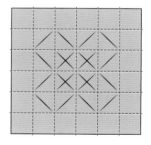

3 Fray the cut fabric edges with a nail brush or toothbrush, or wash the piece in a washing machine and dry in a tumble drier. ▼

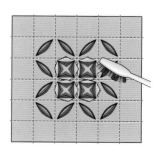

FORMING PLEATS

There are many types of pleat, some of which are shown on page 120. The technique here describes knife pleats, which are all folded in the same direction, but the principles are similar for other types of pleat.

1 Decide on the width each pleat is to be and mark short lines to this measurement across the fabric top and bottom using a temporary marker – these are the fold lines (shown in red and blue on the diagram below). ▼

2 Working from the right-hand edge (or left if left-handed), pinch the fabric at the first mark (red on diagram) and fold it so that it laps up against the second mark (blue). Pin in place. Now pinch the 3rd set of marks and fold to meet the 5th line. Pin in place. Repeat along the fabric width. ▼

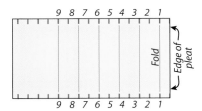

3 Tack (baste) all the pleats in place along the top and bottom of the fabric and then sew on the machine. For soft pleats leave the pleats unpressed; for crisp pleats press with an iron. ▼

BRIGHT IDEA

USE PATTERNED FABRIC FOR A SOFTER PLEATED EFFECT. OR TRY ALTERNATE STRIPS OF CONTRASTING FABRIC TO CREATE A STRIKING DESIGN.

This elegant bag by Lynne Edwards was created using two fabrics strip pieced together and then pleated to produce a two-tone effect.

SEWING TUCKS

For the best results the straight stitching along the length of a tuck needs to be neat so use a straight stitch foot and a needle plate with a round hole on the sewing machine.

1 Begin by making pleats as described in the technique on the previous page but make the pleats narrow, about ½in (1.3cm) wide. Using matching thread, sew a line along the base of each pleat through both layers of fabric. ▶

2 Further stitching can be done nearer the edge of each tuck if desired (shown in red for clarity). Pinch each pleat in turn, folding the others out of the way, and stitch along the edge. ▶

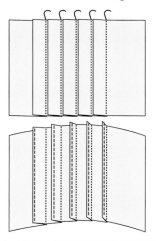

SEWING TWISTED TUCKS

These tucks are made in the same way as normal pin tucks but are sewn at the top, twisted in the opposite direction halfway down their length, and then sewn at the bottom facing the other way. This creates a wave-like pattern and a highly textured look. These twists can occur several times down the length of the tuck and be kept in place with stitching or a trim.

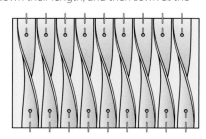

SEWING CORDED TUCKS

These tucks have a more prominent three-dimensional quality because of the piping cord used. Begin by making pleats as described on the previous page but make the pleats narrow, about ¼in (6mm) wide, or a width sufficient to house the piping you are using. Pin the piping in place along the pleat. Using matching thread and a zipper foot, sew a line along the base of each pleat through both layers of fabric, encasing the cord.

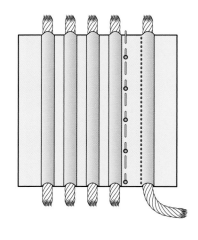

WEAVING FABRIC STRIPS

The technique here describes using strips of the same width but try experimenting with variable widths in the same piece of work.

1 Choose three fabrics that work well together and cut strips between 1in–2in (2.5cm–5cm) wide across the straight grain of the fabric. Arrange two of the fabrics alternately, right sides up on a base fabric. Pin the strips to the base fabric down one side and machine tack (baste) to the base. Press the work to ensure the strips are straight and butted against each other and then pin and tack (baste) the other side. ▼

2 Taking a strip of fabric from the third colour, weave it over and under the other two as shown. Continue all the way along the work and when all strips are in place make sure they are nestled together neatly. Pin the strips at the sides and machine tack (baste) the edges as before. ▼

BRIGHT IDEA

IF YOU DO NOT WANT RAW EDGES CUT THE STRIPS ½IN (1.3CM) WIDER AND PRESS A NARROW HEM DOWN BOTH SIDES. USE TEMPORARY BASTING GLUE TO KEEP THE HEMS IN PLACE AS YOU WORK.

3 Protect the cut edges of the strips by machine sewing a zigzag stitch along each vertical and horizontal join. Remove tacking (basting) on the outer edges and use the panel as desired. ▼

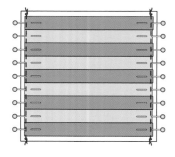

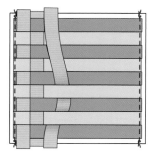

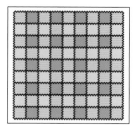

QUILT ART

Quilt art, or fibre art, uses patchwork , appliqué and quilting plus techniques from many other media to create art objects. Quilt art is more often based on the ideas, experiences and imagery of the creator than on traditional patterns and blurs the boundaries between numerous art forms. There are no rules and this liberated attitude allows you to explore techniques, being led by what inspires you to create unique pieces of work.

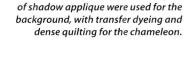

People who explore quilt art often call themselves fabric artists and many base their work on mixed media ideas, combining processes and techniques from many arts and crafts, including embroidery, painting, dyeing, printing, stamping and felting. Many of the techniques covered in this book can be used as a starting point to create your own quilt art, in particular appliqué techniques, crazy patchwork, free-motion quilting and decorative quilting. Dyeing, painting and printing on fabric are subjects in their own right and there are many excellent books on the subject. Specialist fabrics are worth exploring, particularly shrinkable fabric, water-soluble fabric and printable fabric. The pictures shown on this page are by kind permission of Kindred Spirits, a group of fibre artists based in Devon, UK.

'Chameleon' by Sarah O'Hora. Layers of shadow applique were used for the background, with transfer dyeing and dense quilting for the chameleon.

'Driftwood' by Val Thomas. The calico base for this piece was rust dyed using bits of rusty metal. The free-machine quilting was inspired by driftwood found on the beach.

'Under the Surface' by Dot Carter. This was created with fabric strips woven through hessian and stitched heavily. Needle punching, hand dyeing and screen printing techniques were also used.

'Notes from a Different Country' by Vineta Cable. Synthetic felt, polyester fabric and cotton waste were used in this piece, created with transfer dye, needle felting and machine and hand quilting.

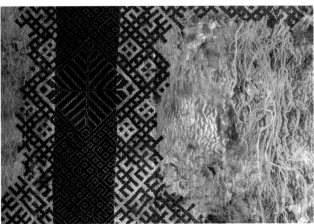

USING SASHING

Sashing, also referred to as lattice or setting strips, is used to frame or separate pieced blocks or parts of a quilt design. Well-planned sashing can unify a quilt design, linking blocks and colour schemes together and is very useful in a sampler quilt where different-sized blocks may be used (see page 48). Sashing can be used to increase the overall size of a block or quilt. This is useful if you are planning a pieced border as the size can be increased to a measurement that is easier to divide equally – see Using Borders on page 130. There are various types of sashing and the main ones are illustrated opposite, with the techniques explained overleaf.

Sashing should always balance with the actual quilt, so the type of sashing used and the proposed width should be carefully considered so it doesn't overwhelm the quilt design. The width of the sashing will depend on many factors, including the size of the patchwork blocks and whether the sashing is to be pieced or plain. The first diagram, right, shows an example of over-dominant sashing. When choosing a sashing width, a quarter of the block width often works well. Widths of 2in–2½in (5cm–6.3cm) are commonly used. Where possible, cut sashing strips along the lengthwise grain of the fabric. A narrow sashing is very useful for framing smaller blocks to bring them up to the size of their companions in a quilt.

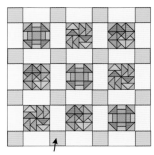

Here, the sashing is too wide in comparison with the blocks and dominates the design.

Narrow sashing can be used to increase the size of smaller blocks, to make them the same size as other blocks in the quilt.

PLAIN SASHING

Sashing can be just strips in a solid or print fabric, sewn to the quilt top with butted or mitred seams. These strips can frame individual blocks or be used only vertically or horizontally to separate areas of a quilt. Using a fabric with a graded colour that shades from light to dark can look very effective. Plain sashing also gives opportunities for quilting.

SASHING WITH SETTING SQUARES

Simple fabric strips can be made more interesting by the addition of cornerstones or setting squares, sometimes called 'posts'. These are often plain squares in a contrasting colour but could be pieced, perhaps in a four-patch or nine-patch arrangement or as quarter-square triangles.

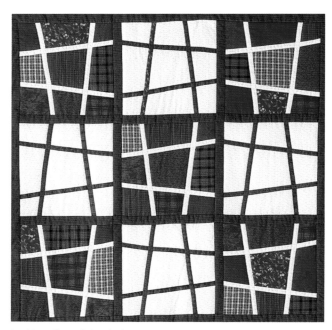

In this quilt made by Shirley Prescott, a narrow, plain sashing in a contrasting colour frames the simple but elegant blocks.

The Pineapple blocks used in this quilt by Sue Fitzgerald are separated and yet linked by cream sashing with green and salmon setting squares.

PIECED SASHING

Sashing can also be pieced in more complicated patterns to create secondary designs within a quilt. Half-square triangles are popular for this and can create interesting effects depending on the tonal combinations. Many simple block designs also make attractive sashing – try Churn Dash, Friendship Star and Seminole patterns. There are many books and magazines filled with examples of pieced sashing so, for ideas, remind yourself to look at the sashing and not just the blocks.

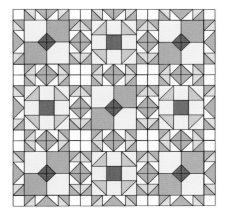

Plain sashing

Vertical sashing

Horizontal sashing

Sashing with setting squares

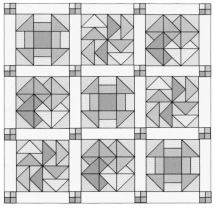

Sashing with pieced setting squares

Pieced sashing in Seminole pattern

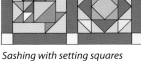

Pieced sashing with half-square triangles

Pieced sashing with stars

Pieced sashing with friendship stars

>>> **related topics...** *Sewing Intersecting Seams 55 • Sewing Half-square Triangles 80 • Sewing Triangle Corners 82* >>

THE TECHNIQUES

SEWING PLAIN SASHING

It doesn't matter whether you add the sashing to the sides of the blocks first or to the top and bottom as long as it is consistent on all blocks. In the example shown the sides are added first. Where blocks are of different sizes the sashing width will need to vary to bring all the blocks up to the same finished size. Plain sashing can also be sewn with mitred corners using the same technique as Sewing a Mitred Border on page 135.

1 Decide on the width of your sashing and cut lengths to fit the blocks. With right sides together, pin and sew the sashing strips to the blocks using ¼in (6mm) seams and then press towards the darker fabric. ▼

3 Once the blocks are joined in a unit, cut a length of sashing in the same width as before and long enough to fit across the unit. With right sides together pin and sew in place using the same seam allowance and press. ▼

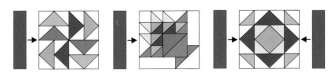

2 With right sides together pin and sew the blocks together using the same seam allowance, and press. ▼

4 Continue in this way for the rest of the blocks and sashing strips. ▶

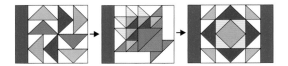

SEWING SASHING WITH SETTING SQUARES

This technique is essentially the same as for plain sashing but with squares added between the strips. In this method care needs to be taken to align seam junctions accurately.

1 Decide on the sashing width and cut lengths to fit the blocks. With right sides together, pin and sew the strips to the blocks using ¼in (6mm) seams and then press towards the darker fabric. ▼

3 With right sides together, pin sew the sashing strips with setting squares in place, matching seams carefully. Sew together using the same seam allowance, and press. ▼

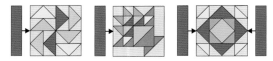

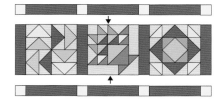

2 With right sides together, pin and sew the blocks together, using the same seam allowance and press. Cut lengths of sashing to fit the top and bottom of the blocks, allowing for seams. Cut squares in a contrasting colour the same width as the sashing. Join the strips and squares together as shown and press. ▼

4 Continue in this way to complete the rest of the quilt and sashing strips. ▶

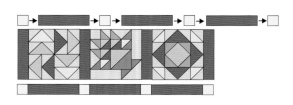

SEWING PIECED SASHING

Work methodically when sewing pieced sashing. Calculate how many pieced sashing strips you will need and cut all your fabric pieces out before you start to sew them together. A star pattern is shown here.

1 Decide on the width of your sashing and cut lengths to fit the blocks. Using ¼in (6mm) seams, create the vertical pieced sashing strips first by sewing triangles to each end of the sashing strips – see Sewing Triangle Corners on page 82. ▼

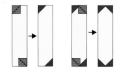 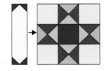 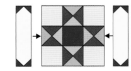

2 Sew the pieced sashing strips to the blocks in horizontal units, using ¼in (6mm) seams and press. ▼

3 Create the horizontal pieced sashing strips in the same way as the vertical strips but with a square sewn to each end. ▼

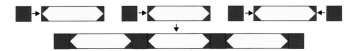

4 Sew the horizontal sashing strips to the blocks using the same seam allowance, taking care to match seam junctions accurately, and then press. ▼

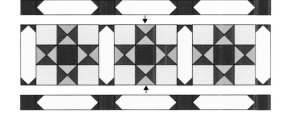

5 Continue in this way, piecing the rest of the sashing strips and joining them to the blocks. ▶

Star sashing is used beautifully in this quilt made by Pam and Nicky Lintott. The stars are positioned at the intersections of the Log Cabin blocks, creating a focal point in the centre. The sashing stars are in a paler fabric, which contrasts well with the earthy tones and also reveals some attractive long-arm quilting.

USING BORDERS

Borders can serve many functions in a quilt design. At their simplest they can be plain strips of fabric that frame the quilt centre, drawing attention to intricate piecing or elaborate appliqué. Plain borders can also provide areas for detailed quilting. If a print is used for the border it can be the same fabric as used in the piecing and so unify the quilt design. In medallion quilts (see page 40), borders are used as frames, drawing the eye outwards. Borders can also be pieced – anything from simple squares and rectangles to classic blocks and complicated patterns that integrate with the quilt top. Some examples are shown overleaf. Of course, a quilt doesn't have to have a border at all but most arrangements do seem to be set off to best advantage with at least one border – rather like a frame that draws attention to a beautiful picture.

Quilt borders can be of variable widths and the size chosen will depend on the patchwork block sizes used and the overall layout and design of the quilt – the aim should always be to create a balanced design. The width of the borders may also be determined by the particular fabric print you are using. For example, a lovely floral print will look its best if the motifs are used 'entire' rather than chopping off flower-heads to fit a narrower measure, so a more generous width than originally planned may be needed.

Borders can be used to tilt blocks at an angle, to create a jaunty look (see tilted settings on page 40). Borders can also be pieced with rectangles at an angle to create the look of a braid. Whole quilts, often called French braid quilts, can be constructed using this technique.

Borders can be constructed in various ways and the most commonly used methods are listed here.

- Straight borders – these are also called square, butted or overlapped borders and are the easiest type to sew.
- Straight borders with cornerstones or posts – these borders are an easy step on from plain borders, with squares in the corners that can contrast with the border fabric colour and provide areas for extra quilting. The squares or posts can also be pieced and four-patch arrangements are common.
- Mitred borders – these are a little more work than straight borders but create a smart 45 degree mitre at each corner of a quilt. Quilt designs using squares and rectangles often benefit from mitred borders, creating a visual break between the quilt top and the border.

APPLIQUÉ BORDERS

Appliqué borders can be sewn to a quilt top with any of the methods described above. These borders can be created quite easily by appliquéing motifs in place on the border strip just as you would for an appliqué block. The motifs can echo those used in the blocks or be different designs. Such borders can be created separately and sewn to the quilt top as butted or mitred borders, and with or without cornerstones. An attractive effect can be created by appliquéing motifs over the junctions of different parts of a quilt, so the appliqué motifs link the different areas.

This scrap quilt by Lynne Edwards features an appliqué border, with floral motifs echoing those used in the quilt. The border is a straight one with nine-patch cornerstones.

PIECED BORDERS

The possibilities for pieced borders are as varied as block designs and these sorts of borders are ideal for using up fabric scraps. Popular pieced border designs include piano key, flying geese and half-square triangles. Using sashing to bring up a block or quilt size can make adding pieced borders easier. Pieced borders can be sewn to the quilt top as straight (butted) strips, with or without cornerstones, or be mitred. They can also be integrated into the quilt design, where the visual presence of the border is created from extended piecing of the quilt top. These sorts of effect can be very rewarding to create, although take more planning and work than straight borders. Refer to the techniques overleaf.

This fun quilt called Mermaid Lagoon, by Lynette Anderson, cleverly creates the impression of a border by the way it is pieced as part of the quilt centre. Half-square triangles were used to create this illusion.

CUTTING BORDERS

Borders can easily stretch, causing a rippling effect and a quilt that is not square. To help prevent this, always try to cut fabric for borders on the straight grain, in lengths as long as possible. If lengths have to be joined a diagonal seam is less noticeable than a straight seam.

QUILTING BORDERS

There are many opportunities for hand or machine quilting in borders. The quilting in borders could be part of the whole quilt top, linking the elements, or the borders could be quilted with separate designs. Over the years many long-format designs have been developed that are ideal for borders, including feather patterns, scroll motifs and cable designs. If a border has cornerstones or posts, these squares can feature square or circular quilting motifs. Many commercial stencils are available for border quilting. See also page 192 for ideas.

This detail from a quilt by Marsha McCloskey shows how a border can be used to showcase some beautiful quilting. A narrow border of strip-pieced triangles (see page 81) links the central panel with the outer wide border.

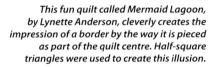

BRIGHT IDEA

IF YOU ARE FOLLOWING A QUILT PATTERN FROM A BOOK OR MAGAZINE, ALWAYS MEASURE YOUR OWN QUILT BEFORE CUTTING FABRIC FOR BORDERS AS THE MEASUREMENTS OF YOUR QUILT MAY DIFFER FROM THOSE IN THE INSTRUCTIONS.

Plain border

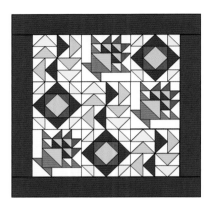

Plain border with cornerstones

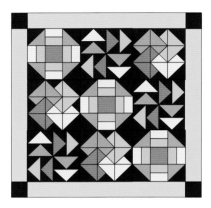

Mitred border

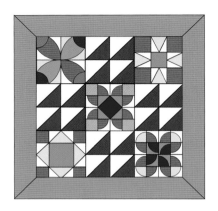

Pieced border – *Piano Key*
A piano key border is perfect for using up scraps. See Straight Strip Piecing on page 67.

Pieced border – *Flying Geese*
Flying Geese units make a striking border. The inner one reverses the direction to create a different pattern.

Pieced border – *Four-patch*
Four-patch blocks make a great border, either straight or on point with setting triangles for a different look.

Pieced border – *Half-square Triangles*
Perfect for using up small scraps, this type of border looks wonderful with Feathered Star blocks.

Pieced border – *Half-square Triangles*
Half-square triangles combined with plain squares create a different four-patch block.

Appliqué border – *Appliqué borders can be straight or mitred. The motifs can straddle the border and central design, linking the elements.*

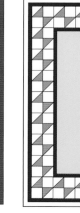

related topics… *Estimating Fabric Requirements 22 • Using Sashing 126*

THE TECHNIQUES

MEASURING FOR BORDERS

In order to cut and sew neat borders the quilt top needs to be measured accurately and the best place to do this is across the centre, as the edges may have stretched.

Measuring for a straight border

1 Ensure the quilt top is square (right angled) and place it flat on a firm surface. Use a tape measure to measure the width across the centre. Decide what width the border is to be and cut the top and bottom border strips to this measurement. Borders can be cut to the exact length or a little extra can be added to allow for the fabric creeping as the border is sewn in place. Trim off after sewing. ▶

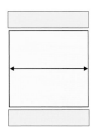

2 To determine the size of the side borders, use a tape measure to measure the height of the quilt across the centre, *plus* the width of the top and bottom borders. ▶

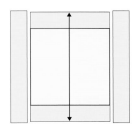

Measuring for a mitred border

Measure the quilt top across the centre, as for a straight border, but add an extra amount to allow sufficient fabric for the mitres to be sewn. Generally, this extra amount is twice the width of the cut border. So, if your border is 2in (5cm) wide, add 4in (10.2cm) in total to the cut border length.

PLANNING A PIECED BORDER

Planning a pieced border that fits the quilt top perfectly takes a little thought and some maths (so a calculator may be handy), but the final result is well worth it.

For a square quilt

1 Measure the quilt along the width and length. Note these measurements and subtract ½in (1.3cm) for the seams that will be needed when sewing the border in place later. ▶

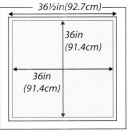

2 Decide on the finished block size required for your border. Ideally this needs to be a size that will divide easily into your quilt measurement. Example: 36in (91.4cm) ÷ 3in (7.6cm) = 12 blocks. This is the *finished* size of each block once the border is pieced, so before sewing the border blocks together seams have to be allowed for. ▶

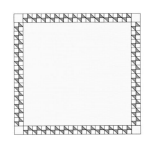

3 The pieced borders will now fit the quilt measurement. Adding corner squares completes the border (see Sewing a Straight Border with Cornerstones overleaf). ▶

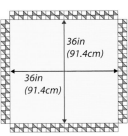

BORDER FIT PROBLEMS

It can sometimes be tricky to create a pieced border that fits the quilt top perfectly. Sometimes, even if the maths seems correct, the border ends up a little smaller or larger than expected. Try the following solutions in these cases.

- If the border is just a fraction too short the careful use of the steam iron can produce that little extra length needed.
- If the border is too long or too short and the seams in the border don't align with seams in the quilt top, check the pieced border against the quilt and use a pin to mark problem seams, unpicking these and re-sewing them.
- A pieced border that is too long can be made to fit the quilt by the addition of a narrow plain border to the quilt, which can then be trimmed down to the correct size when the pieced border is completed and the finished length is known.

- A pieced border that is too short to fit the quilt but where an extra block would make it too long, can be made longer by the addition of 'spacers', that is, thin strips of fabric. Sewing these at either end of the border in the same colour as the border will be least noticeable. Repeat designs like Flying Geese can be broken at the corners and midway by spacers.

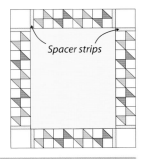

Spacer strips

BRIGHT IDEA

IF THERE ARE MANY SEAM JUNCTIONS TO ALIGN ALONG A PIECED BORDER AND QUILT TOP, SEW THE BORDER IN PLACE FROM THE CENTRE OUTWARDS. FOLD THE QUILT IN HALF AND MARK THE SIDES AT THE CENTRE POINTS WITH A PIN. FOLD THE BORDERS IN HALF AND FINGER CREASE THE CENTRE. ALIGN THE CREASE WITH A PIN ON THE QUILT AND BEGIN SEWING FROM THIS CENTRE POINT, WORKING OUT TO THE EDGE EACH TIME.

SEWING A STRAIGHT (BUTTED) BORDER

This type of border is very popular as it is easy to sew. It doesn't matter whether you sew the top and bottom borders on first and then the side borders, or vice versa, as long as it is consistent throughout a quilt.

1 Once the border strips are cut, pin and sew them to the quilt top. Place the top border right sides together with the quilt top and sew together with a ¼in (6mm) seam. Press towards the darker fabric. Trim the edges flush with the quilt top. Add the bottom border in the same way. ▼

2 Now sew on the side borders, checking the length measurement one final time before you begin. Press to the darker fabric. Trim the edges flush with the quilt top. ▼

3 When all of the borders have been sewn on, check the measurement of the quilt and trim if necessary so all corners are square. ▼

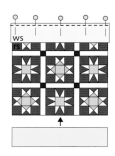

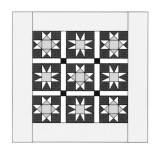

SEWING A STRAIGHT BORDER WITH CORNERSTONES

Cornerstones not only look good in a quilt but are also useful to introduce an accent colour or a pieced unit.

1 Measure the quilt across the centre width and then the length to determine the length of the borders. Cut border strips to these lengths in the width of your choice. Cut four corner squares in the same measurement as the border width. ▶

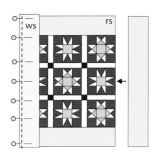

3 Using ¼in (6mm) seams, sew the cornerstones to each end of the remaining border strips and press. ▶

4 Sew the top and bottom borders to the quilt using ¼in (6mm) seams, aligning cornerstone seams carefully, and then press. ▶

2 Sew the two side borders to the quilt using ¼in (6mm) seams and press. ▶

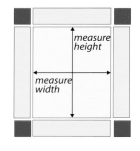

MAKING A TILTED BLOCK

Borders can be used to tilt a patchwork block to the left or right, to create movement in a quilt.

1 Make your block and add a wide border. ▼

2 Place a large square ruler on the block (or a template) and angle it so the four corners touch the edges. Cut out the square. ▼

3 Once cut and placed straight, the block will be tilted. To tilt another block in the opposite direction, rotate the ruler. ▼

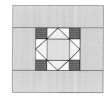

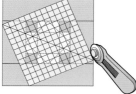

SEWING A MITRED BORDER

Mitred borders look very professional and are useful if you want to continue a print pattern neatly around a quilt.

1 Measure the quilt as described in Measuring for a Mitred Border (see page 133) and cut the borders to this measurement, plus extra to allow for the mitres – generally, the width of the cut border strips x 2. ▶

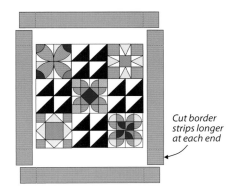

Cut border strips longer at each end

3 Fold the quilt top in half diagonally, right sides together, folding and pinning the border seam allowances towards the quilt top. Pencil a 45 degree line from the end of the stitching to the opposite side. Sew along this line. Turn the work to the right side and check the mitre is lying flat. Repeat with the other corners. ▶

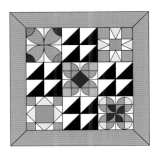

2 Sew the two side borders to the quilt, using ¼in (6mm) seams, starting and finishing ¼in (6mm) from each corner and making sure the extra amount projects at either end. Press seams open. Now sew the top and bottom borders to the quilt, in the same way, starting and finishing ¼in (6mm) from each corner. Press seams open. ▼

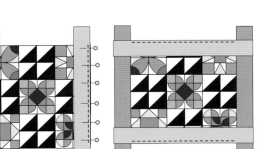

4 When all corners are mitred, trim the seam allowances to ¼in (6mm) and press seams open. Check that the front looks neat and flat. ▶

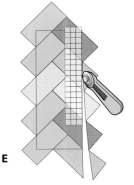

BRIGHT IDEA

PIECED BORDERS CAN SOMETIMES PART AT THE EDGE SEAMS OR STRETCH, SO ADD A LINE OF 'STAY' MACHINE STITCHING AROUND THE EDGE TO STABILIZE THE BORDER. USE A LONG STITCH LENGTH SO IT CAN BE EASILY REMOVED LATER.

SEWING A BRAIDED BORDER

Braids are composed of rectangles and are sewn together at a 45 degree angle and from bottom to top, as shown in the sequence. Place all your rectangles in the correct colour order before sewing to avoid sewing the pieces in the wrong order.

1 Cut sufficient rectangles in the size and colours you require. With right sides together, sew piece 2 to piece 1 (A). Press the seam outwards (B). ▼

A piece 2 ws — piece 1 rs   **B** rs

3 When the braided border is finished use a rotary cutter and ruler to trim the edges as shown (E). Make sure the outer points are aligned on a straight edge before cutting. ▶

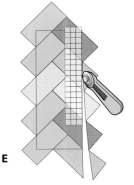

E

2 With right sides together, sew piece 3 to piece 1 (C). Open and press seam (D). Continue adding pieces on alternate sides in this way to the length required. ▼

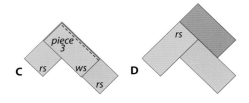

C piece 3 / rs ws rs   **D** rs

ATTACHING TEMPORARY BORDERS

Temporary borders may need to be attached to a quilt top when hand or machine quilting using a hoop or frame, in order that the hoop or frame has fabric to grip on to (see page 198). Attach widths of plain fabric in the same way as described above for sewing on straight borders but use a much longer stitch length, so the stitches and fabric pieces can easily be removed later.

Appliqué

Appliqué has long been a wonderful way to express creativity and has evolved into a fascinating and varied technique which makes the perfect companion to patchwork and quilting. The term appliqué comes from the French word appliquér, which means 'to put on' or 'to apply'. In its simplest form, appliqué is the technique of placing one shaped piece of fabric over or within another and sewing it in place. Appliqué opens up a new world to the patchworker, allowing for many more possibilities than just piecing alone.

Centuries ago all appliqué was done by hand but, with the invention of the sewing machine in 1846 by American entrepreneur Elias Howe, the technique was developed, taking advantage of the speed of machine compared to hand. Today, appliqué is a flexible and inventive art form. Advances in quilting notions and adhesives have made appliqué techniques easy to do and some wonderful effects achievable even for beginners.

Whether you want to appliqué a simple motif on to clothing or create a whole quilt of appliqué blocks you will find what you need in this section. There is advice on fabrics and threads to use for appliqué, finding motifs and using templates, plus instructions on all the major forms of hand and machine appliqué, including traditional methods such as needle-turn appliqué and appliqué persé and more modern developments such as fusible web appliqué. You can also explore the exciting design possibilities of bias-strip appliqué and the delicate effects that can be achieved with shadow appliqué.

FABRICS AND THREADS FOR APPLIQUE

For the patchwork and quilting purist 100 per cent cotton fabrics are the ones of choice for appliqué. They crease fairly easily so can be turned under readily, they don't fray too badly, they wash well and are available in a limitless array of gorgeous solid colours and fabulous prints. In reality, any fabric can be used for appliqué. Some may need more care and coddling but for many people, particularly quilt artists, it is those unexpected fabric types – the shiny silks, the delicate sheers, the strokeable velvets and the sturdy denims – that bring a new dimension to appliqué.

We are spoilt for choice today with all the gorgeous threads available. As you discover applique techniques, experiment with new threads too.

Those new to appliqué should start with cotton fabrics until more familiar with the techniques. When choosing unusual fabrics for appliqué a particular approach may be needed, for example silks and satins fray easily so protecting their edges will be more important than with felt, which doesn't fray. If a project will need laundering then using good-natured fabrics with similar properties is a good idea.

Most appliqué techniques secure one fabric piece to another by hemming the edges or protecting cut edges in some way but fabrics don't have to be attached to the background fabric around all edges. Felt, suede, lace and netting can be attached only at specific points to create a three-dimensional look. The use of varied fabric types is not only exciting but blurs the lines between ordinary appliqué and quilt art.

NEEDLES FOR APPLIQUE

It is important to use the right needle for the right job in patchwork and appliqué – see Using the Right Needle on page 23 for general advice on needles for hand and machine sewing. If sewing appliqué by hand use a Sharps or Betweens size 8–10. For machine appliqué (such as satin stitch) use a Universal 70/10 or Embroidery 75/11.

THREADS FOR APPLIQUE

Traditionally, threads used for appliqué should match or tone with the fabric colours, particularly for needle-turn appliqué where the appliqué edges are turned under and hand stitched in place. These stitches are not meant to show so use a fine sewing thread, such as a 50 or 60 weight. Colours such as grey and beige usually blend in well.

In some forms of appliqué, such as fusible web appliqué, the motif edges are raw but covered by stitches. This may be simple running stitch, more decorative blanket stitch or machine satin stitch. If these stitches are intended to blend in with the appliqué then match the thread to the fabric colour. However, you may want the thread to be on show and in this case a more decorative thread can be used in a thicker weight, such as a stranded embroidery cotton or perle cotton. Variegated embroidery cottons can look fabulous, especially for colourful projects for children. For extra pizzazz try metallic threads too.

When using embroidery and specialist threads, consider the thread thickness, for example, a fine blanket stitch will be difficult to achieve with a thick perle cotton. Try to match the stitches and thread with the scale of the project – a large, bold motif may suit thick thread and chunky stitches.

For machine appliqué, a 40 weight thread is normally sufficient, or use a 30 weight for a heavier look. Machine embroidery rayon threads look wonderful for satin stitch as their lovely sheen is emphasized by the stitch. Threads used in the bobbin are normally polyester or polycotton in a 50 or 60 weight, and because they aren't usually seen any subtle colour will do. Bobbin colour needs to be considered for three-dimensional appliqué as the thread may show – see page 148.

Multicoloured threads are great for edging appliqué motifs and can unite fabric colours.

> > **related topics...** *Fabric Types 14 • Embellishments 17 • Using Colour 19* > > >

THE TECHNIQUES

CALCULATING FABRIC FOR APPLIQUE

The easiest way to calculate how much fabric you need for appliqué work is to draw the motif within an easy geometric shape, such as a square or rectangle, and then measure the geometric shape.

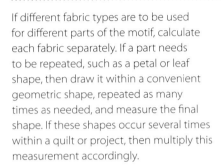
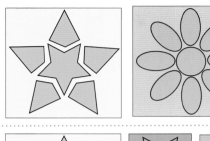

If different fabric types are to be used for different parts of the motif, calculate each fabric separately. If a part needs to be repeated, such as a petal or leaf shape, then draw it within a convenient geometric shape, repeated as many times as needed, and measure the final shape. If these shapes occur several times within a quilt or project, then multiply this measurement accordingly.

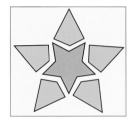

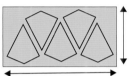

Amount of fabric needed for a repeated shape

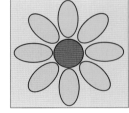
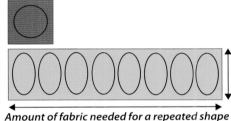

Amount of fabric needed for a repeated shape

PREPARING FABRICS FOR APPLIQUE

Preparing fabrics for appliqué is really all about getting them to a state where it is easy to attach them to the background fabric. This will depend on the specific fabric and the appliqué method you want to use. Today we are fortunate to have so many products to help with this and freezer paper and fusible web (see pages 151 and 152) are two popular products that work well and make appliqué very easy.

- Wash fabrics if you are in doubt about their colourfastness or shrinkage. Press to remove any creases.
- You may want to select a specific area of a printed fabric to feature in the appliqué. This 'fussy cutting' is made easy using clear plastic templates as you can see through the plastic when you position it over the area you want on the fabric.
- If the background fabric is to form a quilt block with the appliqué motif in its centre, ensure the background piece is about 4in (10.2cm) larger than the finished size required, to allow it to be squared off and attached to other blocks.

- To centre the appliqué piece within the background fabric, fold the background piece in half and then in half again and lightly mark the centre with a pencil, or finger crease the folds. Find the centre of the motif in a similar way or use a ruler. When positioning the appliqué motif on the background fabric, these two centre points need to match up. Sometimes working by eye is easier.
- If the appliqué design has several parts, prepare them all and position them on the background fabric to check they will layer and fit correctly before you begin to fix them in position.

BRIGHT IDEA

GENERALLY, YOU DON'T HAVE TO WORRY ABOUT FABRIC GRAIN FOR APPLIQUÉD MOTIFS BECAUSE ONCE ATTACHED TO THE BACKGROUND FABRIC THE MOTIF WILL BE STABLE AND THEREFORE SHOULD NOT WARP. HOWEVER, IF IN DOUBT, MATCH THE GRAIN OF THE APPLIQUÉ PIECE TO THE GRAIN OF THE BACKGROUND FABRIC.

CREATING EFFECTS

When choosing fabrics for appliqué the overall effect of the design can be enhanced by using fabrics in certain ways. Here are some things you might consider.

- Use fabric patterns to create depth in an appliqué design. Things appear smaller as they recede so if you use fabrics with larger prints in the foreground and those with smaller motifs further away you can create a more three-dimensional look. In a similar way light and dark fabrics can be used to create depth. Darker colours tend to 'recede', that is they appear to be farther away, while brighter colours will appear nearer the foreground.
- Use fabrics with different finishes to create different effects. For example, silks and satins could be selected for stained-glass appliqué to mimic the effect of shiny stained-glass windows.
- Use decorative embroidery stitches on appliqué fabrics to echo the design theme. For example, you could add French knots to flower centres or a line of decorative stitches to delineate the centre of a leaf.

Try unusual embellishments with appliqué. For example, you could use sequins in shadow appliqué, trapping them under the sheer layer.

Use ricrac braid, decorative trims and ribbons on appliqué to emphasize or outline certain areas. You could also try adding beads for highlights.

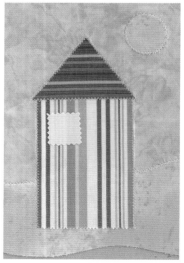

Use specific prints to echo the appliqué theme. For example, use a striped fabric for a colourful beach hut or a spotted fabric to suggest a snowy sky.

Use the motifs within a fabric pattern as a feature. For example, you could use an entire flower motif in an appliqué persé effect.

MOTIFS AND TEMPLATES

Motifs for appliqué can be anything you choose and many books are available with libraries of images. Computer software programs for quilting also have a wide range of motifs. Common images include flowers, leaves, birds, butterflies, animals, insects and geometric shapes, and of course motifs can be combined to create more complex patterns. You can also create an appliqué motif from an image you have seen (see page 143 for technique).

Although you can draw and cut fabric shapes freehand or by eye for appliqué work, templates are normally used as this not only makes appliqué work more accurate but also allows you to reproduce a design as many times as needed. You may use the motifs provided here, enlarging or combining them however you wish and create templates from them.

APPLIQUE MOTIFS

Here is a range of simple decorative motifs suitable for appliqué. You could enlarge these and use them in your work. See overleaf for ideas for combining different motifs to create unusual patterns. Don't forget that appliqué motifs can also be reversed or 'flipped' to create an opposite image. Pairing or mirror imaging is a useful design technique.

BRIGHT IDEA

THERE ARE MANY APPLIQUE SHAPES AVAILABLE PRE-CUT IN PLAIN AND PRINTED FABRICS FROM QUILT SHOPS AND WEB STORES. SHAPES INCLUDE HEARTS, STARS, FLOWERS, LEAVES AND GEOMETRICS.

CREATING COMBINED PATTERNS

Appliqué motifs can be combined to create more intricate and interesting designs. Try repeating a motif in a row or mirror imaging it to create matching pairs. A scanner and computer are very useful for this – see page 34.

FINDING MOTIF IDEAS

Ideas for appliqué patterns and motifs are endless and there are many books devoted to the subject. Everywhere you look there are ideas that can be turned into appliqué. Try some of the following sources for inspiration.

- **Books** – These are an amazing resource, particularly those that show decorative styles through the ages, and sourcebooks for historical motifs. Children's books and colouring books often have simplified drawings and images that can be turned into appliqué motifs. Look at all sorts of craft books too, particularly card-making books.

- **Magazines** – Specialist magazines, including patchwork and quilting magazines of course, are brimful of ideas, projects and useful tips but can encourage your brain to look at a motif in a different way and create something unique of your own. There are also many house and home-style magazines available that are filled with images you could adapt. Try wildlife and gardening magazines too.

- **Catalogues** – All sorts of catalogues can yield inspiration. Look at wallpaper and curtain patterns, bed linen and crockery.

- **Museums** – Places that specialize in fabrics and wall decorations will have objects to inspire you.

- **High street shops** – Design plays a large part in many everyday objects so keep an eye open for images, particularly in greetings card shops and book stores.

- **Websites** – Even the most cursory browse online via some of the most popular search engines will yield masses of ideas. You can also find many copyright-free images that can be turned into appliqué motifs.

BRIGHT IDEA

TAKE A PENCIL AND SMALL SKETCH PAD WITH YOU WHEN YOU ARE OUT AND ABOUT SO WHEN YOU SEE SOMETHING THAT MIGHT MAKE A GOOD APPLIQUÉ MOTIF YOU CAN DO A QUICK DRAWING. YOUR SKETCHING SKILLS WILL QUICKLY IMPROVE AND WRITING NOTES ON THE SKETCH WILL HELP TOO.

related topics... *Using Templates 26 • Using Technology 34*

THE TECHNIQUES

USING TEMPLATES FOR APPLIQUE

Templates for appliqué are used to create the correct shape for a design and are useful if you plan to use the motif several times in a piece of work. Generally, appliqué templates need a ¼in (6mm) seam allowance added all round if the edges of the shape have to be turned under, such as for needle-turn appliqué and freezer paper appliqué. Seam allowances are *not* required on templates being used for fusible web appliqué or machine satin stitch appliqué, where an edging stitch will protect the cut edges.

Templates for appliqué can be made from various materials and common ones used are freezer paper, thin card and template plastic – see Making a Simple Template on page 27 and Making a Multi-Part Template on page 28 for detailed instructions.

TURNING AN IMAGE INTO AN APPLIQUE MOTIF

You may not be able to find just the appliqué motif you want but could draw your own. This process is easier if you have a computer and scanner but is also possible with just a sheet of paper, pencil and eraser. If you are inspired by an existing image, remember to respect the copyright of the original designer. You may use the image supplied here.

1 Choose your image – this might be a photograph you have taken or a drawing you have made of an object. I took a snapshot of an orchid so no copyright applied. The image needs to show a simplified shape as far as possible, that is, the most recognizable view – usually face on for a flower such as this. The second flower, shown from almost a back view, would not make a good shape for appliqué. ▼

2 Draw or trace the shape you want, simplifying the different sections. In the photograph the flower centre is a little too complicated for appliqué so just the outline was drawn. ▼

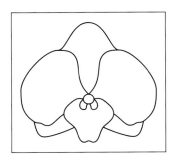

3 Using a pencil, draw the flower shape on to a piece of thin card. ▼

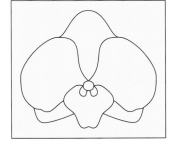

4 Cut out the separate shapes that make up the flower. If the flower is to appear this size, the centre will be too fiddly for appliqué, so cut it out with the lower 'lip'. You could define this area in other ways, such as with decorative stitches. You now have the templates you need, ready to transfer the shapes on to fabric in the appliqué method of your choice. ▼

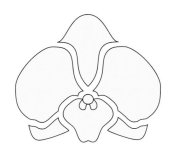

Here the orchid is created as an appliqué in coloured felt. The edges could be left raw or edged with running or blanket stitch.

This second version of the felt orchid shows the appliqué with edges finished in running stitch and blanket stitch.

NEEDLE-TURN APPLIQUE

This is a traditional method of hand appliqué. Essentially each appliqué piece has a seam turned under all round with the needle as the piece is being stitched into place on the background fabric. This is slightly different to freezer paper appliqué (see page 151), where the seam allowance is already turned and in place *before* the appliqué is sewn to the background. You could also pad or stuff the appliqué shapes as they are being sewn – see 3-D Appliqué on page 148.

The seam allowance used in needle-turn appliqué is usually ¼in (6mm) but this may change depending on the size of the appliqué piece being stitched and the type of fabric being used. Smaller pieces may only need an ⅛in (3mm) allowance to reduce bulk, while thicker fabrics or those that fray easily may need more than ¼in (6mm). Once you have learned the technique there is an easy project on page 150 to practise your skills on. You could also enlarge one of the motifs on page 141 and create your own project.

The needle-turn appliqué in this quilt by Lynette Anderson creates a neat effect that works well with the pieced blocks and decorative stitching.

BRIGHT IDEA

INSTEAD OF USING THE NEEDLE, SOME PEOPLE FIND THAT A TOOTHPICK HELPS TO TURN EDGES UNDER AND FORM SMOOTH APPLIQUE CURVES.

SEW AND CUT APPLIQUE

This method of appliqué is similar to needle-turn appliqué but the appliqué fabric is tacked (basted) into place on the background first and the edges are then trimmed, turned and stitched. This method is useful for appliqué designs with many pieces that need to be cut from the same fabric – see technique on page 147.

GATHERED EDGE APPLIQUE

When sewing appliqué by hand, as in needle-turn appliqué, this gathered technique is very useful for appliquéing circles, ovals and other uncomplicated, smooth-edged shapes. Essentially a running stitch is worked around the shape and gathered up over a card shape. The gathers follow the shape and once pressed form a firm edge around the appliqué with a seam allowance – see technique on page 147.

This Apple Tree Farm quilt by Lynette Anderson uses many different appliqué techniques, including needle-turn appliqué and stuffed appliqué, creating a bright and charming design.

>> related topics... *Using Templates 26 • 3-D Appliqué 148* > > >

THE TECHNIQUES

SEWING NEEDLE-TURN APPLIQUE

The technique is called 'needle-turn' because the needle is used to turn or stroke the seam allowance under as the appliqué is stitched into place. The easiest way to create the appliqué shapes is to make templates. Advice on sewing neat curves and points follows.

1 Using your template, trace the appliqué shape centrally on to the right side of the fabric using a light pencil or water-soluble marker. Mark the shape again freehand (or use a seam guide circle – see page 13) ⅛in–¼in (3mm–6mm) further out all round for the seam allowance (A) and cut out the fabric on this outer line (B). ▶

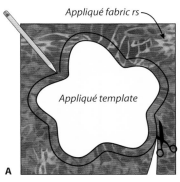
Appliqué fabric rs

Appliqué template

A

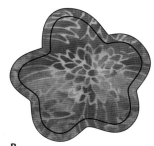

B

2 If the position of the appliqué on the background fabric is crucial you will also need to draw the same appliqué shape on the right side of the background fabric in the correct position and orientation. ▼

3 Position the appliqué fabric shape right side up on the background fabric in the position you require (or matching the drawn shapes with pins). Pin or tack (baste) the appliqué piece in place. ▼

BRIGHT IDEA

IF YOUR APPLIQUE MOTIF HAS A SPECIFIC 'TOP' OR NEEDS TO BE TURNED A CERTAIN WAY, YOU COULD MARK THIS WITH A DOT USING A REMOVABLE MARKER ON BOTH FABRICS TO HELP REMIND YOU WHICH WAY IS UP WHEN MATCHING UP THE SHAPES.

IF YOU HAVE MANY SHAPES TO POSITION YOU COULD PREPARE A MASTER TEMPLATE ON TRACING PAPER. PIN THIS ON YOUR FABRIC AND USE IT AS A GUIDE, SLIPPING THE SHAPES BENEATH IT, INTO THE CORRECT POSITIONS.

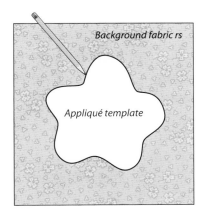
Background fabric rs

Appliqué template

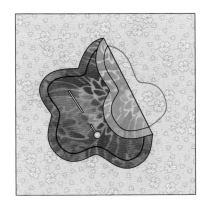

4 Turn the seam allowance under in one area of the appliqué shape so the marked line is covered and begin to sew the appliqué in place. Use thread to match the appliqué fabric, making tiny unobtrusive slipstitches or blind stitches at right angles to the appliqué edge. As you proceed, use the tip of the needle to turn or stroke the seam allowance under. ▶

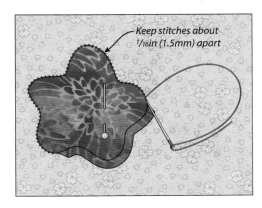
Keep stitches about ¹/₁₆in (1.5mm) apart

5 If there are any tight curves in your appliqué shape, clip them a little (not into the marked line though) to allow the hem to be folded under more easily. Similarly, clip tight V-shapes will need to be clipped. Once the appliqué is sewn in place on the background fabric, finish off the thread at the back of the work, remove pins or tacking (basting) and then press.

SEWING CURVES AND POINTS

Appliqué motifs come in all shapes and sizes, many with acute angles and tight curves, so the following diagrams should help you to manipulate the seam allowance to produce neat work.

INNER CURVES

For inner (concave) curves, clip the seam allowance regularly to about ⅛in (3mm), making sure you don't cut into or past the seam line. When these curves are folded over and finger pressed, they will then fan out and sit neatly, reducing bulk.

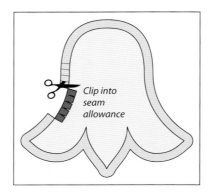

OUTER CURVES

For outer (convex) curves, clip the seam allowance in the same way as for inner curves but also snip out little notches of fabric, which will reduce the fabric bulk and encourage the seam to lie flat when pressed.

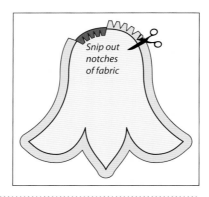

INNER CORNERS AND POINTS

For inner corners and points where acute angles occur, clip the seam allowance to about ⅛in (3mm) or nearly to the stitching line and fold over the allowances, angling them as shown in the diagram.

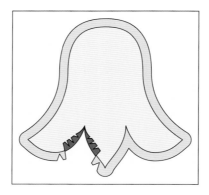

OUTER CORNERS AND POINTS

For outer corners and points, clip the seam allowance and trim the seam fabric to reduce bulk. Fold back the allowance at the point first, followed by the adjacent sides.

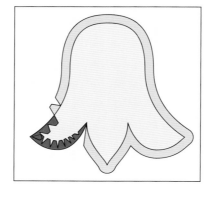

Appliqué is a good technique for creating work with a folk-art quality, as this piece by Clare Kingslake shows. Here a needle-turn method has been used, with echo quilting radiating out from the design all round.

SEW AND CUT APPLIQUE

This method of appliqué is similar to needle-turn appliqué and is useful for appliqué designs with many pieces that need to be cut from the same fabric. Essentially the appliqué fabric is tacked (basted) in place first and then the edges are trimmed and sewn.

1 Mark the appliqué design on the right side of the fabric and then tack (baste) the whole design to the background fabric at least a ¼in (6mm) inside the drawn lines all round. Now work the appliqué by hand or by machine. ▼

2a **If working by hand**, use small, sharp scissors to cut away the appliqué fabric ¼in (6mm) away from drawn outline, turning the seam under and stitching it in place as you go, using the same technique as needle-turn appliqué. ▼

2b **If working by machine**, tack the fabrics together as step 1. Using either machine satin stitch or straight stitch sew on the drawn line all round (the diagram shows both versions). Cut the appliqué fabric away with sharp scissors. ▼

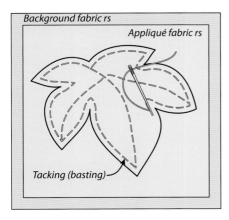

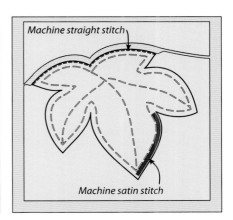

GATHERED EDGE APPLIQUE

This technique uses stiff card to gather up fabric shapes such as circles, ovals and other uncomplicated, smooth-edged shapes.

1 Make a template from stiff card of the shape to be appliquéd. Place the template on the wrong side of your appliqué fabric (pinned if need be) and use a pencil to draw around the shape. Remove the card. With a doubled length of sewing thread, sew a running stitch all around the fabric shape, slightly on the *outside* of the drawn line. Leave long lengths of thread at the ends. Trim the fabric around the shape to within ⅛in–¼in (3mm–6mm) of the running stitch all round. ▼

2 Place the card template on to the back of the fabric, take the two ends of thread and pull to gather up the fabric around the edge of the card. Press the gathered shape with an iron to crease the edges firmly all round. Remove the card. The appliqué shape is now ready to be sewn to the background fabric in a method of your choice. The gathered thread can be removed before or after stitching. ▼

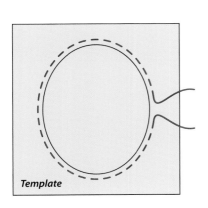

BRIGHT IDEA

USE WELL-WORN OR PREVIOUSLY WASHED FABRIC FOR THIS
TYPE OF APPLIQUÉ AS THE EDGES GATHER UP EASILY.

3-D APPLIQUE

As a variation on the basic method of appliqué, you could add a little more dimension by using a small amount of polyester stuffing or a layer of wadding (batting) or other thick fabric to pad the appliqué, slipping this between the appliqué and the background fabric. Take this one stage further and create a true three-dimensional look by making a shape and filling it with polyester stuffing and attaching it to a background fabric. Depending on the fabrics you choose, padded appliqué effects look really charming on folk-art designs and on projects for children, while three-dimensional work can look very contemporary or whimsical depending on the shapes used.

Preparing three-dimensional appliqué shapes is easy (see the technique opposite) and can become a feature on a quilt, or be used to embellish household textiles, clothing or to create toys and dolls. Flower petals and leaves are easy to make and varying the shapes will allow you to create a wide range of different flowers. Simple leaf and petal shapes can be seen on page 141, so you could enlarge those shapes on a photocopier and sew them as three-dimensional elements.

These starfish make a perfect subject for stuffed appliqué. They can be stuffed with small amounts of polyester filling (fiberfill) or wadding (batting). French knots add a tactile quality.

Needle-turn appliqué, blanket stitch appliqué and three-dimensional work give a tactile quality to a quilt – as this piece by Lynette Anderson shows (see it in full on page 144). The apples are given extra dimension by being padded and it's great fun seeing a design build up in this way.

>> **related topics...** *Fabric Special Effects 118 • Stuffed Quilting 226*   >> >>

THE TECHNIQUES

CREATING PADDED APPLIQUE

In this method the appliqué is lightly padded with a layer of wadding (batting) or some other material. One method for padding appliqué is to tack (baste) a layer of wadding beneath the appliqué piece before you begin to stitch it in place, making sure that the wadding is slightly smaller than the shape. An alternative method is to stitch

the appliqué to the base fabric as you would for needle-turn appliqué but leave a little gap to insert a tiny amount of stuffing using a toothpick or small crochet hook. Spread the stuffing out in a thin layer and sew up the gap with tiny stitches.

BRIGHT IDEA

AN OLD BLANKET MAKES A GOOD MATERIAL FOR PADDING AND CAN BE BOUGHT QUITE CHEAPLY AT CHARITY SHOPS OR THRIFT STORES. AN OLD WOOLLEN JUMPER CAN BE USED TOO — WASH AT A HIGH TEMPERATURE TO MILL OR FELT IT AND CUT IT INTO USEFUL SECTIONS.

SEWING THREE-DIMENSIONAL APPLIQUE

This form of appliqué takes padded appliqué one stage further, where shapes stand proud of the fabric. In this case the shapes are created first. Soft toys are often made with 3-D appliqué attached.

Method 1 – Use a template of the shape you require to mark a piece of fabric on the wrong side. Place a second piece of fabric right sides together with the first and use matching thread to sew them together along the marked line, leaving a gap to turn the shape through to the right side. If your shape is not symmetrical then the template must be reversed for the second shape. Cut the shapes ¼in (6mm) further out all round. Turn through, push the edges out smoothly all round and press the seams. Stuff the shape with polyester stuffing or tiny scraps of fabric offcuts. Turn the gap edges to the inside and slipstitch the gap closed. The shape can now be sewn in place on the background. ▶

Trim fabric for seam allowance

Sew on marked line

Fabrics right sides together

Leave gap

Method 2 – If the back of the three-dimensional shape will not be on show you can also prepare it as above but this time sew all around the edge of the shape, leaving no gap. With sharp scissors cut a small slit in the centre of the shape at the back, through one layer of fabric only. Turn the shape through and press the seam. Stuff as before and sew up the slit. Sew the shape to the background fabric from the wrong side of the background fabric. ▼

Sew up slit

Three-dimensional appliqué can be any shape you want and is very effective, especially when used on a fun soft toy like this chicken, made by Mandy Shaw.

make it now
Flower Power Tote

This bag is easy to make and could be used for a shopping trip, a day at the beach or just to store fabrics. The appliqué is a mixture of needle-turn and fusible web. Choose two bright batiks and a contrasting cream fabric. This bag has a 3in (7.6cm) depth created by sewing across the bottom corners.

profile

Skills practised: Needle-turn appliqué; fusible web appliqué; big stitch quilting; simple bag making
Finished size: 13in x 17½in (33cm x 44.5cm) excluding handles
Fabrics: One fat quarter each of two batiks; half a fat quarter of cream fabric for appliqué; lining fabric ½yd (0.5m); wadding (batting)
Threads: White and pale variegated perle cotton and machine threads

METHOD

- Cut an 11in x 18in (28cm x 45.7cm) piece of main batik. Cut a 3in x 18in (7.6cm x 45.7cm) strip from the second batik. Sew together along the long side with a ¼in (6mm) seam and press the seam open. Make a second pieced panel for the bag back but reverse the fabric colours.

- Use the flower template on page 251, preparing twelve petals using fusible web appliqué (see page 152). Fuse in place on the front panel, ensuring the circle shape will cover the petal ends. Stitch the circles in place with needle-turn appliqué (see page 145).

- Using one strand of perle cotton quilt around the petal edges and circles ⅛in (3mm) from the edge. Add variegated French knots in the centres.

- Make up the bag and handles as described on page 249.

FREEZER PAPER APPLIQUE

Freezer paper was originally a food wrapping material but was discovered by patchworkers in America in the 1970s and put to good use. Because freezer paper has a shiny, plastic-coated side it will stick to fabric when ironed, and can be removed and reapplied several times. It is thin enough to allow designs to be traced on to it and cut out. Instead of turning the appliqué seam under as you stitch it, freezer paper allows you to iron seams before the appliqué is sewn to a background fabric. It can be used in a similar way to the paper templates in English paper piecing. Freezer paper can be bought in rolls and in pre-cut sheets. The white waxy paper used to wrap reams of photocopying and printer paper can be used in a similar way.

>> related topics... *Using Templates 26 • English Paper Piecing 51 • Sewing Curves and Points 146* >>>

THE TECHNIQUES

FREEZER PAPER UP OR DOWN?

Freezer paper can be used shiny side up or down. When it is used shiny side *up*, the seam allowances are pressed on to the paper and temporarily stuck to it. The appliqué can then be sewn in place. The paper can be removed either just before all stitching is finished or after, by cutting a slit in the back of the appliqué.

When freezer paper is used shiny side *down*, the fabric is stuck to the paper but not the seam allowance. The allowance is pressed over the edge of the freezer paper to crease the seam all round. When all the edges are firmly creased, the paper can be removed and the appliqué sewn in place.

APPLIQUE USING FREEZER PAPER

The freezer paper appliqué method described here uses freezer paper shiny side up. A mini iron (see page 13) is a useful tool to have if you plan to do a lot of appliqué, as its smaller sole plate allows easier access to restricted areas of fabric.

1 Using a pencil draw or trace your pattern on to the smooth, non-shiny side of the freezer paper. Cut out the pattern on the drawn line. Place your appliqué fabric wrong side up. Place the freezer paper shape on top of the fabric shiny side up. Draw around the shape with a pencil. Cut out the fabric shape ¼in (6mm) further out than the drawn line all round, to allow for turnings. ▼

2 Place the freezer paper pattern shiny side up on the wrong side of the fabric within the marked shape. Pin in place if need be. ▶

Freezer paper

3 Using the point or side of the iron, turn the seam allowance over on to the paper all round and press into place, easing around curves to keep them smooth. If the pattern is tightly curved, clip the fabric at intervals to allow the edges to follow the curve more easily. The freezer paper will re-stick several times so you can peel the seam off it and re-stick it as necessary. ▶

Seam turned over and pressed/stuck on to freezer paper

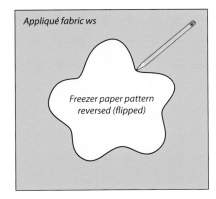

Appliqué fabric ws

Freezer paper pattern reversed (flipped)

FUSIBLE WEB APPLIQUE

Fusible web, also referred to as iron-on adhesive, is a brilliant man-made product that has many uses in patchwork and appliqué. It is made of an ultra-thin sheet of adhesive backed with a special paper. The adhesive melts when heated so when the web is placed between two fabrics the heat of an iron causes the glue to melt and fuse the fabrics together. Once fused, it forms a secure bond and prevents edges fraying.

Various manufacturers produce fusible webs and the specific type you use may depend on what is available in your area and your experience of using a particular brand. The most common ones are SteamASeam2 and Bondaweb (also known as Vliesofix in Europe and Wonder Under in the USA). Many brands are available via website stores. Fusible webs rely on the heat of an iron to melt the adhesive but brands do vary in their ease of use, so always read the manufacturer's instructions before use.

Most fusible webs can be washed and dry-cleaned. Over time and laundering, though, the fabric edges may still fray a little (and some fabrics are more susceptible than others) so it is a good idea to edge the appliqué pieces by hand or machine, unless you want that attractively rustic frayed look – see page 157 for examples and instructions.

STORING FUSIBLE WEB

The backings on fusible webs vary and some detach from the web more easily than others, which means you need to be careful how you store them. For fusible web available by the yard or metre, you could roll it up and store it in a rigid postal tube along with the manufacturer's instructions, with a label on the outside identifying the web. Alternatively, cut the web into A4-sized sheets and store in a plastic folder.

This festive wall hanging has squares fused on point to create a mosaic background, while the trees and moon are given more definition by a blanket stitch edging.

FUSIBLE WEB WEIGHTS

Fusible web is available in rolls in various widths (useful for hems, ribbon and so on), by the yard/metre in most quilting shops and fabric stores and in pre-packaged sheets. It is also available as pre-cut shapes and motifs. There are different weights of fusible web for different types of work, for example there is a heatproof type that is useful for place mats and table linen. If in doubt use the weight that is closest to the fabric you are using.

- **Lightweight web** – This is suitable for appliqué that will not receive too much wear and tear. It doesn't create undue thickness and is very easy to sew through.
- **Medium weight web** – This is slightly thicker and will form a firmer bond and, although it makes the fabric sandwich thicker, it is still easy to sew through by hand or machine. This is the weight commonly used for appliqué.
- **Heavyweight web** – This is the thickest type and can form a very strong bond between fabrics. It makes fabrics much more rigid, although this is an advantage if you want to create three-dimensional objects such as bowls. This rigidity makes fabrics more difficult to sew through so bear this in mind. It may also leave a gum residue on machine needles so these may need to be changed more often.

>> related topics... *Using Templates 26 • Raw-edge Appliqué 157* > > >

THE TECHNIQUES

FUSING A SINGLE MOTIF

Using fusible web to fuse a single, one-piece motif is easy. In a nutshell using any fusible web is a five-stage process: trace, stick, cut, peel and press. You can also use this technique to fuse fabric shapes into place for stained-glass appliqué. If you want your work to be easy to quilt, try using fusible web only as a narrow border around the edge of the shape.

1 Use a pencil to trace the heart shape on to the paper (smooth) side of the fusible web. Note: if the shape isn't symmetrical the shape will need to be reversed (flipped) before you trace it into the web – see technique overleaf. When the shape is traced, roughly cut out the shape about ¼in (6mm) further out all round. ▼

2 Place the shape on to the wrong side of the appliqué fabric with the fusible web (rough) side down (some webs have a backing sheet that has to be peeled off). Apply the iron to fuse the shape into place (usually about ten seconds but check the instructions). Allow to cool. ▼

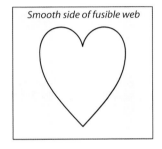

Smooth side of fusible web

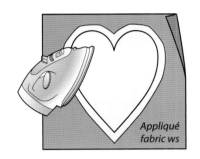

Appliqué fabric ws

BRIGHT IDEA

IF YOU DON'T HAVE ENOUGH FUSIBLE WEB FOR A DESIGN (AND SIMPLY CAN'T WAIT TO BUY MORE!) YOU CAN 'PATCH' SMALL PIECES TOGETHER TO COVER THE BACK OF THE FABRIC. CUT THE WEB PIECES WITH STRAIGHT LINE JUNCTIONS AND BUTT THEM TOGETHER.

3 Cut carefully around the shape on the marked line and peel the backing from the web. Place the appliqué shape right side up on to the background fabric (also right side up) in the correct position and fuse into place with the iron. ▼

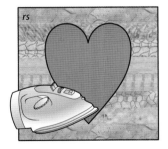

rs

Using Fusible Web

✓ Fusible web bought by the yard or metre should come with a sheet of manufacturer's instructions. Make sure this is included when you buy the product and read this at home before you start using the fusible web.

✓ There are various fusible webs on the market so try out a few and decide which you like best.

✓ Draw the design on the paper side of the web and use sharp scissors to cut the web. You might want to keep a pair of scissors just for this task to avoid blunting your fabric scissors.

✓ Avoid using fusible web on any fabrics with coatings on them – wash these fabrics beforehand to remove any sizing that may have been used to stiffen the fabric.

✓ Fuse the web to the fabric using a medium to hot iron with no steam for about 5–10 seconds (check manufacturer's instructions). The iron temperature will also depend on the fabric you are using – a more delicate fabric will require a cooler temperature.

✓ When fusing your pieces of fabric to the background fabric, position them where you want them, making sure the background fabric is crease free, and press without moving the appliqué piece.

✓ The fused area will retain the heat of the iron for a while and will be very hot, so take care. Allow the fused pieces of fabric to cool completely – the glue will then be set and the bond strong.

✓ If any of the glue from the web gets on your iron it can be removed with a commercial iron cleaner. You could protect the ironing board with a large sheet of greaseproof paper or baking parchment.

✓ There is also a spray glue that can be used as a fusible web.

REVERSING SHAPES

Fusible web is fused to the back of a fabric and the shape is cut out and fused to another fabric or a background fabric. However, some shapes are not symmetrical and therefore need to be reversed (or flipped over) so they appear the right way round once fused. For symmetrical shapes this flipping isn't necessary because the shape will appear the same either way. Some fabrics look the same from the right side and the wrong side (most batiks do), so you don't have to worry about flipping problems. In this case, simply use fusible web in the normal way and then use the reverse side of the fabric as the right side.

The bird motif shown here is not symmetrical, so if you want it to face towards the left it would need to be flipped. Draw the shape, flip it over and trace it that way on to the fusible web. Creating a template from plastic is useful as you only need to flip the template over and draw around it. ▼

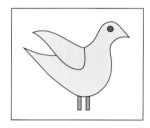

You can use this facility to reverse templates to your advantage. For example you can flip the bird template to create a partner for the first bird. ▼

You can also use just a few templates to create a combination of shapes that appear different. For example, this design uses only uses three templates – one flower, one leaf and one oval – but each can be flipped and rotated to create the impression of a more complicated design. ▼

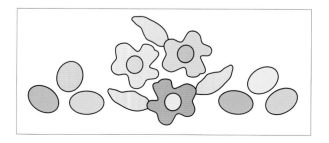

FUSING MOTIFS WITH MANY PARTS

Some designs are made up of more than one shape and some parts will need to be fused first, followed by others that overlap. A diagram of the finished pattern will help you, especially if you number the parts to remind you of the fusing order. If you are new to appliqué the simple tulip design shown below would be ideal to practise your skills. Only one tulip shape is needed, produced three times, with the right-hand flower tilted and duplicated as a reversed or flipped image for the left-hand flower. The leaf is repeated once as a reverse (flipped) image. For fusible web appliqué no seam allowance is needed but if you wanted to use the design for needle-turn appliqué or freezer paper appliqué then add a ¼in (6mm) seam allowance all round.

The stems are strips of ricrac braid but you could use bias strips (see page 177). These need to be fused or sewn into place first, so the raw ends will be covered. Fuse the rest in place as follows: 1 stems; 2 flowers; 3 right leaf; 4 left leaf. The dashed line shows where the left leaf should overlap the right leaf.

After fusing the edges in the sample shown above, they were decorated with three strands of stranded cotton (floss) and hand blanket stitch. Chained feather stitch decorates the leaf centres (see page 245 for working these stitches).

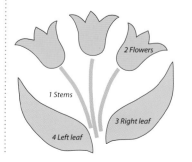

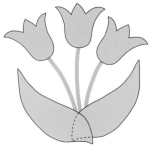

Daisy Cot Quilt

This little quilt uses fusible web appliquéd flowers on a background of pieced squares. Fresh, contemporary fabrics have been used but the design would suit any style and colours and could be scaled up to any size.

profile

Skills practised: Piecing squares; fusible web appliqué; blanket stitch edging; straight borders; machine and hand quilting; binding
Quilt layout: 5 x 3 appliqué squares, with two borders
Finished size: 46in x 30in (117cm x 76cm)
Fabrics: Fifteen 8½in (21.6cm) squares (white and cream); fifteen 7½in (19cm) print squares for appliqués; white border fabric 2in (5cm) wide x 140in (355cm); print fabric 2½in (6.3cm) wide x 155in (394cm); backing fabric; wadding (batting); binding 2½in (6.3cm) wide
Threads: Anchor perle cotton multicolour 1304; stranded cottons in mid green and cream and machine threads

METHOD

- Piece together the 8½in (21.6cm) white and cream squares in a 5 x 3 layout.
- Using the template on page 251 (enlarged) and fusible web, appliqué a daisy in each square. Edge the daisies with blanket stitch (see page 245) using one strand of perle cotton.
- Embroider flower centres with a circle of whipped running stitch (see page 247) in three strands of green stranded cotton, whipped with cream.
- Add the borders (see page 134). Make a quilt sandwich (see page 188). Machine quilt in the ditch between the squares and across flower petals. Hand quilt a loop pattern in the borders using variegated thread.
- Bind the quilt to finish (see page 238).

EDGING APPLIQUE

As you have seen with needle-turn appliqué, motifs and patterns can be attached to other fabrics with fine and unobtrusive slipstitches. This section looks at further treatments of appliqué motifs, including edging the motifs with decorative hand or machine stitches or deliberately leaving the edges ragged or frayed. Edging a motif with stitching not only gives a decorative quality but, if you have used fusible web to attach the appliqué, will make the cut edges of the fabric more secure and long lasting, especially if the item is to be laundered frequently.

Traditionally, certain stitches are used to attach or edge appliqué, including slipstitch or blind stitch, running stitch or topstitch, zigzag stitch, satin stitch and blanket stitch. You could experiment with many other stitches, such as chain stitch, herringbone stitch and long stitches for a more folk-art look. Refer to pages 245–247 for working these stitches. Edges can be worked by machine or by hand, depending on your preference and the effect you want to achieve. Choosing threads for edging appliqué is an enjoyable part of this process – see page 138 for advice.

Applique motifs can be edged with almost any stitch you like. One that covers the edge well is best, such as the blanket stitch used here.

Blanket stitch is a traditional edging for appliqué and this design by Lynette Anderson shows how charming it can look.

>> related topics... *Using Templates 26* • *Fusible Web Appliqué 152* • *Useful Stitches 245* >>>

THE TECHNIQUES

RAW-EDGE APPLIQUE

Raw-edge appliqué deliberately leaves edges raw, using very simple stitches to fix the appliqué in place, which can create a lovely rustic look. It is also perfect for fabrics that do not fray, including felt or faux suede materials such as Ultrasuede.

Cut your appliqué motif to the size and shape desired. Pin or tack (baste) in position on the background fabric and sew around the edge with a machine or hand stitch. (It could be fused into place with fusible web if desired.) The stitches used can be anything you like – a running stitch, intermittent long stitches, machine topstitch or wide machine zigzag. Sewing several rounds can look attractive. Stitches can blend with the fabric or make a feature of them by using vivid colours, shiny rayons, metallic threads or variegated threads. Using a tear-away stabilizer behind the background fabric will help to keep the work stable while you are stitching. Tear this away when you have finished, or leave in place for additional body.

These two appliqué motifs are in felt, so the edges can be left raw without fear of fraying. The appliqué was attached to the background fabric with simple stitches: the bird above with machine top stitch and the one on the left with a hand running stitch and long stitch.

FRAYED-EDGE APPLIQUE

You can go one stage further from raw-edge appliqué and make a feature of the edges by deliberately fraying them, which can look very 'arty' and attractive and is great for wall hangings. Some fabrics lend themselves to this treatment better than others so have fun and experiment. Denim works well and some solid-dyed fabrics have colourful edges that show up well when frayed; others, such as silk dupions and satins, may have differently coloured warp and weft threads, resulting in a frayed edge in a different colour, as below.

For frayed edge appliqué, sew or fuse the appliqué motif on to the background fabric as described above but leave the edges free. Again, the stitches can become an embellishment in their own right. Use a fingernail or nail brush to fray the edges. You could take this technique further and try chenilling (see page 119).

ZIGZAG STITCH EDGING

Zigzag stitch can be worked by hand but using a sewing machine is quicker. Zigzag stitching can also be used to couch threads, cords and ribbons in place. The instructions below for working zigzag stitch also apply to satin stitch. Sewing machines have various zigzag stitches so experiment first to find a stitch width and length you like. A wide, long zigzag will stand out more than a short, narrow one.

ZIGZAG ON STRAIGHT EDGES OR GENTLE CURVES

When zigzag stitching around straight edges or gentle curves follow the shape smoothly, as shown below. The needle needs to pierce the appliqué and the background fabric and follow the appliqué edge all round. Some people prefer that most of the stitch occurs on the appliqué, only entering the background fabric by a thread or two. Others prefer to have equal amounts on each side, especially if using a specialist thread. When stitching is finished, take the ends of the thread through to the back and tie off, or feed into the layers. ▼

ZIGZAG AROUND TIGHT CURVES

For stitching around tight curves, pivot the work to follow the shape.
- When sewing on a tight outer curve, as shown in the diagram below, stop the machine with the needle in the fabric on the outside of the curve and then pivot or turn the work a little. Move on a few more stitches and pivot again. The tighter the curve, the more often you will have to pivot, otherwise your curves will be stepped or jagged.
- When sewing on a tight inner curve stop with the needle on the inside of the curve and then pivot. ▼

ZIGZAG AT CORNERS

If the appliqué shape has sharp angles or corners the machine can be stopped at these points and pivoted to keep the edges neat. Finish off neatly as before.
- When stitching around an *outer* corner stitch up to the corner and stop the machine with the needle in the background fabric to the *right* of the shape. Lift the presser foot, pivot the work as shown so the next side to be stitched is in line and then continue stitching. ▼

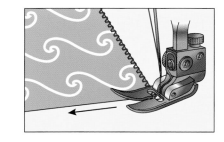

- When stitching around an *inner* corner stitch exactly up to the corner and stop the machine with the needle in the background fabric to the *left* of the shape, as shown. Lift the presser foot, pivot the work so the next side to be stitched is in line and then continue. ▼

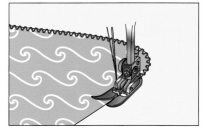

This piece by Gail Lawther shows how a beautifully worked satin stitch edging on appliqué in a contrasting colour can become the focal point of a design. The appliqué could also have been edged with a zigzag stitch by machine or a tight blanket stitch by hand.

SATIN STITCH EDGING

For many people, satin stitch by machine is the method of choice for appliqué. On most machines satin stitch is really just a tight zigzag with a shorter stitch length, so can be sewn in a similar way to that described for zigzag edging opposite. However, satin stitch and zigzag stitch are actually formed in slightly different ways, so if your machine has a dedicated satin stitch then use that rather than a zigzag. Study your sewing machine manual for settings for satin stitch.

Machine Satin Stitch

✓ *If you have a dedicated satin stitch on your machine select that, otherwise set your machine for a zigzag stitch with a stitch width of about ⅛in–¼in (3mm–6mm). About three-quarters of the satin stitch should be over the appliqué and the other quarter on the background fabric. If the stitch length is too short the machine may get stuck or clump the stitches.*

✓ *Satin stitch can pull on the fabric and cause it to pucker so use a tear-away stabilizer to help stiffen fabric. Spray starching may also help. To work well, satin stitch needs the correct tension and your machine may have automatic tension controls. Generally, a tension of about 3 works well. Ideally, the bobbin thread should not appear on the top – if it does then lower the top tension to a smaller number. You should see some of the top thread pulling through to the back.*

✓ *Practise on spare fabric first before moving on to your project.*

✓ *Decide how you want to work corners in satin stitch. You may want to keep the needle in the fabric and pivot or adjust the needle position – see zigzag stitch diagrams opposite.*

✓ *If the appliqué design has several parts, stitch the edges of the parts that are beneath others first.*

✓ *Satin stitch can be tapered to a point by gradually adjusting the stitch width as you sew. Some machines have this facility.*

✓ *Thread the needle with thread in a matching colour or complementary colour 60 weight embroidery thread. Use 50 or 60 weight cotton or polyester thread in the bobbin. If the bobbin thread shows through on the right side then match the top and bobbin thread colours.*

✓ *Use an open-toe foot and a Universal 70/10 needle in the machine. If the satin stitching looks jagged at the sides, change the needle to an Embroidery or Sharps.*

BLANKET STITCH EDGING

Blanket stitch is a very popular way of edging appliqué motifs. Many sewing machines today have attractive blanket stitch settings but many people love the appearance of hand-sewn blanket stitch because it creates a charming, folk-art look. It also looks lovely when worked with variegated threads, as shown in the Daisy Cot Quilt project on page 155.

Blanket stitch and buttonhole stitch are worked in the same way, with the spacing for buttonhole being much closer (see page 245 for working blanket stitch). When turning sharp corners, such as the points on leaves, make one extra tiny stitch on the spot at the corner to keep that long corner stitch in place.

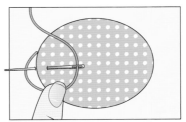

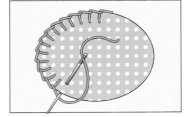

A blanket stitch edging on appliqué is very enjoyable to do. It can be done by hand in spare moments and brings a rustic charm. It can also be done by machine if your machine has blanket stitch as a decorative stitch.

OTHER APPLIQUE EDGINGS

If you love embellishing your work you could edge appliqué motifs with all sorts of braids, ribbons and trims. These can be sewn in place invisibly with tiny slipstitches and matching thread, or with decorative threads and embroidery stitches. They can also be sewn or couched in place by machine.

There are thousands of trims available today, many of which could be used as an edging or even an appliqué in their own right, such as the frayed-edge trim used in the ice cream cone shown here. Ricrac braid is great for edging appliqué as it can be made to curve. If the ricrac frays at the ends, turn the ends under and stitch in place.

REDUCING BULK

Once your appliqué motifs are in place you may wish to quilt the work, in which case the multiple layers may prove a problem. You may simply wish to lessen the overall bulk of the project and reduce the potential for puckers. Both of these problems can be reduced by trimming away some of the background fabric. Removing background fabric may, however, weaken the work and some people prefer to leave it intact.

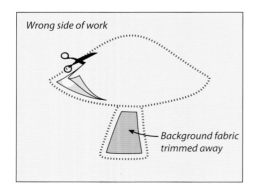

Wrong side of work

Background fabric trimmed away

To reduce bulk, turn the work so the wrong side is facing you and, using a small pair of sharp scissors, trim away the base fabric to within ¼in (6mm) of the seam allowance or appliqué edge. ◀

BRIGHT IDEA

DON'T LIMIT YOURSELF TO USING DECORATIVE STITCHES TO EDGE YOUR APPLIQUE. ADD STITCHES ON TOP OF YOUR APPLIQUE TO DRAW THE EYE TO A PARTICULAR AREA.

APPLIQUE PERSE

This appliqué technique involves cutting out specific pictorial motifs from fabrics and appliquéing them to a background fabric, which is usually plain. The technique is also called broderie persé, because people in 18th century England thought it resembled rich Persian embroidery. The technique was used then to get the most use out of expensive fabrics. Animals, birds, trees, flowers and figures were favourite motifs. Various ways of featuring appliqué persé were used, including tree of life designs, medallion-style arrangements and all-over patterns of individual motifs.

CHOOSING FABRICS AND MOTIFS FOR APPLIQUE PERSE

This picture gives some idea of what parts of a fabric could be used for appliqué persé work. Motifs outlined in blue could be used as they are 'entire'; those outlined in orange could not be used – this might be because they are too small, or that parts are overlapped by other motifs or are missing for other reasons, such as being too near the edge of the fabric.

- Choose fabrics with clearly defined motifs, which can be cut out entire and which are not overlapped by other motifs.
- Choose fabrics with decent-sized motifs as very small ones will make the appliqué work too fiddly.
- Add any details needed, such as butterfly antennae, flower stems and insect legs, with embroidery stitches after the appliqué is attached.

SEWING APPLIQUE PERSE

Appliqué persé can be done by hand or machine and is worked in the same way as needle-turn appliqué (see page 144) and fusible web appliqué (see page 152), so refer back to those subjects for detailed instructions. The only real difference is that you 'fussy cut' the appliqué fabric to encompass a specific motif. If using fusible web (shown in the diagram here), no seam allowance is needed. If using a needle-turn technique, allow the usual ¼in (6mm) seam allowance around each motif. ▶

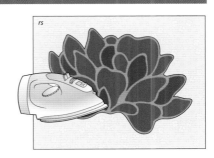

This detail from a wall hanging by Anne Davis and Julia Muxworthy shows appliqué perse motifs being used in both lower corners to link the border with the rest of the wall hanging. The peony motifs have been placed and sewn most beautifully so they spill over. Quilting further unites the main panel with the border.

HAWAIIAN APPLIQUE

Hawaiian appliqué is a very distinctive type of appliqué where traditionally bold, symmetrical designs are created using bright, plain fabrics. A large central pattern, called *kapa lau* by the Hawaiians, is first created by folding paper into eighths and cutting out an intricate design that radiates out from the centre. The design is then recreated in fabric by folding and cutting the fabric in the same way. Patterns were inspired by nature and include flowers, leaves and fruit.

Traditional fabric colours used for Hawaiian appliqué were bright, solid-dyed primaries against white or cream.

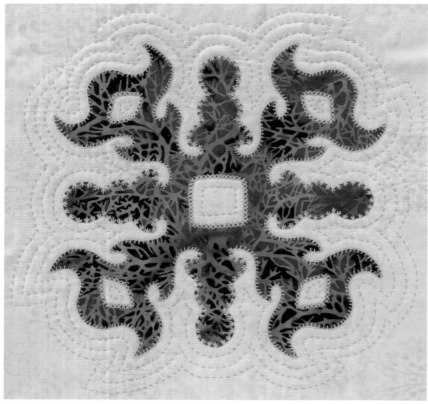

Traditionally, Hawaiian designs use bright, plain colours but today's fabrics are hard to resist and batiks do seem to follow the spirit of these colourful Pacific islands. Here, cross stitch, blanket stitch and chicken foot stitch (fern stitch) have been used.

Another distinctive feature of Hawaiian appliqué is the bold colouring used, normally two solids – a primary such as red, green, blue or orange – combined with white. Today, printed fabrics are popular too. Traditionally, Hawaiian designs only used a simple plain border, if any, but you could create a border design using a similar paper-folding technique if you wish. The quilting pattern in Hawaiian appliqué is almost always echo quilting, following the outline of the design and working outwards in a thread matching the fabric colour. Tahitian appliqué is similar to Hawaiian appliqué but the designs are based on a quarter fold not eighths. The finished quilts are 90in x 108in (228cm x 274cm); they could be worked on plain or printed fabric and are not quilted.

APPLIQUÉ METHODS FOR HAWAIIAN APPLIQUE

Once the pattern is created and cut out of the fabric the appliqué itself can be done in several ways.

- You could use a needle-turn appliqué method, tucking the seam allowance under all round and stitching in place, described on page 165.
- You could use freezer paper to turn under the seam allowances, temporarily sticking them to the freezer paper – see page 151 for the full freezer paper technique.
- You could use fusible web to fuse the pattern to the background fabric and then machine satin stitch it in place.

>> related topics... *Needle-turn Appliqué 144 • Sewing Curves and Points 146 • Freezer Paper Appliqué 151 • Fusible Web Appliqué 152* > > >

THE TECHNIQUES

MAKING A PAPER PATTERN

If you want to experiment with creating Hawaiian appliqué designs from paper, use cheap, thin paper that can be folded easily – newspaper will do. Once you have decided on the pattern and want to create a template for cutting fabric use a thicker paper.

1 Cut a square of paper a little larger than your appliqué design needs to be. Fold the square of paper from the bottom to the top (A), then fold the right edge to the left (B) and finally fold it diagonally, upper right to lower left (C). Make the creases sharp. ▼

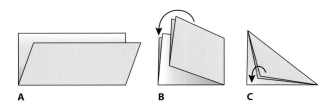

A   **B**   **C**

BRIGHT IDEA

IF YOU PLAN TO USE A NEEDLE-TURN APPLIQUÉ METHOD YOU NEED TO ENSURE THAT YOU HAVE ALLOWED ENOUGH FOR A SEAM ALLOWANCE. ONCE YOU HAVE DRAWN YOUR DESIGN, DRAW IT AGAIN ¼ IN (6MM) FURTHER OUT (SHOWN IN RED ON THE DIAGRAM, RIGHT). IF THE DESIGN IS CUT ON THIS LINE YOU WILL HAVE SUFFICIENT TO TURN UNDER ALL ROUND.

2 Draw your design on the triangle, remembering that the folded corner is the point the design should radiate out from. See also the Bright Idea below. If using a template, trace the design on to the folded paper. Shade the design area roughly with a pencil and mark a little cross near the corner point (D). Add a seam allowance if needed (E). Staple the paper layers together outside the design area to hold them in place. ▼

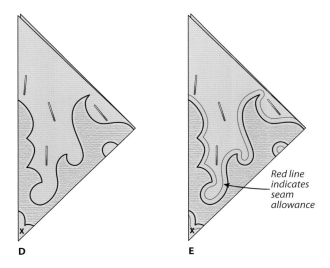

D   **E**

Red line indicates seam allowance

3 Cut out the pattern along your marked lines using sharp, paper-cutting scissors. At this stage you can adjust the design by cutting some parts a little bigger or smaller (remembering seams need to be allowed for). Make sure the design is connected on all folds, otherwise when unfolded some parts will be in pieces. ▼

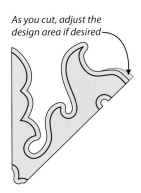

As you cut, adjust the design area if desired

4 Open out the paper to check you like the result. If the pattern is not interesting enough re-fold the paper very carefully and cut out more areas. If using the pattern as a template, cut out one-eighth of the design – your shaded area will make this easy. ▼

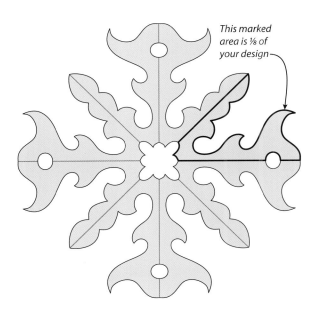

This marked area is ⅛ of your design

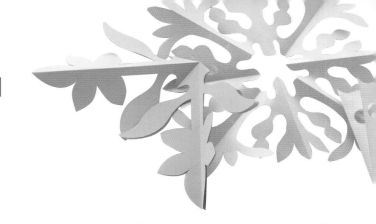

PAPER PATTERNS

If creating your own Hawaiian appliqué designs from scratch, make the design from paper first (see previous technique), to see if you like the finished result and to create a template to work from. This will also allow you to check the overall shape and see if there are any sharp corners that might cause difficulties when you come to stitch the design. It is easier to turn over seam allowances on gentle curves. Remember, too, that if using needle-turn appliqué to stitch the design in place you will need to allow for ¼in (6mm) seams all round. Three designs are provided below for you to use – enlarge or adapt them as you wish. Seam allowances are included.

When creating patterns, paper can be bought in large sheets from stationery suppliers. You could also buy a roll of cheap lining paper used for papering walls and ceilings.

DEVELOPING DESIGNS

A Hawaiian appliqué design with several interlocked patterns or repeated motifs can be created using the same technique, although this is a more complicated procedure. An easy way to develop a design is to use the same pattern to create numerous square blocks, piecing them together in the traditional way. The blocks could all be identical in colour and orientation or all different. The appliqué design could also be rotated 45 degrees on some blocks to create a more dynamic look – see diagrams below for examples. You could also use the three designs provided above to create a quilt with varied patterns.

Traditionally, Hawaiian designs had plain or no borders, but you could create a pattern to complement the central design. The easiest way is to cut up part of the original paper pattern to create a new template.

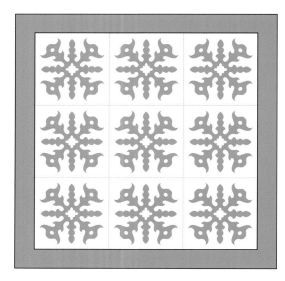

SEWING HAWAIIAN APPLIQUE

Traditionally this type of appliqué was sewn into place using a needle-turn technique, where a seam was turned under all round the design. Needle-turn appliqué is described in detail on page 145 but the basics are shown below.

1 Cut your square of appliqué fabric a little larger than your design and fold it in the same way as you did in step 1 of Making a Paper Pattern (see page 163), making sure the edges match and the folds are even, and ironing the fabric creases well between folds. Use your paper template (the one-eighth segment) to mark the pattern on the fabric. Match the edges and the corner point of the pattern with the corner of the fabric. Draw around the template to transfer the shape. Position the fabric bias direction on the side of the triangle that has one thick fold. ▶

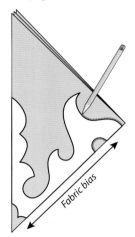

2 Pin the layers of fabric together so they don't move and then cut out the shape using sharp scissors. When the design has been cut out leave the fabric folded while you prepare the background fabric. ▶

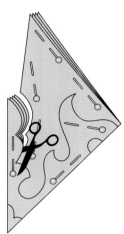

3 Cut your background fabric to the size required. Fold and press it into eighths as for the appliqué fabric. Open out and place on a flat surface. Open out the appliqué design carefully to avoid stretching. Put the appliqué on the background, aligning the grain lines and matching up the creased lines and centre point. Pin the fabrics together from the centre outwards. Tack (baste) the fabrics together about ½in (1.3cm) away from the edges. ▼

4 With small, sharp scissors, clip just up to but not into the seam allowance on tight curves and corners. Now use a needle-turn technique to turn a ¼in (6mm) seam (or less) under all round, stitching into place with small, close stitches in a thread colour to match the top fabric. When the appliqué is sewn in place remove all the tacking stitches carefully and press the work. The appliqué is now ready for quilting. ▼

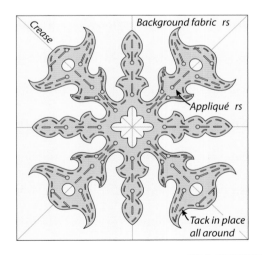

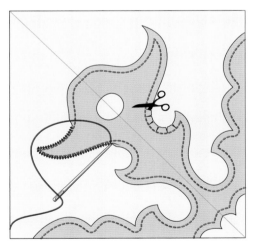

QUILTING HAWAIIAN APPLIQUE

Traditionally this type of appliqué is echo or contour quilted, which means following the lines of the design out in a radiating, wave-like pattern using thread that matches the fabric colour – see page 216 for technique. You may find quilting easier if you cut away the background fabric within the appliqué design, to reduce layers and thus bulk. Turn the appliqué over to show the wrong side and with small scissors, cut away the background fabric to within ¼in (6mm) of the stitches. ▶

REVERSE APPLIQUE

In this technique a shape is cut in an upper layer of fabric and the seam allowance turned under and stitched down to reveal the fabric layer beneath. It is the opposite of normal appliqué – instead of adding fabric you are removing parts of it. Reverse appliqué often features many layers of fabric and creates an interesting recessed look and adds shape, colour and texture to a project.

The technique can be a little tricky and a successful result is more likely to be achieved if you are careful which fabrics you use – those that resist fraying are the easiest. Reverse appliqué can be done by hand or machine and both methods are described opposite. If working by hand, a seam allowance needs to be turned under all round. If working by machine the most common method is a satin stitch edging, in which case no seam allowance is needed. Excess fabric can then be trimmed away.

This is a genuine mola design from the San Blas Islands worked in reverse appliqué. Five layers of fabric have been used here, all decorated with hand stitching.

MOLA WORK

The Kuna Indians on the San Blas Islands, off the coast of Panama, use a reverse appliqué technique to create their mola work. Mola means 'shirt' or 'clothing' and the mola is part of the traditional costume of the Kuna women. Many layers of cloth are stitched together, with geometric designs cut out to expose underlying fabric colours. For some decades now these brightly coloured molas have featured other designs, including birds, flowers and animals. The largest pattern is cut from the top layer of fabric, with progressively smaller motifs cut from the subsequent layers.

The quality of a mola is judged by several factors, including the number of layers, the width and evenness of fabric cut-outs, the fineness of the stitching, colour combinations and embroidery. Today, mola blouses are still worn as part of the traditional costume but molas are also made into pillows, wall hangings, place mats and framed pictures.

Reverse Appliqué

✓ If you are new to the technique use just two or three layers of fabrics until you have developed your skills and confidence.

✓ If you are a beginner use closely woven fabrics such as 100 per cent cottons as these resist fraying and take a crease well.

✓ When learning the technique select a simple design without too many sharp points or angles.

✓ If working on a large design, increase the amount of tacking (basting) used to keep the layers in place and stabilized while stitching takes place.

✓ When choosing fabric colours, placing dark colours on top of light ones will avoid seam allowances showing through.

✓ Fabric combinations are endless but try strong plains combined with small prints or try using a pieced fabric for the lower layer to create an unexpected look.

✓ Use a removable stabilizer at the back of the work when machine satin stitching to avoid puckers.

✓ Keep your master design handy so you can check your work.

✓ When working with many layers you can reduce bulk by trimming off excess fabric from the back of the work after the appliqué is finished.

> > related topics... *Using Templates 26 • Needle-turn Appliqué 144 • Sewing Curves and Points 146 • Satin Stitch Edging 159* > > >

THE TECHNIQUES

REVERSE APPLIQUE BY HAND

This description for reverse appliqué by hand uses just two fabric layers but once you are familiar with the technique you can use many more. Turning in the seam allowance on the top fabric uses the same technique as needle-turn appliqué.

1 Cut your two fabrics to the size required (allowing at least 2in (5cm) extra) and layer them together, right sides up. Press them together using spray starch between the layers to make them more secure. Draw the design in pencil on the top fabric using a template or dressmaker's carbon paper to trace the design. ▼

2 Pin the fabrics together and then tack (baste) through both layers of fabric around the shape, about ½in–1in (1.3cm–2.5cm) outside the drawn line (see Bright Idea below). You could add more tacking (basting) if the design is a large one. ▼

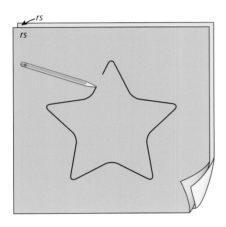

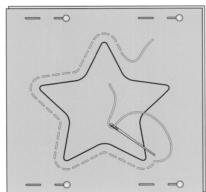

BRIGHT IDEA

YOU MIGHT FIND IT EASIER TO CUT OUT THE SHAPE *BEFORE* PINNING AND TACKING (BASTING) THE FABRIC LAYERS TOGETHER. RE-POSITION THE TOP FABRIC ON THE LOWER FABRIC WHEN THE SHAPE HAS BEEN CUT OUT, THEN TACK (BASTE) TOGETHER.

3 Using sharp scissors, cut away the design from the top fabric ¼in (6mm) *inside* the drawn line, following the shape (the seam allowance). You could mark this first if you prefer. Do *not* cut into the lower fabric. If the design has curves and angles, snip the seam allowance regularly up to but not into the drawn line. ▼

4 Using a thread that matches the top fabric, take small slipstitches through to the bottom layer of fabric, turning the seam allowance under as you go. Work your way around the design until all raw edges are hidden. ▼

5 When all stitching is finished remove the pins and tacking (basting). If you wish the work to have greater stability then leave the fabric layers in place. Alternatively, turn to the wrong side and trim away the excess second layer fabric.

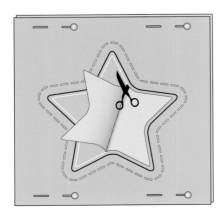

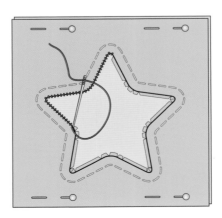

WORKING WITH MULTIPLE LAYERS

If working with three or more layers of fabric, follow the same process as described on the previous page. Think about the design and plan all the stages before you begin cutting and sewing. The following points should also help.

- Press and then layer all the fabrics, tacking (basting) them together through all the layers. A little spray starch will help keep the layers together.
- Mark the design on the top layer of fabric. Cut out the shape, being careful to cut through only the top layer of fabric. Turn under the seam allowances and sew as described before. Diagram A below shows the blue as the top fabric layer, cut away and sewn to reveal the second white layer.
- After the first layer of reverse appliqué is finished, put your master pattern back in place and draw the second part of the design on the second fabric layer (the one just revealed). In the case of the swan this would be the areas in yellow, shown in diagram B. Cut away the newly drawn shape being careful to only cut through the second layer. Repeat the cutting and sewing process. At each stage you need to sew through all fabric layers.

- You might find it easier to make templates of all the parts of the master design. Number them with the fabric layer – 1 for the top layer, 2 for the second, 3 for the third and so on. As you work down through the layers you then only need to select the relevant template and position it according to the master design before drawing around it.
- Put the pattern back in place and draw the next part on the third layer of fabric (the lemon colour on the swan). Repeat the cutting and sewing process.
- Repeat the process for the fourth layer (orange). The bottom layer (the black on the swan) should remain intact to act as a foundation for all the other layers.
- Additional pieces of fabric can be added to a layer by cutting the shape required, turning the exposed edges in and sewing it in place right side up with neat little slipstitches. The eye of the swan could be done in this way.
- You can 'jump' fabric layers if required, cutting through more than one layer. In this case turn under the seam allowance on the upper layer, folding it under to encompass the cut edge of the layer below.
- If a fabric layer is cut by mistake you can repair it by inserting a piece of matching fabric. This must be larger than the cut-out area. If the area is quite small you can use your needle to poke it into place, making sure it is flat and that any subsequent stitches pass through it to anchor it.

A

BRIGHT IDEA

REVERSE APPLIQUE IS PERFECT FOR FEATURING SPARKLY FABRICS. THOSE THAT ARE SEQUINNED OR HEAVILY EMBROIDERED WILL PROVIDE SOME STUNNING EFFECTS WHEN REVEALED BY THE CUT LAYERS.

B

1st (top) layer of fabric	4th layer
2nd layer	5th (base) layer
3rd layer	

This elegant block, made by Pam Croger during a Lynne Edwards' sampler quilt course, is a good example of reverse appliqué using several layers of fabric.

REVERSE APPLIQUE BY MACHINE

The method for reverse appliqué by machine is essentially the same as for hand reverse appliqué but the cut edges are not turned under but satin stitched instead. Using a tear-away or other form of removable stabilizer will help prevent the puckering that sometimes occurs with satin stitch. You could also secure the cut edges using a close buttonhole if your sewing machine has that facility. The description below shows just two layers of fabric plus a stabilizer.

1 Cut your fabrics to the size required (allowing extra for finishing) and layer, right sides up with tear-away stabilizer beneath. Press and then draw the design on the top fabric using a template or dressmaker's carbon paper to trace the design. ▼

2 Pin the fabrics together and then tack (baste) through all layers of fabric around the shape, about ½in–1in (1.3cm–2.5cm) outside the drawn line. Add more tacking (basting) if the design is a large one. ▼

3 Using a small pair of sharp scissors, cut away the design from the top fabric just inside the drawn line (about ⅟₁₆in/1.5mm), following the shape – there is no seam allowance in this method. Do not cut into the lower fabric. ▼

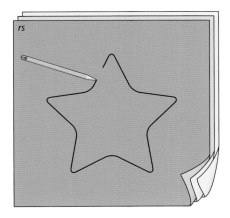

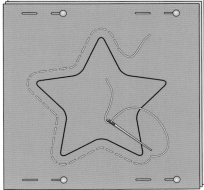

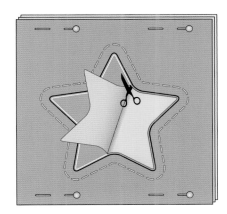

4 Select a close satin stitch on your machine and sew around the shape, covering the raw edges and stitching through all layers (see Satin Stitch Edging on pages 158–159 for more advice). ▼

5 When all stitching is finished remove the pins and tacking (basting). If you wish the work to have greater stability then leave the fabric layers in place. Alternatively, turn the work to the wrong side and trim away the excess second layer fabric. If working with three layers of fabric a second design can now be marked on the second fabric layer and the process repeated to reveal the third layer, and so on.

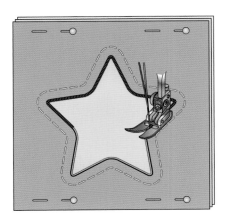

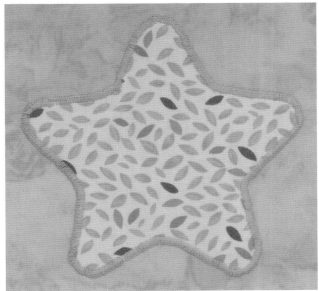

SHADOW APPLIQUE

No fabric is safe from the avid patchwork, quilting and appliqué fan, and shadow appliqué is a wonderful technique that uses delicious transparent fabrics such as silk gauze, chiffon and georgette to create beautiful and delicate effects. In this appliqué technique, an appliqué design is sandwiched between a background/ base fabric layer and a top, transparent fabric layer. Stitches are then worked around the appliqué outline, through all layers. The sheer top layer can be left in place or trimmed away from the edges of the appliqué motif.

A veritable bouquet of sheer fabrics that are perfect for shadow appliqué work. Many quilt shops and online stores sell 'taster' packs of mixed colours.

Shadow appliqué has a delicate appearance as the motifs and colours are softened by the transparent fabric. It is thus very suitable for a range of projects, including clothing, particularly evening wear, and household items, such as cushions and curtains.

FABRICS FOR SHADOW APPLIQUE

The fabrics used for the top sheer or transparent layer can include net, voile, organza, nylon, organdie, tulle, chiffon or georgette. Sheer fabrics have some wonderful finishes, including crystal, pearlized and gilded. Others are available with jewels or sequins attached to the fabric.

The fabrics used for the appliqué design and the base or background fabric can be anything you like, from completely plain to densely patterned – indeed, patterned fabrics once covered by the sheer fabric can yield some attractive results. When choosing fabrics for the appliqué remember that the colours will be toned down and lightened by the sheer layer, so choose bright or distinctive colours and try out the effects before you cut your appliqué shapes.

You can be as inventive as you like with materials used for shadow appliqué and once you are familiar with the technique experimenting can be great fun. Try overlaying one sheer fabric with another. Ribbons and trims can also be used.

Flower motifs are perfect for shadow appliqué. Here, a Mackintosh rose design was used to decorate a simple drawstring bag. The shadow layer was edged with a trim glued into place.

COLOUR COMBINATIONS

If a white or very pale sheer fabric is used for the top layer then the colour of the fabric beneath (both the appliqué fabric and the background fabric) will be lightened in tone. Some interesting colour combinations can be achieved by using a coloured sheer as the top layer as this will change the hue of the lower fabric. Refer also to the colour wheel on page 19 for more details about colour combinations.

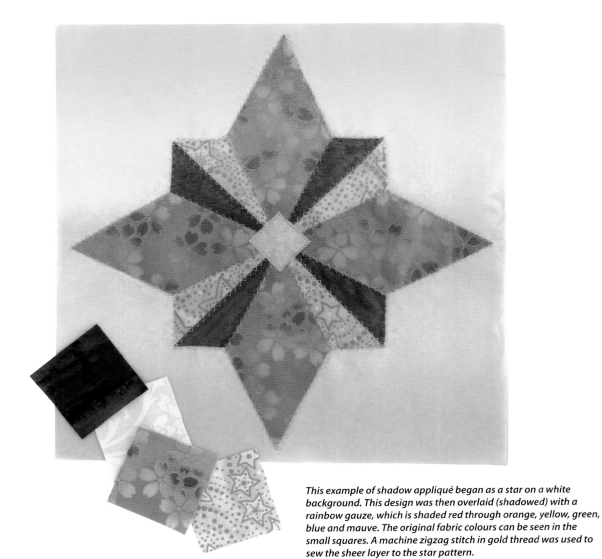

This example of shadow appliqué began as a star on a white background. This design was then overlaid (shadowed) with a rainbow gauze, which is shaded red through orange, yellow, green, blue and mauve. The original fabric colours can be seen in the small squares. A machine zigzag stitch in gold thread was used to sew the sheer layer to the star pattern.

Shadow Appliqué

✓ *If you are new to shadow appliqué then for your top sheer layer use net, nylon, organdie, voile or organza as these fabrics are easier to handle, being a little stiff.*

✓ *When you are more experienced with the technique you could try chiffon or georgette, which are a little softer and floppier.*

✓ *Experiment with recycled fabrics – even old net curtains can be used. Bridal shops and those that make and sell ballet clothes may have small offcuts you could use.*

✓ *Use fabric scraps to experiment with colours and the different combinations and effects that can be achieved.*

✓ *Choose bright colours for the base fabric and/or appliqué as this will be muted by the top transparent layer of fabric.*

✓ *Simple appliqué shapes work best, resulting in a clean, pure look that is very attractive.*

✓ *You could use a glue stick to fix the appliqué shapes on the background fabric or fusible web for more lasting security.*

✓ *For a subtle look, match your thread colour to the appliqué/ sheer colour.*

✓ *To create details, such as flower stamens and veins on leaves, you could use a darker or contrasting thread. Decorative embroidery stitches could also be used.*

✓ *If trimming away parts of the gauze, leave a wide margin in case the fabric frays, or oversew it securely or cover with a trim.*

>>> related topics... *Marking Fabrics 25 • Fusible Web Appliqué 152 • Edging Appliqué 156* >>>

THE TECHNIQUES

SEWING SHADOW APPLIQUE

This technique creates a beautiful, delicate look and can be quite addictive! The instructions assume the use of fusible web to fix the appliqué shapes to the background fabric but you could use a glue stick for a quicker result. The appliqué design can be marked on the fabric either freehand or using templates or another marking method of your choice.

1 Iron your fabrics if necessary to remove any creases, being *very* careful if ironing the transparent fabric to avoid shrivelling or scorching it. Mark your appliqué design on your fabric (or fabrics if using more than one). Back the appliqué fabric pieces with fusible web and cut out the shapes on the marked lines. ▼

2 Peel off the backing from the fusible web and position the appliqués where you want them on your background fabric. Press with an iron to fuse the appliqué into place and allow to cool. ▼

3 Cut your transparent fabric so it is slightly larger than the background fabric. Place the sheer fabric on top of the background/appliqué, smooth it flat and pin or tack (baste) the layers together. ▼

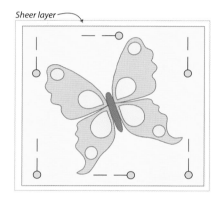

Sheer layer

SHADOW APPLIQUÉ PLUS

If you like being creative you can experiment with unusual materials under the shadow layer, such as the metallic flakes used in the centre of the flower in this sample. Sequins would also look good. A visit to your local paper crafting store should provide other ideas, but remember that unusual materials may not be washable.

4 Stitch around the appliqué shapes, through all layers, just inside the shape. Normally a matching thread is used for this stage. You can now choose whether to cut away the sheer fabric from the background or leave it in place. If cutting it away use small, sharp scissors and trim very carefully. Do not cut into the stitches around the appliqué and leave at least ¼in (6mm) all round to allow for fraying. You can now add any extra details required with surface embroidery, such as the butterfly antennae and any other decorative embellishments. ▼

make it now
Butterfly Bag

This sweet little bag is perfect to show off some shadow appliqué. It could be used as an evening bag or to store favourite pieces of jewellery. Batiks were used for the butterflies with yellow gauze for the shadow layer. The gauze was trimmed to a curved shape and edged with ricrac but could cover the whole bag front if desired.

profile

Skills practised: Fusible web appliqué; shadow appliqué; simple bag making
Finished size: 11in x 10in (28cm x 25.4cm) excluding handles
Fabrics: Fat quarter of print fabric for bag outer and handles; scraps of batik for appliqué; yellow gauze; fat quarter of lining fabric; wadding (batting)
Threads: Stranded cottons to suit appliqué and machine threads to match fabric
Embellishments: Ricrac braid and four buttons

METHOD

- Cut two pieces of bag fabric 12in (30.5cm) square. Use the template on page 251 to cut the large butterfly parts from batik fabrics and use fusible web appliqué (see page 152) to fuse the shapes on to the bag front piece. Add smaller butterflies too if desired.

- Cut a piece of gauze to fit over the butterflies and use quilting stitches to sew it in place all round the butterflies. Sew the antennae using long stitches and finishing with French knots (see page 246).

- If trimming the gauze to a shape, use a short machine stitch to sew the shape first before trimming excess gauze and edging with ricrac.

- Make up the bag, the lining and handles as in steps 1–4 of the Flower Power Tote bag on page 249. The handles could be sewn between the layers of the bag or attached on the outside with buttons.

INLAID APPLIQUE

Normal appliqué, such as that described in fusible web appliqué on page 152, is a *laid on* approach, where a shape is laid on top of another fabric and stitched down. In *inlaid* or inlay appliqué, the same pattern is traced on two different fabrics and both are then cut out carefully, with one shape laid seamlessly into the other and sewn into place. This technique is most attractive if two contrasting fabrics are used and two mirror-images can be produced from one marking and cutting procedure.

Inlaid appliqué works very well with felt as the edges do not fray, so if you are a beginner this would be a good fabric to start with – the hand technique described opposite uses plain and patterned felt. Inlaid appliqué can also be done by machine, where the junction between the two fabrics is covered by machine satin stitch. There are also variations possible with inlaid appliqué. For example, the inlaid part may be edged with decorative cord or floss silk couched into place. In the past, strips of cut silk or narrow ribbon were stitched over the edges to keep them flat.

These two mirror-image inlaid appliqué cushions make an attractive pair. One has cord couched in place while the other is edged with whipped running stitch.

>> related topics... *Using Templates 26 • Freezer Paper Appliqué 151 • Edging Appliqué 156*   > > >

THE TECHNIQUES

INLAID APPLIQUE BY HAND

This is the simplest form of inlaid appliqué. The featured design needs to be marked and cut out identically on two fabrics. Using felt has the advantage of not fraying.

1 Iron your two fabrics if necessary to remove any creases. Mark your design on the right side of both fabric pieces, making sure that the shapes are *identical* – using a template will ensure this.

2 Cut out the design with sharp scissors, either on each piece of fabric in turn, or layer the fabrics together, pinning securely, and cut through both layers simultaneously. Alternatively, use masking tape to fix the fabrics to a cutting mat to keep them flat and steady while you use a sharp craft knife to cut out the design. Follow the marked line accurately. ▼

3 Now swap the two shapes over, putting the cut shape of one fabric into the hole of the other fabric. ▼

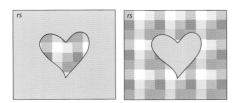

4 Sew around the edges of the shape to secure the shape to the background. Stitches used can vary – try invisible slipstitching or a decorative stitch such as cross stitch. Before sewing the shapes into place, it is helpful to stabilize the fabrics (so the inlaid part doesn't keep falling out of the hole as you stitch it in place). Iron a thin, fusible interfacing to back the whole area of inlaid fabric.

INLAID APPLIQUE BY MACHINE

A feature of the machine method is that satin stitch or another decorative machine stitch is worked along the design edge, covering any cut edges.

1 Prepare your two fabrics as described in steps 1–3, left. Once the pieces are fitted together, back the whole piece with fusible interfacing to stabilize the work. The interfacing must cover the area where the pieces fit into one another. ▼

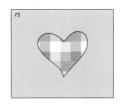

2 Using a wide machine satin stitch, sew all around the design shape, covering the raw edges of both fabrics. ▶

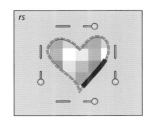

BRIGHT IDEA

YOU COULD EXPERIMENT WITH OTHER DECORATIVE MACHINE STITCHES. USE THOSE THAT ARE WIDE ENOUGH TO COVER BOTH FABRIC EDGES AND DENSE ENOUGH TO PREVENT FRAYING.

INLAID APPLIQUE WITH FREEZER PAPER

One way to create perfectly identical shapes for inlaid appliqué is to use freezer paper. One of the fabrics needs to be flipped (reversed) compared to the other fabric, so it is important that at least one of the fabrics looks good from either the right or wrong side. Plain solids and many batik fabrics can often be viewed from either side.

Back each piece of fabric with freezer paper so the freezer paper is stuck to the wrong side of each fabric. Using a glue stick, glue the two pieces of freezer paper together. Mark your design on the right side of one of the fabric pieces, and cut out the design through all layers simultaneously. Peel off the freezer paper and swap the shapes over, putting the cut shape of one fabric into the hole of the other fabric. Remember that one of the fabrics will need to be flipped – both its cut-out parts and the background. The shapes will fit into the opposite background fabric holes exactly and create a smooth surface.

BIAS STRIP APPLIQUE

Stained-glass appliqué and Celtic appliqué are two techniques that use bias strips to outline the parts of a design in a bold and highly distinctive way. The fabric strips are cut on the bias to take advantage of the 'give' or stretch of that fabric direction, allowing the strips to be curved more easily. The bias strips can be handmade or bought and can be sewn in place, fused or attached by a machine satin stitch. Stained-glass appliqué mimics the look of stained-glass windows, where the parts of the design are interconnected and lead off to the edges of the design. Celtic appliqué does not tend to connect to the edges, having designs that are more self-contained. The intricate knots of Celtic art are popular motifs.

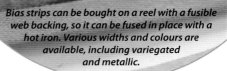

Bias strips can be bought on a reel with a fusible web backing, so it can be fused in place with a hot iron. Various widths and colours are available, including variegated and metallic.

STAINED-GLASS APPLIQUE

Stained-glass appliqué was inspired by the stained-glass windows seen in churches and grand houses, where bold, colourful shapes are used to build up an image and outlined with strips of lead. Fabric bias strips are used in this form of appliqué to mimic the lead. Colours tend to be jewel-like, to mimic glass. This type of appliqué is also very effective used over a wholecloth panel or pieced work, to perhaps frame a view or represent window and door frames.

   For ideas on stained-glass appliqué designs look at stained-glass windows in churches and civic buildings, wrought iron work and the glass creations of Art Nouveau artist Louis Comfort Tiffany. Bold shapes work best, where parts of the design can retain their shape when outlined by the bias strips. The strips don't have to be black but can be any colour you like or be created from patterned fabric. If the design is a geometric one with straight edges, such as the wall hanging design shown here, you could use ribbon instead of bias strips. The project on page 182 features a more organic flower design, which does require bias strips.

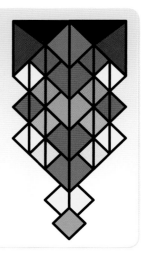

Stained-glass appliqué can create stunning images, especially in the hands of a talented designer like Brenda Henning. The marbled fabrics used here cleverly convey the translucent look of brilliantly coloured stained glass. The piece was made by Beke Jameson (see Suppliers on page 253).

CELTIC APPLIQUE

This form of appliqué is inspired by the wonderfully intricate patterns of Celtic art – the spirals, knots, fret and key patterns and zoomorphic motifs seen on ancient stone crosses and in illuminated manuscripts of the medieval period. Celtic designs can also be used as quilting patterns – see page 204. A feature of Celtic appliqué is that the bias strips interlace, winding over and under each other in a seemingly never-ending pattern. They do not normally connect to the edges of the background fabric as stained-glass appliqué does.

Celtic appliqué ideas can come from many sources and there are commercial patterns available. The designs can also be contemporary ones. A knot pattern could be sewn just with bias strips, as the little pillow on the right has been, or the areas of the knot could be filled with coloured appliqué. Celtic patterns are also perfect for creating larger designs by repeating and mirroring motifs to build up a more complex design.

A simple knot design is easy to achieve with fusible bias strips and here is teamed with a pretty fabric and some simple echo quilting.

Even a simple Celtic design is often quite flexible: fill the areas of the knot with appliqué or multiply the motif to create a more complex pattern.

BIAS STRIPS

Bias strips are very useful in patchwork and appliqué and can be used for many designs, particularly as plant stems in appliqué work. You can make your own bias strips and either stitch or fuse them in place, or buy ready-made tape that has a fusible web backing. Making your own bias strips will allow you to use any fabric or even pieced fabrics – see technique overleaf. There are two gadgets that make this process easier and quicker – a bias bar and a bias maker. These are available in various widths, with the ¼in (6mm) and ½in (1.3cm) widths being the most useful.

DESIGN CONSIDERATIONS

- Don't have design elements that are too small and fiddly. Choose the bias strip width that will be in scale with the overall design.
- If sewing stained-glass appliqué make sure all shapes have 'exit' lines leading off to the sides of the design, and that they don't float and finish in mid-design.
- You don't have to use solid colours for bias-strip appliqué – try bias strips made from patterned fabric. Although stained-glass windows often use bright, plain colours, artists such as Tiffany and Galle produced their own glass with patterned, multicoloured and iridescent effects.
- Batik fabrics change colours and shapes across the fabric, so can be useful in creating an interesting look to a design. Some fabrics are graded in colour and these too can be used to create a different look.
- There are books of stained-glass and Celtic appliqué patterns you could use for inspiration. Try childrens' colouring books too for bold patterns with easy shapes. Wallpaper pattern books may also give you ideas.

Any appliqué motif can be adapted for bias strip appliqué – enlarge the motif and use a thick black marker pen to outline the design areas to get some idea of how a finished design might look. This contemporary-style butterfly appliqué started out this way.

>>> related topics... *Using Fabric Grain 23 • Marking Fabrics 25 • Fusible Web Appliqué 152 • Satin Stitch Edging 159* >>

THE TECHNIQUES

MAKING BIAS FABRIC STRIPS

The method for making bias strips for stained-glass and Celtic appliqué is the same as making strips to create bias binding for a quilt. The important thing is that the strips of fabric must be cut on the fabric bias so they are stretchy – one time when bias edges are a blessing, not a curse!

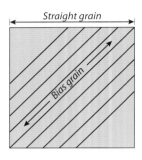

Straight grain

Bias grain

1 Decide what width your bias strips need to be. Place your fabric on the cutting board and determine which way the bias grain is running (it will be stretchy). Use a rotary cutter to cut parallel lines across the fabric in the bias direction. ◄

2 Place two strips right sides together at a 45 degree angle and sew a ¼in (6mm) seam. Continue to join strips in this way until you have sufficient for your needs. Press seams to one side. ▶

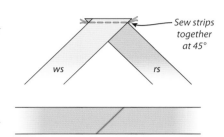

Sew strips together at 45°

ws   rs

BRIGHT IDEA

TO CALCULATE THE LENGTH OF BIAS STRIP REQUIRED, USE A LENGTH OF STRING OR WOOL, FOLLOWING THE LINES OF THE DESIGN. MEASURE THE STRING AND ADD A BIT MORE.

3 Now that you have your lengths of bias-cut strips the edges can be pressed under to create bias binding. You can do this yourself or use a bias maker – see below. The flat bias-cut fabric strips can also be turned into bias tubing using a bias bar or bias press bar.

USING A BIAS MAKER

Once you have cut your fabric strips on the bias this handy tool provides a quick way of turning the edges under. Your fabric strip needs to be ¼in (6mm) wider than the finished size of the tape, which will be the size of the narrow end of the tool. You could use spray starch before you begin to create sharper creases.

Begin to feed the fabric strip into the tool, guiding it along through the slit in the top of the tool with a pin. As it emerges from the other end you will see that it is folded at each edge. Press this folded strip with an iron to set the creases and slowly pull the tool away from the iron, moving the iron along the folded strip. ▼

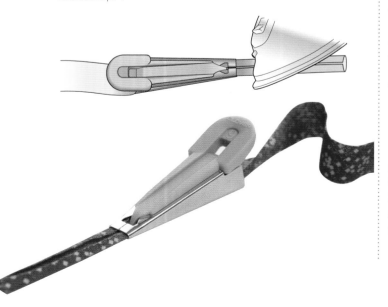

USING A BIAS BAR

Using a bias bar helps to turn bias-cut strips into a tubular form. The bars come in different widths so choose the width you need your finished bias strips to be – ¼in (6mm) and ½in (1.3cm) are the most commonly used sizes.

1 Bias fabric strips need to start off wider than the finished width: to calculate this, double the finished width and add ½in (1.3cm) for the seam. So if you want the finished tape to be ¼in (6mm) wide: ¼in (6mm) + ¼in (6mm) + ½in (1.3cm) = 1in (2.5cm) wide. If you want the finished tape to be ½in (1.3cm) wide: ½in (1.3cm) + ½in (1.3cm) + ½in (1.3cm) = 1½in (3.8cm) wide. With wrong sides facing (right sides out), fold the fabric in half lengthwise and machine a ¼in (6mm) seam along the length. Trim the allowance to a scant ⅛in (3mm). ▶

rs

2 Push the rounded end of the bias bar inside the fabric tube – it should be a snug fit. Turn the tube so the seam lies flat on the bar and press with an iron. If your strip is a long one, keep threading the tube on to the bar and pressing, slipping the pressed section off the other end. The strip is now ready to use. ▶

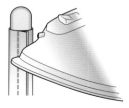

SEWING STAINED-GLASS APPLIQUE

Stained-glass appliqué could use homemade bias strips or commercial bias tape, which may be fusible or sew-on. These instructions are for sew-on strips – see overleaf for using fusible strips. The project on page 182 has a more intricate design.

1 Draw the design full size on paper and number the shapes. Transfer the design to the right side of your background fabric using the method of your choice. Do not transfer the numbers, only the outline shapes. You could use coloured pencils to colour your paper design, indicating the shades of fabrics you plan to use. ▼

2 Cut the numbered shapes from your paper pattern and use the pieces as templates to cut out the shapes in the fabrics you have chosen for the appliqué. No seam allowances are needed. If some pieces are the same colour and next to each other cut the piece out as one shape. An easier way is to use fusible web to back your fabrics so when they are cut out you can fuse them into place on the background. The project on page 182 was made with fusible web. ▼

3 Put the fabric shapes in position on your background fabric and tack (baste) them in position, recreating the overall design shape (or fuse them if you have used fusible web). You could also keep the shapes in position using tacking (basting) glue. ▼

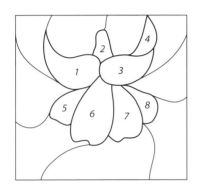

4 At this stage you need to plan which areas of bias strip need to be applied first, so all starting and finishing points are covered. Some lines will need to be covered by others, while some may end outside the design area, to be trimmed off or sewn into a seam later. One way of ensuring the correct order is to plan the route using coloured pens to denote what lines are sewn 1st, 2nd, 3rd and so on. The diagram here shows the order of stitching for this design. ▼

5 If using sew-on bias strips, start with the lines shown in turquoise on the diagram. Pin or tack (baste) the strip in place, folded side down. The bias stretch will allow you to ease the strip around curves but pin inner curves first to avoid puckers. Make sure the outer edges extend past the planned edge of the design. Stitch the strip in place with little hem or slipstitches. Where the raw ends of a strip will be covered by another strip, butt the end up against the shape. If using fusible bias strips, see overleaf. ▼

6 Once the first strips have been sewn in place, add the second set (shown in red in the diagram with step 4). Then add the third set (green), and so on. If a curve is too acute, form a single little pleat to mimic a mitre. Remove tacking (basting) when all stitching is complete. Add any details with embroidery. Trim the design to the required size. ▼

Sewing order
Petals are shown in pale grey so coloured lines can be seen more clearly.

———— 1st
———— 2nd
———— 3rd
———— 4th
———— 5th
———— 6th

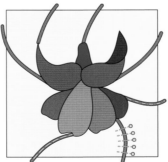

USING FUSIBLE BIAS TAPE

Fusible bias tape is a very useful product that relies on the heat of an iron to melt the glue on the back of the tape and fuse it to the ground material. For additional security the tape should then be stitched in place with tiny stitches in thread matching the tape.

Use the tape in the same way as sew-on bias strips but instead of pinning and stitching in place the tape can be fused immediately with a hot iron following the lines of the pattern. If you use the nose and side of the iron you will find that the tape can curve around acute angles (a mini iron is useful here). If fusing to delicate fabrics, use a thin fabric as a press cloth. Press from the back of the work too, to help the glue melt and fuse. You will still need to plan your route carefully to ensure that the parts of the design that stand forward are fused last. Follow the diagram with step 4 on the previous page.

SEWING CELTIC APPLIQUE

This technique is very similar to stained-glass appliqué except that the route of the bias strips is planned to wind over and under other areas of the design to create an unending look. You could also fill parts of a design with fabric, as described in stained-glass appliqué.

1 The knot pattern shown below has three distinct paths, which could be strip-appliquéd in three different colours or in a single shade, as shown. ▼

2 Use dressmaker's carbon paper to trace the design through the centre of the strips, shown here in red for clarity (A). Leave small gaps where one line goes under another. Transfer just those thin lines on to the right side of your fabric (B). The marked design will eventually be covered by bias strips but you could use an erasable marker if you prefer. Now prepare bias strips (see page 178) in the width and colour needed – a design may use more than one width and several different colours so plan ahead. You may need to join bias strips together to ensure they are long enough. ▼

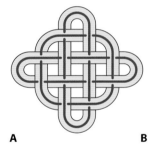

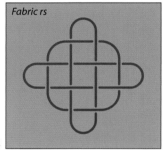

A   B

Fabric rs

3 Place the bias strip seam side down, centrally over the marked line of the design at a point where it will eventually be covered by another length of bias strip. Pin or tack (baste) in place if you wish or just sew directly into place with tiny stitches and matching thread. ▼

4 Continue stitching the bias strip in place, easing it around curves. If the strip passes *under* another line then just continuing sewing. If the strip passes over another line in the design leave a 'bridge' or gap for the 'under' strip to pass through later on. ▼

5 When the strip needs to go under a bridge, feed the end through, flatten the strip and stitch in place. Sew up the gaps in the upper strip. To start a new part of the design or new strip, hide the end under a bridge. Continue this way all round. To finish, tuck the end of a strip under the stitching or fold under and sew down. ▼

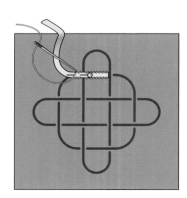

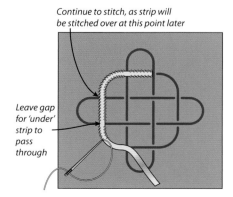

Continue to stitch, as strip will be stitched over at this point later

Leave gap for 'under' strip to pass through

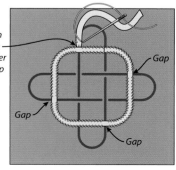

If starting a new part of the design or strip, hide the end under a bridge (gap in stitching)

Gap

Gap

Gap

CELTIC APPLIQUE WITH MACHINE STITCH

Instead of using hand stitches to secure the bias strips in place or fusible tape you could use machine satin stitch or a narrow zigzag. As described in Sewing Celtic Appliqué opposite, leave gaps in the machine stitching for the 'under' strips to pass through. Take care to start and stop satin stitch neatly and use the same stitch width throughout. Using a stabilizer under the fabric before you begin to stitch will minimize the undulations that can occur with dense satin stitch. See page 159 for more on working satin stitch.

This wall hanging by Gail Lawther makes a wonderfully bold yet stylish statement. This piece is an example of appliqué edged with machine zigzag stitch, but the appliqué pieces could also have been edged with satin stitch or blanket stitch.

FUSIBLE WEB CELTIC APPLIQUE

Instead of using bias strips for Celtic appliqué you can cheat and create the illusion of strips using fusible web appliqué and some carefully placed machine satin stitch. See page 153 for using fusible web.

1 Cut your appliqué fabric larger than the design and fuse fusible web on to the back. Trace the design on to the back, that is, the paper side of the web, and then cut out the design all round with sharp scissors. Carefully cut out the 'holes' in the design too. ▼

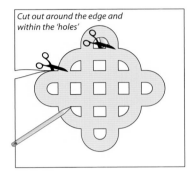

Cut out around the edge and within the 'holes'

2 Take a piece of contrast background fabric and fuse the appliqué design to the right side of this. With a pencil lightly draw in the lines showing where the 'unders' and 'overs' should go (shown in red on the diagram below for clarity). ▼

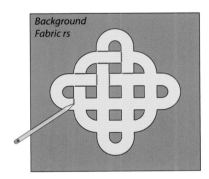

Background Fabric rs

3 Begin to satin stitch on your lightly marked lines, starting and stopping where the design goes under and over. The satin stitching is shown in red here for clarity. Once finished, the design will look as if the fabric is weaving under and over. ▼

make it now
Stained-Glass Fuchsia

This wall hanging was made using silk dupion to mimic the shine of coloured glass. Refer to the bias strip techniques on pages 179 and 180.

METHOD

- Enlarge the template on page 252 to full size and make two copies. From one copy cut out the flower shapes. Cut background fabric 15in x 19in (38cm x 48cm) and use pins to mark out a rectangle 8¼in x 12¼in (21cm x 31cm) – see diagram on page 252.
- Cut 3in (7.6cm) squares of fabric in the chosen colours and apply fusible web. Mark the shapes on the paper side of the web, cut out and position on the background. Fuse into place.

profile

Skills practised: Bias-strip appliqué; bagging-out; making hanging loops
Finished size: 13½in x 21in (34.3cm x 53.3cm)
Fabrics: Assorted scraps of silk each about 3in (7.6cm) square; background fabric; fusible web; fusible bias strip 5½yd (5m); backing fabric; wadding (batting)
Threads: Hand sewing thread in dark green and purple
Embellishments: Five seed beads

- Fuse the bias tape in place around the edges of all the shapes, following the diagram order. Lightly draw in the 1st round of lines (turquoise on diagram) by eye or trace, using the uncut template. Strip ends not covered by other strips need to be turned under and stitched down.
- Sew the stamens using purple thread and whipped backstitch, with a purple seed bead on each end.
- Make up with or without a border – see page 249.

SHISHA

Shisha embroidery, also known as mirror work, is an Indian technique where small pieces of mirrored glass or shiny metal are attached to fabric. Shisha work originated in Persia and the shiny glass pieces were thought to ward off or reflect away the evil eye. The technique is a form of appliqué that creates a bright, sparkling look and originally was used to decorate and create focal points on many items, including clothing, wall hangings, domestic textiles, curtains and torans (door hangings).

Shisha embroidery is easy to do and can be worked randomly or in patterns on fabric.

Originally, shisha work used mica flakes and then hand-blown mirrored glass cut into small pieces, usually round but sometimes square and triangular. A distinctive framework of stitches was developed to hold the mirror in place and cover the sharp edges. The stitches worked around the edge can be decorative ones, such as herringbone, cretan or fly stitch (see page 245 for working these stitches). Safer reflective materials are used today, including sequin shisha, which are large, flat sequins, and plastic shisha. Little embroidered rings are also available, which are placed over the mirror and stitched in place with tiny stitches. Various types of thread can be used for shisha embroidery, such as stranded embroidery cotton and perle cotton in a number 5 or 8 gauge. You could also use the shisha stitch to attach jewels, coins and flat beads to fabric.

WORKING SHISHA STITCH

The initial framework of stitches (shown in pink in the diagrams below) is used to anchor the subsequent stitches around the edge of the mirror (shown in green). The tightness of the initial framework determines how much of the mirror shows – a loose tension allows more mirror to show.

1 Hold the mirror in place with a spot of craft glue or double-sided tape. Knot the thread and begin at the back of the work, bringing the needle through to the front and crossing the mirror in the grid-like sequence, looping each thread as you cross it, as shown in diagrams A, B and C. ▼

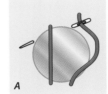  

2 Now start the outer ring of stitches – these are shown in green in diagrams D, E, F and G below but are normally the same colour as the initial framework. Follow the sequence shown, working all around the edge. These outer stitches will pull on the inner framework to reveal more of the mirror. To finish, secure the thread firmly on the back of the work. ▼

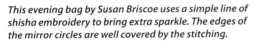

This evening bag by Susan Briscoe uses a simple line of shisha embroidery to bring extra sparkle. The edges of the mirror circles are well covered by the stitching.

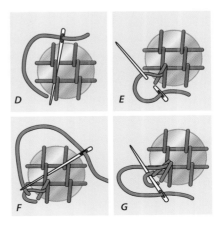

Quilting

At its most basic, quilting is used to secure the layers of a quilt top, wadding (batting) and backing, but it can do much more than this and over the centuries quilting has become as much a part of the creative process as patchwork and appliqué. In its many forms, quilting is increasingly used to complement and accentuate pieced work with a highly decorative and sometimes tactile quality. Quilting designs can be stitched by hand or machine or a combination of both, and be anything from simple straight lines to intricate patterns, and some wonderful techniques have been developed to showcase different effects and threads.

This section looks at a wide range of quilting techniques, as well as the basics on choosing and marking designs and preparing to quilt. You might prefer the slower but calming techniques of hand quilting, including big stitch, Japanese sashiko and Indian kantha work. You can explore the creative possibilities of machine quilting, including the all-over patterns created by free-motion machining. Raised quilted work has many fans, and techniques such as corded quilting and stuffed quilting create stunning padded effects, especially when combined with densely quilted areas.

Of course, quilting doesn't have to be a hand running stitch or a machine straight stitch. You can tie the layers together with bright threads or shiny beads and buttons. You can also use some fabulous decorative stitches for quilting to bring a new dimension to your work.

PREPARING TO QUILT

Before you start quilting, whether by hand or by machine, ensure that you have the correct materials and equipment for the job. The quilt or project will need to be prepared for quilting. Some people prefer to mark the quilting pattern before the quilt sandwich is prepared, while others like to do this after – see page 194 for marking designs. The top needs to be secured in a sandwich with wadding (batting) and backing fabric. For some projects you may think that a quilt-as-you-go method, that is, quilting blocks as they are made – see page 222 – is suitable.

CHOOSING THE RIGHT MATERIALS AND EQUIPMENT

There are many quilting techniques but for most you will really only need needles, threads, a thimble and a sewing machine. Quilting stencils are useful for marking designs. See pages 10-13 for general information on patchwork, appliqué and quilting supplies.

The thread used for the quilting in this quilt by Christine Porter echoes the blue in the blocks and shows up well against the pale fabric. A curved quilting design also provides contrast against the linear patchwork.

Quilting threads – Threads used depend on the type of quilting and each section gives details of choices. The colour of the thread can match the fabric or contrast with it, depending on the effect you want to achieve. The greater the colour contrast and the bigger the quilting stitch, the more the quilting will draw the eye.

For hand quilting, as a general rule, use 100 per cent cotton quilting thread as it is thicker than ordinary sewing thread. For a more decorative effect try using embroidery threads and crochet cottons.

For machine quilting, 100 per cent cotton thread is a popular choice for both the top thread and in the bobbin. Nylon monofilament thread is often used as it is nearly invisible and is available in clear for light fabrics and tinted for darker fabrics. Avoid using hand quilting thread as it has a wax coating that can damage the tension discs on a sewing machine.

Needles – These depend on the type of quilting you want to do and the fabrics and threads you are using, see also page 23. A curved needle may help when tacking (basting) the quilt layers together.

For hand quilting use Quilting needles (or Betweens), which are short and strong enough to make several stitches through the quilt layers. The shorter the needle, the shorter the hand-quilted stitches can be, so start with a size 7 or 8 and work up to a shorter size 12. Big stitch quilting often uses thicker threads, so a needle with a larger eye may be needed. Italian quilting requires a large-eyed tapestry needle or bodkin to thread thick yarn through narrow channels.

For machine quilting, needles need to be sharp to pierce all the quilt layers. The size of needle used will depend on the thickness of wadding, so try a 75/11 for thin wadding and increase to a 80/12 or 90/14 for thicker ones. There are also needles designed to work with special threads. Insert a new needle at the start of each new project.

Pins – Quilting pins and safety pins can be used to secure the layers of the quilt sandwich together. Curved safety pins are easier to insert than straight ones. Consider that pins may get in the way if you intend to quilt within a hoop.

Spray glue – Spray glues are useful for fixing the layers of a quilt sandwich. These can usually be removed by washing or dry-cleaning . They are useful for smaller projects and are designed to be sprayed on to the wadding (batting). Avoid contact with the right sides of fabrics. Always read the instructions for the product.

Sewing machine – Any sewing machine can be used but newer machines will have helpful features, such as the following.
- A large throat area between the needle and motor, so it is easier to move a bulky quilt through the opening.
- A walking foot or other fabric-feed mechanism, for keeping the top and bottom layers of the quilt moving through the machine at the same rate. An open-toe walking foot will allow better visibility when quilting, especially in the ditch.
- Feed dogs that can be dropped down or covered for free-motion quilting.
- A darning or quilting foot, which is useful for free-motion quilting.

CHOOSING BACKING FABRIC

In most cases the quilting done on the front of the quilt will show on the back. Backing fabric is usually chosen to coordinate or link with the front of the quilt and is normally calico or plain or printed cotton in a similar weight to the quilt top, although you might choose a different backing material depending on what the quilt is being used for. For example, a child's quilt that is meant to be soft and snuggly might use a soft fleece or mink backing.

For a large quilt the backing may have to be pieced, although there are extra wide fabrics, 60in (152cm), 90in (228cm) and 108in (274cm) wide, available if you want to avoid this. A pieced backing does add an extra dimension to a quilt and is great for using up fabrics left over from piecing the quilt top. The piecing might be simple strips, large squares or a combination of both – see examples below.

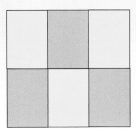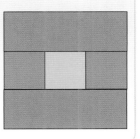

CHOOSING WADDING (BATTING)

There are various types of wadding made from different materials and blends, and the sort you choose depends on the type of quilting you intend to do and how the item will be used. Some waddings are fine for machine quilting but are more difficult to hand quilt through, while others work best for tied quilts. Some need to be quilted at quite tightly spaced intervals, such as 3in (7.6cm), while others may only need to be quilted every 10in (25.4cm) or so. The thinner the wadding, the easier it is to hand quilt through. See page 16 for more on wadding choices.

If a piece of wadding isn't large enough it can be joined to another piece by butting the straight edges together and working a ladder or herringbone stitch or machine zigzag stitch along the edges.

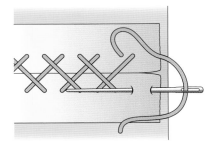

THE QUILT SANDWICH

Before quilting can begin, a quilt has to be assembled in three layers – a top, a middle of wadding (batting) and a backing – and these must be secured prior to quilting. The sandwich can be secured in various ways, the main ones being tacking (basting), pinning, safety pinning, gluing or using plastic tacks from a tacking gun. Whichever method you choose it needs to ensure that the quilt sandwich is smooth and fastened at regular intervals so that none of the layers move or wrinkle during the quilting. The quilt sandwich could be prepared on the floor or a very large table.

The wadding and backing need to be at least 2in (5cm) larger than the quilt top to allow for the size reducing as the quilting is done. If sending the quilt to a long-arm quilting service, check the size they require as 4in–6in (10.2cm–15.2cm) larger may be preferred.

>>> related topics... *Estimating Fabric Requirements 22 • Preparing Edges and Squaring Up 234*

THE TECHNIQUES

PREPARING A QUILT SANDWICH

This method assumes the use of tacking (basting) or safety pins to secure the layers but the principles are the same for other methods. A tacking gun shoots plastic tacks through the layers and requires a plastic grate to protect the carpet. The quilt top can be marked before or after preparing the sandwich.

1 Prepare the backing fabric by trimming off the selvedges and pressing. If pieces have to be joined, avoid a central seam as this will receive wear if a quilt is folded for long periods. Press seams open. Prepare the wadding (batting), making sure it is flat and large enough to fit the quilt. Iron the quilt top, ensuring that seams are lying flat and that the edges are straight and square. Trim if necessary.

2 Find an area large enough to lay out the quilt and place the backing fabric right side down, squared and with wrinkles smoothed or patted out. Use low-tack masking tape at points around the backing to fix it to the surface (or use pins if on a carpet). Put the wadding on top of the backing fabric, centring and smoothing it, and tape/pin in place. Place the quilt top right side up on top of the wadding, centring and smoothing it, and tape/pin in place. ▼

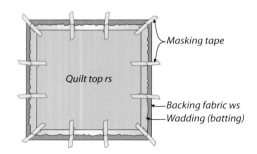

Masking tape

Quilt top rs

Backing fabric ws
Wadding (batting)

3 Begin to tack (baste) the layers together, working from the centre outwards in a grid (A) or radiating pattern (B). You may find that a curved needle will help this process. The finished lines of tacking (basting) need to be about 4in (10.2cm) apart to secure the layers firmly. Alternatively, use safety pins to secure the layers (C). When the layers are secured remove the tape. ▼

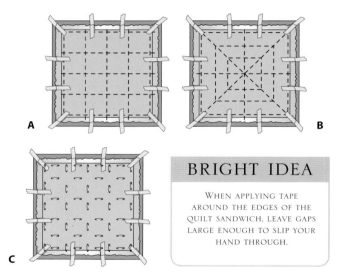

A

B

C

BRIGHT IDEA

WHEN APPLYING TAPE AROUND THE EDGES OF THE QUILT SANDWICH, LEAVE GAPS LARGE ENOUGH TO SLIP YOUR HAND THROUGH.

USING A SPRAY GLUE

Spray glues should be used *lightly* and be sprayed on to the wadding (batting). Always read the manufacturer's instructions for the product you choose to use. Long-term effects of glue on fabric are not known so it is best to wash the finished quilt to remove any glue used. For a large project that may take some time to quilt it might be wiser to use the tacking (basting) or pinning method.

1 Work in a well-ventilated area. Protect the floor or surface from over-spray with scrap paper. Prepare the quilt sandwich following steps 1 and 2 above.

2 Carefully turn back half of the wadding (batting). Shake the can of adhesive really well and, spraying *lightly* from a distance of about 10in (25.4cm), spray the half of wadding that is turned back. Roll the wadding back over the backing fabric and smooth in place. Repeat with the other half. ▶

Backing fabric ws

Spray glue on this half of wadding

3 Now position the quilt top right side up on top of the wadding and smooth in place. Turn back half of the quilt top. Shake the adhesive well and spray the half of the wadding that is showing. Carefully fold the quilt top back over the wadding and smooth in place. Repeat with the other half of the quilt top, spraying the remaining half of the wadding. ▼

Spray glue on this half of wadding

Fold back quilt top

CHOOSING QUILTING DESIGNS

There are so many wonderful quilting designs you can use to enhance your patchwork and appliqué projects. This section gives ideas on what to quilt and makes some suggestions on how blocks might be quilted. Obviously, there isn't room here to show you lots of different permutations but there are many books available (see Further Reading on page 252).

CHOOSING WHAT TO QUILT

As with all aspects of patchwork, appliqué and quilting, people have their favourites. You might get the most pleasure from perfect piecing or adventurous appliqué or intricate quilting, so think about this when deciding how much quilting and what type to do. If quilting isn't your thing then the layers of the quilt can simply be held together with machine quilting in the ditch or tied quilting, or the quilt can be sent away to a long-arm quilting service to produce something wonderful for you. Even if you like quilting you might have a preference for hand quilting rather than machine or vice versa, or love combining the two. So choose what gives you the most pleasure.

A successful quilt will look balanced, and good planning will avoid some areas being quilted to death while others look bare. Don't rush when deciding what to quilt – there is nothing wrong with quilting some basic areas – in the ditch, outlining and so on – and then making other decisions as you go along.

What to Quilt?

When deciding what to quilt the following ideas might help.

✓ Do a colour drawing of your block or quilt top, or take a photo and print it, and sketch in quilting ideas with a pencil. If you make several photocopies before you begin sketching you can try out a number of ideas.

✓ Cut out basic shapes, such as circles, ovals, squares, kites, stars or hearts, in thin tracing paper and place these on your design to see what might work.

✓ The fabrics used may help you decide what patterns to quilt, so look for motifs used in the fabric – stars, hearts, circles, flowers and leaves occur often.

✓ If the quilt design is a single repeated block, look for patterns that occur when the blocks meet, such as stars, diamonds or circles, which might provide inspiration for a quilting pattern.

✓ If the pieced top is an intricate one with lots of small pieces, an all-over quilting pattern might work best, such as those produced on a long-arm quilting machine.

✓ Contour or outline quilting might be all that is needed to emphasize appliqué motifs. Alternatively, work the outline of the appliqué motif in quilting in plain blocks.

✓ Choose patterns and motifs that complement the style of the quilt. If you have used traditional colours and fabrics, then choose traditional motifs. If your project has a contemporary look, abstract patterns might work well.

✓ Consider the borders – a quilting pattern can be extended into the borders to produce a satisfying and coherent look to a quilt.

✓ Plan your quilting according to the fabrics being used, for example, quilting will not show up as well on densely patterned fabrics, whereas it will stand out clearly on plain fabrics.

✓ Resist adding too many different quilting patterns to a single project as this may detract from the finished result.

An abstract quilting design can look most effective if it echoes the patchwork design, as in the landscape on this stylish bag by Susan Briscoe. Straight or zigzag lines are very easy to quilt.

TYPES OF QUILTING PATTERN

There is no doubt that quilting can enhance a quilt and bring a new dimension to it and before choosing a marking method you need to decide what type of quilting to do. Some examples of commonly used types are shown below. Some are more suited to machine techniques, while others can be worked by hand. See pages 215–216 for instructions.

In-the-ditch quilting

This type of quilting follows the seam lines of patchwork blocks and is the least visible as it is normally done with matching or invisible thread. It is also useful for securing the basic areas of a quilt prior to more detailed quilting.

Crosshatched (grid) quilting

This is simple linear quilting, which is quick and easy to do. Straight and diagonal grid patterns not only hold the quilt layers in place well, but are also good at emphasizing specific areas of a quilt.

Outline (contour) quilting

This follows patchwork and appliqué shapes and is normally done a consistent distance away from the shape, usually ¼in (6mm) or ⅜in (1cm). Using the width of the machine walking foot is the easiest way to achieve a consistent spacing.

Echo quilting

This is similar to contour quilting but repeated lines are quilted outwards, like waves lapping out from a shore. It is a feature of Hawaiian appliqué and is a really easy way to quilt a design. It can be done by hand or machine.

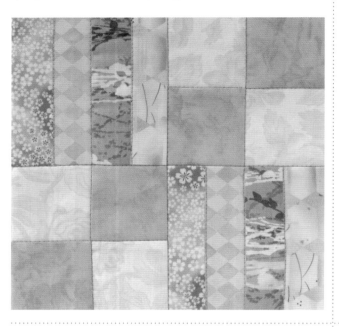

Motif quilting

Quilted motifs may be small pictorial patterns or larger, elaborate ones that can be used in the centre of medallion quilts. The motifs may be in a specific style, such as Celtic or Art Nouveau. Motif patterns can be used to quilt border corners or sashing keystones.

All-over quilting

This is normally worked by free-motion quilting using a freehand doodling technique or a repetitive pattern can be built up using a long-arm quilting machine. Such patterns could also be worked by hand quilting.

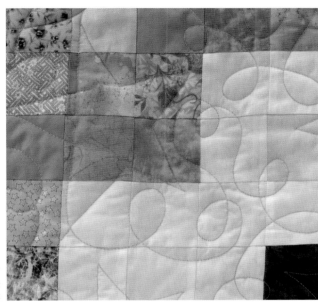

Repeat pattern quilting

These are quilting patterns that repeat regularly within a quilt. They are often linear and so are useful for borders. Cable and feather patterns are common examples and can be quilted by hand or machine. Many templates are available commercially.

Vermicelli quilting

This is a free-motion technique where tight curving lines are stitched in meandering, uninterrupted patterns. This type of quilting may be referred to as stipple or infill quilting. You could also work seed stitches in a similar way, randomly over parts of a quilt or block.

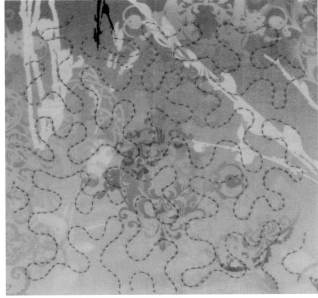

QUILTING BLOCKS AND BORDERS

The wonderful thing about quilting is how it can change the look of a patchwork block or group of blocks, emphasizing the pattern or creating a visual complement to it. For example, curved and circular quilting patterns work well with linear blocks, while linear or grid quilting patterns can bring a new dimension to curved patchwork designs. Setting identical blocks together in a quilt can create new opportunities for quilting. Some examples of quilting patterns for blocks and borders are shown below and opposite.

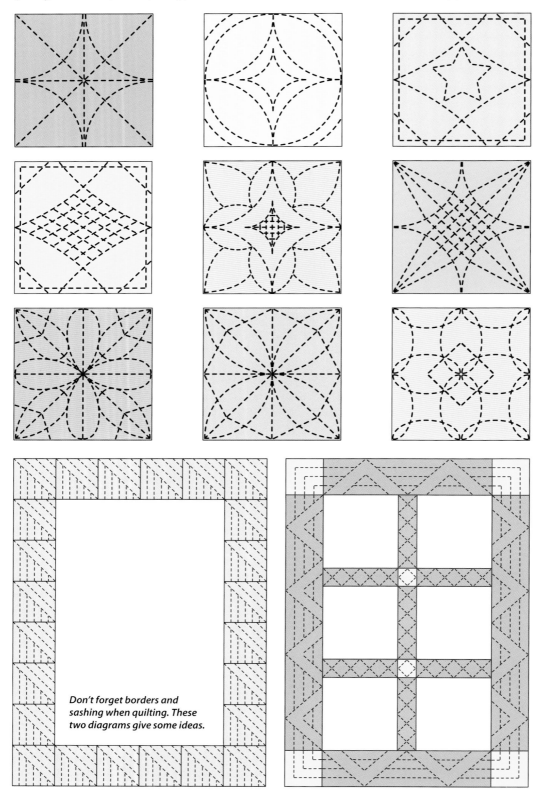

Don't forget borders and sashing when quilting. These two diagrams give some ideas.

Tumbling Blocks could be quilted with lines to accentuate the linear pattern or curves as a contrast.

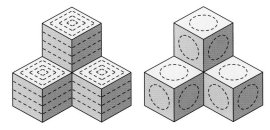

Inner City is another tessellating block that can be quilted with lines or curves.

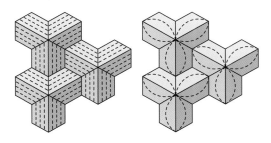

A Spinning Star block singly and in a group of four, quilted in a simple linear pattern to accentuate the star design. The space created by the junction of four blocks allows for further quilting.

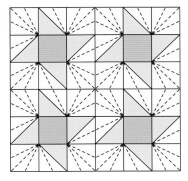

Rail Fence is a very linear design but curved quilting can add a different dimension, breaking up the lines.

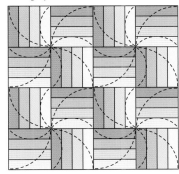

The same Spinning Star block but this time quilted with curved lines and spirals to suggest movement.

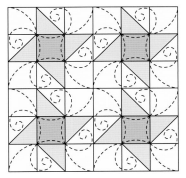

Log Cabin is another strongly linear design. Piecing can be complemented by an easy, all-over diagonal pattern.

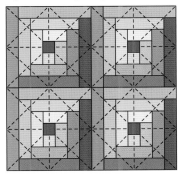

Plain blocks alternating with appliqué blocks create opportunities for motif quilting.

Plain blocks alternating with simple pieced blocks can be quilted to link the whole design together.

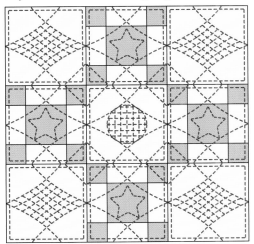

MARKING DESIGNS

Once you have chosen the quilting designs for your quilt or project, in most cases you will need to mark it on to your quilt top. This section shows a variety of ways to mark patterns ready for the exciting stage of quilting. Some people prefer to mark quilting patterns before assembling the quilt sandwich, particularly if they are intricate designs, while others prefer to mark after the sandwich is prepared.

CHOOSING A MARKING METHOD

In some cases no marking at all is needed. For example, if machine quilting in the ditch you can simply follow the seam junctions, or if contour quilting you can use the machine foot to follow the patchwork pieces ¼in (6mm) away from each seam. Seed stitches worked by hand can simply fill a shape or area. Simple linear quilting often requires very little marking, maybe just the use of a ruler and chalk or masking tape, or a hera tool to produce a temporary crease in the fabric. Where marking has to be done there are an increasingly large number of methods to choose from and the main ones are described on page 25. There are some questions you might ask before you choose a marking method:

- How long will the quilting take me and how much will the project be handled? Chalk markings may rub off during lengthy quilting.
- Do I intend to hand quilt or machine quilt? Machine quilting stitches are normally closer together and will disguise marks more readily than hand quilting.
- What fabrics do I need to mark? The fabrics may be densely patterned or a combination of dark and light, which means that marked lines might not show up.
- What is the end use of my project and will it be washable? If it is a wall hanging only to be dusted off occasionally and never washed, then avoid markers that will show.
- Have I used a particular marking method before? If not test it thoroughly before use. Use it on different types and colours of fabric, wash it, iron it and see what happens.

Plastic stencils are easy to use and quite versatile, creating quilting designs that are satisfying to stitch.

MARKING METHODS

The following tools and materials are the most useful for marking quilting patterns – see page 25 for details.

- Pencils
- Marking pens
- Chalk
- Rulers
- Masking tape
- Tracing paper
- Hera
- Needle marking
- Dressmaker's carbon paper
- Compasses and flexicurves
- Perforated paper
- Stencils
- Templates
- Freezer paper

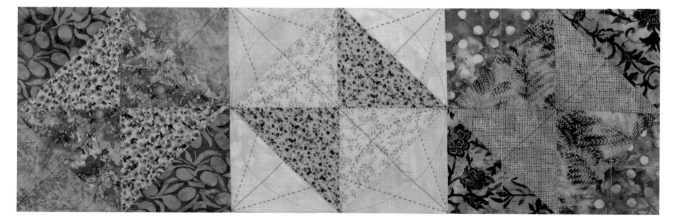

If you are new to quilting, start with easy designs of simple straight lines and gentle curves. Mix hand quilting with machine quilting to practise the techniques. Machine quilting in the ditch and diagonally across blocks will stabilize the quilt layers prior to hand quilting.

>> related topics... *Marking Fabrics 25 • Using Templates 26*   > > >

THE TECHNIQUES

TRACING

Designs can be traced on to light-coloured quilt tops but need to be marked before wadding and backing are added. Prepare the design on paper to the size required. Go over the lines in a dark felt-tip. Place the paper pattern so a light source shines through it. A light box is good but you could use a window. Position the quilt top on the pattern and tape in place. Using a suitable marker (usually a removable one) trace all of the lines. Move the paper pattern and quilt top periodically if required.

USING PLASTIC STENCILS

Plastic stencils are available commercially in many shapes, sizes and combinations or you could create your own.

1 Check the stencil pattern you wish to use will fit into the space on your quilt top. Fix the quilt top on a firm surface, position the stencil and use a suitable marker to draw along the lines cut out of the stencil. ▼

2 Remove the stencil and connect the lines with further marking if you feel it is needed. ▼

3 A mirror image can be created by flipping the stencil over, positioning it where required and drawing it again. ▼

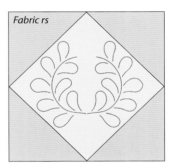

BRIGHT IDEA

CREATE STENCILS WITH TEMPLATE PLASTIC. DRAW THE DESIGN AND CUT OUT THIN LINES USING A DOUBLE-BLADED KNIFE. LEAVE UNCUT 'BRIDGES' IN PLACES.

4 When repeating the pattern for a border or to build up complex designs, ensure that when the stencil is moved the pattern intervals remain constant. Most commercial patterns have little marks to guide you. ▶

Align marks when moving the stencil

USING TEMPLATES

Quilting templates can be very simple shapes or more complex patterns. The technique described here can be used for any type of template. This quilted bird motif has details within the outline that need to be sketched in freehand after the outline is drawn. If you're worried about your drawing skills cut the template into smaller parts. Make a copy of the template to keep as a master.

1 Place the template on the fabric and mark lightly around the outline with a suitable marker. ▼

2 Cut just the wing shape from the template and use it as a separate template to mark the wing on the fabric. ▼

3 Draw the other details by eye (shown here as thin red lines). Add a French knot eye. Work the legs in backstitch. ▼

HAND QUILTING

Hand quilting and machine quilting use different techniques and both take practice to master. Hand quilting generally has a softer appearance than machine quilting. Originally, of course, all quilting was done by hand but sewing machines today have many features that bring a handmade look to quilting. The thread used for quilting can be a contrasting colour to the fabric or blend with it and may be solid, variegated or metallic.

If you are new to hand quilting you may only be able to make one or two stitches at a time but this will increase with practice. Using Betweens needles, which are short and strong, will allow you to make the quilting stitch a reasonable size on the front and back of the work. Because the needle needs to be pushed into the work as vertically as possible, using a thimble will help. Get into the habit of frequently checking the back of the work to make sure your stitches are catching the backing too. The overall size of the stitches doesn't matter as much as making them the same, even spacing. Hand quilting can be done with or without a frame – neither is compulsory but they do require slightly different techniques, described opposite and overleaf.

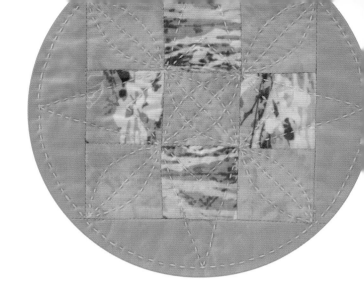

Hand quilting can be charmingly simple or more elaborate. Experimenting with different thread types is great fun.

Hand Quilting

- ✓ The three layers of the quilt sandwich need to be smooth and taut so don't skimp on tacking (basting) or pinning when securing the layers together.
- ✓ Waddings (battings) made from polyester, silk or wool are easier to hand quilt through than cotton wadding.
- ✓ Stitching in the ditch can be done by hand or machine and is a good way to stabilize the layers of a quilt before going on to add further quilting.
- ✓ Using a thread in a slightly darker shade than the fabrics will help bring dimension to a quilt top.
- ✓ If your quilt top is made up of many pieced shapes of varying patterns and colours it would be best to choose a more neutral thread colour or an invisible thread.
- ✓ Specialist threads, such as metallics, need a little more care. If hand quilting, work with shorter lengths.
- ✓ Work can be hand quilted with or without a hoop or frame – try both ways to see which you prefer.

This pretty cushion made by Elaine Hammond uses hand quilting in a loose vermicelli pattern to resemble seaweed to add decorative elements to the sea-themed appliqué.

>> related topics... *Attaching Temporary Borders 135 • Preparing a Quilt Sandwich 188*

THE TECHNIQUES

HAND QUILTING WITHOUT A FRAME

Quilting without a frame makes a project more portable and allows you to hold or gather up the fabric between the thumb and finger of one hand while quilting with the other hand. Begin quilting in the centre of the quilt top or block and work outwards. Where it is possible, avoid changing direction and sewing in the reverse direction: fabric is pushed ahead of stitching and changing direction like this can cause ripples. If using a hoop or frame see the technique overleaf.

1 Use a Quilting or Betweens needle and a length of quilting thread about 12in–18in (30.5cm–45.7cm) long. Make a small knot at the end of the thread. Put the needle into the quilt top and wadding (batting), a little way from where you wish to start quilting, and bring it up to the surface again (A). Pull the thread so that the knot pops through the top layer into the wadding. Make a backstitch and take the needle through into the wadding again (B). Now bring the needle up to the surface where you want to start quilting (C). ▼

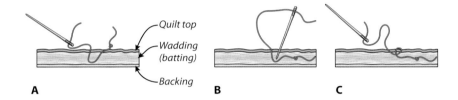

Quilt top
Wadding (batting)
Backing

A   **B**   **C**

2 Hand quilting is achieved with a rocking action of the sewing hand. Position your non-sewing hand under the fabric. Wearing a thimble on the first or middle finger of your sewing hand and on the underneath hand is advisable. Forming your sewing hand into a C shape will help achieve the correct action. Push the needle vertically through the layers until the tip touches the finger underneath. Using this finger and a rocking motion, push the tip of the needle back upwards through the top layer. Swing the needle head over the fabric, forwards and then back as vertically as you can into the fabric. Repeat this action to put as many stitches on the needle as you comfortably can. ▶

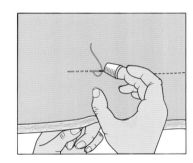

3 Now pull the needle through the layers so the stitches sit snugly, making slight indentations in the layers. Continue making the running stitches in this way, keeping them a similar size and spacing and following your marked lines until the quilting is complete. When working without a frame take care to monitor your stitch tension – it is easy to tighten the stitches too much and so cause the fabric to pucker. If seam junctions are too thick to quilt through make one stitch at a time or use a stabbing motion until the seam is passed.

BRIGHT IDEA

IF YOU HAVE DIFFICULTY PULLING STITCHES THROUGH THE LAYERS, CUT THE FINGERS OFF AN OLD RUBBER GLOVE AND USE ONE ON THE FOREFINGER OF YOUR SEWING HAND FOR A BETTER GRIP.

FINISHING HAND QUILTING

To finish off hand quilting, wind the thread twice round the needle and make a knot in the thread close to the surface of the fabric (A). Insert the needle into the wadding (batting), running it 1in (2.5cm) or more away from the stitching (B), and pop the knot beneath the surface of the top fabric. Cut off the thread level with the quilt top (C). ▼

A   **B**   **C**

MOUNTING WORK IN A HOOP OR FRAME

Quilting within a hoop or frame, which can be done for hand and machine quilting, ensures that the quilt sandwich stays taut and smooth and can help achieve more even hand stitches. For small projects a lap hoop will suffice but for larger bed quilts a floor frame will be needed.

Using a hoop – Mark the quilt top with your quilting design and place the quilt sandwich in the hoop, with the area you want to quilt in the centre. Tighten the screw so the quilt sandwich is flat but not too taut, and begin quilting. The hoop will need to be moved as you complete an area of quilting. Some quilting hoops have a lap table attached to support the hoop. If not, rest the edge of the hoop on a table or chair arm as you stitch. ▼

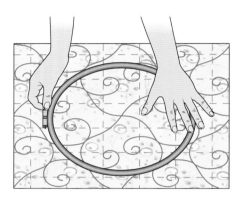

If you have areas of quilting near the edge of the quilt sandwich you will need to temporarily attach borders of plain fabric all round so the hoop has enough fabric to grip on to (see page 135). ▼

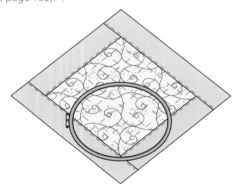

Using a frame – When using a frame, consult the manufacturer's instructions, as frames vary a little. Generally, the quilt sandwich first needs to be tacked (basted) or pinned on to the two roller bars at the top and bottom of the frame to maintain a tension in that direction. ▼

The sides of the quilt sandwich also have to be under tension and to do this pin fabric strips or bias tape to the sides of the quilt, wrapping the strips around the side stretcher bars and pinning them in place as shown. These will have to be moved periodically as you complete sections of quilting and roll the quilt over the frame. ▼

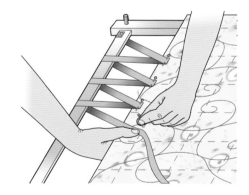

The hand quilting on this decorative patchwork border by Petra Prins blends subtley into the design while echoing the shape of the individual squares on point. Curved line quilting contrasts with the linear patchwork.

HAND QUILTING WITH A HOOP OR FRAME

If the quilt sandwich is contained within a quilting hoop or frame you will not be able to gather the fabric between your thumb and finger, so the hand quilting technique has to be slightly different. Some quilters find that a stabbing motion is easier than a rocking one. Do not fix the quilt sandwich drum tight in the hoop or frame – a little 'give' will help your stitching technique.

1 Position your non-sewing hand under the hoop or frame with your middle finger where the needle will be coming through. Wearing a thimble on the first or middle finger of both hands will help. Position the needle vertically on the quilt top (A). Push the needle through the layers until the tip touches the underneath finger. Move the needle backwards and flatter, so the tip is now pointing upwards. Push the tip upwards with the underneath finger and, as it emerges on top, position your thumb in front of it (B). Push the needle tip along the fabric a short way. You will now have one stitch on the needle (C). ▼

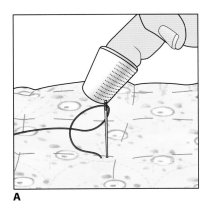

A

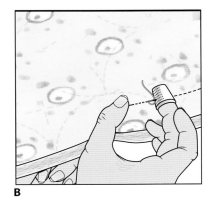

B

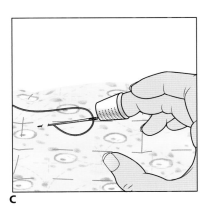

C

2 Now push the needle tip downwards with your thumb so it re-enters the fabric again. Repeat the action of pushing the needle vertically through the layers until the tip again touches the underneath finger. Repeat this process to load several more stitches on to your needle, or as many as you feel comfortable with (D). Pull the thread through the fabric (E). Begin loading the needle with stitches again and continue in this way following the marked pattern until the quilting is complete. ▶

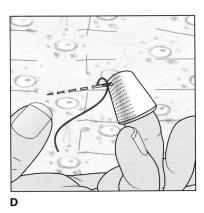

D

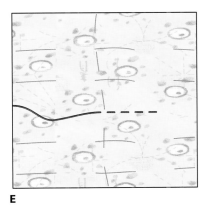

E

BIG STITCH QUILTING

Big stitch quilting is just that, quilting with nice big stitches. As a quilting technique it has two advantages: it is very easy for beginners to do as fewer stitches are stitched than in normal hand quilting, and it showcases some of the gorgeous threads available today. It is the perfect way to learn the soothing joys of hand quilting, without the angst of tiny stitches. Big stitch quilting isn't a shy violet that blends delicately into the patchwork fabrics – big stitch *wants* to be seen and is wonderful for folk-art style quilts and children's quilts.

THREADS FOR BIG STITCH

Big stitch quilting is suitable for thicker threads, such as perle cottons and metallics and some lovely effects can be created with variegated threads. In fact, any thread that can be sewn through fabric can be used – so experiment!

If you plan to do a lot of big stitch quilting with thick threads and like to add decorative stitches and embellishments then consider completing this stage before adding a backing fabric. Add the backing after all the decorative work and then machine quilt in the ditch or around motifs to secure the layers in the traditional way. See also page 228 for Decorative Quilting.

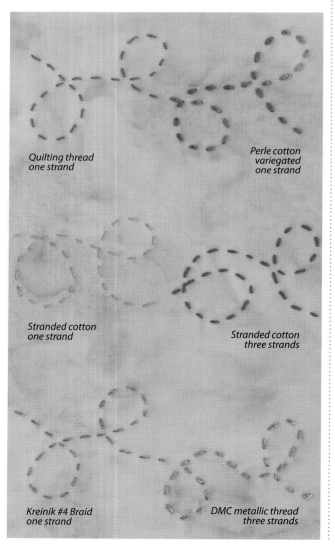

Quilting thread one strand

Perle cotton variegated one strand

Stranded cotton one strand

Stranded cotton three strands

Kreinik #4 Braid one strand

DMC metallic thread three strands

THE TECHNIQUES

STARTING AND FINISHING BIG STITCH

If big stitch quilting with the same type and thickness of thread as for hand quilting, start and finish in the same way, by popping the starting and finishing knots inside the wadding (batting). If using thicker threads a different approach will be needed.

When starting, take the thread through from the back of the work to the front, leaving a tail of about 3in (7.6cm). Quilt for a few stitches (A), then park the needle in the fabric and thread the tail with a second needle. Make one or two backstitches with the tail thread and run the thread along inside the sandwich for a little way and trim off. Finish quilting in a similar way, taking one or two backstitches, before burying the thread in the wadding (B). ▼

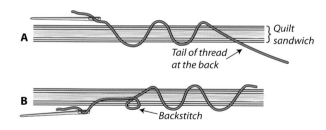

A

Quilt sandwich

Tail of thread at the back

B

Backstitch

WORKING BIG STITCH

As with normal hand quilting, the evenness of the stitches in big stitch quilting is more important than the closeness. Generally between four to eight stitches per inch (2.5cm) is fine, and will depend on the type and thickness of thread and what you feel comfortable with. As with normal hand quilting, several stitches can be taken on the needle at once, which will help keep the stitches even. Choose a needle suitable for the thread you are using, probably a Sharps or Betweens with a larger eye if you are using thicker thread. Work as for normal hand quilting

Four stitches to 1in (2.5cm)

Eight stitches to 1in (2.5cm)

You can be as creative as you like with threads for big stitch quilting – here are some examples of threads worked in big stitch and shown at actual size.

make it now
Welcome Cards

Big stitch quilting is ideal for experimenting with different threads. You could use the designs here as greetings cards or new baby cards, adding stick-on messages or letters for the baby's name.

profile

Skills practised: Marking a quilting pattern; big stitch quilting; whipped big stitch; French knots
Finished size of motif: 3½in (8.9cm) diameter
Fabrics: For one card 5in (12.7cm) square of cream fabric; wadding (batting) 5in (12.7cm) square
Threads: Stranded cotton in pinks and pale green for pink card; variegated blues and mauves for blue card
Card mount: Double-fold card with aperture
Embellishments: Ribbons and toppers as desired and double-sided adhesive tape

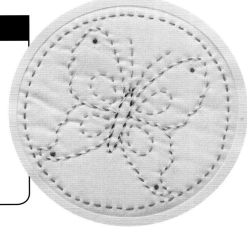

METHOD

- Use the templates on page 251 to mark the design on your fabric. Back the fabric with wadding (batting) and tack (baste) in place.
- Work big stitch quilting on all the lines of the design. For extra definition whip the big stitch around the outline of the butterfly wings and body and the bird's beak. Add French knots on the wings. Work the legs in backstitch.
- Press and mount into a double-fold card, adding embellishments as desired.

WHOLE CLOTH QUILTING

Whole cloth quilting is quilting – normally by hand – that is stitched in an intricate design on one single, large piece of fabric. This subtle and elegant form of quilting not only holds the three layers of the quilt together but adds light and shadow, texture and dimension, especially if worked on a fabric with a sheen. The patterns usually have a central design with repeated floral and/or geometric motifs surrounding it. This type of quilting, sometimes called English quilting, requires skill as the quilting stitches need to be small and even enough to make visually strong lines that form the pattern.

Whole cloth quilting became popular in France and then England, where Welsh whole cloth quilters achieved wonderful results on cotton sateen. Whole cloth quilting is sometimes referred to as Durham quilting because the style was used by quilters in Durham and the north-east of England from around 1900 onwards.

In whole cloth quilting the quilting pattern is drawn on the fabric. A pencil could be used on light-coloured fabric and chalk on dark colours, or use a water-soluble marker. Today there are pre-printed whole cloths for quilts and cushions available with the quilting pattern already in place. The pattern can be washed out after quilting is finished.

Fabric colours for whole cloth quilting can be pale and subtle or bold and bright, including indigo and red. Solid colours tend to show the quilting off to best advantage but some whole cloth quilts use printed fabrics or subtly variegated fabrics. Whole cloth quilting can be taken a step further by adding trapunto work, where some of the motifs in the quilting pattern are padded with additional wadding (batting) or stuffing – see page 226.

PREPARING TO QUILT

Designing and marking a whole cloth quilt requires experience and practice but the basic points to consider are as follows.

- Ensure the fabric you plan to use is suitable, with no flaws. Wash and iron it, making sure it is colourfast. Square up the fabric, if possible with the cut edges even with the grain. Decide which side of the fabric you want to use.
- Use a suitable marker to mark the edge of the quilt at least 1in (2.5cm) in from the raw edge. To ensure symmetry, fold the fabric in quarters and mark vertical and horizontal folds. Fold diagonally and mark the diagonals.
- Decide on your central design and pin a paper copy in place temporarily.
- Decide on the width of the outer border, balancing this with the central design size. Choose the motif or pattern to be used in the outer border and work out how many repeats will be needed – you may have to adjust a pattern to fit. Once you know how the pattern will work, the outer border width can then be decided.
- Plan the rest of the patterns between the central design and the border, seeing how they look when added to the space. Enlarge or reduce patterns to fit. Continually check how the design is building, taking your time to stand back and study it.
- Add any background fillers needed to bring balance and detail to the whole design.
- If adding trapunto work you will now need to look at the whole design and decide which parts could be shown three-dimensionally in this way.
- Once happy with the design, mark all of the patterns and motifs including background grid patterns.
- Prepare the quilt sandwich and begin to quilt from the centre outwards.

Using a fabric with a slight sheen emphasizes the beauty and intricacy of whole cloth quilting. A solid-coloured fabric will draw attention to the quilting more than a pieced fabric would.

WHOLE CLOTH DESIGNS

Traditionally, whole cloth designs are balanced and symmetrical, with the central motif the main focus. Borders are used as frames, keeping the eye within the quilt, and can be of varying sizes and intricacy. Originally, patterns were collected from many sources, including architecture, stone work, ceiling designs, wood carvings, scrollwork, old tapestries and carpets. Start by choosing the central design and build the other patterns outwards from this. Commercial quilting stencils are available in a range of patterns.

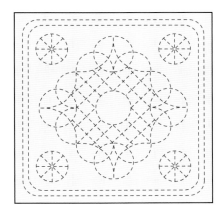
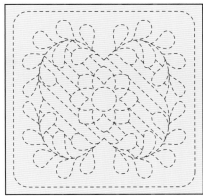

Whole cloth quilting patterns for bed-sized quilts can be those you have created yourself, such as the large design below, or be bought from quilting shops and web stores. Patterns can also be found pre-printed on to fabric, ready for many hours of pleasurable quilting. Smaller designs are perfect to try your hand at whole cloth quilting – these two designs could be scaled up and quilted for cushions.

CELTIC QUILTING

Celtic quilting is the name given to quilting that uses Celtic-inspired designs. Bias-strip appliqué also uses Celtic designs so patterns that are suitable for that technique can also be adapted as quilting patterns. Celtic designs are varied and some of the best examples can be seen in the *Lindisfarne Gospels*, *The Book of Kells* and *The Book of Durrow*, created around the 7th century. Motifs include spirals, knotwork, fret and key patterns, carpet page patterns, lettering and animal and plant designs. Today, Celtic-inspired designs can come from numerous sources and there are many commercial patterns.

Philomena Durcan introduced quilted Celtic designs in 1980 with her book, *Celtic Quilt Designs,* and since then many designers have explored this fruitful source of designs. Celtic designs can be hand quilted with a normal quilting stitch, with big stitch or with more decorative hand stitches. Celtic quilting can also be undertaken by free-motion machine quilting (see page 218).

Threads used for this type of work can be almost anything you choose. The thread colour could blend with the fabric or contrast with it or you could use several different colours within one design. Celtic quilting is very effective on whole cloth, especially glazed cottons, which have a sheen. Try plain solids or variegated fabrics such as batiks. The designs can also be used as all-over patterns on patchwork.

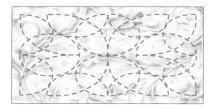

QUILTING CELTIC DESIGNS

Celtic designs are great for relaxing hand quilting and a small motif is the perfect way to practise quilting skills. You could also experiment with more decorative quilting stitches – see page 228. The designs can also be machine quilted, although many would need to use a free-motion technique to cope with tight curves and spirals.

Mark the quilting design, enlarging it if necessary, and prepare the quilt sandwich as on page 188. If you wish, mount the quilt in a hoop or frame. Choose your thread and begin quilting with a knot popped into the wadding.

If quilting a knotwork design with a double channel you may need to 'skip' from time to time when you come to an 'over' or 'under'. To do this, simply feed the needle through the wadding only and bring it back up where the line of the design begins again.

TYPES OF CELTIC DESIGN

Due to their decorative qualities Celtic inspired designs are wonderful for all sorts of patchwork, appliqué and quilting work. Some, such as fret and key patterns, are based on geometric shapes and so can be adapted for patchwork as well as quilting. Others, such as knots, spirals and lettering, can be used for whole cloth quilting and big stitch quilting. With many Celtic patterns the lines of the designs can be doubled to create channels, which makes them suitable for corded quilting and stuffed quilting or trapunto (see pages 224 and 226).

In this quilt simple pieced work has been used by Gail Lawther to showcase some fabulous Celtic quilting designs. See Further Reading on page 252 for details of Gail's books which contain many quilting patterns.

Knotwork designs

Knot designs are wonderful for all sorts of quilting and appliqué work, especially whole cloth quilting, corded quilting and trapunto. Their flowing lines and interlaced patterns are very satisfying to quilt and if the lines are doubled, then channels can be created for corded quilting. Knotwork motifs are also perfect for creating more complex designs as they are easy to rotate, flip and combine. The spaces inside and outside a knot can feature denser quilting, such as seed stitches or vermicelli.

 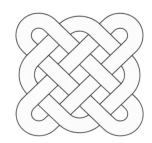

Spiral designs

These are characterized by strongly curved lines, usually spinning out from a central point or points. Often several spirals meet and merge and can form different shapes overall, including circles, ovals, squares and rectangles. A single spiral design can be repeated and rotated to create a more complex design, which could be used as an all-over quilting pattern. Spiral patterns can also be extended and repeated for use in borders and strip quilts.

Fret and key patterns

These sorts of patterns are very old and are found all over the world, dating back to ancient civilizations including those of Egypt, Greece and Rome. The patterns can be simple or be built up into complex designs. They can be used as stand-alone motifs or all-over patterns. Their geometric basis means they can be adapted for patchwork too as the second diagram shows.

 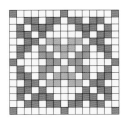

Nature designs

Biomorphic motifs are a highly distinctive feature of Celtic design and some fabulous motifs can be found, not just from ancient sources but also in contemporary art. Animals, birds, fish, plants and fantasy creatures are all portrayed, sometimes recognizably but often in more fantastical forms, with creatures twisting and turning in highly decorative poses. The dragon here has been adapted from a Gail Lawther design.

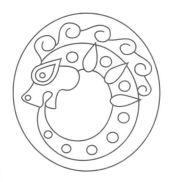 

Carpet page patterns

The Anglo-Saxon illuminated manuscripts of the 7th and 8th centuries featured a wealth of designs that filled whole pages. These often looked like colourful carpets, hence the name. They were based on a subtle mathematical grid and contained combinations of patterns, including fret and key, knots, spirals and animals. Using these patterns for patchwork, appliqué and quilting means simplifying them and extracting useful elements.

Lettering

The early illuminated manuscripts are filled with exuberant designs for lettering – highly decorative and embellished with gold. Simpler Celtic lettering is more suitable for quilting and there are many computer fonts you might try. There are lots of books on the subject and a web search will yield plenty of choices.

SASHIKO

Japanese sashiko is centuries old and was originally a form of darning. By the 18th century it had developed as a rural domestic craft and was practised by the wives of fishermen and farmers as a way of thickening work jackets and prolonging the life of the fabric. The word sashiko (pronounced 'sash(i)ko' with the i almost silent) means 'little stab' or 'little pierce'. Traditionally sashiko was worked by hand with white thread on indigo fabric. A huge range of patterns and motifs has been developed over the centuries and most are based on an imperial grid. Family crests were also popular motifs to be stitched as sashiko.

Originally, sashiko was sewn by hand and its distinctive look can really only be achieved by hand. Because the stitches are meant to be larger than normal quilting stitches (between four and eight to 1in/2.5cm) it is a wonderfully rewarding way to practise your quilting skills. Sashiko patterns can be machine sewn but the lines will be continuous and somewhat harder in style, although sewing machine manufacturers are working on ways to achieve the spaced running stitch look of sashiko.

Sashiko is a very versatile form of quilting – it looks beautiful in its own right, it combines well with patchwork blocks and the designs can also be used as all-over quilting patterns. Patterns can also be distorted to create even more designs.

Sashiko can be worked with the same needles and threads as normal hand quilting but using authentic materials is part of the experience for many people.

NEEDLES AND THREADS

Normal quilting needles can be used for sashiko, including Embroidery types or Betweens but if you enjoy sashiko by hand then special needles can be bought, which are very sharp, thick and rigid.

Sashiko can use the same threads as normal quilting but aim for the thicker ones, such as perle cotton No.5 or 8. Threads can be used doubled to achieve a nice, chunky stitch. For an authentic look specialist sashiko threads are available. These are thick, strong and come in different weights and colours, including variegated. Traditional colours were white and indigo but modern sashiko uses a wider palette.

Some beautiful projects, from small items to large quilts, can be created with sashiko. These little bags by Susan Briscoe have a small amount of sashiko. The blue bag shows the nowaki pattern (see opposite) and the red bag showcases matsukawabishi (see overleaf) and a pattern called komezashi.

SEWING SASHIKO

Sashiko patterns can be marked in a similar way to other quilting designs and care needs to be taken to mark accurately. Tracing is a good method if you are using light-coloured fabric. Light boxes can be expensive so try taping the design to a window with the fabric right side up on top and use a pencil lightly or an erasable marker. If you are new to sashiko, an easy way to try it is with a kit or pre-printed fabric squares, which, once stitched, could be made up into projects such as cushions or bags.

Sashiko generally uses only two layers of fabric but wadding (batting) can be used between the layers if desired. The traditional sewing action is different to normal hand quilting in that the needle is held still while the fabric is fed on to it several stitches at a time in a pleating action. This means that a quilting hoop or frame isn't used. Sewing is done from side to side, rather than from the centre outwards. Experiment for yourself and see which technique works for you.

SASHIKO PATTERNS

There are hundreds of sashiko patterns to choose from based on various shapes, including squares, circles, spirals, diamonds, hexagons, wave patterns, steps and weaves. Much of the beauty of sashiko lies not just in the way the patterns are stitched but also in the way they can be combined, especially when dense patterns merge into airy ones. The direction and sequence in which sashiko patterns are sewn is important to create the neatest work and to be economical of thread and stitching time. When following patterns from books or magazines the stitching sequence is normally colour coded to help you see which lines to stitch first, second and so on. Susan Briscoe provides a wonderful library of designs in her sashiko books and explains how to stitch over 100 patterns. A few popular designs are shown below. Red dots show where to start stitching, with arrows indicating the direction. Dotted lines show where thread should be loosely stranded across the back of the work.

Raimon (lightning spiral)

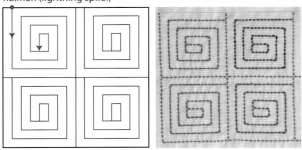

Asanoha (hemp leaf)

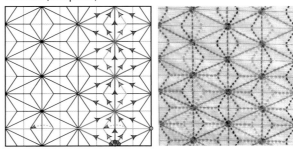

Seigaiha (ocean waves)

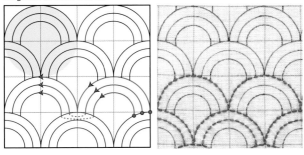

Shippō tsunagi (linked seven treasures)

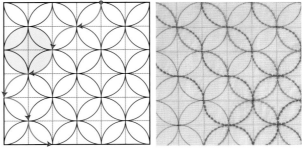

These two patterns, *mitsuba* (trefoil), right, and *nowaki* (grasses), far right, can be seen on the Sashiko Placemats on page 210. If you enlarge these patterns by 400 per cent they could be used to mark your own placemats, or you could use another sashiko pattern of your choice. ▶

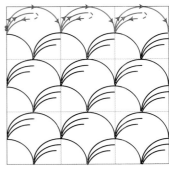

>>> **related topics...** *Marking Fabrics 25 • Enlarging and Reducing 27 • Hand Quilting 196 • Machine Quilting 212* >>

THE TECHNIQUES

SASHIKO BY HAND

Sewing sashiko by hand creates a very distinctive, traditional look. See opposite for machine sewing sashiko. Sashiko is not sewn with tiny quilting stitches – between four to eight per 1in (2.5cm) is fine. Ideally, the spaces between the stitches need to be the same length as the stitches. The *matsukawabishi* (pine bark diamond) pattern is used below as an example.

1 Select your pattern and, if need be, enlarge it to the size required. Transfer the pattern to your fabric and create a quilt sandwich in the normal way. Choose your thread and begin quilting with a knot on the back of the work. Sashiko doesn't have to be reversible like normal Western quilting, but if you are using wadding (batting) then the knot could be popped into the wadding as normal.

2 Sashiko can be stitched by keeping the needle still and feeding the fabric on to it, several stitches at a time, in a pleating action. Alternatively, you can use a normal hand quilting method. Wherever possible, work sashiko in long, continuous lines, from side to side. Follow the route suggested by the pattern you are using or take time to devise the most efficient way of completing a design. For the pattern shown here, begin stitching at a red dot and hand stitch the pathway shown in red. ▶

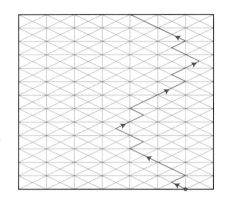

3 Once the red pathway is stitched, begin again at a green dot and follow a green pathway. Do not crowd stitches in on top of each other and where several stitches meet leave a little gap – see Sewing Neat Sashiko opposite. ▶

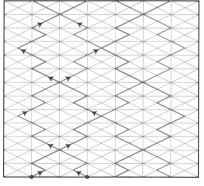

4 Continue in this way until the whole pattern is complete. The grid used for this pattern is a rectangular one on a 2:1 ratio – for example ½in (1.3cm) high x 1in (2.5cm) wide. ▶

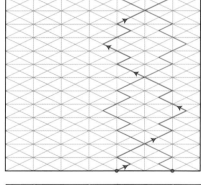

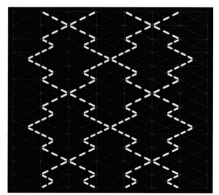

5 Finish off with a knot at the back of the work, as shown here, or by popping the knot through into the wadding as with normal hand quilting. ▶

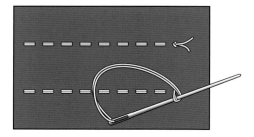

SEWING NEAT SASHIKO

For the neatest and most authentic looking sashiko bear in mind the following points, particularly when hand sewing sashiko. If you can, try to stitch the same number of stitches in each section of a design.

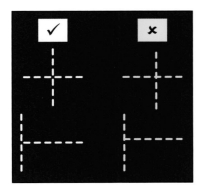

Patterns will look neater if you space the sashiko stitches so that they don't touch each other.

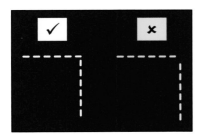

Angled shapes will be more clearly defined if a stitch is made right into the corner.

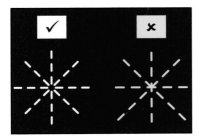

If several pattern lines cross each other, space the stitches to leave a gap at the crossing point.

When moving from one line of the pattern to another strand the thread loosely across the back to avoid puckering.

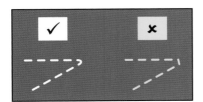

When changing direction sharply leave a little loop on the back of the work to avoid the stitches pulling too tight and causing puckering.

SASHIKO BY MACHINE

Sashiko can be stitched by machine but the line stitched will appear almost continuous, without the distinctive gaps between the stitches (although machines are now being produced to mimic sashiko more accurately). Machine sewing is quicker and useful for larger projects. Some people find that sewing sashiko from the back of the fabric works well. The design can be marked on lightweight fusible interfacing, fused to the back of the fabric. Thicker thread would be used in the bobbin with this method.

Another difference between stitching sashiko by machine compared to by hand is that the directions a pattern is stitched in may be different. For machine sewing select the longest, easiest route, with as few twists and turns as possible. The diagrams below are of the *matsukawabishi* pattern: the first shows the hand quilting route; the second shows the machine quilting route.

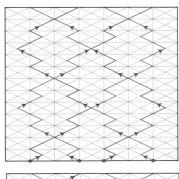

Sashiko by hand – stitching direction for the matsukawabishi *pattern.*

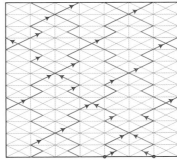

Sashiko by machine – stitching direction for the matsukawabishi *pattern.*

SEWING SASHIKO MOTIFS

There are many wonderful oriental-inspired images that make fabulous motifs for sashiko quilting and three are shown here. Mark them as you would any quilting pattern and stitch them as sashiko, keeping the stitches even and nicely spaced.

Plum blossom

Bamboo

Chrysanthemum

make it now
Sashiko Placemats

Sashiko is perfect for creating stylish placemats. Medium-weight sashiko threads were used but you could use perle cotton. The amount of sashiko you stitch is up to you – the white sashiko mat has one-third sashiko to two-thirds print fabric, while the variegated mat reverses these ratios.

profile

Skills practised: Sashiko quilting; machine sewing
Finished size: 10in x 15in (25.4cm x 38cm)
Fabrics: Dark blue cotton for sashiko; a coordinating print; thin wadding (batting); backing fabric
Threads: White sashiko thread and variegated sashiko thread in medium weight

METHOD

• Decide what size your sashiko stitching is to be and cut a piece of blue fabric 2in (5cm) larger all round. Mark your sashiko design on the fabric using the patterns on page 207. (You could cheat a little and buy a pre-printed panel.) Stitch the sashiko. Start and finish at the edges to reduce the number of knots on the back. Trim the finished piece to size, plus 1in (2.5cm) all round for seams.

• Cut print fabric to the size required. If your sashiko is to be one-third of the mat, cut the print twice as wide, plus seam allowances. If your sashiko is to be two-thirds of the mat, cut the print half as wide, plus seam allowances. Join the sashiko and print fabric pieces together using a ½in (1.3cm) seam allowance and press. Cut out wadding (batting) the same size.

• Cut print fabric for the backing, plus seam allowances. Make up with a bagging-out technique as described on page 235.

KANTHA QUILTING

If you enjoy hand quilting then you will enjoy kantha embroidery, which is also called Indian quilting. India and Pakistan are rich sources of many forms of quilting and embroidery. Kantha is popular in Bangladesh and West Bengal in India and is characterized by bright multi-coloured running stitches, similar to sashiko quilting. Kantha decorates all sorts of items, including wall hangings, clothing, decorative objects and household textiles. It displays highly decorative motifs and patterns, including gods and goddesses, the tree of life, flowers, plants, birds, animals, fish and geometric shapes. Another Indian technique that is very popular is shisha embroidery, also called mirror work (see page 183).

In its simplest form kantha embroidery is worked on multiple layers of fabric, originally recycled sari fabrics, with rows of running stitch, which often fill the area of a motif. Designs and motifs can be highly elaborate and complex and often tell a story. The stitches do not have to be small and their evenness is more important than their size.

Almost any shape you choose could be worked in kantha quilting – try using appliqué motifs, which often have simplified outlines. Mark and stitch kantha quilting in the same way as hand quilting.

Here is a small selection of kantha motifs for you to try. These can be enlarged and arranged as you desire, perhaps in a simple design for a little picture, as shown below.

MACHINE QUILTING

Machine quilting, as with hand quilting, takes practice to master but there are some techniques that even beginners can do easily and quickly. Some people machine quilt for ease and speed while others develop it as a means of creative self-expression. There is a wide range of machine quilting, including everything from just outlining patchwork blocks in straight stitch to stitching dense and intricate patterns and curves. The effects that can be achieved with machine quilting can be spectacular and are well worth learning. Machine sewing creates a more solid line compared with the interrupted nature of hand sewing, although sewing machine manufacturers are constantly improving their products to be as versatile as possible.

Machine quilting can be broadly divided into machine-guided stitching and free-motion stitching. In machine-guided stitching the feed dogs are up and the machine guides the fabric through; this stitching method allows you to stitch straight lines and gentle curves. In free-motion stitching the feed dogs are dropped, allowing the fabric to be guided by you, which means that more intricate stitching is possible, with tighter curves and freehand patterns. Work can be machine quilted while in a hoop to keep the quilt surface firm and this can be useful for free-motion quilting.

NEEDLES AND THREADS

Machine quilting needles or Sharps are very sharp and pierce through all layers of the quilt sandwich easily. The needle size will depend on wadding (batting) thickness, so try a 75/11 for thin wadding and 80/12 or 90/14 for thicker ones. If working with specialist threads, such as rayons or metallics, use a needle suitable for the type of thread.

For machine quilting, use 100 per cent cotton thread for the top thread and in the bobbin. Monofilament nylon thread is useful for stitching in the ditch as it is nearly invisible. Specialist threads, including rayons and metallics, are popular in quilting – choose those rated for machine work and of a suitable weight, such as a 50 weight thread for normal sewing and a 40 or 30 weight cotton for machine quilting.

STITCH LENGTH

Stitch length on the majority of machines refers to the length in millimetres of each individual stitch that makes up the pattern. For machine quilting most people use a stitch length of about 10–12 stitches per inch (2.5cm) but this may need to be varied depending on the fabric and threads you are using. The thicker the fabric, the longer the stitch length required.

Flowers, curves and swirls are among the many freehand patterns used in the machine quilting on this brightly coloured quilt made by Katharine Guerrier. Curved patterns contrast very well with linear patchwork.

MACHINE TENSION

Machine tension is the tightness the stitches are formed under and affects how the work looks from the front and back. There are two tension adjustments that can be made – at the top and in the bobbin. The bobbin thread tension is controlled by a screw on the bobbin case, which can be loosened or tightened, but is usually left as standard. The top tension is controlled on most machines by a dial, the position of which varies.

The upper and lower tensions should balance, so thread used in the bobbin should not show on the top of the work, and vice versa. Tension problems will be more noticeable if you are using a different colour thread in the bobbin to the top. If the bobbin thread is showing through on the top, the tension is too tight, so loosen it by selecting a lower number. If the top thread is showing through on the back and even creating loops, the tension is too loose, so tighten it by selecting a higher number.

BRIGHT IDEA

IF YOUR MACHINE CUTS CORNERS OR SKIPS WHEN YOU PIVOT AT CORNERS, TRY SHORTENING THE STITCH LENGTH.

MACHINE QUILTING TOOLS

There are a few sewing machine accessories that will make machine quilting easier. Most modern machines already have these accessories but if not they are usually easy to buy – ask at your nearest sewing machine shop or contact the manufacturer. Your machine manual will usually have pictures identifying these accessories.

Walking foot or even-feed foot – This foot is needed for machine-guided quilting and feeds the layers of a quilt through the machine more evenly by feeding the fabric layers through from the top, as the feed dogs do at the bottom. This helps prevent puckering and the quilt backing from shifting. It works on the same principle as the built-in dual feed foot described below. Sewing machines usually have a walking foot available though it may need to be bought separately.

Walking foot

Darning foot – This is a type of presser foot that is useful when free-motion quilting. It is often made from clear acrylic to allow a good view of the stitching area.

Dual-feed foot – This foot may also be called an integrated or built-in dual feed system, and many modern machines have this. It helps to ensure even stitching by feeding the fabric layers through from the top, as the feed dogs do at the bottom. It is normally behind the presser foot.

Darning foot

Quilting guide – This is a useful gadget that acts as a guide when machine quilting parallel rows of stitching. It is an angled rod that is available with most machines, usually made of metal but may be plastic.

Throat plates – Using a straight stitch throat plate instead of the zigzag throat plate is helpful when free-motion sewing.

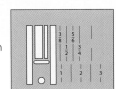

Zigzag throat plate

Straight stitch throat plate

Machine Quilting

✓ When tacking (basting) the quilt sandwich together, avoid using long stitches that the machine foot could catch on. If using pins, avoid placing them along seams or quilting lines.

✓ When quilting in the ditch invisible thread will show the least.

✓ Stitch more slowly when using specialist threads such as metallics. Machine brands vary so if your machine doesn't like a certain type try another.

✓ If a thread breaks frequently, check the needle type and size being used – it may be the wrong one or too small for that thread. It may also be coming off the spool too quickly, so try the spool vertically if possible.

✓ Before making the first stitch, hold the top thread down to avoid the thread knotting.

✓ If your stitching isn't looking neat, try the following things. Make sure the needle is fitted correctly and you are using the correct foot. Re-thread the machine and check the bobbin area. Check your tension is correct. Try not putting the thread through the thread guide above the needle.

✓ Because quilting tends to push the fabric slightly ahead of the stitches and can cause rippling, try to plan the direction of your quilting, stitching in a consistent direction.

✓ If working on a large, heavy quilt that is difficult to manoevre, place a small table or ironing board next to the sewing machine table to help support the quilt.

✓ Plan your quilting so there are as few starts and stops as possible – this is called continuous line quilting.

>>> related topics... *Marking Fabrics 25 • Preparing a Quilt Sandwich 188 • Mounting Work in a Hoop or Frame 198* >>

THE TECHNIQUES

PREPARING TO MACHINE QUILT

Prepare and mark your quilt top and make up the quilt sandwich. If your project is a large one it will need to be supported, especially at the back and side, so use an extra table or ironing board if need be. You could also roll the sides of the quilt inwards to reduce bulk. To do this, lay the quilt sandwich out flat, right side up. Roll each side in towards the centre and secure with large pins, safety pins or quilting clips (A). If the quilt sandwich is quite thin, fold the sides in, pleating like an accordion (B). ▼

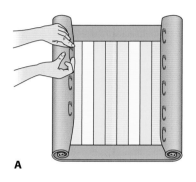
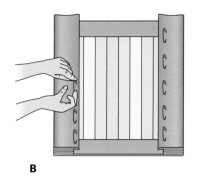

A **B**

STARTING AND FINISHING

Where possible, start and finish machine quilting at the sides of a project, and then you don't need to worry about finishing off ends neatly. However, this won't always be possible so there are two ways of starting and finishing so your machine quilting looks neat.

- Start and finish by sewing several stitches on the spot – newer machines will have this function or simply set the stitch length on your machine to zero. Thread ends can then be trimmed off close to the fabric.
- Start and finish stitching as normal and when a line of stitching is finished take the thread ends to the back of the work, tie them together in a knot and use a needle to feed the ends into the wadding (batting) out of sight.

This quilt by Pam and Nicky Lintott has primary coloured patches linked by a white background quilted with an all-over pattern of swirls worked on a long-arm machine.

QUILTING IN THE DITCH

The 'ditch' in this term means the ditch between seams. Quilting in the ditch not only allows you to secure the layers of a quilt together but is also an easy machine quilting technique for beginners to learn. The important thing is to keep your sewing line straight, watch where the needle is going, and keep in the ditch all the time to avoid wandering off. Using an invisible thread is helpful here as any slight meanderings won't show so much. Most modern machines have a stitch-in-the-ditch foot available, if required, which has a guide in the centre to keep you in the seam ditch.

• Try to start your ditch quilting with a seam that runs in the lengthwise grain with the wadding (batting) and lining as this will help avoid stretching and distortion. Let the walking foot do the work and don't pull or push the quilt. If you can, try to start and finish at the edges of the quilt, as you will have fewer loose ends to deal with later.

• If you have pressed your seams to one side then one side of the seam will sit slightly higher than the other because this side will have three layers of fabric compared to one layer on the other side of the seam allowance. If you machine quilt fractionally on to this lower side your machine will find the stitching easier and the stitches will be hidden or not show as much as they would when sewing on the 'high' side. ▼

• When quilting in the ditch watch where the needle is piercing the fabric, following the seam lines between blocks, or even between patches for denser quilting. The quilting lines are shown in red on the diagram below for clarity. Tie off and bury thread ends neatly, especially if they occur within the centre of the quilt. ▼

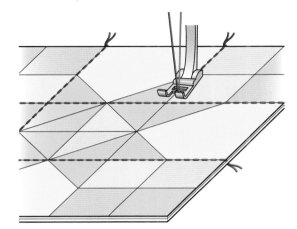

QUILTING IN A GRID OR HATCHED PATTERN

Working machine quilting in parallel lines in a grid or crosshatched pattern is easy and can look very effective in areas of plain fabric. The lines to quilt could be marked with a pencil or masking tape. Use the width of the sewing machine foot as a guide for quilting or fix a quilting guide to your machine. To attach the guide consult the manual for your machine.

Using the machine foot – To quilt narrow parallel lines (no wider than the machine foot), stitch the first line and then move the machine foot so it is aligned with the first row of quilting. Lower the presser foot, stitch the second row and then repeat the process as necessary.

Using a quilting guide – To quilt wider parallel lines, stitch the first line and then raise and move the machine foot to one side so the quilting guide is aligned with this first row of quilting and just touching the fabric surface. Tighten the guide's screw to hold it in place. Lower the presser foot, stitch the second row and then repeat the process as necessary.

Quilting in a grid pattern – Stitch and align as above but work at right angles to your first set of rows. It is often easier to begin in the centre of the fabric and work out to the sides.

Quilting in a crosshatched pattern – Work as above but with lines at 45 degree angles or at another angle of your choice. A rotary ruler normally has markings for 30, 45 and 60 degree lines and can be used to mark angled lines.

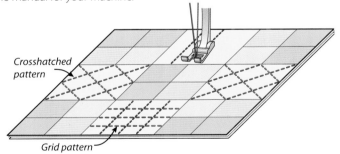

Crosshatched pattern

Grid pattern

If you have a lot of grid or crosshatch quilting to do, or need to stop and start to avoid certain areas (see the trapunto example on page 226), it is best to tie off thread ends in batches as you proceed, to avoid having to deal with a mad spaghetti of threads at the end.

OUTLINE OR CONTOUR QUILTING

This is another easy form of machine quilting which is commonly used to outline patchwork blocks or quilt a contour around an appliqué shape or pieced motif. This quilting is normally worked a consistent distance away from the shape, usually ¼in (6mm) or ⅜in (1cm). Using the width of the machine walking foot is the easiest way to achieve a consistent distance.

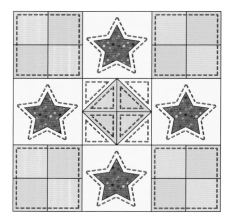

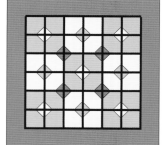

BRIGHT IDEA

Before quilting, prepare a small sandwich about 6in (15.2cm) square of similar fabrics and wadding (batting) used in the quilt as a test piece to check stitch length, tension and thread colour.

ECHO QUILTING

Echo quilting is similar to contour quilting but repeats the contour lines outwards, like waves lapping out from a shore. The quilted lines are normally the same distance apart, so using the width of the machine walking foot is the easiest way. You could also move the needle position to achieve a slightly wider space. Echo quilting is a feature of Hawaiian appliqué.

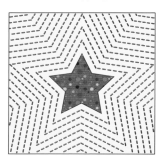

QUILTING ORDER

A quilt is usually a combination of quilting patterns and the order these are stitched in can make a difference to the ease with which the project is sewn. Every quilt is different but an example of a quilting order is shown in the diagrams below of the Floral Lap Quilt project. In the project, see opposite, the quilting thread colour for stages 2, 3 and 4 was a medium olive green.

Stage 1 – in the ditch quilting

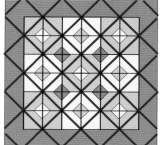

Stage 2 – diagonal quilting

Stage 3 – oval quilting

Stage 4 – smaller elements

Stage 1 – 'Anchor' the layers at regular intervals by quilting in the ditch first (shown as purple lines on the diagram above). In this case the ditch quilting does not extend into the border, which means the starting and stopping points need to be finished off neatly.

Stage 2 – Grid or diagonal quilting (shown in dark green) will further stabilize the quilt layers and in this project can be stitched right across the quilt, which means there are no thread ends to finish off.

Stage 3 – By this stage the quilt is quite stable, which makes the slightly trickier curved quilting easier (shown in blue). An oval was chosen because it is easier to stitch than a tighter circle. A freezer paper template was used to mark the ovals.

Stage 4 – The final stage of quilting consists of small squares (shown as yellow lines), to fill the corners and edges and add a little more definition to the centre of the quilt.

make it now
Floral Lap Quilt

Sometimes you fall in love with a fabric and have to make something to show it off. This bright print is teamed with two other colours to echo the colours in the print. The blocks are big and bold too, quilted with easy machine quilting.

profile

Skills practised: Simple piecing; mitred border; simple machine-guided quilting; binding
Finished size: 44½in (113cm) square
Fabrics: Bright print ½yd (0.5m); light fabric ½yd (0.5m); dark fabric ¾yd (0.75m); wadding (batting) 50in (127cm) square; backing fabric 50in (127cm) square
Threads: Machine quilting thread to suit fabrics

METHOD

- Make five print blocks and four light triangle corner blocks (see page 82). Piece together in three rows of three and press.
- For the mitred border use the dark print and cut four pieces 6½in (16.5cm) wide x 46in (117cm) long (joining strips as necessary). Sew to the quilt top as described on page 135 and press. Square up the finished top, trimming as necessary.
- Make a quilt sandwich of the top, wadding (batting) and backing (see page 188). Quilt in the ditch with invisible thread between the large blocks. Use machine quilting thread to quilt the pattern shown on the diagrams opposite.
- Remove tacking (basting) or pins and trim the top ready for binding. Using the print fabric or light fabric, cut 2½in (6.3cm) wide strips, joining them together into a 190in (483cm) length. Double bind as described on page 238.

FREE-MOTION QUILTING

Free-motion quilting is a form of machine work where you decide exactly where the machine sews. When the feed dogs are lowered or covered, the machine is no longer able to feed the fabric through, which allows you to steer the work in whatever direction you like. Free-motion or free-hand quilting takes practice. Try drawing on a piece of paper by moving the paper and not the pencil and you'll get an idea of the technique. However, the results are well worth it and, once mastered, the technique allows great creativity.

PREPARING YOUR MACHINE

A special presser foot called a darning foot is used for free-motion quilting. This foot, which may also be called a free-motion or embroidery foot, is spring loaded so it can move up and down with the needle – see example here. If your machine doesn't have one ask at your local quilting shop or your machine manufacturer. Alternatively, use an open-toe free-motion foot to allow you to see the stitching area – see example.

Darning foot

You must drop or disengage the feed dogs for free-motion quilting, so check your manual for how to do this. Modern machines usually have a simple sliding device. If you can't drop the feed dogs due to the age of your machine then cover them so they cannot engage with the fabric. Tape a rectangle of thin card securely to the needle plate. Punch a hole in the card for the passage of the needle.

Open-toe free-motion embroidery foot

Using a straight stitch throat plate rather than a normal zigzag plate can be helpful for free-motion work. The straight stitch plate helps to form more regular stitches, with less skipping, as the smaller hole allows less room for the fabric to be pushed into the hole (see examples on page 213).

FREE-MOTION DESIGNS

Free-motion or free-hand designs can be anything you choose – geometric shapes, circles, spirals or pictorial motifs. The patterns can be quilted within a specific block or border or repeated over whole areas of a quilt. Sashiko patterns can be used too. The density of stitching can be of your choosing and will depend on the time available and the overall balance of quilting you wish to achieve. A few patterns are supplied here for practice on paper first, if you are new to the technique.

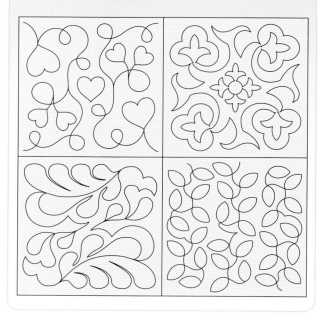

A loose and relaxed free-motion pattern of swirls, stars and hearts was used on this beautifully coloured quilt, made by Lynne Edwards.

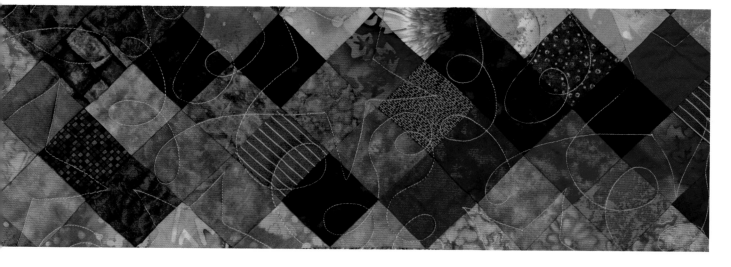

>> related topics... *Marking Fabrics 25 • Preparing a Quilt Sandwich 188* > > >

THE TECHNIQUES

FREE-MOTION QUILTING BASICS

This technique takes practice to master. Make up some small practice quilt sandwiches and aim at first just to feel comfortable with the technique and enjoy the process. Many people find it very liberating. Take some time to study the design you wish to quilt, planning which directions you want to go in. It is also helpful to stabilize the quilt first by quilting in the ditch of the blocks and borders. If you don't want this stabilizing quilting to remain in the quilt use water-soluble thread, which can be washed out later.

1 If you are quilting a specific shape or motif this will need to be marked on the quilt top in the usual way. Prepare the quilt sandwich. Meandering and stipple patterns don't usually require marking as they are meant to be free-flowing and random. Lower or disengage the feed dogs on the machine and disengage the dual-feed foot if your machine has one. Attach the free-motion foot and select a straight stitch with the needle in the centre position. Stitch length in free-motion quilting is determined by the speed you are quilting at and the movement of the quilt by your hands but set the length at zero anyway as this stops the feed teeth from moving.

2 Lower the presser foot where you want to begin quilting. Hold the end of the top thread, make a stitch and pull the top thread to bring up the bottom thread. This prevents the bobbin thread from being caught in the stitching underneath. Sew a few stitches on the spot to secure.

3 Place your hands in a C-shape on either side of the presser foot and begin to stitch, pressing down to move the quilt around and keeping the speed of the machine as consistent as you can. Alternatively, try bunching the quilt up in one hand and use your thumb and index finger on the other hand to encircle the stitching area. Move the quilt with your hands, don't turn it, and aim to create even stitches of a uniform length. To finish off, work several stitches on the spot and trim the thread ends. Once comfortable with the technique, move on from practice pieces to quilting your actual project. ▼

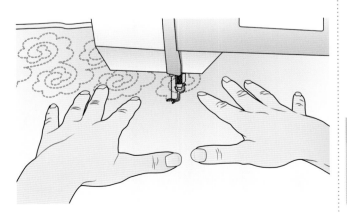

FREE-MOTION STIPPLING

A popular type of free-motion quilting is called stippling, also referred to as vermicelli quilting. This is a free-form, random pattern where the quilting line meanders in swirls and loops that do not cross each other, rather like the shapes of a jigsaw puzzle. Its random nature means that no marking of the quilt top is necessary. The pattern may be dense or loosely spaced, where it is sometimes referred to as meandering quilting. It can look very attractive if stitched as a companion to corded quilting, throwing them into high relief. Some modern machines have a built-in stippling stitch and computerized patterns.

Set up your machine and the quilt as described in steps 1 and 2, left. Begin free-motion quilting in an unending pattern of tight curves and loops that do not cross. Work from one corner, across and down the area to be quilted, keeping stitches a consistent length and the pattern a consistent density.

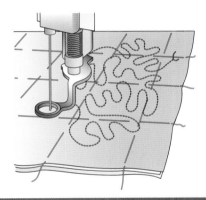

FREE-MOTION MOTIFS

Free-motion quilting can follow any shape or pattern. Simply mark the pattern or motif on the quilt top and follow the lines. A motif with a 'one-way, no stopping' route will be easier to stitch (A). Appliqué motifs can also be used as the basis for motif quilting (B) and can be rotated and reversed to create variety.

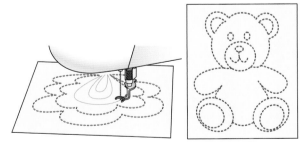

BRIGHT IDEA

PRACTISE FREE-MOTION QUILTING BY FOLLOWING THE DESIGN ON A LARGE-PRINT FABRIC, OR DOODLE YOUR OWN DESIGN AND FOLLOW THAT.

LONG-ARM QUILTING

Long-arm quilting is achieved by a sewing machine that has an extended area between the back of the machine and the sewing head. In other words, it has a long arm. The machine has pairs of wheels that allow it to be moved around and, unlike a normal sewing machine, the head moves while the quilt is kept still, suspended between rollers. Long-arm machines can be hand operated or computer controlled, with a wide range of patterns available via software. Patterns can also be customized and enlarged or reduced.

A simple long-arm quilting pattern is often all that is needed to finish a quilt.

Long-arm machines take skill and practice to operate, with the operator needing to be adept at various functions, including making sure that all the layers of the quilt sandwich are properly loaded and attached, that patterns are positioned correctly and that the top and bottom tensions are correct.

The quilt sandwich is attached to the machine, with the top edge of the backing attached to the take-up roller and the bottom edge to a roller on the opposite side, so the backing can be made taut. The wadding (batting) is positioned at the top edge of the backing, with the rest left free. The top edge of the quilt top is attached to the backing and wadding, with the bottom edge fixed to another roller. Attaching the layers in this way means that the backing and wadding need to be about 4in–6in (10.2cm–15.2cm) larger on all sides to allow for fabric take-up by the machine.

WHY LONG-ARM QUILT?

There are many reasons why people use a long-arm quilting service. For many patchworkers the thrill is in the piecing, not the quilting, and using a long-arm quilting service means that their pieced work is returned in a short time, fully and expertly quilted, and even bound if they want. Other people are not confident in their machine quilting skills, especially if the quilt is a large one, and so prefer a professional to handle this aspect. For some, a lack of time makes sending a quilt away a sensible proposition. Keen stitchers may simply have too many tops to quilt and prefer to get a project finished rather than have it lying around unfinished. A big bonus with long-arm quilting is that you do not need to tack (baste) the quilt layers together beforehand, as each of the layers are loaded on to the machine separately. If you want to do your own quilting but really hate spending time preparing a quilt sandwich then a long-arm quilting service can do this for you.

The cost of long-arm quilting varies but most companies base their fees on quilt size and the density or intricacy of the patterns required. Quilting may be custom or edge to edge. Extras may be offered, such as sourcing the backing and wadding and binding the quilt. Quilts can also be semi-quilted and returned to you to complete as you like.

This example of long-arm quilting from Pam and Nicky Lintott shows how this form of free-motion work can enhance the overall design of a quilt beautifully.

LONG-ARM QUILTING PATTERNS

There are lots of patterns available for long-arm quilting, many of which are pantograph designs. Patterns can be simple or complex, pictorial or abstract, all-over or focused on specific areas. Choosing a pattern will depend on various factors, including the ratio of plain blocks to pieced ones, the theme of the quilt and the type of thread selected. A browse on the internet will reveal a huge selection or you may be happy for the long-arm quilter to select an appropriate design or work freehand. A few examples of edge-to-edge patterns are illustrated below, which The Quilt Room (see Suppliers on page 253) kindly allowed us to show.

USING A LONG-ARM QUILTING SERVICE

- Always consult with the long-arm quilter and find out what they require before you choose and prepare backing and wadding (batting). For example, they may request a certain type of wadding be used, for example, a low-loft one that is hard-wearing and washable, with low shrinkage percentages.
- Ensure backing and wadding (batting) are 4in–6in (10.2cm–15.2cm) larger all round.
- Ensure all seams are secure, particularly at the edges, and don't leave selvedges in seam allowances of backings as these can pucker when the quilt is washed.
- Press the quilt top well and ensure seams are lying flat. Don't prepare the quilt sandwich as the layers are loaded separately on to the long-arm machine.
- Ensure that the backing is straight and squared.
- Tie off loose threads close to the fabric as these can get caught on the machine foot. For the same reason don't have tacking (basting) stitches too large or loose.
- Choosing backing fabric that matches the thread will minimize tension problems.
- If you want a backing fabric that shows the quilting, choose one that is not too 'busy'. Solid colours and tones show quilting to best advantage.
- If posting your quilt, remember to insure it.

A few examples of long-arm quilting patterns.

QUILT-AS-YOU-GO

Quilt-as-you-go is a method of working where quilt blocks or small sections of a quilt are quilted before they are joined together. This method has two main advantages: it avoids having to manipulate a whole, large quilt when hand or machine quilting and it makes the individual blocks very portable.

The method can be used to join blocks together edge to edge or with the use of sashing strips. It does require slightly more backing fabric and wadding (batting) so remember to allow extra. You also need to give some thought to the quilting patterns used as some additional quilting may be needed to extend the patterns between blocks. Any quilting done with the quilt-as-you-go method needs to end about ½in–¾in (1.3cm–1.9cm) from the outer edges of the blocks to allow for the joining process.

Patchwork blocks made for a sampler quilt, as this one was by Pat Mitchell, can be sewn using a quilt-as-you-go technique.

THE TECHNIQUE

QUILT-AS-YOU-GO

1 Once the blocks have been padded, backed and quilted, they can be joined together, usually in rows. Put two blocks right sides together, pin the wadding (batting) and backing back out of the way and stitch the block fronts together by machine or hand. Press seams open, taking care with the wadding in case it melts under the heat of an iron. Continue for all the blocks. ▼

2 With the joined blocks right sides down, release the wadding but keep the backing fabric out of the way. Trim the wadding pieces so their edges butt together and then stitch them together using ladder stitch or herringbone. ▼

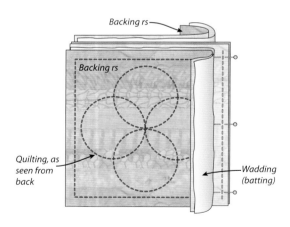

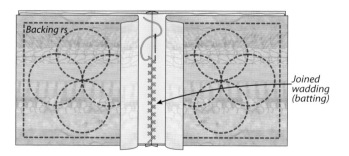

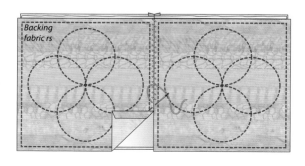

3 Release the backing pieces. Create a folded edge on each piece of backing fabric and butt these edges together. Finger press and pin in place. Check that the front of the work looks smooth and flat and slipstitch the backing fabric pieces together. If you prefer, you could have one folded edge of backing fabric slightly overlapping the other. Repeat this for all the blocks in a row and then sew the rows together in a similar fashion. Finish any quilting as needed. ▶

BRIGHT IDEA

THE QUILT-AS-YOU-GO METHOD ALSO ALLOWS YOU TO MAKE QUILTS THAT ARE FULLY REVERSIBLE.

TIED QUILTING

The layers of a quilt can be secured by tying rather than stitching and this method can create a distinctive and charming look to a quilt. Machine and hand quilting are usually quite closely spaced, giving a flat appearance to a quilt but tying the layers together is done at wider intervals, giving a quilt a puffier look. This method is also excellent for a quilt with thicker layers. The knots in tied quilting can be tied on the front of the quilt or on the back and can be made in various ways, constructed to blend in or stand out as decorative features in their own right. Tying a quilt can be done by machine by stitching on the spot several times through all layers.

THREADS FOR TIED QUILTING

Threads need to be strong enough to hold the quilt layers together without breaking, so use a sturdy thread such as perle cotton or crochet cotton. The thread used for tying can be matched to the quilt colours or used as a contrast to create artistic effects. For example, an area of dark blue night sky on a quilt could use white or silver knots to represent stars.

THE TECHNIQUES

TIED QUILTING WITH KNOTS

Make a quilt sandwich as normal and use long pins to fix the layers together at the points you want the ties to be. If the quilt top has a wide border add pins here too. Thread your needle with a long length of strong thread and make a stitch through all the layers, twice, over the pin. Cut the thread, leaving a 3in (7.6cm) tail at each end. Tie the ends together securely in a square or reef knot (right over left and then left over right) – see diagram A below. Remove the pins as you go.

USING BUTTONS AND BEADS

You could also use buttons, beads and charms to tie a quilt. Flat buttons can be tied in the same way as thread, as shown below. If using a button with a shank, first stitch the button in place, leaving tails of thread at the back and then knot the threads securely and trim ends.

If using beads to tie the layers together choose a strong type that will not shatter or break – wood or metal are the most durable. Sew the bead in place with strong thread and tie securely in a knot at the back of the work.

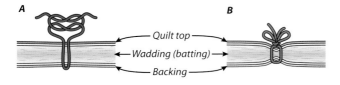

TYING BOWS

Bows create a really decorative effect on a quilt or project and you could emphasize this by using narrow ribbon or cord instead to make a real feature of the bows. If you want to tie a bow instead of simple knotting you will need to leave longer tails, at least 5in (12.7cm). Once you have tied the bow, then tie a square or reef knot in the centre of the bow, to make sure it is secure and doesn't come undone – see diagram B above.

SAFETY TIP

IT IS BEST NOT TO USE BEADS OR BUTTONS FOR QUILTS THAT WILL BE USED FOR BABIES AND YOUNG CHILDREN AS THEY COULD BECOME A CHOKING HAZARD OR SCRATCH DELICATE SKIN.

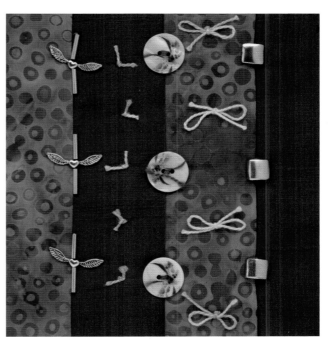

Examples of tied quilting from left to right: beads and charms, knotted thread, buttons, thread knotted and tied in a bow, and metal beads.

CORDED QUILTING

Cotton piping cord or quilting wool and a large bodkin are needed for corded quilting.

Corded quilting is also known as Italian quilting and is a method of quilting where channels are stitched and then padded by running lengths of cord or wool yarn through them from the back of the work. Corded quilting creates an attractive raised look and many designs can be quilted this way simply by quilting a second parallel line ¼in (6mm) away from the first. Celtic designs look very striking worked as corded quilting, especially intricate knots. Stuffed quilting (see overleaf) is similar to corded quilting in the effect created but shapes rather than narrow channels are stuffed.

The channels for corded quilting can be created by various hand stitches, including a normal quilting stitch, backstitch or stem stitch. If you prefer machine stitching then a straight stitch can be used and this will create the firmest line and the sharpest edge to the channel. The cord or wool is normally threaded through from the back of the work with a large, blunt-ended needle or bodkin, so it is helpful to use a backing fabric with a looser weave. This fabric cannot also become the back of your quilt as it will have holes in it, so use a normal backing and wadding (batting) after all the corded quilting is finished. Traditionally, corded work was left unpadded. A shadowed effect can be created with corded quilting by using a sheer fabric as the top layer and selecting coloured cords or yarns to thread through.

CORDS

The cord normally used for corded quilting is a cotton piping or special quilting wool. Thick knitting wool yarns are also suitable. Pre-wash cord so it does not shrink when the quilt is laundered. Whatever you use must be thick enough to fill the stitched channel or the corded effect will not be seen, but not so thick that it is difficult to thread or where the cord distorts the fabric.

Corded quilting together with areas of stuffed quilting are used on this sumptuous cushion by Pauline Ineson. The corded quilting around the edge echoes the shape of the central petals.

>> related topics... *Marking Fabrics 25 • Hand Quilting 196 • Stuffed Quilting 226* >>>

THE TECHNIQUE

CORDED QUILTING

Corded quilting is a technique that creates raised lines on the front of the work that catch the light and cast shadows. Channels are normally ¼in (6mm) apart but could be narrower for a more pronounced look. If the cord or wool you plan to use isn't thick enough then use a doubled length.

1 Mark the design on the front of your fabric using an erasable marker. Place this fabric together with the backing fabric and pin or tack (baste) together. Lines are usually quilted ¼in (6mm) apart and it is helpful to mark the channels like this so you can see exactly where to stitch. ▼

2 If your design has lines that cross, decide beforehand which channel goes under and which goes over. These points are marked * on the diagram below. You need to stop, skip and start again at these areas in order that the cord can be fed smoothly along the channels. Quilt the lines by hand or machine. ▼

3 Cut cord or wool longer than the channel to be stuffed and thread it into a large-eyed blunt needle or bodkin. Insert the needle from the back of the work into the channel and work it along the channel until a cross-over point or a sharp bend. Bring the needle out at the back and gently pull the cord along the channel. Allow a little ease, re-insert the needle, leaving a loop, and continue to stuff the channels. If your needle and cord will not pierce and enter the backing fabric, cut a tiny slit in the fabric. Leave cord tails on the back at the start and finish of the lines stuffed – these can be tacked (basted) together and trimmed later. ▼

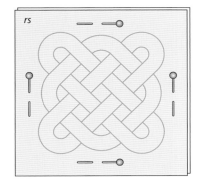

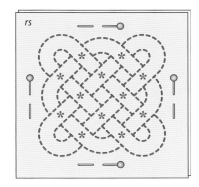

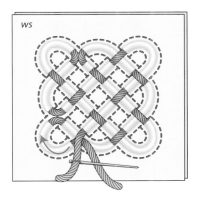

Even the smallest amount of corded quilting can look most attractive. This little bridal bag by Gail Lawther features an elegant border in a Celtic pattern.

STUFFED QUILTING

Stuffed quilting is a beautiful addition to patchwork and appliqué and is a rewarding skill to master. Two layers of fabric are joined together with a stitched design, which is then stuffed to create raised areas. When stuffed quilting also incorporates corded quilting it is called trapunto but many people use the term just to mean stuffed quilting. *Trapunta* in Italian means 'quilt', while *piqué cordé* is the French term for trapunto work. Boutis quilting uses similar techniques but is usually reversible, which normal stuffed quilting is not. After the stuffed quilting is finished, wadding (batting) and backing are added, so allowing quilting in the normal way.

Trapunto work is shown to best effect on pale-coloured fabrics with a slight sheen or glaze and all white or cream quilts can look stunning. The stuffed shapes can be abstract, geometric or pictorial, including flowers, foliage, fruit, shells and feathers. The raised appearance of the technique can be emphasized even further by densely quilted areas around the trapunto. This surrounding quilting can be worked by hand or machine and three popular patterns are grid, stipple and echo quilting. Whole cloth quilting (see page 202) often features elaborate trapunto work, creating lovely three-dimensional effects that catch the light and contrast beautifully with flat, densely quilted areas. Adding a decorative stitch around the stuffed shape or cord couched in place can further highlight the effect, as can using satin stitch to stitch the trapunto shapes.

Stuffed quilting requires the use of a backing fabric, through which the stuffing is inserted. This fabric could be a loosely woven one such as muslin, which will allow the fabric threads to be parted for the stuffing to be inserted, or a fabric in which small slits can be cut and sewn up later. Stuffed quilting can be worked in two ways – stitched and then stuffed or stuffed and then stitched; both are described opposite.

Trapunto

- ✓ If you are new to stuffed quilting start with easy shapes, such as large circles or regular geometric shapes.
- ✓ Light-coloured fabrics with a slight sheen work best for trapunto work, emphasizing the three-dimensional look.
- ✓ The stitching that outlines the shapes can be done by hand but the denser quality of machine stitching works better, resulting in a smooth, well-defined outline.
- ✓ Polyester filling (fiberfill) is the easiest material to use for stuffing but layers of wadding (batting) can also be used.
- ✓ Use a blunt-ended tool for stuffing, such as a wooden cuticle stick or blunt-ended toothpick.
- ✓ Relate the size of the stuffing to the area to be stuffed – small pieces for corners and tips of designs and larger pieces for wider areas. As you stuff, keep checking the front of the work to see how it is looking.
- ✓ Don't over-stuff shapes as this will make them look out of balance with the flat areas and may distort the surrounding fabric. Using an embroidery hoop may help.
- ✓ Don't press the finished stuffed areas or you will flatten them. To remove creases, hold the iron just above the work and use steam.
- ✓ For maximum effect surround areas of stuffed quilting with densely worked normal quilting, for high relief.

This trapunto flower was created with the reversed stuffed method and edged with whipped quilting. Needle-turn appliqué completes the simple design, with a background of crosshatched quilting.

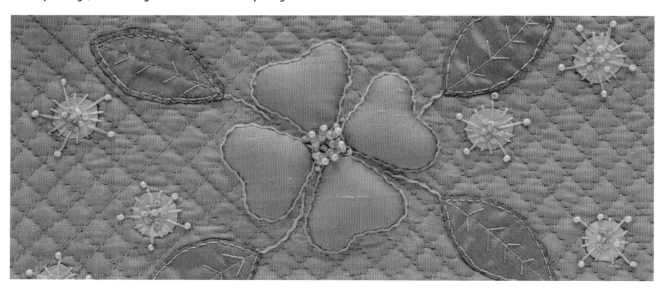

>> related topics... *Marking Fabrics 25 • Hand Quilting 196 • Machine Quilting 212 • Corded Quilting 224* >>>

THE TECHNIQUES

STUFFED QUILTING

In this method the shape is outlined with stitching and the stuffing is done from the back of the work through a medium-weave fabric or via little slits cut in the fabric. You can use a thread that matches or tones with the top fabric. You may find that placing the work in a hoop will help.

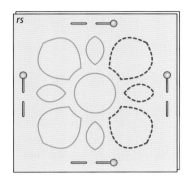

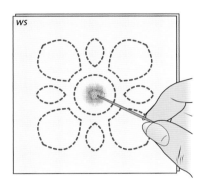

1 Mark the design on the right side of the top fabric using an erasable method. Cut a medium-weave fabric and pin or tack (baste) in place under the top fabric. If working on a quilt where quilting is to show on the back then do the general quilting after the trapunto is finished. If the project will not have the back on show, such as a cushion or bag, then the quilting can be done at this stage by placing wadding (batting) between the backing and top fabric.

2 Carefully sew around the marked shape or shapes that are to be stuffed. If you want to couch cord around the shape do it now (see overleaf for couching). ◄

3 Turn the work to the back and use a blunt-ended needle to tease apart some threads of the medium-weave fabric. If the weave won't allow this then cut a small slit with sharp scissors. Take small quantities of stuffing and insert it through the gap, beginning stuffing at the tips, corners and perimeters of a shape. As you add more stuffing, blend the pieces together to avoid clumps and use your fingers on the front and the back of the work to model the shape. ◄

4 When all the stuffing is finished, use a needle to tease the threads of the backing fabric back into shape so they hold the stuffing. If you have cut a slit, use ladder stitch or herringbone to close the gap. ▼

REVERSED STUFFED QUILTING

In this method the stuffed areas are prepared first and then outlined with stitching. Once all the trapunto is finished you can add wadding (batting) and backing to the quilt as normal.

1 Mark the design on the right side of the top fabric using an erasable method. Mark the design again but in reverse on the back of the fabric, matching it up in the same place as the front design. ▼

2 Cut a piece of high-loft wadding (batting) just slightly larger than the area to be raised and pin it in place on the back of the design, covering the area. You could tack (baste) it in place or use a dab of craft glue. ▼

3 Using a walking foot and thread to match the quilt, stitch around the shape from the front. Turn the work to the wrong side and using small, sharp scissors, carefully cut away excess wadding around the shapes close to the stitching. ▼

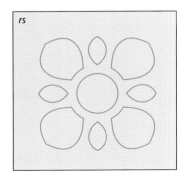

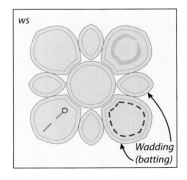

Wadding (batting)

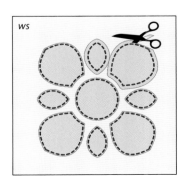

DECORATIVE QUILTING

Quilting doesn't have to be a plain running stitch or machine straight stitch. There is a whole world of possibilities once you consider using decorative hand and machine stitches. Add to this the potential for using braids, cords, tapes, ribbons and other trims, not to mention beads, buttons and charms, and you have an exciting world of quilting that promises to take a piece of work into the extraordinary. Mixed media effects are increasingly popular and allow your creativity free rein.

Using decorative hand quilting along seams is an attractive way to quilt a project and add embellishment. Add further interest and texture with trims and braids couched into place.

The boundary between quilting and embroidery is blurring all the time and mingling these techniques allows you to use some fabulous threads and different fabrics for patchwork, including those with a thicker pile or more open weave. This section can only hint at what is available but shows some decorative hand stitches you might try for quilting and some of the decorative stitches achievable by machine. Couching can also be used to quilt a project and add embellishment to your work.

DECORATIVE HAND QUILTING

There are so many wonderful stitches to experiment with in patchwork, appliqué and quilting projects, and it's also fun to add variations or additions. There are many stitches to choose from on pages 245–247, and many wonderful books on the subject (see Further Reading on page 252).

Threads for decorative quilting can be the same as those used for the other hand-quilting techniques or you could branch out and try others, such as perle cottons, metallics, rayons, bouclés, crochet cottons and all sorts of variegated threads. Any thread that can be sewn through the quilt sandwich can be used. Most of us have some gorgeous threads we couldn't resist buying but are unsure what to do with – now is the time to find out.

DECORATIVE MACHINE QUILTING

Most sewing machines have a range of decorative stitches that can be used for quilting. A simple zigzag stitch can take on a new look depending on its width, length and thread used. If you are only quilting through the top layer of the quilt then it is best to use a tear-away stabilizer beneath your quilt top.

Threads for decorative machine quilting can be the same as for normal machine quilting but experiment to judge the effect. A thicker thread, such as a 30 weight, will show up better than a thinner one. A shiny rayon thread will catch the light and be more noticeable than a cotton thread. Normal bobbin thread (50–70 weight) can be used in the bobbin. The machine needle used will depend on the fabric and thread you are using but generally use a size 75/11 for 40 weight threads and a size 80/12 for 30 weight.

COUCHING

Couching is essentially laying a length of thread, cord, braid, ribbon or other trim on to the surface of fabric and securing it in place with hand or machine stitches or glue for projects that don't need to be washed. Couched designs include simple outlines, geometric patterns and swirling motifs. Couching adds a wonderful three-dimensional, tactile quality and allows you to try many different fibres, including metallic braids, bouclés, chainette, unusual knitting yarns – even leather and chain. Quilt artists create many dazzling effects with couching.

Some lovely effects can be achieved with decorative quilting stitches, especially when stitched on shiny silk, as Gail Lawther did for these cushions. The pale cushion uses sashiko quilting, while the dark blue cushion has herringbone stitch and fern stitch.

>> **related topics...** *Marking Fabrics 25 • Preparing a Quilt Sandwich 188 • Machine Quilting 212* >>>

THE TECHNIQUES

DECORATIVE QUILTING BY HAND

Quilting with decorative stitches can be worked by hand along seam junctions or as patterns and motifs within blocks and borders. Choose a thread type and weight suitable for the fabric you are using. If the stitches are to follow a pattern or motif then mark this on your quilt top in the normal way. If the decorative stitches need to secure the layers of the quilt then stitch a practice piece to check what the stitches look like from the back of the work. Start and finish off with a quilter's knot as normal. If the thread is too thick for this, take a tiny backstitch and run the thread inside the wadding (batting) for some distance before trimming it.

DECORATIVE QUILTING BY MACHINE

Decorative machine stitches can be worked along seam junctions or as patterns within blocks and borders. Select the right thread and needle for the fabric you are using and mark the pattern on the fabric if required. Practise on spare fabric first. Start and finish by sewing several stitches on the spot, or tie loose ends in a knot and use a needle to lose the ends inside the quilt.

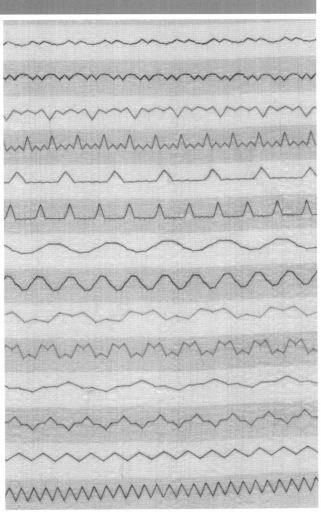

Standard sewing machines have a surprising number of decorative stitches. You can increase the range of these by experimenting with stitch width and length.

BRIGHT IDEA

KEEP A NOTEBOOK BY YOUR SEWING MACHINE TO JOT DOWN THE DETAILS OF THREAD PROGRAMME/STITCH LENGTH AND WIDTH YOU USED FOR A PARTICULAR PROJECT. SO IF IT'S WEEKS OR MONTHS (OR YEARS!) BEFORE YOU RETURN TO THE PROJECT YOU WILL HAVE A RECORD OF HOW THE STITCHING WAS ACHIEVED.

Small projects are ideal to practise decorative quilting techniques. Here some ricrac braid has been couched with long stitches in a contrasting colour. Beneath this a twisted metallic braid has been couched in a freehand pattern using small stitches in a toning thread.

COUCHING BY HAND

Couching is best done before adding wadding (batting) and backing, because the ends of the material being couched can be secured neatly at the back. For best results, strengthen the base fabric with a fusible stabilizer.

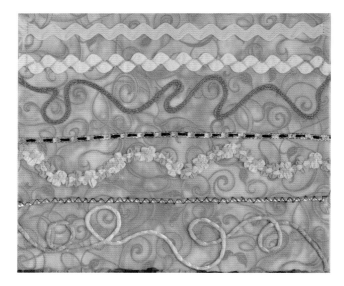

The hand stitches used for couching may depend on the width of the material being couched and whether you want the couching stitches to also sew through the quilt layers. For example, a wide ricrac braid could be secured with small stitches for an invisible look or larger stitches in a pattern to draw attention to the couching. When couching a narrow metallic braid, oversew along the braid from one side to the other with small stitches in matching thread or use a contrasting thread and sew at an oblique angle.

1 To couch by hand, lay the cord or braid along the line marked on your fabric, pinning in place. ▶

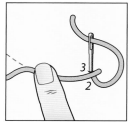

2 Using your couching thread, make small stitches over the laid thread. ▶

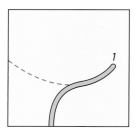

3 Continue to anchor the laid thread in this way along its entire length. ▶

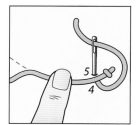

COUCHING BY MACHINE

On a sewing machine a zigzag stitch is the easiest to use for couching but if you have a machine with other decorative stitches with side-to-side actions then try those too. Cord creates a three-dimensional quality to the surface and can blend in with the background fabric or stand out from it, depending on the thread type and colour you use. For a more noticeable effect use a thread in a contrasting colour. For best results when couching by machine, use an embroidery or narrow braiding foot with a groove underneath in a similar width to the cord you are using. Your machine may have a presser foot that can feed the cord under the foot or through a hole in the top of the foot.

1 Mark the design you wish to be couched. Use a zigzag width that will just cover the width of the cord or braid you are using. It is a good idea to practise with some scrap fabric and a short length of cord.

2 Leave a short tail of cord at the beginning and secure by stitching on the cord. Slowly zigzag stitch over the cord and turn the fabric when needed to keep the drawn line under the centre of the foot. At the end of the line, secure the stitching and cut the cord, leaving a short tail. Take the cord tails to the back of the work or into the wadding (batting) with a large-eyed needle. ▼

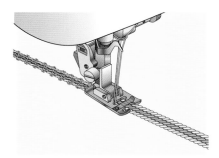

If there is a sharp angle or point in the design, stop with the needle down on the inside of the line, pivot so the point in the design is at the side of the needle and reduce the stitch length to zero. Sew two stitches to secure the cord and stop on the inside of the line. Pivot again to point in the right direction, reset the stitch length and continue on.

BRIGHT IDEA

When sewing with trims that fray, seal the ends with Fray Check liquid or a spot of clear nail varnish. Allow to dry before continuing to sew or couch.

make it now
Scented Sachet

A sampler of decorative stitches has been made up as a sachet filled with pot-pourri. The central panel is pieced with half-square triangles but any patchwork block could be used. Stitches used include cross, chain, open chain, fern, feather, herringbone, blanket, crossed herringbone, sheaf stitch and French knots (see pages 245–247).

profile

Skills practiced: Half-square triangle patchwork; mitred border; machine quilting; decorative quilting
Project layout: Half-square triangles with mitred border
Finished size: 11in (28cm) square
Fabrics: Pastel prints for centre panel; border fabric 2½in x 44in (6.3cm x 111.8cm); wadding (batting) 12in (30.5cm) square; backing fabric
Threads: Variegated stranded embroidery cotton
Embellishments: Four buttons (optional)

METHOD

- Piece the centre panel with patchwork of your choice (see page 80 for stitching half-square triangles). The panel shown is 7½in (19cm). Add a mitred border (see page 135). Cut wadding (batting) larger than the sachet front, place behind the patchwork and machine quilt in the ditch.
- Enlarge the pattern above by 500 per cent or the size required and mark the design. Using threads to suit your fabrics, work decorative stitches of your choice. Sew a button in each corner if desired.
- Make up as a cushion (see page 249), filling with pot-pourri before closing the final gap.

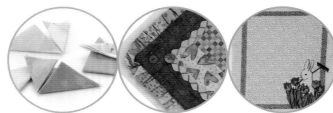

Finishing Off

By now most of the work needed to create a wonderful patchwork, appliqué or quilted project is done and all that remains is to add the finishing touches to your work. This section looks at some of the many edge finishes that can be given to quilts, from ultra-simple 'bagging-out' and utilitarian binding to decorative edges such as scallops and prairie points. Advice on labelling work, caring for quilts and exhibiting quilts is also given. A library of stitches commonly used in patchwork, appliqué and quilting is illustrated on pages 245–247 and there is some useful information on page 250, which will be helpful for the mathematically challenged (author included!). Further Reading on page 252 suggests some books you may find helpful. There are so many fabulous books and magazines available on all aspects of patchwork, appliqué and quilting that you will no doubt build your own library of favourites.

FINISHING EDGES

The edges on a quilt or other project can receive a lot of wear and tear so it makes sense to finish a project with a strong and durable edging. Binding is a popular method but the edges can be finished in many ways to complement the quilt. Finishing edges is usually done after all quilting is completed, as quilting can affect the overall size and even the shape of the quilt top. This section looks at how to prepare a quilt for an edging and how to stitch different types of edging to bring an extra 'wow' factor to your work.

PREPARING EDGES AND SQUARING UP

Preparing quilt edges carefully not only ensures that the quilt is square but will also make the task of applying binding or other edgings easier. If you have been checking measurements as you were making the quilt, any mismatches will be minimal but there always seems to be the need for further adjustments, no matter how careful you are. See technique below.

Once the quilt sandwich has been prepared (see page 188) and all quilting is finished, check that the quilt is square and hangs correctly. This is important if the quilt is to be displayed on a wall or exhibited at a show. Press it and fold in half along the length to see if the two edges match. If one side is longer than the other see the suggestions opposite for correcting this.

PREPARING EDGES

1 Ensure the quilt is smooth and crease-free, pressing it if need be. Before adding any edging to a quilt, use the sewing machine to tack (baste) the quilt layers together, sewing a *scant* ¼in (6mm) from the raw edge of the quilt top. Stitch along each side separately and leave long tails of thread at beginning and end.

2 Check the quilt is square. If it is only slightly out of true, use method A or B described in Squaring up a Quilt, right, to bring it back to square. If it is considerably out of true then use method C before proceeding with edge trimming.

3 Using a large rotary cutting mat, rotary cutter and large square ruler, carefully trim the wadding (batting) and backing evenly with the edges of the quilt top, making sure the quilt is square by aligning the edge with the side and top of the ruler as shown in the diagram. Move the quilt as necessary to continue trimming, aligning it with a previously cut edge to ensure it all stays straight and square. When finished, check the quilt is still square. ▼

SQUARING UP A QUILT

A quilt that is not square can be corrected in various ways. Prepare the quilt as shown left, with a machine-tacked (basted) line along the sides, then use one of the following methods.

A If one side is only slightly longer than the other you may be able to trim the long side slightly to even it up. This is only possible with a plain border, not one with blocks right up to the edges where points or parts of the block might be cut off.

B If the length difference is small (less than 1in/2.5cm), then the longer side can be shortened by pulling gently on the bobbin thread of the machine-tacked (basted) line to slightly pull up the fabric. Ease any small gathers, tie off the threads and press.

C If a quilt is more out of true, then blocking will help to straighten it. Lay the pressed quilt out flat on a clean sheet on the floor, ideally on a carpet. Start at one corner and pull the edges of the quilt so they are square, checking with a rotary ruler, and pin in place into the carpet. If blocking on a non-carpeted surface, use a low-tack tape. Using two rulers will help ensure the corner is square. Move to the next corner and repeat. Secure the side between these two corners. Continue in this way all around the quilt. Mark the quilt all round so you have a line to trim against later. Leave the quilt in place for a day or two to help the fabric set in this position. If the quilt needs a lot of persuasion to be squared, spray it lightly with clean water as you block (provided it is colourfast). Leave until dry and then trim edges as necessary.

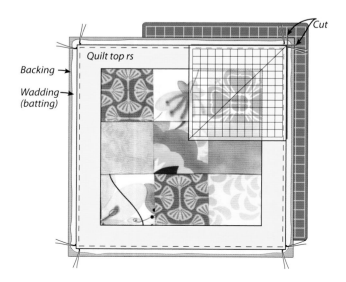

Cut

Quilt top rs

Backing →

Wadding → (batting)

BRIGHT IDEA

RE-STITCH ANY OF THE TACKING (BASTING) THAT MAY HAVE BEEN CUT OFF DURING THE SQUARING-UP PROCESS AS IT WILL HELP TO KEEP THE LAYERS STABLE AS YOU ADD THE BINDING.

BAGGED-OUT EDGE

Probably the simplest way to form a secure edge on a quilt is by 'bagging-out', that is sewing the quilt top and backing together with right sides facing and then turning out though a gap. This is a useful method if your project has lots of decorative hand quilting or couching, where the back of the quilt looks untidy or bulky. The quilting and any embellishing required can be done through the quilt top alone, with the wadding (batting) tacked to the backing fabric. Alternatively, the quilt top and wadding can be tacked together before quilting and embellishing and the backing added after. In either case the normal 'quilt sandwich' stage is a little different so some forward planning is required. This technique is useful for bags and cushions to create neat and secure edges.

SEWING A BAGGED-OUT EDGING

1 Place the quilt top right sides together with the backing fabric, layer the wadding (batting) on top and pin together, ensuring all layers are smooth. The backing/wadding can be either slightly larger than the quilt top, or flush. Sew with the quilt top uppermost.

2 Sew a ¼in (6mm) seam all around the edge, leaving a gap along the bottom for turning the quilt through; this will need to be about 12in (30.5cm) long, so the bulk of the quilt can be pulled through the opening. Before turning through, trim the backing down to the same size as the quilt top and trim the wadding to within ⅛in (3mm) of the stitched line. Clip the corners to reduce bulk.

3 Turn through to the right side (bag-out) and smooth out the quilt. If any quilting is to be done now, tack (baste) the layers together, complete the quilting and press and sew up the gap. If quilting was done previously, then smooth out the quilt, press the seam and slipstitch the gap closed. For extra security and a firmer edge, topstitch all the way around the quilt, about ⅛in– ¼in (3mm–6mm) from the edge.

Sewing a knife edge – A knife edge is similar to bagging-out but is done from the right side and by hand. Simply fold the quilt top edges under by ¼in–½in (6mm–1.3cm) and the backing fabric edges under by the same amount and then slipstitch them together all round. This type of edging would not be durable enough for a bed quilt but would be fine for decorative projects.

TURNED-OVER EDGE USING THE BACKING

Another easy way of finishing a quilt is to sew a turned-over edge by wrapping the backing fabric around to the front of the quilt, covering the edges. The backing fabric is thus seen from the front of the quilt and gives the appearance of binding.

SEWING A TURNED-OVER EDGE

1 Pin the backing out of the way and trim the wadding (batting) to the same size as the quilt top. Trim the backing to twice the width you want the edge to be, so for a ½in (1.3cm) wide edge, trim the backing 1in (2.5cm) wider all round than the quilt top. Start at one corner and fold over the backing as shown and then trim off the small corner. ▼

2 Fold the backing over so the raw edge meets the edge of the quilt top. Fold again so it overlaps the quilt top. Pin in place. Do the same on the other side of the corner, checking the two sides are meeting in a neat mitre. Continue to fold and pin all the way round the quilt and then stitch the backing down using matching thread and invisible slipstitches. ▼

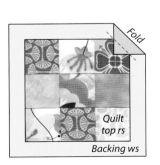

Quilt top rs

Backing ws

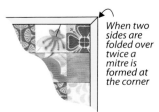

When two sides are folded over twice a mitre is formed at the corner

Bagging-out is a really useful technique for smaller projects, forming a neat and secure edge that is quick to stitch.

BINDING AS AN EDGING

Binding a quilt edge with fabric is the most popular way of finishing a quilt and creates a neat appearance. Bias binding is available commercially but the range of colours, patterns and quality is very limited so it is far more satisfactory to make your own. The binding can be a plain fabric to complement the rest of the quilt, a print to echo fabric used in the quilt, or be pieced to use up the last scraps of fabric. It is a good idea to choose the binding fabric after the quilt is finished so you can judge which best complements the quilt. The technique for making binding can also be used when creating bias strips for bias strip appliqué.

There are some aspects of binding to consider before you start choosing and cutting fabric so ask the following questions.

- Is the binding just for straight edges or to curve around corners? If for straight edges then the fabric can be cut on the straight grain. If intended to curve, cut the fabric on the bias so it can be eased around corners more easily.
- Is the binding to be single or double? A double binding (often called French-fold binding) has two layers of fabric so is more durable than a single binding, but uses more fabric.
- Is the binding to be sewn in place with straight corners or mitred corners? The corners may form part of the overall quilt design so the blocks used for the quilt top and the way they have been sewn together may help you decide.
- Is the binding to be from one fabric or be pieced? You may have fabric left over from the quilt top and a pieced binding is a good way to do this. Alternatively, the quilt may be 'busy' enough and a plain fabric will work best.

Calculating width – The finished width of a binding is normally ¼in (6mm), ⅜in (1cm) or ½in (1.3cm) and is sewn with a ¼in (6mm) seam allowance. The following formula is useful:
Finished width x 2 + seam allowance x 2 = width required.
So for a single binding finishing ½in wide: ½in x 2 = 1in + ¼in seams x 2 = 1½in (3.8cm) cut width.
For a double binding finishing ½in wide: ½in x 2 = 1in + ¼in seams x 2 = 1½in x 2 (fabric is doubled) = 3in (7.6cm) cut width.

For double-fold binding many books and magazines suggest a 2½in (6.3cm) cut width for a finished binding width of ⅜in (1cm). This is a useful measurement as most pre-cut strips and Jelly Rolls™ are this width.

Calculating length – To calculate the length of binding needed, measure your finished quilt top around all sides. Add 8in–10in (20.3cm–25.4cm) to this measurement (to allow for corners and overlapping at the finish) and this is the length of binding needed. See opposite and overleaf for binding techniques.

This quilt by Lynette Jensen uses a binding with mitred corners in the same fabric as the border, which ensures that the pieced central area remains the centre of attention.

BRIGHT IDEA

TAKE CARE THAT THE BINDING AND SEAM USED DON'T INTERFERE WITH PIECED BLOCKS AT THE QUILT EDGE AND CAUSE PARTS OF BLOCKS TO BE LOST IN THE SEAM. A ¼IN (6MM) SEAM IS A SAFE ONE TO USE.

MAKING BIAS BINDING

1 Press the fabric and cut sufficient strips in the width you require. If a single fabric is being used then aim for as few joins as possible. For straight binding, cut the fabric from selvedge to selvedge. If using a fabric with a definite linear pattern to the print it is better to follow the design line or the binding will look crooked. For bias binding cut the fabric into strips at a 45 degree angle.

2 Join the strips together into the length required. Place the strips as shown and sew them together diagonally, which looks neater than straight junctions. Trim off excess fabric to within ¼in (6mm). ▼

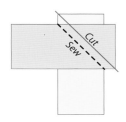

3 Once all seams have been sewn, press open. Fold the binding in half along the length and press. It is useful to press a diagonal hem at one end of the binding before beginning to sew it in place. ▼

Fold and press

SEWING SINGLE BINDING WITH STRAIGHT CORNERS

The same technique can be used for double-fold binding but using a double layer of fabric. If a generous ¼in (6mm) seam is used, when the binding is folded over the three layers at the edge of the quilt, the binding width will end up ⅜in–½in (1cm–1.3cm). When sewing on binding, a walking foot will help to sew through several layers. Use thread to match the fabric.

1 Prepare your binding in the width and length required, fold it in half along the length, wrong sides together, and press. Turn in a ¼in (6mm) seam along each long edge and press.

2 With the quilt right side up, open out the binding and place it on the quilt, aligning it at one corner and along raw edges. Pin in place and use a ¼in (6mm) seam (or following the pressed line) to sew the binding to the quilt through all layers along one side. Trim the binding flush with the edge of the quilt. ▼

3 Fold the binding over the edge of the quilt to the back, folding under the pressed seam allowance. Pin in place and then slipstitch the binding to the backing fabric. Repeat this with a second strip of binding on the other side of the quilt. ▼

4 Repeat with the other two sides but this time start and stop about ½in (1.3cm) from the end of the quilt edge. Working from the back, turn the edges under to hide raw ends and slipstitch into place. Press the edge carefully all round. ▼

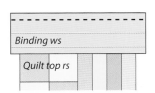

Binding ws

Quilt top rs

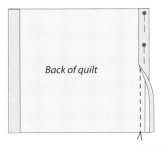

Back of quilt

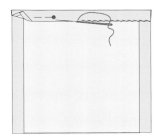

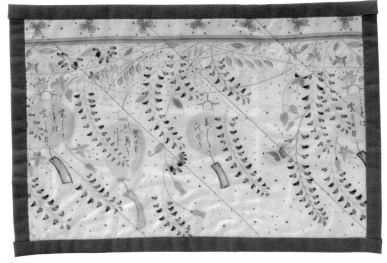

A tablemat is soon finished off neatly with straight corner binding.

BRIGHT IDEA

AVOID HAVING THE JOINS IN A LENGTH OF BINDING AT THE CORNERS. TO DO THIS, DO A 'DUMMY RUN' BEFORE PINNING THE BINDING, LAYING THE BINDING AROUND THE QUILT TO SEE WHERE JOINS OCCUR.

SEWING DOUBLE BINDING WITH MITRED CORNERS

This is the most popular way of finishing a quilt. The technique can also be used for single binding. Use a walking foot on your machine and threads to match your fabrics. Using a generous ¼in (6mm) seam will give a finished binding width of approximately ½in (1.3cm), taking into account the thickness of the quilt sandwich.

1 Prepare your binding in the width and length required. With wrong sides together, fold the binding in half along the length and press.

2 With the quilt right side up, start about halfway along one side and pin the binding along the edge, right side down and aligning all raw edges. Leave about 8in (20.3cm) of binding free at the start. Stitch the binding to the quilt through all layers using a generous ¼in (6mm) seam until you near a corner when you should stop a seam width away from the end. ▼

3 Remove the work from the machine and fold the binding up, northwards, so it is aligned straight with the edge of the quilt and the corner is at 45 degrees (A). Hold the corner and fold the binding back down, southwards, aligning it with the raw edge and with the folded corner square (B). Pin in position and begin sewing again, from the top and over the fold, continuing down the next edge. Repeat this process with the other corners. ▼

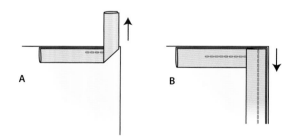

4 When you are nearing the starting point stop about 6in (15.2cm) away. Fold back the beginning and end of the binding, so they touch and mark these folds with a pin (C). Open out the binding and join the ends with a diagonal seam (D). Press the seam open and re-fold it (E). Finish stitching the binding in place. ▼

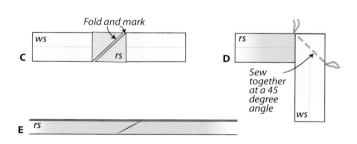

5 Fold the binding over to the back of the quilt and slipstitch it in place all round with tiny slipstitches and matching thread (F). If sewing a single binding the raw edge will need to be folded under before being slipstitched in place. When you reach a corner, manipulate the mitre so it folds neatly and then secure it with tiny stitches (G). ▼

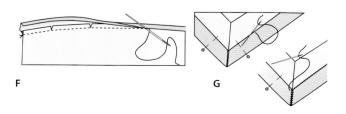

BRIGHT IDEA

INSTEAD OF USING HAND STITCHES, BINDING CAN BE MACHINE SEWN TO THE BACK OF THE QUILT. TO DO THIS, THE BINDING NEEDS TO BE SLIGHTLY WIDER SO THE MACHINE-SEWN SEAM DOESN'T SHOW ON THE BINDING AT THE FRONT. USE TOP THREAD TO MATCH THE BINDING AND THREAD IN THE BOBBIN TO MATCH THE FRONT OF THE QUILT.

PIPED EDGE

Adding piping to a quilt or project can create an elegant and professional finish. Piping cord can be used to create filled piping to form an edging all around a quilt or piping can be flat fabric, which can be inserted between the border and the binding or between the quilt top and an inner border. Piping in a contrasting colour will have the most impact. Piping can be bought ready-made but colours are limited so it is better to make your own to suit your project. The piping could also be pieced.

Fabric for piping can be cut on the straight grain or bias if the piping has to curve. The width of the fabric needs to be twice the width of the seam allowance, plus enough to wrap around the cord you are using. To calculate the total length of piping required, measure the sides of the quilt and add about 6in (15.2cm). Sew lengths of fabric together at 45 degree angles until you have the length required – see Making Bias Binding on page 237. Cord that is 1⁄16in (1.5mm) wide is a useful size, and a 2in (5cm) fabric width will be sufficient to cover this and allow a flat area for the seam.

Piping can also be flat rather than filled with cord. Flat piping is simply a fold of fabric and it can act as a mini border or frame, especially when used within a quilt rather than at the edge. Flat piping is sewn in place in a similar way to filled piping (see below).

Piping, whether flat or filled with cord, can bring additional colour and pattern. The spotted coral fabric here is flat binding between two seams, while the outer edge is a filled binding.

SEWING A PIPED EDGING

When sewing piping you will need to use a piping foot or zipper foot on your sewing machine. Prepare the fabric strips for the piping in the same way as for bias binding.

1 Prepare the length of fabric required. Fold it in half along the length, wrong sides together and finger press. Wrap the fabric strip around the piping cord so that the cord is in the crease (A). Use a piping or zipper foot and thread to match the fabric, sew along the strip with the needle slightly away from the piping to prevent the stitching being seen once it is sewn in place. Trim the piped strip to 1⁄2in (1.3cm) from the edge of the piping cord, or to the seam allowance you require (B). ▼

2 Place the piping in position on the right side of the quilt top, aligning the raw edges of the piped strip with the raw edges of the quilt top. Layer the backing fabric on top. Sew the piping to the edge (C). Trim the piped strip off in line with the ends of the quilt. Repeat on all four sides of the quilt. Alternatively, continue sewing the piping in place all round in a continuous strip. If the piping is to curve around a corner, clip the seam allowance of the piped strip so it can be eased into position more easily. ▼

3 Once within about 4in (10.2cm) of the starting point, trim the cord so the ends butt or twist together and tack (baste) or glue in position. On one end of the fabric strip turn under a 1⁄4in (6mm) seam (straight or at an angle depending on what you have used before to sew the strip). Lay the other end of the fabric strip inside to overlap by 1in (2.5cm) or so (D). Fold the fabric strip over as before and continue to sew the piping in place. ▼

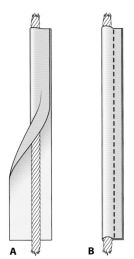

A   **B**

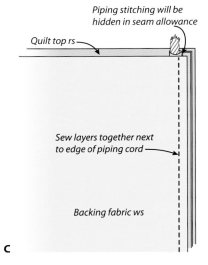

Piping stitching will be hidden in seam allowance

Quilt top rs

Sew layers together next to edge of piping cord

Backing fabric ws

C

D

PRAIRIE POINTS EDGE

Prairie points are a form of folded patchwork and are a great way to add texture to a project. They can be single-fold or double-fold and can be made individually and assembled into a row or be made in a continuous arrangement (see page 112). A prairie point or sawtooth edging creates an interesting edging to a quilt. It is also an excellent way of using up fabric scraps.

When used as an edging, prairie points can overlap each other by half their length or not overlap at all. Calculate how many prairie points are needed for each side of a quilt, as follows.

For no overlap – For single-fold or double-fold points, the base width of the triangle will be the same size as the starting square, while the height will be half the size. For example, a starting square of 4in (10.2cm), once folded will produce a triangle 4in (10.2cm) across the base and 2in (5cm) high. Triangles need to overlap each other by ¼in (6mm) in order that they meet at the bases once sewn into place, and have a ¼in (6mm) seam allowance at the bottom (see diagram). A 4in (10.2cm) prairie point will end up 3½in (8.9cm) long. So divide the quilt side measurement by 3½ to determine how many points are needed. For example, a quilt measuring 70in (178cm) square will need twenty prairie points along each side. ▼

For half-length overlap – Here, each triangle will overlap its neighbour by half its base length (see diagram). A 4in (10.2cm) wide prairie point, once overlapped, will cover a 2in (5cm) wide space, so for a 70in (178cm) wide quilt thirty-five points will be needed (70 ÷ 2 = 35). ▼

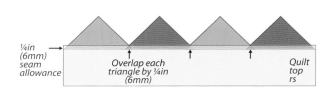

¼in (6mm) seam allowance — Overlap each triangle by ¼in (6mm) — Quilt top rs

¼in (6mm) seam allowance — Overlap each triangle by half their length — Quilt top rs

ADDING A PRAIRIE POINT EDGING

1 Calculate how many prairie points you will need for the quilt or project. Prepare the prairie points as described on page 112. The backing and wadding (batting) need to be flush with the edge of the quilt. Pin the backing out of the way temporarily. Pin the prairie points in position along the top edge of the quilt, right sides together and raw edges aligned. Make any adjustments needed so the final triangles at each side align with the sides of the quilt. Tack (baste) in place and then sew the row of prairie points in place with a ¼in (6mm) seam. Remove pins. ▼

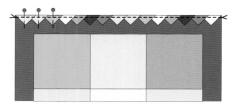

2 Pin and tack another row of prairie points at the side of the quilt and sew as before. Repeat on all sides. ▼

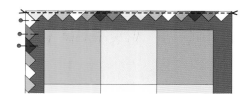

3 Clip each corner to reduce bulk and then fold the rows of prairie points outwards and press. ▼

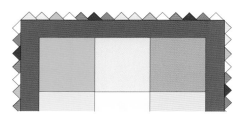

4 Turn the work over and fold the wadding and backing fabric back into position. Fold under a ¼in (6mm) seam on the backing fabric and slipstitch in place all round. Finish any quilting required. ▼

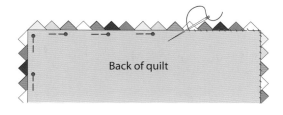

Back of quilt

SCALLOPED EDGE

A scalloped or clamshell edge looks very pretty and can be created in a similar way to a prairie point edging by using individual scallops, or the quilt edge can be cut in a scalloped pattern and binding applied to the curves. Both techniques are described below. Scalloped edges look very attractive on quilts made for children. Deep scallops also provide additional scope for appliquéd motifs and quilting.

ADDING AN INDIVIDUAL SCALLOPED EDGE

1 Cut two U-shaped pieces of fabric, place right sides together and sew around the curved edge, leaving the straight edge open. Clip the curved edge, turn through to the right side and press. ▼

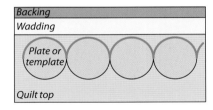

2 Pin the scallops in position along the edge of the quilt, in a similar way to a non-overlapped prairie points edging. A shell shape at an angle on the corner will create a rounded shape. ▼

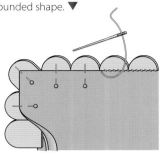

MARKING A SCALLOPED EDGE

Marking and cutting a scalloped edge accurately is important for a neat finish. The curves may be single, creating humps, or alternating for a wavy edge.

To mark curves for a humped edge place plates or circular templates as shown and mark a line along the template edges as shown by the green line. ▼

To mark and cut a wavy edge with inner and outer curves, place circular templates as shown and mark a curving line along the edges as shown by the green line. ▼

BRIGHT IDEA

WHEN CALCULATING HOW MUCH BINDING WILL BE NEEDED FOR A SCALLOPED EDGE, LAY STRING OR YARN AROUND ALL THE CURVES. MEASURE THE STRING AND ADD 12IN (30.5CM) EXTRA FOR CORNERS.

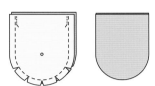

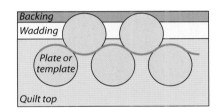

BINDING A SCALLOPED EDGE

Applying binding to a scalloped edge is the same in principle as for a straight edge (described on page 238). The technique here assumes a double-fold binding with the backing and wadding (batting) already trimmed but you could sew the front of the binding in place first before trimming the edges. When binding a scalloped edge, the binding strip will need to be cut on the bias to ease around curves smoothly.

1 With the quilt right side up, start halfway along one side in the middle of a curve, leaving a length of binding free at the start. Pin the binding in place, aligning its edges with the edges of the quilt and easing it around the curve. Where a scallop dips, clip into the seam for about ⅛in (3mm) and along the curves where necessary. On tight curves use more pins than usual to position the binding accurately. You could pin one side and corner and then stitch before moving on to the next side. ▶

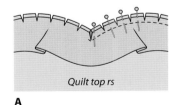

Quilt top rs

A

2 Stitch the binding carefully to the quilt to ensure the fabric is curving neatly using a ¼in (6mm) seam. When you reach a dip, pivot the machine. Remove pins as you go. Press the binding outwards. ▼

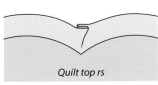

Quilt top rs

B

3 Fold the binding over to the back of the quilt and begin to slipstitch it in place all round with tiny slipstitches and matching thread. When you reach a dip, fold the binding into a little tuck and slipstitch the edges under. Continue this way all round the edging and then press. ▼

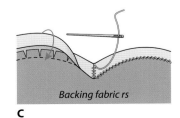

Backing fabric rs

C

GATHERED EDGE

Gathered or ruffled edges look very attractive, particularly on baby quilts and cushions. They are also useful for some types of quilt that do not have a standard border-type edge, such as puffed patchwork. For a softly gathered look choose fine, soft fabrics or lace. To make gathers form a firmer, almost pleated, edging, choose crisper fabrics that hold their shape well.

Ruffles are normally formed from a strip of fabric folded in half along the length. A gathered edge can be sewn in place between the front and back of a quilt, as shown here, or can be in the form of a gathered tube sewn to the outside edge of the quilt, as in the Puffed Play Quilt on page 108. Gathers may be gentle or full – the fuller the gathers, the more fabric length will be required.

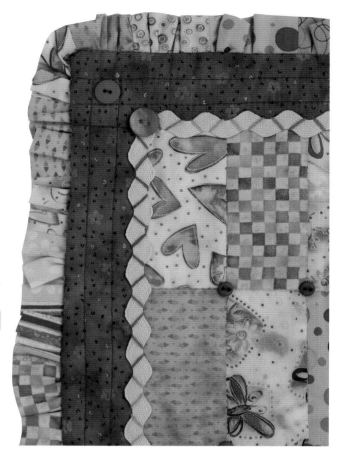

A frilled edge brings an extra dimension to a project. Here, it was sewn in place with a bagged-out edging.

SEWING A GATHERED EDGE

1 Decide on the width of your ruffles and then double this and add ½in (1.3cm) for a gathering/seam allowance. For the length of the gathered trim, measure your quilt or project around all the edges and double this measurement or triple it for very full gathers. Cut a fabric strip to these measurements, joining strips as necessary and pressing seams open. Sew the strip together along one short end to make the strip into a complete circle. Fold the fabric strip in half all along its length and press.

2 Using a strong thread, hand or machine sew two rows of gathering stitches ¼in (6mm) apart and ¼in (6mm) in from the raw edges of the strip. On the machine a gathering stitch is an extra long stitch, such as that used for machine tacking (basting). Take the circle off the machine and make a pencil mark at the raw edge of the circle at four equidistant points (shown by the red lines on the diagram below). ▼

3 Pull on the bobbin threads to gather up the fabric, arranging the gathers evenly along the length to fit around the quilt. Pin the ruffle in position around the quilt, right sides together, with raw edges together and the ruffles facing inwards. Position the marks made earlier at the corners of the quilt so it's easier to arrange the gathers equally on all sides. Place the backing fabric right side down on top of the ruffles and pin in place so all raw edges are aligned. Sew all layers together ½in (1.3cm) from the raw edge all round, leaving a gap for turning the quilt through. ▼

4 Turn the quilt through, making sure the frill is now pointing outwards all round the edges and press. At the gap, turn back a seam on the quilt top and on the backing fabric and pin against the frill, making sure the frill is sandwiched. Slipstitch the gap closed with small stitches through all the layers. ▼

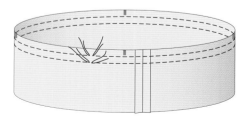

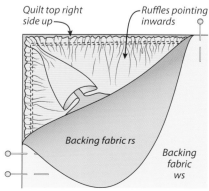

Quilt top right side up

Ruffles pointing inwards

Backing fabric rs

Backing fabric ws

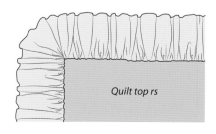

Quilt top rs

FINAL TOUCHES

At this stage your quilt is complete, apart from a few finishing touches. This section looks at labelling your creation, how to add a hanging sleeve or loops, how to care for finished quilts and some points to consider if exhibiting or displaying your work.

MAKING A HANGING SLEEVE

Essentially a hanging sleeve is a tube of fabric sewn to the back of the quilt, either during construction or at the end. It is useful for displaying a quilt and will certainly be needed if the quilt is to be exhibited or entered for a competition. Making a hanging sleeve between 4in–5in (10.2cm–12.7cm) deep will ensure that a wooden pole can be fed through the sleeve. A sleeve can be made with a single piece of fabric but a tube is better at protecting the back of a quilt.

1 Cut a piece of fabric as wide as the quilt and twice the finished depth of the tube plus 1in (2.5cm) for seams. So for a 4in (10.2cm) deep sleeve cut the fabric 9in (2.9cm). Turn under a ½in (1.3cm) hem on each short end and stitch. Fold the fabric in half lengthwise, right sides together, and sew together. Turn to the right side and press the seam so it is centred along one side.

2 Pin the sleeve to the back of the quilt, with the long seam facing inwards, positioning it just below the top of the quilt. Slipstitch the sleeve in place, along the top and bottom, through the backing and wadding (batting) but not through to the front of the quilt. Don't stitch it flat against the quilt but allow some space for a pole or flat baton to be inserted. ▶

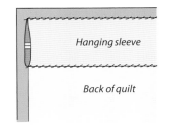

Hanging sleeve

Back of quilt

LABELLING WORK

Adding a label to a quilt or other piece of work doesn't take long but can be of immense interest to other people. This could include the name of the maker, the date the quilt was started and finished, the occasion it was made for and the recipient. It's also useful to note any specific care instructions.

The easiest and quickest method of labelling is to write on a piece of fabric with a fine-tipped permanent fabric pen and then sew this label to the quilt, or fuse it in place with fusible web. Another method is to mark the details in pencil, then sew them by hand with backstitch or stem stitch. Pretty labels can be bought from quilt shops and web outlets. Details can be stitched on to a fabric label by sewing machine and some modern machines can be programmed to stitch a label. Labels can also be printed on fabric via a computer – see page 34.

MAKING HANGING LOOPS

Hanging loops or tabs can be used to display a quilt and can form a decorative part of a wall hanging. Loops can be incorporated during the sewing process or be features in their own right, sewn in place as separate units, perhaps with button detailing. Choose the width and number of loops to complement the quilt or project and achieve a balanced look.

1 Decide how many loops you want and what width and length they should be. It is quicker to make one single long tube and cut it into separate lengths. The fabric needs to be twice as wide as the finished loop, plus ½in (1.3cm) seam allowances. Create the tube by folding the fabric in half along its length, right sides together, and sew together with a ½in (1.3cm) seam. Turn through to the right side and press the long seam so it is centred. Cut the tube into equal lengths. ◀

2a Turn in the ends of each loop and sew together neatly. Fold each loop in half and position across the back of the quilt or project, spacing them evenly. Sew into place with small stitches and matching thread. ▼

Back of project

2b Loops can also be attached so they show from the front of the work. Prepare loops as before and turn under a hem at the short end of each, either straight or in a point, and press. Stitch one end of the loop in position on the back of the quilt and fold the other half over to the quilt front and stitch in place. Add buttons if desired. ▼

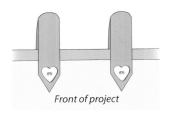

Front of project

CARING FOR QUILTS

Well-made quilts should stand the test of time but there are some things you can do that will protect your hard work and keep it looking its best for many years to come.

Storage – Try to store quilts flat whenever possible, ideally on a bed covered with a sheet to keep out sunlight. Make sure the area is dry and free from moths and other insects. Avoid packing in plastic but use a cotton pillowcase or sheet. Don't fold so the folds are flat, which will create stubborn creases, but pad with rolls of wadding (batting) covered with acid-free paper. Try not to fold a quilt along seam lines as these may weaken over time. Shake the quilt out from time to time and re-fold it along different lines.

Cleaning – If you own a vintage or antique quilt then avoid washing if possible. Dust can be removed by a *very* gentle vacuuming, placing an open-weave cloth or net between the nozzle and the quilt to avoid fabric being sucked upwards. If in doubt, seek the advice of a fabric specialist or conservationist. Cleaning normal quilts can usually be done by washing machine if your machine is large enough. Use a delicate, low temperature programme and a mild washing agent. Spin only for a short time to remove excess water. Depending on the materials the quilt was made from it might be safest not to tumble dry.

If the quilt is to be washed by hand, use a mild washing agent in a bath of warm water, agitating the quilt gently with your hands. Rinse the quilt several times and then press out as much water as you can while the quilt is still in the bath, using towels to absorb excess water. The quilt will still be very heavy as it is removed from the bath so get help to lift it if need be.

Dry quilts flat if possible, outside on a warm day, using towels beneath to protect from dirt and soak up excess moisture. Place a sheet on top to protect from birds. Avoid hanging a large quilt on a clothes line as the moist weight will strain the fabric and stitches.
Pressing – Once dry, if the quilt needs to be pressed, use a cool iron without steam as using a hot iron might damage specialist threads and also cause polyester wadding to bond to the fabric.

EXHIBITING WORK

Shows and exhibitions can be valuable learning experiences, and great fun, especially if you are part of a quilting group that likes to stage regular exhibitions of their work. Work can be exhibited almost anywhere – in town halls, churches, museums and libraries to name but a few. Work can also be entered in local, regional, national and international quilt shows and competitions, which usually have a wide variety of categories and prizes, both for beginners and experienced quilters.

If entering a competition, be organized and plan your approach. Consider the following points.

- Obtain an entry form early to familiarize yourself with the rules, date and venue. Look carefully at the form and decide which categories would suit your skills. There will usually be many categories, listed in various ways, for example, by quilt type, such as bed quilt, cushion, wall hanging, and by quilt style, such as traditional or contemporary.
- Check for specific requirements that need to be fulfilled, for example, it may be a requirement that a certain fabric range is used or certain techniques used.
- Check closing dates for competitions and return entry forms in plenty of time.
- Quilts and other projects are judged on many points, such as design, use of colour, techniques and quality of finish so consider all of these as you make your piece.
- Competition organizers usually require some specific information. For example, you may need a title to identify your piece. You will also need to write a short description of it, including the size, the fabrics used and why, the techniques used and why, and the inspiration. A high-resolution digital photograph of your work is usually required.
- Prepare your entry well, making sure that it is clean, has a hanging sleeve and hangs straight, has an exhibition label attached to the back and that all sewing looks neat and finished properly.
- When sending the quilt to the exhibition, rolling it with the right side outwards and packing it in a tube with bubble wrap will minimize creases. Hand delivery may be safest but not always possible so, if posting, insure the quilt against loss or damage and obtain proof of delivery.

USEFUL STITCHES

There are hundreds of stitches that can be used in patchwork, appliqué and quilting, both functional and decorative, and throughout the book many have been explored. This section looks at some of the most useful hand stitches that can be used for patchwork and also those that bring an attractive decorative quality to appliqué and quilting. Simple stitches are also increasingly being used for 'stitcheries', that is, hand-stitched pictorial motifs. The stitches are shown alphabetically within sequenced diagrams.

BACKSTITCH

Backstitch is a very versatile stitch and can be used to 'draw' parts of a stitched motif, to add single stitches for emphasis and to outline areas. It can also be 'whipped' with another thread, to strengthen the line or add a second colour (see whipped running stitch on page 247).

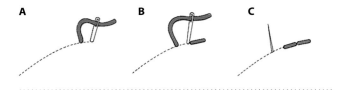

BLANKET STITCH

This is the stitch most often used to edge appliqué motifs, especially in fusible web appliqué. It is also ideal for decorating seams on crazy patchwork. When stitched tightly together, the stitch can be used for buttonholing or as the edging stitch in shisha work.

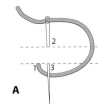

CHAIN STITCH

This stitch is used in many forms of embroidery. It can be worked in straight or curved lines and as a single detached stitch. It could also be used in crazy patchwork and decorative quilting. Open chain stitch is a variation where each loop is stitched with the ends spaced further apart.

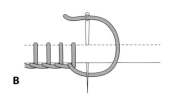
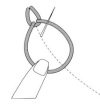

CHAINED FEATHER STITCH

This attractive stitch is useful for decorative quilting and embroidery. It was used in the tulip design on page 154.

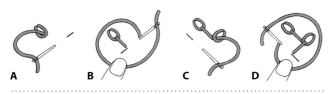

COUCHING

Couching is a way of securing a length of thread, cord, braid, ribbon or other trim on to the surface of fabric with small hand stitches. It can also be done by machine – see page 230.

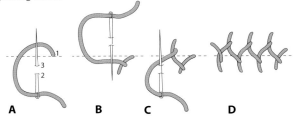

CRETAN STITCH (OPEN)

This stitch can be used as a decorative filling stitch but when worked in an open format, as here, it can be used as a decorative quilting stitch.

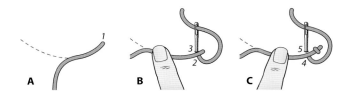

CROSS STITCH

This embroidery stitch can be used in many ways – as an edging, a filling and individually in decorative quilting.

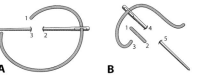

FEATHER STITCH

This stitch creates a very attractive look and can be used as a quilting stitch, especially for small projects. It looks lovely in crazy patchwork too. Marking parallel guidelines, as shown in diagram C will help when forming a line of stitches.

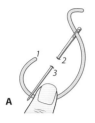
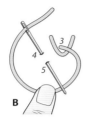
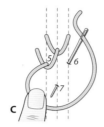

FERN STITCH

This is an easy decorative stitch that can be used for edging appliqué motifs, crazy patchwork or as part of a stitchery design. When worked on its own this stitch is sometimes called chicken foot stitch and is used as an edging in Hawaiian appliqué.

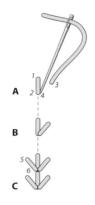

FLY STITCH

This embroidery stitch is useful for creating dense lines of pattern. Single stitches can also be worked as random spot fills.

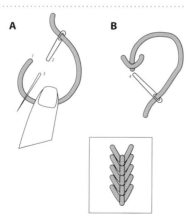

FRENCH KNOT

These are such useful little knots and easy to form. Use them for decorative stitching, focal points and infills. Wrap the thread around the needle once or twice, hold the thread firmly and reinsert the needle, pulling the thread through to the back. For bigger knots use a thicker thread. Narrow ribbon can also be used to create French knots.

HEMMING STITCH

A basic stitch worked with small stitches and thread matching the fabric for invisible or 'blind' hemming. Run the thread inside the fabric fold where possible, emerging at intervals.

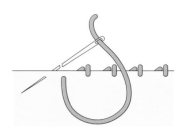

HERRINGBONE STITCH

This is a versatile stitch that can be used as an edging or decoratively, especially in crazy patchwork. Additional stitches can be worked to create a more complex look.

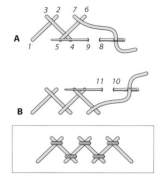

LADDER STITCH

This is a joining stitch that is used for invisibly closing gaps. It is worked like the rungs of a ladder joining two fabrics, with the thread run invisibly into the folded fabric edges and the 'rungs' pulled tightly. Use a thread colour to match the fabric.

LAZY DAISY STITCH

This stitch is really a detached chain stitch (see page 245). It is often worked in circles for flower effects.

OVERSEWING OR WHIP STITCH

This stitch is used to stitch two fabric edges together, particularly when sewing up gaps where quilts or other projects have been bagged-out through a gap. Fold the fabrics inwards to create folded edges and stitch together with matching thread and small stitches (they are shown larger here for diagrammatic purposes).

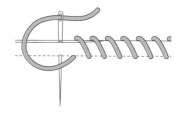

QUILTING OR RUNNING STITCH

This is really a running stitch and is worked by taking the needle in and out of the fabric at regularly spaced intervals in any direction required. See page 197 for more on quilting stitches.

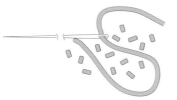

SATIN STITCH

This stitch can be used to edge applique motifs to prevent fabric fraying, though is more often worked by machine. It can also be used as a filling stitch in decorative stitching. Work the stitches side by side closely together.

A   B

SEED STITCH

This is also called seeding and is often used as a quilting infill. Work small stitches randomly in different directions.

SHEAF STITCH

This stitch is easy to work, with three or five satin stitches 'tied' together with a single horizontal stitch, which could be worked in a different colour. It can be stitched singly or along a line or curve and is useful for crazy patchwork.

A   B   C

SLIPSTITCH

This is simply tiny stitches used to secure fabric or trims in place and is really a hemming stitch.

STEM STITCH

This stitch is useful for 'drawing' lines, such as flower stems or leaf veins, on applique motifs and stitcheries.

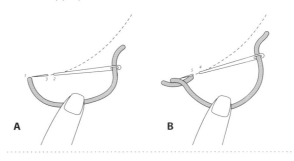

A   B

TOPSTITCH

This is usually done by machine but can be hand worked. It provides additional security on hemmed or folded edges and creates a neater, flatter edge. Work the stitches about ⅛in (3mm) from the edge.

WHIPPED RUNNING/QUILTING STITCH

This stitch creates a stronger line than running stitch alone and can look very decorative if the whipping is done in a different colour, creating a twisted look. Use a round-ended needle for the whipping. The Welcome Cards on page 201 use a whipped quilting stitch to outline the motifs. Backstitch can also be whipped this way, as can many other stitches.

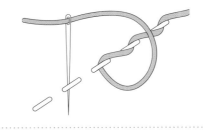

PROJECT MAKING UP

We all lead busy lives today and although the creation of a quilt is a wonderful goal the joys of patchwork, appliqué and quilting can just as easily be experienced by making smaller items. Throughout the book the Make It Now projects allow you to explore many of the techniques and are quick to create.

SEMINOLE SCARF

Seminole patchwork is ideal for creating a scarf, as described on page 73, and you can make as many or as few bands as you like.

1 Once your scarf bands are complete and sewn together press the scarf front and check it is straight. Cut a piece of backing fabric the same size as the scarf front. If the scarf is for winter use cut a piece of wadding (batting) 1in (2.5cm) smaller all round than the backing fabric.

2 Place the scarf front right side up on a flat surface. Pin and then tack (baste) the prairie points in position on the right side of the scarf front, with the triangles pointing inwards (see Adding a Prairie Point Edging on page 240). Place the backing fabric on top, right side down and pin together all round, sandwiching the prairie points between the layers. If using wadding, place that on top of the backing fabric.

3 Using a ¼in (6mm) seam, sew all round the edge of the scarf, leaving a small gap for turning though along one long side. Remove pins and tacking (basting). Turn through to the right side and check the prairie points are neatly facing outwards. Press and then sew up the gap with tiny slipstitches. ▼

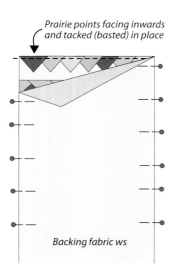

Prairie points facing inwards and tacked (basted) in place

Backing fabric ws

PUFFED PLAY QUILT

The puffed play quilt on page 108 could be made any size and colours you like. Once all the puffs and plain blocks are sewn together make up as follows.

1 Cut backing fabric the same size as the quilt top (or a little larger and trim it down after sewing if you prefer). Pin the front and back right sides together and sew together around the edge using a ½in (1.3cm) seam and leaving a large gap for turning through. Turn through to the right side and sew up the gap.

2 To make a frill to go all around the edge of the quilt, measure all four sides of the quilt, add these together and double the measurement. The quilt shown is 28in square, so 28in x 4 = 112in x 2 = 224in, which is about 6¼yd. In metric this would be 71cm x 4 = 284cm x 2 = 568cm, which is about 5¾m. Prepare a length of fabric 6¼yd (5.7m) and 4½in (11.4cm) wide, joining lengths together as necessary.

3 Fold the fabric strip in half all along its length, right sides together and sew together down the long side. Turn through to the right side and press the tube. Using a long length of strong thread (at least 112in/284cm), work a gathering stitch down the centre of the tube (if you pass the thread over a wax block it will help to prevent tangles – see page 12) and gather up the frill so it fits all around the edge of the quilt. ▼

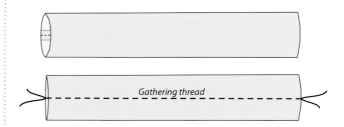

Gathering thread

4 Pin the frill in place all round, sewing it to the edge of the quilt with hand stitches through the centre of the frill. Turn each end under neatly and slipstitch the edges together. Remove the gathering thread once the frill is sewn in place. Alternatively, make a frill and sew it in position as you make up the quilt – see page 242 for technique.

FLOWER POWER TOTE

The bag on page 150 is 17in (43cm) wide, 12in (30.5cm) tall and 3in (7.6cm) deep, created by sewing across the bottom corners. The handles are 30in (76cm) long.

1 Create the front and back panels of the bag in the size you require. Sew the front and back together along the bottom. Cut thin wadding (batting) slightly larger than the bag piece and pin to the wrong side. Quilt to secure the two layers but do not quilt within 1in (2.5cm) of the top and bottom. Trim the wadding top and bottom to leave ½in (1.3cm) unpadded – this will allow the top to be turned over easily later. Trim the sides flush with the bag panel. ▼

Bag panel (front and back joined)

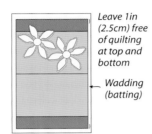

Leave 1in (2.5cm) free of quilting at top and bottom

Wadding (batting)

2 To make the lining bag, use the outer bag panel to cut out a piece of lining fabric and a piece of wadding a little larger all round. Quilt to secure the two layers but not within 1in (2.5cm) of the top and bottom. Trim the wadding top and bottom to leave ½in (1.3cm) of lining bag panel unpadded. Trim the sides flush with the lining bag panel.

3 Fold the bag outer panel in half, right sides together, and sew up the sides with a ¼in (6mm) seam. Repeat with the lining panel but using a ½in (1.3cm) seam. Create corners if required by sewing across the corners (like a sugar bag). Place the inner bag inside the outer, wrong sides together, aligning edges. Pin in place. ▼

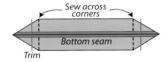

Sew across corners

Bottom seam

Trim

4 The handles are made of a single tube cut into two. Cut fabric 4in (10.2cm) wide x length required. Fold in half along the length right sides together and sew together with a ½in (1.3cm) seam. Turn through to the right side and cut into two pieces. Take webbing 1½in (3.8cm) wide and as long as the handle. Cut a strip of wadding 1in (2.5cm) wide and as long as the handle and glue to the webbing. Feed the webbing/wadding inside a handle and stitch down the centre to secure. Repeat for the other handle.

5 Place the bag handles between the inner and outer bag, at least 1in (2.5cm) inside the bag. Pin in place and check for length and position. Turn the top of the outer bag and inner bag over by about ½in (1.3cm) all round, sandwiching the handles. Tack (baste) in place and sew around the top ⅛in (3mm) from the top. Sew a cross shape over the handle ends where they extend inside the bag. Remove tacking (basting) and press.

STAINED-GLASS FUCHSIA

The fuchsia design on page 182 could be made up as a framed picture or wall hanging, with or without a border. The instructions here include a pieced border.

1 When all the bias-strip appliqué is complete create a border around the design with 1in x 3in (2.5cm x 7.6cm) oblongs of silk in mixed colours. Join the oblongs together in strips or back them with fusible web and fuse to the background. Add bias strips along all the edges, securing the strips with tiny stitches and matching thread.

2 Trim the front to within 2½in (6.3cm) of the oblong border. Cut a piece of backing fabric the same size as the front and a piece of wadding slightly smaller and make up the hanging with a bagged out edge and hanging loops – see pages 235 and 243. The loops used were 2in (5cm) wide x 6in (15.2cm) long.

SUMMER CUSHION

The cushions on page 53 are made using the simple envelope or Oxford type, where the cushion pad is inserted via the back of the cushion, which is made up of two overlapping fabric pieces.

1 Cut two pieces of backing fabric as deep as the cushion front and three-quarters as wide. Fold over ¼in (6mm) twice for a hem on one short side of each piece. Stitch the hems and press. ▼

Backing fabric piece *Hem*

Backing fabric piece *Hem*

2 Place the cushion front right side up and the backing fabric pieces on top, right side down, with all outer edges aligned and the backing fabrics overlapping across the centre. Sew together around all four sides. Trim seams and clip corners to reduce bulk. Turn the right way out and press seams. Insert the cushion pad and arrange the overlap neatly. ▶

Overlap

USEFUL INFORMATION

This section contains some handy tables you may need, and will take some of the stress out of the maths. . .

IMPERIAL TO METRIC CONVERSIONS

To convert inches to centimetres multiply the inch measurement by 2.54.
To convert centimeters to inches divide the centimetre measurement by 2.54.
To convert feet to metres multiply the foot measurement by 0.3048.
To convert metres to feet multiply the metre measurement by 3.28084.

STANDARD QUILT SIZES

Bed size	Mattress size
Crib	23in x 46in (58cm x 117cm)
Toddler	30in x 57in ((76cm x 145cm)
Twin (Single)	39in x 75in (100cm x 190cm)
Full (Double)	54in x 75in (137cm x 190cm)
Queen	60in x 80in (152cm x 203cm)
King	76in x 80in (193cm x 203cm)

DOUBLE BINDING

Finished width	Cut size
¼in (6mm)	2¼in (5.7cm) wide
⅜in (1cm)	2½in (6.3cm)
½in (1.3cm)	3½in (8.9cm)
⅝in (1.6cm)	4¼in (10.8cm)
¾in (1.9cm)	4¾in (12cm)
1in (2.5cm)	6½in (16.5cm)

REDUCING AND ENLARGING BLOCK SIZES

Use this formula to **enlarge** a block pattern:

desired size ÷ original size x 100 = enlargement %

For example, to enlarge a 3in block to a 9in block:
9 ÷ 3 = 3,   3 x 100 = 300,   so enlarge by 300%.

Use this formula to **reduce** a block pattern:

desired size ÷ original size x 100 = enlargement %

For example, to reduce a 12in block to a 4in block:
4 ÷ 12 = 0.33,   0.33 x 100 = 33,   so reduce by 33%.

NUMBER OF TRIANGLES FROM A SQUARE OF FABRIC

The following table shows the size a square has to be to cut half-square triangles or quarter-square triangles. The formulas are: for half-square triangles add ⅞in (2.2cm) to the required finished size; for quarter-square triangles add 1¼in (3.2cm).

Finished block size	Cut square for ½-square triangles	Cut square for ¼-square triangles
2in (5cm)	2⅞in (7.3cm)	3¼in (8.2cm)
2½in (6.3cm)	3⅜in (8.5cm)	3¾in (9.5cm)
3in (7.6cm)	3⅞in (9.8cm)	4¼in (10.8cm)
3½in (8.9cm)	4⅜in (11.1cm)	4¾in (12cm)
4in (10.2cm)	4⅞in (12.4cm)	5¼in (13.3cm)
4½in (11.4cm)	5⅜in (13.6cm)	5¾in (14.6cm)
5in (12.7cm)	5⅞in (14.9cm)	6¼in (15.9cm)
5½in (14cm)	6⅜in (16.2cm)	6¾in (17.1cm)
6in (15.2cm)	6⅞in (17.4cm)	7¼in (18.4cm)
6½in (16.5cm)	7⅜in (18.7cm)	7¾in (19.7cm)
7in (17.8cm)	7⅞in (20cm)	8¼in (20.9cm)
7½in (19cm)	8⅜in (21.1cm)	8¾in (22.2cm)
8in (20.3cm)	8⅞in (22.5cm)	9¼in (23.5cm)
8½in (21.6cm)	9⅜in (23.8cm)	9¾in (24.7cm)
9in (22.9cm)	9⅞in (25cm)	10¼in (26cm)
9½in (24.1cm)	10⅜in (26.3cm)	10¾in (27.3cm)
10in (25.4cm)	10⅞in (27.6cm)	11¼in (28.5cm)
11in (27.9cm)	11⅞in (30.1cm)	12¼in (31.1cm)
12in (30.5cm)	12⅞in (32.7cm)	13¼in (33.6cm)

SEWING MACHINE NEEDLE SIZES

European	American
60 (thinnest)	8
65	9
70	10
75	11
80	12
90	14
100	16
110	18
120 (thickest)	19

NUMBER OF SQUARES FROM A FAT QUARTER

Based on a fat quarter 20in x 17in (50.8cm x 43.2cm)

Square size	No. of squares
2in (5cm)	80
2½in (6.3cm)	48
2¾in–3in (7cm–7.6cm)	30
3½in–4in (8.9cm–10.2cm)	20
4½in–5in (11.4cm–12.7cm)	12
5½in–5¾in (14cm–14.6cm)	9
6–6½in (15.2cm–16.5cm)	6
6¾in–8in (17.1cm–20.3cm)	4

DIAGONAL MEASUREMENTS OF SQUARES

The following table gives the size of a square when it is turned 45 degrees or on point. The mathematical formula is: multiply the length of one finished side by 1.414 and round up to the nearest ¼in (6mm).

Block size	Diagonal size
2in (5cm)	2⅞in (7.3cm)
2½in (6.3cm)	3½in (8.9cm)
3in (7.6cm)	4¼in (10.8cm)
3½in (8.9cm)	5in (12.7cm)
4in (10.2cm)	5⅜in (13.6cm)
4½in (11.4cm)	6⅜in (16.2cm)
5in (12.7cm)	7⅛in (18cm)
5½in (14cm)	7⅞in (20cm)
6in (15.2cm)	8½in (21.6cm)
6½in (16.5cm)	9¼in (23.5cm)
7in (17.8cm)	9⅞in (25cm)
7½in (19cm)	10¾in (27.3cm)
8in (20.3cm)	11¼in (28.5cm)
8½in (21.6cm)	12⅛in (30.8cm)
9in (22.9cm)	12¾in (32.4cm)
9½in (24.1cm)	13½in (34.3cm)
10in (25.4cm)	14⅞in (37.7cm)
11in (27.9cm)	15¾in (40cm)
12in (30.5cm)	17in (43.2cm)

TEMPLATES

Some of the small projects throughout the book use templates and these are given here at a half size for your use. Enlarge them by 200 per cent, or to another size of your choice. See page 26 for using templates.

Daisy Cot Quilt Template (page 155)

Flower Power Tote Templates (page 150)
Add ¼in (6mm) seam allowance all round if using needle-turn or freezer paper appliqué.

Welcome Cards Templates (page 201)

Butterfly Bag Templates (page 173)

Floral Lap Quilt Template (page 217)

Summer Cushion Templates (page 53)
Add ¼in (6mm) seam allowance. The finished layouts are also shown.

Stained-glass Fuchsia Templates (page 182)

Make two full size copies (enlarging by 400 per cent) – one to cut up and use as templates for all the shapes and one as a guide for positioning the bias tape and border. Stitch the stamens with whipped backstitch or stem stitch with a seed bead at each end.

Fusing Diagram

Fuse or sew the bias tape in place in the following order:

1st   3rd
2nd   4th

Mark the outer edge of the design with pins. Bias tape lines in blue must extend past this pin-marked rectangle. Edges will be covered by the border later.

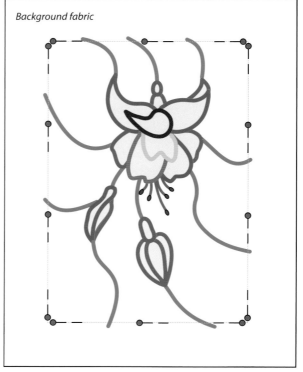

Background fabric

FURTHER READING

There are many wonderful books and magazines on patchwork, appliqué and quilting. Some of those I found most useful are listed here but there are many more to choose from.

BEYER, Jinny *The Quilter's Album of Patchwork Patterns* Breckling Press, 2009

BRISCOE, Susan *21 Terrific Patchwork Bags* David & Charles, 2003

BRISCOE, Susan *21 Sensational Patchwork Bags* David & Charles, 2006

BRISCOE, Susan *The Ultimate Sashiko Sourcebook* David & Charles, 2005

BRISCOE, Susan *Japanese Sashiko Inspirations* David & Charles, 2008

BRISCOE, Susan *Compendium of Quilting Techniques* Search Press, 2009

BROWN, Pauline *The Complete Guide to Quilting Techniques* Reader's Digest, 2006

CHAINEY, Barbara *The Essential Quilter* David & Charles, 1993

CHAINEY, Barbara *The Essential Quilter Project Book* David & Charles, 1997

CHAINEY, Barbara *Quilt It!* David & Charles, 1999

CHAINEY, Barbara *Fast Quilts from Fat Quarters* David & Charles, 2006

DAVIS, Julia & MUXWORTHY, Anne *Easy Japanese Quilt Style* David & Charles, 2009

EDWARDS, Lynne *The Sampler Quilt Book* David & Charles, 1996

EDWARDS, Lynne *New Sampler Quilt Book* David & Charles, 2000

EDWARDS, Lynne *Making Scrap Quilts to Use it Up!* David & Charles, 2003

EDWARDS, Lynne *Stash-Buster Quilts* David & Charles, 2006

EDWARDS, Lynne *Cathedral Window Quilts* David & Charles, 2008

EDWARDS, Lynne *The Essential Sampler Quilt Book* David & Charles, 2010

FRANSES, Chris *Little Book of Patchwork: Log Cabin* David & Charles, 2001

FRANSES, Chris *Little Book of Patchwork: Stars* David & Charles, 2001

GAUDET, Barri Sue *Quilt a Gift* David & Charles, 2009

GUERRIER, Katharine *Scrap Quilt Sensation* David & Charles, 2007

GUERRIER, Katharine *The Encyclopedia of Quilting and Patchwork Techniques* Quarto Publishing, 1994

HAMMOND, Elaine *The Absolute Beginner's Guide to Patchwork Quilting & Appliqué* David & Charles, 1997

INESON, Pauline *How to Create an Heirloom Quilt* David & Charles, 2010

KRENTZ, Jan *Diamond Quilts & Beyond* C&T Publishing Inc, 2005

LAWTHER, Gail *Celtic Quilting* David & Charles, 1998

LAWTHER, Gail *More Celtic Quilting* David & Charles, 2004

LAWTHER, Gail *Fun & Fabulous Patchwork & Appliqué* David & Charles, 2007

LINTOTT, Pam (consultant) *The Quiltmakers* David & Charles, 2009

LINTOTT, Pam and Nicky *Jelly Roll Quilts* David & Charles, 2008

LINTOTT, Pam and Nicky *Layer Cake, Jelly Roll & Charm Quilts* David & Charles, 2009

LINTOTT, Pam and Nicky *Jelly Roll Inspirations* David & Charles, 2009

MALONE, Maggie *5,500 Quilt Block Designs* Sterling Publishing Co Inc, 2004

MARTIN, Judy *Ultimate Rotary Cutting Reference* Crosley-Griffith Publishing Co, Inc, 1997

PAHL, Ellen (editor) *The Quilters Ultimate Visual Guide* Rodale Press, 1997

PORTER Christine *Quilts Beneath Your Feet* David & Charles, 2009

PORTER, Christine *Tessellation Quilts* David & Charles, 2006

SEELY, Ann & STEWART, Joyce *Color Magic for Quilters* Rodale Press, 1997

SEWARD, Linda *The Complete Book of Patchwork, Quilting and Appliqué* Mitchell Beazley, 1987

SHAW, Mandy *Quilt Yourself Gorgeous* David & Charles, 2008

SINGER Sewing Reference Library *The Quilting Bible* Creative Publishing International, 1997

TINKLER, Nicky *Quilting with a Difference* Traplet Publications, 2002

TINKLER, Nicky *The Quilter's and Patchworker's Stitch Bible* Search Press, 2006

WOLFF, Colette *The Art of Manipulating Fabric* Krause Publications, 1996

Magazines

British Patchwork & Quilting Traplet Publications www.pg@traplet.com

Fabrications: Quilting for You Grosvenor Shows Ltd www.grosvenorshows.co.uk

Fons & Porter's Love of Quilting New Track Media LLC www.fonsandporter.com

Magic Patch Les Éditions de Saxe www.edisaxe.com

McCall's Quilting New Track Media LLC www.mccallsquilting.com

Popular Patchwork My Hobby Store Ltd www.myhobbystore.com

SUPPLIERS

UK

Coats Crafts UK
Tel: 01484 681881
www.coatscrafts.co.uk

The Cotton Patch
Tel: 01217 022840
www.cottonpatch.co.uk

Creative Crafts & Needlework
Tel: 01803 866002
www.creative-crafts-needlework.co.uk

Creative Grids (UK) Limited
Tel: 01455 828667
www.creativegrids.com

D&S Sewing Machines
Tel: 01626 369840
www.dandssewingmachines.co.uk

The Eternal Maker
Tel: 01243 788174
www.eternalmaker.com

Euro Japan Links
Tel: 02082 019324
www.eurojapanlinks.com

Pelenna Patchworks
Tel: 01639 898444
www.pelannapatchworks.co.uk

The Quilt Room
Tel: 01306 877307
www.quiltroom.co.uk

Sewing the Seeds (Beke Jameson)
Tel: 01803 294808
www.sewingtheseeds.co.uk

The Silk Route
Tel: 01252 835781
www.thesilkroute.co.uk

Step by Step Patchwork Centre
Tel: 01769 574071
www.stepbystep-quilts.co.uk

USA

The City Quilter
Tel: 212 807 0390
www.cityquilter.com

Coats & Clark
Tel: 800 648 1479
www.coatsandclark.com

Connecting Threads
Tel: 800 574 6454
www.connectingthreads.com

DMC
Tel: 201 589 0606
www.dmc.com

eQuilter.com
Tel: 877 322 7423
www.equilter.com

Fat Quarter Shop
Tel: 866 826 2069
www.fatquartershop.com

Hancocks of Paducah
Tel: 800 845 8723
www.hancocks-paducah.com

Jo-Ann Stores Inc
Tel: 888 739 4120
www.joann.com

Moda Fabrics/United Nations
Tel: 800 527 9447
www.modafabrics.com

ACKNOWLEDGMENTS

There are so many people to thank for their invaluable help in producing this book. Firstly, David & Charles for offering me the opportunity to write this book, in particular Ali Myer and Jane Trollope. To my commissioning editor Cheryl Brown, who managed to whip me along at a brisk pace to meet the many deadlines but still remain my friend at the same time. I wouldn't have made it without you. To Heather Haynes, my project editor: having another editor check my work was initially daunting but I'm so glad Cheryl suggested you Heather – thank you for all your hard work, you've been wonderful. Thanks to Jeni Hennah and James Brooks for your help with the many, many stages of the proofs. My thanks to Sarah Underhill, Sarah Clark and the design team at D&C – as always, it's great working with you all. A big thank you to Ethan Danielson for his wonderful diagrams and to Karl Adamson and Kim Sayer for the lovely photography.

Big thanks to my long-time friend Sue Cleave, who was always at the end of a phone or email with support whenever I flagged and whose input and encouragement was much appreciated.

To all of the many wonderful authors I have worked with over the years who were so full of helpful advice and support, in particular Joan Elliott, Susan Briscoe, Gail Lawther, Pauline Ineson, Pam and Nicky Lintott, Julia Davis, Anne Muxworthy and Lynette Anderson. A special thank you to Lynne Edwards for her soothing support, technical advice and Foreword for this book. Thanks so much Lynette, for the loan of your two gorgeous quilts on pages 131 and 144. Thanks to Cara Ackerman at DMC for the fabulous threads.

Last but not least, love and thanks to my family, in particular my son Rory who had to put up with a stressed, overworked mother for long, long months. To my dear dad, niece Cassie and sister-in-law Val, who had to admire every piece of stitching I showed them, and of course my sister Jan, who had to listen to me droning on interminably about deadlines, page layouts and repro dates. Thanks for your faith in me.

CONTRIBUTORS

The work of some talented people appears in this book, for which the author is very grateful. Some details about them have been provided below, with website addresses where relevant.

Lynette Anderson – Lynette lives in Australia and is a prolific designer and stitcher. Some of her charming designs can be seen in her book *It's Quilting Cats and Dogs*. www.lynetteandersondesigns.typepad.com

Susan Briscoe – A highly talented designer, textile artist and teacher who has written many quilting books. She specializes in Japanese designs and sashiko. www.susanbriscoe.co.uk

Julia Davis – A skilled quilter and co-author of *Easy Japanese Quilt Style*, Julia runs Step by Step Patchwork Centre with Anne Muxworthy. www.stepbystep-quilts.co.uk

Lynne Edwards – Lynne is an internationally renowned quilter, teacher and expert in a wide range of techniques. She has written many definitive works, particularly on sampler quilts and cathedral window techniques. The work of some of Lynne's pupils can also be seen in this book: Birgitte Bennett, Pauline Bugg, Janet Covell, Pam Croger, Margery Dench, Sue Fitzgerald, Mary Harrowell, Heather Jackson, Jenny Lankester, Pat Mitchell and Shirley Prescott.

Joanna Figueroa – A talented designer and quilt maker and founder of Fig Tree & Co. Joanna designs the gorgeous Fig Tree fabrics. www.figtreeandco.com

Carolyn Forster – A popular quilt maker, teacher, author and fabric designer, Carolyn's quilts are valued worldwide. www.carolynforster.co.uk

Katharine Guerrier – Katharine is a renowned expert with a superb sense of colour and design. She is a talented teacher and has written many inspiring books. www.katharineguerrier.com

Elaine Hammond – Elaine is a well-known and talented quilter who is skilled in many techniques. In 1985 she jointly started the influential *Patchwork and Quilting* magazine.

Brenda Henning – Brenda is a quilter and teacher living in Alaska. Many of her designs, including the appliqué one shown on page 176, are available in kit form. www.bearpawproductions.com

Pauline Ineson – Pauline is an award-winning quilter who specializes in machine sewing and appliqué techniques. www.paulineineson.co.uk

Beke Jameson – Beke runs Sewing the Seeds and creates lovely quilts for her shop. She stitched the appliqué design on page 176 from a Bear Paw kit. www.sewingtheseeds.co.uk

Lynette Jensen – A leader in the international quilting community and founder of Thimbleberries, Lynette is an acclaimed teacher and fabric and quilt pattern designer. www.thimbleberries.com

Kindred Spirits – Examples of the fascinating work of fibre artists Val Thomas, Vineta Cable, Dot Carter and Sarah O'Hora can be seen in this book. www.kindredspirits.co.uk

Clare Kingslake – Clare is an expert in appliqué techniques and exquisite hand work. Her first book, *Folk Quilt Appliqué* will be published by David & Charles in 2011. www.clarespatterns.co.uk

Gail Lawther – A highly talented designer and textile artist and an expert on many techniques. Gail has written many books on quilting and appliqué. www.gaillawther.co.uk

Pam and Nicky Lintott – Pam and Nicky are authors of many quilting books, particularly on using pre-cut fabrics to create fabulous quilts. www.quiltroom.co.uk

Marsha McCloskey – Known worldwide as a skilled teacher and prolific author, Marsha specializes in feathered star designs. www.marshamccloskey.com

Anne Muxworthy – a talented quilter and co-author of *Easy Japanese Quilt Style*, Anne runs Step by Step Patchwork Centre with Julia Davis. www.stepbystep-quilts.co.uk

Christine Porter – A highly respected teacher and author whose stunning quilts have won many awards. wwwchristineporterquilts.com

Petra Prins – Petra is a devotee of medallion-style quilts. She runs a quilt store in Amsterdam specializing in reproduction fabrics. www.dutchquilts.com and www.petraprinspatchwork.nl

Mandy Shaw – A charismatic and talented quilt maker and designer, Mandy is the author of *Quilt Yourself Gorgeous*. www.dandeliondesigns.co.uk

ABOUT THE AUTHOR

Linda Clements spent many years nursing in intensive care but, after completing her MA in creative writing and degree in publishing and book production, she switched careers in 1990 and is now an experienced project editor and writer, specializing in craft and particularly quilting titles. Over the years, Linda has contributed her writing skills to many of the David & Charles titles, particularly in the cross stitch list, as well as penning stories in her spare time and writing a non-fiction book, *The Spirit of Christmas Past*, which was published in 1996. Her main passion, however, is quilting, and she has been in the fortunate position of being able to learn and improve her skills from some of the best quilting teachers via her editorial work. Linda lives in Totnes, Devon, with her science-mad son, Rory, and two demanding cats, Kiki and Boo Boo.

INDEX